Lincolnshire People and Places

Terence Leach at the Methodist chapel at Raithby, John Wesley's 'earthly paradise' in 1975 and 1993.

Lincolnshire People and Places:

Essays in Memory of Terence R. Leach (1937-1994)

Edited by

Christopher Sturman

Lincoln
The Society for Lincolnshire History and Archaeology
1996

Jews' Court
Steep Hill
Lincoln LN2 1LS

ISBN 0 903582 05 8

Printed by Technical Print Services Limited, Nottingham.

Foreword

Easter in 1994 was darkened for many Lincolnshire people by the shadow of Terence Leach's serious illness; he was in hospital for several weeks and to everyone's distress died on 16 April. The tiny parish church of St Chad in Dunholme was packed for Terence's funeral on 22 April. Despite the solemnity of the occasion it was also a celebration of a life richly lived and a thanksgiving for this 'man of Lincolnshire'. How apt it was, therefore, that we sang the famous valedictory lines by another son of Lincolnshire:

And may there be no sadness of farewell
When I embark . . .

At this time plans were made by the Society for Lincolnshire History and Archaeology for a more permanent memorial to Terence (he had been a member of the Society and its predecessors for over thirty years, its chairman 1980-82, Hon. Secretary of the Local History Committee for many years and its Chairman 1980-93, Hon. Editor of the *S.L.H.A. Newsletter* 1986-90, and Joint Editor of *Lincolnshire Past & Present* 1990-93). An annual lecture in his memory was planned and at the same time a memorial volume was proposed.

At first it was suggested that this might be a companion volume to *Some Historians of Lincolnshire* (1992) which published lectures delivered in a series devised by Terence in 1989, but it soon became apparent that, a more substantial volume, and one which recognized the breadth of Terence's many interests, would be more appropriate. I am therefore exceedingly grateful to those - both Terence's friends and the admirers of his work - who responded positively to my initial enquiry and whose contributions (in some cases after many reminders and editorial requests for rewriting!) are printed here. I must also express my appreciation to Paul Roper and Carol Cook of Technical Print Services Ltd., for the patient and helpful way they have dealt with a book which has been put together almost chapter by chapter during the last eight months.

Terence loved the county of his birth: when returning to Lincolnshire he would always comment to Joyce, 'Back in God's country!' His knowledge of Lincolnshire was, like Sam Weller's of London, 'extensive and peculiar'; he amassed over the years a remarkable collection of Lincolnshire books. Moreover, he was willing to share and communicate, often with ebullience and wry humour, his passion for all things Lincolnshire: the bibliography of his writings is extensive but many will also remember what an excellent excursion guide he was. (He also had a genius for organization, relished committee work, and was prepared willingly to undertake tasks - such as the manning of a book stall at a thinly-attended day-school - which many consider thankless!)

The contributions to this volume reflect and actively develop Terence's wide-ranging enthusiasms: Lincolnshire houses, family portraits, John Wesley, Sir Joseph Banks, Tennyson, Lincolnshire historians, Lincolnshire books, and so on. They mirror the local historian's fascination with people and places and with the landscapes evolved, from the patrician house and park to the seemingly ordinary village, from agricultural improvement to land reclamation and sea defence; however various, they all suggest that intangible identification with a particular locality which more than anything characterizes a local historian such as Terence Leach.

Finally, should the title of this memorial volume strike a chord in any reader's mind, the 'echo' is obvious, that of Terence's sadly unfinished *Lincolnshire Houses and Their Families.*

Christopher Sturman

February 1996

Contents

Abbreviations Used:

A.A.S.R.P.	*Associated Architectural Societies' Reports and Papers*
L.A.A.S.R.P.	*Lincolnshire Architectural and Archaeological Society Reports and Papers*
L.A.O.	Lincolnshire Archives Office
L.A.O.R.	Lincolnshire Archives Office *Archivists' Report*
L.C.	*Lincolnshire Chronicle*
L.H.	*Lincolnshire Historian*
L.H.A.	*Lincolnshire History and Archaeology*
L.N.Q.	*Lincolnshire Notes and Queries*
L.R.S.M.	*Lincoln, Rutland and Stamford Mercury*
L.R.S.	Lincoln Record Society
P.R.O.	Public Record Office

Illustrations.

Copyright of these is acknowledged in parentheses after the caption. The Society for Lincolnshire History and Archaeology is grateful to those individuals, libraries, museums, and archives, who have generously allowed material from their collections to be reproduced in this volume.

Cover illustration: Part of the area north of Lincoln surveyed by Andrew Armstrong, published 1779.

Terence Leach: An Appreciation

> DUNHOLM, a scattered village, on the banks of a rivulet, 6 miles N.E. by N. of Lincoln, has in its parish 411 souls, and about 2190 acres of land, which was made freehold at the enclosure, by an allotment to the Bishop of Lincoln, the lord of the manor. *Mickleholm*, a large farm, 1 mile E, is the property of Robert and John Munn. *Dunholm Lodge* is a farm belonging to the Rev. Fras. Swan, B.D., *prebendary of Dunholm*, who purchased it, in 1832, of the Thorpe family. The Church (St. Chad) is an ancient structure, with a massive tower, and contains a monument and kneeling figure of Robert Grantham... who died in 1616. The vicarage... is in the patronage of the Prebendary of Dunholm, and incumbency of the Rev. Charles T. Swan... The *Church* was restored, at the cost of £600, in 1852-'3, when a handsome stained glass window was inserted at the east end. The Wesleyan Reformers have a chapel here. Four poor people of Dunholm participate in *Grantham's Charity*... The other poor parishioners have... yearly *rent charges*...

This description of Dunholme was published in White's *Directory of Lincolnshire* in 1856 just over eighty years before Terence Leach was born in the village. Despite the distance in time its themes resonate with associations relating to his many interests and preoccupations. These interests - church and chapel, landownership, social relations - were not only historical material preserved in the pages of a century old reference book, but part of a meaningful continuum linked to the living and developing village community of which he was an active part.

The institutions of village life, which White's *Directory* records, were the means through which the community functioned, expressed its ideals and to a greater or lesser extent moved towards their realisation. These institutions were nothing without the people who were part of them, who made them work and for whom they existed. The Directory entry for Dunholme shows the farmers, tradesmen and craftsmen of the mid-nineteenth century village: the landlady of the Lord Nelson; the Rev. Charles Trollope Swan, the vicar, and his parish clerk; also the village bricklayer. Among them is William Twell, a cow leech, standing out for the relative unusualness of his occupation, but a vital part of the local community he served. The fact that he was one of seven generations of Terence's family to live in Dunholme has an appropriateness which goes beyond the merely coincidental.

Terence's appreciation of this continuity was expressed in the dedication of his history of education in nineteenth century Dunholme to his grandfather, Harry Twell, and his mother, both former pupils of Dunholme School. His realization that interesting facts and associations needed to be set in a wider context to give them real meaning and significance, and his own debt to the village school for the sound basis it had provided for his future life and work, is seen also in the dedication of *Alas! Poor Dunholme School* (1981) to Miss D. M. Wilmore, sometime its Headmistress, 'In Gratitude'.

Terence spent the whole of his life in Dunholme, apart from periods of National Service and as a student. His roots can be said to have been firmly fixed there, yet he grew in response to outside stimuli and his vision was always wider than the boundaries of his parish. There was a symbiotic relationship between his local interests and the wider world, which nurtured his service to the local community. This was seen in his work to establish the Dunholme Old School Centre, when the old village school building ceased to be used in 1984. In *Alas! Poor Dunholme School* Terence showed how the school, with its parish library and night school had contributed to the social life of the village. Its development as a recreational centre for the village, including the provision of adult education classes in local history taught by Terence, continued the building's traditional role in a way which was attuned to current needs. This creative recall of the past and the way it was linked to present needs typified the approach through which Terence realised his aspirations in practical terms.

Terence's appreciation of the reality of past problems as seen, for example, in the title of his history of Dunholme School, stimulated him to find the means to overcome present difficulties in pursuit of his goals. This was nowhere more apparent than in his efforts to ensure that the Methodist chapel at Raithby - a place which was to John Wesley 'an earthly paradise' - was preserved for posterity. The first issue of the journal of the newly formed Lincolnshire Methodist Society, published in October 1963, had contained a note by its Editor, Terence R. Leach, about the need to repair this chapel. Further details were promised in the next issue of the journal, where an account of the chapel's history provided the justification for action to remedy its 'poor state' as well as material on its legal position.

The two hundredth anniversary of the opening of Raithby chapel by John Wesley in 1779 had been a cause of celebration, but the series of lectures named after its builder, Robert Carr Brackenbury, begun in 1980, ensured that the chapel remained in occasional use, continued to be in the public eye, and that money was raised for its support. Terence's creative influence is evident in the way the local Methodist circuit, the Lincolnshire Methodist History Society, the Tennyson Society and the Society for Lincolnshire History and Archaeology came together to arrange the lectures. For four of the fourteen years up to 1993 in which they were held Terence was either the lecturer or shared the programme with another speaker. The subjects of his lectures 'Writers in Spilsbyshire' (1980), 'Squire, Preacher, Poet and Mystic - Robert Carr Brackenbury of Raithby and His Contribution to the History of Methodism' (1988), 'Willingham and All the Rawnsleys' (1989) and 'Revesby Abbey' (1993) - are a reminder that, behind Terence's efforts to preserve and conserve the material remains of the past, he remained concerned with the people who used and built them. His work to save Raithby chapel came to fruition in 1994, when its restoration was completed at a cost of nearly £49,000, but sadly he died just over a month before its rededication.

Terence's interest in Raithby was encapsulated in the booklet *John Wesley's Early Paradise* (1993) which he published in support of the maintenance of the chapel. It was an interest which began in the late 1950s when, as a student at Westminster College Oxford, he had browsed through the *Arminian* and *Wesleyan Methodist Magazines* in pursuit of Lincolnshire material and had come across an obituary of Robert Carr Brackenbury. This began a search for material on him. 'Little did I realise', Terence wrote some thirty years later, 'how many hours of my life would be devoted to that particular quest...'. It was, uncharacteristically for Terence, a quest he did not complete by the publication of a biography of Brackenbury.

The influences which led Terence to Westminster, the Methodist teacher training college, also reflected his Lincolnshire village background. Brought up as a Methodist, Terence played a full part in the worship and social life of the Methodist church in Dunholme and had gone to Westminster College to study Religious Education and English with the full support of the minister and local Methodist community. While the origins of his remarkable collection of Dunholme material cannot be exactly equated with his college dissertation on Dunholme, the cuttings, sale bills and similar papers, often 'emphemeral' material, constitute what is probably a unique collection on any village. It typifies Terence's work in the way in which it takes the day to day currency of village life - socials, chapel teas, church events, school affairs - and through their preservation gives them importance and meaning. By understanding the significance of this village past he believed it was possible to create a viable future.

Weston Cracroft of Hackthorn wrote in his diary in 1860 of the Rev. James Michaelmas Barrett, vicar of Dunholme from 1858 to 1868: 'He doesn't understand that in Lincolnshire many of the best churchgoers attend chapel too.' When Terence used this quotation in his work on Dunholme school it was with a real appreciation of the way in which people in Lincolnshire communities were often eclectic in their approach to village affairs. Institutions, religious or otherwise, could be used constructively with the best elements of each contributing to the creation of a sustainable way of life, enriched from a broad range of sources.

These attitudes are based primarily on intuition rather than ratiocination and because their ultimate concern is to make communities function effectively they are the stronger for being so. They led Terence, product of the village chapel, to office as churchwarden at St Chad's church, Dunholme; to follow his father in his involvement with the village hall; to the production of *Dunholme News* with a circulation approaching 600 and distributed to the whole village; and to serve on the parish council. All this was achieved with the enthusiasm and energy that Terence brought to all things and which he took into the many societies and bodies whose life he enriched.

It was apposite that it should be Mrs Florence Baker who first took Terence, as a schoolboy, to the meetings of the Lincoln Branch of the Historical Association where he was welcomed and his interests encouraged by the Archivist and Assistant Archivist at the Lincolnshire Archives Office, Mrs Joan Varley and Dr Dorothy Owen. As the grandaughter of Henry Winn of Fulletby, chronicler of and participant in the affairs of his village, Mrs Baker was also part of the continuum of Lincolnshire village life which was the framework for Terence's work. Terence notes, in 'Tales of a Lincolnshire Bibliophile', which he circulated at Christmas 1980, that his collection of Lincolnshire books began when in 1953 his father bought him the last copy of her book *The History of Nettleham* (first published 1938).

The link which Mrs Baker helped to create led Terence to work in the Archives Office and to the other societies and groups of both local and national importance to which he gave so much. As well as those which reflected his passionate interest in the history of Lincolnshire, his work for the Tennyson Society brought together his love of English literature and his commitment to the study of Lincolnshire and its people. At a national level membership of the Georgian Society, the Victorian Society, the National Trust, the Ancient Monuments Society and the Society of Architectural Historians of Great Britain reflected the way this commitment was sustained in a wide context. A list of these societies, while quantitatively impressive, could not do justice to the quality of the service he gave to them. Towards the end of his life he became involved in the initiatives which led to the establishment of the Lincolnshire Gardens Trust. This new commitment was indicative of his continuing concern with all that would further enrich the appreciation and understanding of his beloved county of Lincolnshire.

In 'Tales of a Lincolnshire Bibliophile' Terence observed that the book collector is in an 'enviable position - for many collectors of books leave marks of their ownership upon their possession'. These marks can be, he goes on, of 'as much interest as the books themselves'. It was an interest in the people who lived in them which gave his work on Lincolnshire country houses its particular texture, and led to the publication of the two parts of *Lincolnshire Houses and their Families* (1990 and 1991) and the preparation of material which would have been the basis of more publications in the series. His passionate interest in this aspect of Lincolnshire's history also led him to collaborate in the preparation of four parts of *Lost Lincolnshire Country Houses* which appeared in a characteristic burst of energy in a three year period (1990, two in 1992 and 1993).

The publications on Lincolnshire houses and families were the outcome of years of enthusiastic commitment, which had some years earlier motivated his survey of Lincolnshire portraits. The survey was undertaken as a result of a suggestion from the Standing Conference for Local History, another of the national bodies on which he served and where his local interests became associated with national causes. In both its approach and in what it achieved the portrait survey was of national significance. Terence's local base was, in this case, the former Lincolnshire Local History Society, which he also served unstintingly and in fruitful co-operation with Miss Flora Murray, for many years its Honorary Secretary and Treasurer.

Terence's skills as a guide, racconteur and lecturer also brought alive the people of Lincolnshire's past country houses whose faces he came to know so well through the portrait survey. He was able to deploy these skills in a wider context on the tours he arranged and led, which took parties throughout and beyond Lincolnshire, often following a Lincolnshire connection or association and providing him with the opportunity to explore new areas of the country.

Terence's wide interests and association fed back into his thirty-two years as a teacher, first at Sincil Bank Secondary School, Lincoln, and from 1963 until 1992 at William Farr School, Welton, where he became Head of Fourth Year and Senior Teacher. Here, his creativity found expression in the context of a predominantly rural school. It was an environment to which he was well attuned, although he saw his early retirement in 1992 as giving him the liberty to exercise his gifts in ways which were not constrained by contemporary educational preoccupations.

Terence's life and achievements could never be fitted into a merely chronological account. The rich pattern of links and associations of which it was made up cross and recross, moving from a local base into a wider field and then returning, sometimes from a new direction, back to the people of Lincolnshire who both inspired him and whom he served.

This appreciation began with an extract from White's 1856 *Directory* for Dunholme which also evokes one final and all important link. Among the landowners listed at Dunholme were the Swan family who were, as prebendaries of Dunholme, patrons of the living. At the time the *Directory* was compiled a member of the family was also vicar. Terence's booklet on the Wolds village of Sausthorpe, published in 1968, which he described, characteristically, as 'notes' concerned mainly with 'the families who have lived here in the past', shows the importance of the same Swan family in its recent history. Much more importantly, Sausthorpe was the home of Joyce Clements and she recalls how on his first visit there Terence took the opportunity to work on the parish register at nearby Raithby, then still kept in the church, in pursuit of material on the Brackenbury family. Yet, however great Terence Leach's interest in the past, it never detracted from his care to nurture and sustain the quality of human relationships in the present. The marriage of Terence to Joyce at St Andrew's church, Sausthorpe, in 1964 celebrated a partnership which, through mutual support, further broadened and deepened the concern and the commitment on which Terence's life was based, qualities which have benefited and will continue to benefit many people both in Lincolnshire and beyond.

R. W. Ambler

A Bibliography of the Principal Writings of Terence Leach

This bibliography does not include Terence's correspondence to journals and periodicals, his contributions to 'notes and queries' of various publications, nor his reviews of other peoples' work. As he was sometime editor of both *Lincolnshire Past and Present* and the *Society for Lincolnshire History and Archaeology Newsletter*, many short items and much editorial matter in these publications were written by him, and have been deliberately omitted from this list. I would like to thank Joyce Leach for her help with this project.

A Short History of Stoke Rochford Hall (n.d.)
Notes on Dunholme, Lincolnshire (1964).
Brocklesby: A Brief Account of the Pelham Family (1968).
An Elizabethan and his Charity: Robert Grantham of Dunholme, 1541-1618, Dunholme Local History Pamphlets, 1 (1971).
[editor] *Index to a Transcript of the Parish Register of Brant Broughton* (1977).
The Turners and Their Wragby Estates; Kitching Memorial Lecture Given at Bardney, July 1978 (Bardney: Association of Friends of Bardney Abbey, 1978).
Tales of a Lincolnshire Bibliophile (For private circulation, 1980).
Writers in Spilsbyshire: A Lecture Given in Raithby Methodist Chapel, 3 July 1980, The Brackenbury Memorial Lecture (1980).
Alas! Poor Dunholme School: The Story of Education in Dunholme in the Nineteenth Century, Dunholme Local History Pamphlets, 2 (1981).
'Champion of Champions: Samuel Lodge and the history of Scrivels by', in Naomi Field and Andrew White, eds, *A Prospect of Lincolnshire* (Lincoln, 1984), 100-03.
[compiler] *A Welton Miscellany: Some Contributions to the History of Welton by Lincoln* (1984).
[editor] *A Swinethorpe and Harby Miscellany* (1988).
Lincolnshire Country Houses and their Families, Part 1 (Dunholme: Laece Books, 1990).
[with Robert Pacey] *Lost Lincolnshire Country Houses, Volume 1* (Burgh le Marsh: Old Chapel Books, 1990).
'Life in Watkins' Lincoln', in *The Victorian Facade 1859-1918: William Watkins and Son, Architects, Lincoln* (Lincoln, 1990), 30-33.
Lincolnshire Country Houses and Their Families, Part 2 (Dunholme: Laece Books, 1991).
'Edward Trollope and the Lincoln Diocesan Architectural Society', in Christopher Sturman, ed., *Some Historians of Lincolnshire*, Occasional Papers in Lincolnshire History and Archaeology, 9 (Lincoln, 1992), 13-26.
[with Robert Pacey] *Lost Lincolnshire Country House, Volume 2* (Burgh le Marsh: Old Chapel Books, 1992).
[with Robert Pacey] *Lost Lincolnshire Country Houses, Volume 3; Bayon's Manor, Tealby* (Burgh le Marsh: Old Chapel Books, 1992).
John Wesley's Earthly Paradise: Raithby Methodist Chapel, Lincolnshire and Robert Carr Brackenbury (Dunholme: Laece Books, 1993).
[with Robert Pacey] *Lost Lincolnshire Country Houses, Volume 4* (Burgh le Marsh: Old Chapel Books, 1993).
'Lincolnshire Country Houses', in *Welcome to Lincolnshire and South Humberside: Holiday Guide*, (Lincoln: Lincolnshire and South Humberside Tourism, 1994), 8-9.
Lincolnshire Country Houses [4pp leaflet] (Lincoln: Lincolnshire and South Humberside Tourism, 1994).

Dunholme Gossip Sheets

1. *Lincoln Road* (1983).
2. *Scothern Road* (1983).
3. *Ashing Lane* (1983).
4. *Holmes Lane* (1983).
5. *Watery Lane and Holmes Lane* (1983).
6. *Ryland Road* (1983).
7. *Fen Lane and Market Rasen Road* (1983).
8. *The Village Centre* (1983).

Notes For Outings

Unless otherwise indicated, these notes were prepared for outings of the Lincolnshire Local History Society and its successor the Society for Lincolnshire History and Archaeology.

Notes for a Tour for Members of Tennyson House [William Farr School, Welton] (n.d.).
A Tour of the Villages Associated with the Wrays of Glentworth, 17 June 1967 (1967).
[with Ian Beckwith] *The Eighteenth Century Church in Lincolshire: A Tour* (1967).
Brewing and Brickmaking in Dunholme in the Nine-teenth Century: Notes for a Visit to Dunholme on 25th May 1968 of the Industrial Archaeology Group of the Lincolnshire Local History Society (1968).

Notes for an Outing to Skinnand, Brant Broughton and Stragglethorpe on 7th September 1968 (1968).
Sausthorpe (1968).
Outing to Kirkby Green, Thorpe Tilney, Timberland and Linwood Hall, 18th October 1969: Notes (1969).
Notes for an Outing to Scampton, Aisthorpe, Brattleby and Cammeringham, Saturday 30th May 1970 (1970).
[with Hilary Healey and Ian Beckwith] *Notes for an Outing to the Trent-side Villages of Torksey, Marton, Gate Burton, Knaith and Lea* (1971).
Grantham Local History Society. 19 June 1971. Notes for a Tour of the Places Associated with the family of Wray of Glentworth (1971).
Outing to Folkingham, 28 August 1971 (1971).
Notes for a Tour of the Houses and Churches in the Four Parishes Raithby, Aswardby, Langton and Sausthorpe (1972).
Visit to Hainton, April 15th 1972: Notes (1972).
Notes for an Outing to Culverthorpe Hall, Heydour and Kelby, July 1972 (1972).
Outing to Corringham and District, 23rd September 1972 (1972).
Lincolnshire Local History Society: Notes for Outings 1972 [includes notes on Hainton, Alford, Raithby, Aswardby, Sausthorpe, Langton, Culverthorpe, Heydour and Corringham] (1972).
William Farr School, Welton, 1972. Notes for a School Journey to Kirkstead Abbey and Tattershall (1972).
[with John Turner and Enid Ballard] *Notes for an Outing to Snelland, Reasby, Stainton, Rand, Fulnetby and Holton Beckering, 28th April 1973* (1973).
Notes for an Outing to Barholm, Greatford, Casewick and Uffington, June 23rd 1973 (1973).
Notes for an Outing to Little Grimsby and Brackenborough, Saturday 8th September 1973 (1973).
Lincolnshire Local History Society Outings 1973 [includes notes for outings to Snelland, Fulnetby, Reasby, Stainton, Rand, Holton Beckering, Grimsby, Greatford, Barholm, Casewick, Uffington, Boston, Freiston, Little Grimsby and Brackenborough] (1973).
William Farr School, Welton. First Year School Journey. A Journey Through South Lincolnshire (1973).
Lincolnshire Men and Australia: Notes for a Tour June 8th 1974 (1974).
Outing to Caythorpe and Frieston, Saturday 18th May 1974 (1974).
Notes for a Visit to Gunby Hall and South Ormsby, Homes of the Massingberd family [Prepared for outings of the Grantham Local History Society on 6 July 1974 and the Tennyson Society on 13 July 1974] (1974).
Notes for an Outing to Corby Glen, Grimsthorpe Castle and Edenham, Saturday 7th September 1974 (1974).
[with John Turner] *Notes for an Outing to Monastic Sites near the Witham, including Stainfield, Bardney, Tupholme, Stixwould and Bucknall, Saturday 12th October 1974* (1974).
[with Judith Cripps] *Notes for an Outing to Fulbeck, Lincolnshire on 17th May 1975 and an Outing to Apethorpe, Northamptonshire on 14th June 1975* (1975).
The Tennyson Society: Notes for the Lincolnshire Pilgrimage 1975; Raithby, Partney and Dalby (1975).
The Tennyson Society Lincolnshire Pilgrimage 1977: Halton Holgate, the Rawnsley family, Alfred Tennyson and Skegness (1977).
Notes for an Outing to Stainton le Vale, Swinhope and Kirmond le Mire, with Notes on Orford Priory by John Turner (1978).
Notes for the Society's Outing to Stoke Rochford and Easton, 24th June 1978 (1978).
Notes for an Outing to Ashby de la Launde and Bloxholm (1978).
Notes for an Outing to Leasingham May 1978 (1978).
Notes for an Outing to Brocklesby and Great Limber (1980).
Farforth cum Maidenwell, Lincolnshire. Notes compiled by Terence R. Leach for a Visit by Members of the Society for Lincolnshire History and Archaeology April 11th 1981 (1981).
Oxcombe, Lincolnshire. Notes supplied by Terence R. Leach for a Visit by Members of the Society for Lincolnshire History and Archaeology April 11th 1981 (1981).
Ruckland, Lincolnshire. Notes compiled by Terence R. Leach for a Visit by Members of the Society for Lincolnshire History and Archaeology April 11th 1981 (1981).
[with E.H. Rudkin] *Walmsgate, Lincolnshire. Compiled for a Visit by Members of the Society for Lincolnshire History and Archaeology April 11th 1981* (1981).
Worlaby (near Ruckland), Lincolnshire. Notes compiled by Terence R. Leach for a Visit by Members of the Society for Lincolnshire History and Archaeology April 11th 1981 (1981).

Articles

Amateur Historian
'The recording of family portraits', 6, 3 (Spring 1964), 74-78.

Dunholme News
'Dunholme bricks', (Christmas Supplement 1967).
'Drinking at Dunholme - the Leather Bottle and the Lord Nelson', 301-8 (March 1989 - October 1989); 310-13 (December 1989 - March 1990).
'The story of Dunholme spring', 314-18 (April - August 1990).

'Dunholme war memorial', 319-23 (September 1990 - January 1991).
'The story of Dunholme church', 325 (March 1991) and following.

Epworth Witness
'Links - Nettleham, Horncastle and Henry Winn', 1, 1 (October 1963), 13-14.
'"Wesley's Chapel" Raithby by Spilsby', 1, 2 (April 1964), 10-12.
'Forward with the past - visit of the Rev. John Bowmer to Heighington, 22 May 1965', 1, 5 (October 1965), 9-11.
'Obituary: Florence L. Baker', 1, 9 (Autumn 1967), 8-9.
'Samuel Wesley at South Ormsby', 1, 12 (Spring 1969), 13-14.
'The Methodist Squire of Raithby: Robert Carr Brackenbury 1752-1818', 1, 13 (Autumn 1969), 9-15; 14 (Spring 1970), 10-16; 15 (Autumn 1970), 10-14.
'Benjamin Thorold of Harmston', 2, 3 (Spring 1972), 44-48.
'The Brackenburys of Raithby and the Bournes of Dalby - a footnote', 2, 6 (Autumn 1973), 96.

Journal of the Lincolnshire Methodist History Society [formerly Epworth Witness]
'The Boston Methodist Messenger', 3, 8 (Spring 1983), 165.
'The Lincolnshire Methodist History Society; its origins, growth and future', 4, 1 (1988), 22-28.

Lincoln Diocesan Magazine
'Parish life in 1869' [Dunholme, Fiskerton, Reepham, Scothern and Welton], LXXXV, 3 (March 1969), 38-41; 4 (April 1969), 55-57; 5 (May 1969), 72-75; 6 (June 1969), 88-90; 7 (July 1969), 108-10.

Lincolnshire Chronicle
'Lifestyle of a fortunate man', [Sir Cecil Wray], (17 April 1980).

Lincolnshire Historian
'The Preaching Squire - Robert Carr Brackenbury 1752-1818', 2, 11 (1964), 21-28.

Lincolnshire Home and Garden
'Lincolnshire country houses', (September 1993), 10-11.

Lincolnshire Lady
[with Robert Pacey] 'A history of Kettlethorpe Hall', (December 1993), 10-11.

Lincolnshire Life
'Lincolnshire crested china', 7, 12 (February 1968), 56-8.
'Some Lincolnshire rhymes', 19, 9 (December 1979), 34-35.
'George Houghton', 20, 7 (October 1980), 19.

Lincolnshire Past & Present
'The Lincolnshire family portraits index', 1 (Autumn 1990), 11-13.
'Two disasters at Bassingham', 1 (Autumn 1990), 24-25.
'Anniversary treat' [Dunholme Methodist Sunday School 1912], 3 (Spring 1991), 14.
'A Methodist minister's farm' [Rev. Zechariah Taft at Legbourne], 3 (Spring 1991), 7-9.
[with Betty Kirkham] 'Local history at Hogsthorpe and Langham Row', 6 (Winter 1991-92), 23-25.
'Who - and what - was Edmund Boulter?', 7 (Spring 1992), 14-16.
'Christopher Turner, G.F. Watts and the Tennyson statue', 8 (Summer 1992), 13-17.
'Dr. John Connolly (1794-1866) - The Tennyson connection', 8 (Summer 1992), 8-10.
'The Somersby and Bag Enderby Estate', 8 (Summer 1992), 21-6.
'Tennyson's gift to Lincoln Cathedral', 8 (Summer 1992), 17-18.
'A cautionary tale', 9 (Autumn 1992), 16-17.
'Credulity at Metheringham in 1861', 10/11 (Winter - Spring 1992-93), 35.
'A Methodist letter' [from H. Holland of Raithby by Spilsby], 12 (Summer 1993), 20.
'Memorials to servants (1)', 15 (Spring 1994), 10-11.
'The true authorship of the History of Scampton' (Authorial Alternatives, 2), 16 (Summer 1994), 4-6.
'One hundred and fifty years: the origins of the Society for Lincolnshire History and Archaeology', 18 (Winter 1994-95), 3-7.

Medical News [Journal of the Lincoln Postgraduate Medical Federation]

'Lincolnshire country house fires', 13 (Winter 1991-92, 18-19.

Proceedings of the Wesley Historical Society
'The will of Robert Carr Brackenbury (1752-1815)', 33, 6 (June 1962), 125-128.

Society For Lincolnshire History and Archaeology Family History Newsletter
'Methodist ancestors - some sources, part 1', 5 (October 1979), 4-7.
'Methodist ancestors - some sources, part 2}, 6 (January 1980), 6-7.

Society For Lincolnshire History and Archaeology Newsletter
'Parish magazines', 49 (July 1986), 12-13.

Tennyson Research Bulletin
'The Tennysons and the Massingberds', 2, 4 (November 1975), 155-159.

The Village
'More rural rhymes', 20, 3 (Autumn 1965), 80-82.
'The village spring', 21, 2 (Summer 1966), 48-54.

Welton Express
'A local murder', (March 1957).

Eleanor Nannestad

Revesby Abbey Charters

Dorothy M. Owen

The handlist of cartularies published by Dr G. R. C. Davis in 1958 contains a single entry for Revesby Abbey Lincolnshire, a twelfth century list of its charters written on a single membrane of parchment.[1] This and a group of one hundred and fifty documents deposited by the trustees of Lady Beryl Grove's settlement in the Lincolnshire Archives office are almost the sole survivors of this house. The abbey's properties had been granted at the Dissolution, like those of so many Lincolnshire houses, to Charles Brandon, duke of Suffolk, in whose house at Grimsthorpe there remained in 1559 'in the xxxvth tyll wrytynges sealled consernyng Revesby Abbey in a box sygned wyth M.'[2] Unfortunately Robert Glover, Somerset Herald, visiting Grimsthorpe in 1582 to collect material for the Willoughby-Bertie pedigree did not include any Revesby documents among the many early deeds which he abstracted.[3] Others saw some at least of the charters during the next century and have recorded documents which have now disappeared. A small group of them, including the foundation charter, was copied into the Lincoln Cathedral Chapter Acts;[4] Gervase Holles transcribed some of the same documents, from sources he does not name.[5] Sir Henry Spelman possessed ancient copies of the foundation deed and other early charters of William de Roumare III from which the editors of the Monasticon printed them, along with others which seem now to have disappeared '*ex armario comitis de Lindsey apud Grimsthorpe*'.[6] Only a very few documents have survived at Grimsthorpe[7] and none of them was seen by seventeenth century antiquaries.

Meanwhile the principal Revesby estates had passed, when Suffolk's property was divided among his heirs-general after the death of his two sons in 1551, to John Carsey, who held them in right of his wife Margaret, grandchild of Suffolk's sister, and sold them in 1575 to William Cecil, Lord Burghley. With the estates the Cecils obtained a number of charters, which they retained, although Elizabeth, daughter of the second earl of Exeter, took the estates into the family of Howard earls of Berkshire, into which she married. Joseph Banks bought the Revesby property about 1715 from this family who retained such few medieval deeds as they had.[8] When Edward Stanhope, who inherited Revesby from the Banks family, read in the sixth report of the Historical Manuscripts Commission that a number of Revesby deeds remained at Burghley with the Cecil papers, he seems to have applied for permission to have them copied and to have received them as a gift from the marquis of Exeter, along with a number of Kirkstead and Barlings documents which had once been at Grimsthorpe. Stanhope arranged for transcripts of the Revesby deeds to be made by G. F. Warner of the British Museum, who also supplied copies of other Revesby material in the Museum's own collections. Abstracts from Warner's notes, with a little topographical comment, were supplied by the Reverend Frank Besant of Sibsey and these abstracts Stanhope printed in 1889, in an edition limited to one hundred copies.[9]

In 1958, not long before we were married, my husband and I examined and listed the Stanhope trustees' deposit in Coutts Bank, and in 1960 were privileged to carry them back to Lincoln for deposit in the Lincolnshire Archives Office.[10] In 1962 I edited a group of Stickney charters from these documents in *A Medieval Miscellany for Doris Mary Stenton.*[11]

Not all the Revesby documents left Burghley in 1881, for in 1929 Miss Joan Wake, searching for early charters, found there the foundation charter and two other twelfth century charters of the house.[12] Meanwhile, stray charters relating to the outlying estates of the house had appeared from time to time. Before 1848 Sir Charles Anderson acquired a fine grant by Roger of Trehampton, dated 1163, of water meadows at Boleferry near Gainsborough, which is now at Lincoln,[13] Sir Jocelyn Bray deposited in the Guildford Museum three charters of land in Otby in Walesby[14] and in 1954 the Lincolnshire Architectural and Archaeological Society received from Mr A. D. Passmore a gift of a charter of land in Ashby Puerorum, which is now also in the Lincolnshire Archives Office.[15]

Appendix
British Library Egerton MS. 3058

The approximate date of this roll is a little later than 1170: it mentions no charters of William of Roumare III, who succeeded to his grandfather's estates in 1155 but was not of age before 1168, and who in 1172 confirmed his grandfather's gifts to Revesby.[16]

Privilegia sanctorum pontificum privilegia IIII[or]

Primum Anastasii pape de confirmatione ordinis nostri sine sigillo

Secundum Eugenii de confirmatione terrarum nostrarum

Tercium Adriani

Quartum Alexandri

Carte regum

Carta regis Stephani de Folesbi

Alia de Thoft et Rig'

Tercia de teloneo Quatuor de remissione omnium consuetudinum

V de terra in Wilkesbi. Carta ducis H. de confirmatione terrarum nostrorum

Carta regis H. de omnibus rebus nostris. Due carte eius de Folesbi Carta eius de danegeldis.

Carta de via in marisco de Sibecei. Littere regis Willelmo comiti Littere eius Ernaldo de Munbeg

Littere Rogeri Trehanton. Carte tres de teloneo.

Carte clericorum

Carta legati. Confirmacio episcopi et capituli Linc' de rebus nostris. Littere episcopi ad decanos

Testimonium episcopi de terra Alani de Philich. Carta eiusdem Alani in proprio sigillo

Alia in sigillo capituli Linc' de eadem terra. Carta capituli in terra de Kales. Carta capituli qua tradidit nobis Ph. de Crochesbi cum eadem terra Testimonium capituli de terra Radulfi filii Gilberti.

Carta episcopi Dunelm' de terra quam dedit Hugo Pinc'. Alia de stagno.

Carta capituli de Beverl' de terra quam dedit Reinaldus de Enderbi. Littere eiusdem capituli ad capitulum Linc' de eadem terra. Carta prioris de Brill'ton de remocione decimarum.

Carta Galfridi capellani de Thatersal. Carta Willelmi de Mithingesbi. Carta Alexandri et Turstini de Philinh'. Alia carta eorundem. Testimonium abbatis deKirkested de terra Johannis de Maring

Cyrografa inter nos et Kirk'. Divisio inter nos et Kirk'. Cyro' inter nos et Parc', Cyr' abbatis de Neuhus. Carta Willelmi de Mithing' Cyrografia sine .... cyrografia sine ... termino ix

Carta comitum

Prima carta Willelmi comitis de sede abbacie et escambia hominum habitancium in Revesbi et Thoresbi et Schitebi

Carta euisdem Willelmi de Geinesbi. Carta eiusdem de Hagnebi. Carta de remissione rusticorum de Hagnebi. Confirmacio eiusdem de terra Willelmi de Mithig'.

Carta de bosco in Kirkebi. Confirmacio eiusdem de Barra. Confirmacio eiusdem de donacione Osberti de Calz. Carta de eirico. Alia de Ailthein. Carta quo tradidit nobis Ph. de Crockesbi cum terra in Kales. Carta de hiis que dedit primitus. Due carte de omnibus rebus nostris. Carta Willelmi filii comitis de concessu [*sic*] terrararum nostrorum.

Carta eius de Stickeneia. Carte eiusdem de terra Willelmi de Mithigh'. Concessio comitis de Richemond de terra in Summeretebi. Carta comitis Rannulfi de teloneo. Concessio comitis Simonis de terra Sibaldi.

Carte baronum

Carta Radulfe filii Gilberti de grangia in Holebec

Carta eius de medietate dominii sui in Askebi.

Alia de toto dominio suo. Carta de terra in Salmundebi. Carta de terra in Wilkesbi.

Confirmacio eius de terra Giralmi. Carta Constancie uxoris Radulfi filii Gilberti.

Carta Hugonis Vac. Concessio Rogeri de Molbrai de terra quam dedit Willelmus comes in Geisb.'

Confirmacio eius Rogeri de Mow de eadem terra postquam dedit eam nobis Willelmus Tysun.

Confirmacio eius de bosco in Gainesb'. Carta eiudem de clamacione servicii Willelmi Tysun.

Confirmacio eius de terra in Bliburg'. Carta Hugonis de Baiocis de Toresueia.

Alia eiusdem de mansione. Tercia de vi acris terre. Carta Roberti filii Hugonis de remissione de terra in Folesbi. Carta eius de concessu stagni et prati. Carta Osberti de Calz de tribus acris in Dunstal. Carta eiusdem de XII acris. Carta Adami de Munbeg' de octoginta acris in Thorp. Carta eiusdem de iiii bovatis. Confirmacio euis de terra Willelmi Belalnei in Uptun Carta Jordani taxonis de Piscaria. Carta Ricardi de Haia. Carta Reinaldi de Crevequer. Carta eiusdem Reinaldi et Alexandri filii eius. Carta Philippi de Kime de 1 bovata in Scegnesse

Testimonium euisdem Philippi de bosco quod dedit nobis Johannes de Maring.

Carta eiusdem de salina. Confirmacio Roberti de Monasterio de xl acris.

Confirmacio Matthei de Pratariis de salina. Concessio Johannis Malerbe. Concession Ricardi de Haia de terra Willelmi Wifligham ad tempus. Confirmacio Roberti de Mohan'. Concessio Gorbadi de Scaud. Carta eiusdem de xx acris.

Carta militum [de remotis grangiis]

Carta Rogeri de Trehantun de terra in Sumerthebi. Carta eiusdem de piscaria. Carta eiusdem de pratis de Bolefere. Carta Willelmi Tysun de terra in Geinesburg. Carta Alasie de terra iuxta grangiam. Carta de piscaria. Confirmacio de terra Reinaldi. Carta eius de mansione. Carta eiusdem de bosco. Carta eius de loco molendini. Carta Dodonis Bard' de terra in Philigham. Carta Thome Bard' de eadem terra. Carta Alexandri militis de terra quam dedit Osbertus de Calz. Carta Gaufridi de Turs. C. Columbani. C. Roberti Wale de 1 tofto. Carta Willelmi de Belalnei de terra in Uptun. Carta Odonis de sancta cruce. de ix acris. Carta Alexandrie uxoris Odonis de xxvii acris.

Confirmacio Reinaldi de sancta cruce de eadem terra. Carta eius de dimidia cultura. Carta eius de cultura et 1 bovata terre. Carta eius de tofto in Sumertbi.

Carta Petri de terra in Thoresu'. Confirmacio Gervasii de Halton de eadem terra

Carta Rogeri de sancto Martino C. Willelmi filii Fulconis.

Carta Jordani filii Ranulfi de terra in Othebi. Confirmacio Rogeri de Milleia de eadem terra.

De propiquis grangiis

Carta Jacobi de Munsbeg' de Holebec. Carta Ernaldi de Munbegun de Holebec.

Carta Walteri Falconarii. Carta Radulf de Stafenesbeia. Carta Roberti de Tumbi. Carta Hugonis Pincun de terra in Folesbi. Carta eius de stagno. Carta Petri de Scrembi. Confirmacio Roberti Pettephin de eodem stagno. Carta Johannis de terra in Wilkesbi. Carta eius de bosco. Carta eius de Rogero filio Hucce. Carta Willelmi filii Ketel. Cyrografa Normanni de terra in Fulesbi.

Carta Rogeri de Benigwrd de Seggedic. Carta Alani de Kales. Carta Gilberti de Bolonia de Barra.

Carta Simonis de Dunstorp de ii bovatis. Carta eius de una acra et dimidia. Carta Willelmi de Greinesbi de xl acris terre in Stiken' Carta euis de prato. Carta de uno tofto.

Carta euis de xx et una acris. Carta euisdem Willelmi de V acris terre.

Carta euis de xiiii acris. Carta euis de xii acris. Carta Alani Smerehorn. Carta Radulfi de Wassigburg.

Carta Henrici de Clakesbi. Carta Ricardi. Carta Henrici et Alani de Clak' de iiii acris.

Carta Rogeri de Eirico. Carta Giralmi de terra in End'. Confirmacio Radulfi filii Gilberti de eadem terra Carta Sibaldi de terra in Burg Carta Roberti le Calceis. carta Walteri de Lindeseia. Carta Amfridi de Mith'.

Cyrographe cum sigillo ad terminum

C. Hugonis de Baiocis. C. Roberti Marmiun. C. Reinaldi de Crevequer. C. Jordani filii Ranulfi.

C. Rogeri de Millei. C. Dodonis Bardulf. C. Petri. C. Goslin de Torp. C. Rogeri filii Fulconis.

C. Johannis de Maring. C. Willelmi de La Landa de terra in Wiflegham.

Concessio Ricardi de hat'. C. Galfridi Columban'. C. Alani Smerehorn. C. R. de Trehantun.

C. Normanni de Folesi. C. Henrici de Clak' Carta Radulf filii Willelmi. Carta Geroldi de Normanvile. Carta Radulfi de Braibef'

Notes

1 *Medieval Cartularies of Great Britain*, A Short Catalogue (1958), 91-92. This list is now British Library Egerton MS. 3058.

2 L.A.O. Anc. 5/A/1, f. 17^{v}.

3 British Library Harleian MS. 245, fols. 86-107.

4 L.A.O., D & C, A.3.9, ff. 32-36.

5 British Library Add. MSS. 6118, fols. 328-29.

6 *Monasticon Anglicanum*, ed. John Cayley *et al.*, 8 vols. (1817-30), V, 454-56.

7 L.A.O.R., 3-9 *passim*.

8 *Letters and Papers of the Banks Family of Revesby Abbey, 1704-60*, edited by J. W. F. Hill, L.R.S. 45 (1952), xvi-xvii.

9 *Historical Manuscripts Commission, 6th report, 234-45; Abstracts of the Deeds and Charters Relating to Revesby Abbey*, 1142-1539 (Horncastle, 1889).

10 L.A.O. R.A. 1. L.A.O.R., 10 (1958-59), 39-42 and 11 (1959-60), 49.

11 Pipe Roll Society, n.s. 36 (for 1960), 221-34.

12 *Facsimiles of Early Charters from Northamptonshire Collections*, edited by F. M. Stenton, Northamptonshire Record Society, 4 (1930), 1-3, 38, 40. Another Revesby charter is now known in the Northamptonshire Record Office: a notification by William de Roumara to Bishop Alexander, of a grant of all the land of William the clerk of Midingesbeia, 1143x48. A copy is in L.A.O. M.C.D. 1000.

13 L.A.O., And. 1/3/2/1, L.A.O.R., 7 (1955-56), 28-29 and 8 (1956-57), 28-29. The charter was exhibited to the Lincoln meeting of the Archaeological Institute in 1848, *Memoirs Illustrative of the History and Antiquities of the County and City of Lincoln* (1850), xlv. It was subsequently exhibited at Horncastle on the occasion of the Lincoln Diocesan Architectural Society's visit in 1858, *A.A.S.R.P.*, IV, 2 (1858), lxx.

14 Guildford Muniment Room, 85/13/1-8. Photostats of these deeds are at L.A.O. M.C.D. 308.

15 L.A.O.R. 5, (1953-54), 57; D. M. Williamson, 'Ralf son of Gilbert and Ralf son of Ralf', *L.A.A.S.R.P.*, 5, 1 (1953), 19-27.

16 *Honors and Knights' Fees*, edited by W. Farrar, 3 vols. (1924), II, 154-55.

The After-Life of Monastic Houses: The Earthwork Evidence

Paul Everson

It was his passionate interest in Lincolnshire families that fuelled Terence's interest in Lincolnshire country houses. It led to the characteristic accumulation of large amounts of information, and to the particular flavour of the series of booklets on *Lincolnshire Country Houses and Their Families* and *Lost Lincolnshire Country Houses* that he published directly himself towards the end of his life, which passed that information on to others. His disclaimer of these as 'an amateur's work intended for other amateurs' may be realistic of their scope and aspirations, but in practice it greatly underplays their usefulness to all *amateurs* of the county, not least to those resident at a distance, as a source of information and quarry of quotable facts.

Coming from the direction of interest that he did, with its roots in genealogy and documentary and antiquarian sources, when he came to discuss country houses of the sixteenth century it was by reference to the phenomenon of those created on the sites of the county's dissolved medieval monasteries that Terence found it natural to structure his account in the first volume of *Lost Lincolnshire Country Houses* (1990). For that in the documentary record was an obvious and recurrent occurrence. He naturally cites Edward Clinton's mansion on the Gilbertine priory at Sempringham, that is known from pre-war excavations as well as from documentary sources[1] and Sir Vincent Skinner's grandly conceived but ill-fated house of *c.*1610 sited among the conventual ruins at Thornton,[2] but also Knaith Hall (erroneously believed to be on the site of the Cistercian nunnery of Heynings[3]), the Tyrwhitts' Stainfield Hall on the site of the former Benedictine nunnery there, a house evidently belonging to the Wray family at Barlings,[4] and Sir Christopher Willoughby's mansion at Tupholme.

Once the point is taken, and pursued, this handful can be seen as but the tip of the iceberg. Tanner's *Notitia Monastica* (1787), incidentally listing post-Dissolution grantees, confirms this at a general level, and further specific examples are not hard to find. At Bardney, granted to Sir Robert Tyrwhitt, conversion into a secular residence is evidenced through excavations but the house has apparently been abandoned by the mid seventeenth century; there was a country house of later sixteenth-century date on the site of Nocton Priory and a secular successor to the Augustinian house at Thornholme; the Carthusian priory at Low Melwood was succeeded by two phases of country house; Newstead was the principal residence of the Pelhams until their creation of a new emparked mansion and centre for their north Lincolnshire estate at Brocklesby in 1603; at Nun Cotham Sir Edward Skipwith built a secular mansion having been granted the site in 1540, which was sold to Robert Tyrwhitt in 1544, and continued as a residence until well into the seventeenth century.[5] With little work the tally might be extended very considerably.

In contrast to recent discussion of examples with elaborate architectural survivals, archaeologists generally have been rather slow to recognize this phenomenon.[6] In Lincolnshire, few monastic sites have substantial standing monastic remains, and none has a later great house incorporating monastic fabric to compare with Audley End in Essex or Place House at Titchfield in Hampshire, for example: but earthwork survival has been good, in some cases startlingly so, to the extent that several of them, brilliantly captured by aerial photography, have become standard illustrations of medieval monastic precincts.[7] Yet at Nun Cotham, for example, the well-preserved earthworks, which include clear building ranges with appended regularly walled enclosures and large ditched or moated and embanked paddocks, cannot be understood simply as a monastic layout and must rather be the post-Dissolution house and its formal gardens, remodelling and masking the monastic features.[8]

Measured site surveys have strikingly confirmed and elaborated this perception in a series of instances. At Stainfield, rather little of the monastic site can be made out in the earthworks except for the fishponds along the stream and the general area of the precinct, with planned village replanted along its south side. The most prominent earthworks before their destruction in 1980 were the rectangular arrangement of lawn, with L-shaped terrace and embanked enclosure - perhaps a wilderness - that spread up the hillslope south of the house, overlying the abandoned village remains. This formal garden of late sixteenth- or early seventeenth-century type was axially arranged with the south wing of an early house whose plan is recorded. Subsequently the house was extended, principally by service rooms to the north, a brick and stone walled garden was built to the east incorporating water-filled basins or canals, and the principal emphasis and viewpoint was re-oriented to the west, where a splayed vista marked by low earthen banks was created in the parkland, with Lincoln Cathedral as a distant viewpoint.[9] The church was built fully ninety degrees out of orientation to present a symmetrical facade to the visitor: dates on it (1711) and on the stables (1707) date the change.

Barlings was a Premonstratensian house sited on the island of Oxney, across the low-lying land and fen to the west of Stainfield. It is an almost totally unencumbered precinct full of earthworks; a single tall fragment of masonry marks the north-west corner of the crossing and the beginning of the nave arcade of the abbey church. The church's plan can be traced in some detail as an earthwork and the whole cloistral layout made out. Outside this north-east quadrant of the precinct, however, everything is different and unconvincing in purely monastic terms. There are large rectangular paddocks or closes divided by stone walls, complex water features, the foundations of large agricultural buildings - barns or stables - a stone-lined well and the earthwork of a large building of the sort that might be thought of within a monastic context as a separate household such as the abbot's lodging. It may well have been that in origin; but Millicent's drawing of the ruins in the 1720s shows a derelict secular building hereabouts with cross-mullioned windows, an octagonal turret, and door in the north facade with canopied hood. This must be the post-medieval mansion created by Sir Christopher Wray of Glentworth for his wife, Albinia, whom he married in 1623, probably converting an existing monastic building. It perhaps lasted less than half a century as a country house. The paddocks, outbuildings, and water features are likely to go with it, and this realisation changes completely the perception of

Fig. 1: Samuel Buck's east prospect of Kirkstead Abbey, 1726.

the site at an important level. For, rather than a medieval monastery *tout court*, the monument is more reasonably seen now as a post-medieval house and gardens, in one corner of which the ruined abbey church and cloisters were left tucked away.[10]

A measured survey of the earthworks of the Cistercian house at Kirkstead Abbey undertaken by staff of the Royal Commission on the Historical Monuments of England in 1993 has revealed precisely the same pattern.[11] The clearly intelligible earthworks of the abbey church and cloisters, so brilliantly captured in air photographs,[12] lie in a closely defined area of the south-east quadrant of the precinct, but the remaining earthworks comprise the remains of large rectangular stone-walled closes, low terraces and linear water features, all focused coherently on the foundations of a major building situated to the west of the medieval cloisters. This seems plainly to be a post-Dissolution country house, perhaps re-using the monastic Guest House. Parts of this layout of house and gardens can be correlated with the plan of the site made by Stukeley in the early eighteenth century, while the view drawn by Samuel Buck masks off the secular house that probably still stood at that date and shows St Leonard's chapel in the background - surely deliberately (Fig.1).

A variation on the same theme was revealed by measured survey by R.C.H.M.E. staff in 1989 at Tupholme.[13] John Leland records that Sir Christopher Willoughby was resident at the site of the former Premonstratensian house already within a few years of the Dissolution. The survey revealed as rather slight but coherent earthworks a pattern of rectangular walled closes, with a low raised terrace on its east side terminating in a small mount, and the water feature previously categorised as a 'moat' lying integrally within this pattern and therefore best understood as a post-Dissolution ornamental feature. The layout takes its orientation from the quadrangular plan on the southern side of which the surviving fragment of thirteenth-century refectory stands. This evidence suggests very strongly that the monastic church lying on the north of the cloisters was totally demolished, as Cromwell's standing instructions routinely required, and the remaining three ranges were converted into Willoughby's country house, with the north side of the quadrangle closed by a screen wall. The house was surrounded by the elaborate pattern of garden compartments shown by the earthworks, with the gatehouse drawn by Stukeley perhaps located axially in front of the house. When that Tudor house was replaced by the Vyner's new house, Tupholme Hall, that stood beyond the precinct to the north-east in the early years of the eighteenth century,[14] the old building was stripped back to the familiar fragment of thirteenth-century refectory, whose function was to act as a ready-made Gothic ruin and eye-catcher. This ensured its survival until it became an object of antiquarian interest in the nineteenth century, and latterly of statutory protection and finally direct ownership in recent times.

A similar mechanism contributed to the surviving form of remains at Barlings. For that site was bought at the beginning of the eighteenth century by Sir John Tyrwhitt of Stainfield, of whom it was said he 'keeps up the tower', probably as a ready-made Gothic ruin within sight of the re-oriented layout of Stainfield Hall. Samuel Buck's drawing of the ruins, dedicated to Sir John, in practice reverses the view, with the monastic ruins in the foreground and Stainfield Hall a distant feature in the landscape, in precisely the same manner as the equivalent view of Tupholme Abbey dedicated to Robert Vyner (Figs. 2 & 3).

In a comparable but equally characteristic way, it was the presence of a post-Dissolution country house at Kirkstead that led to the survival of what is now St Leonard's church, through the creation of a Presbyterian chapel in the building in line with the religious outlook of that branch of the Disney family who occupied the house. By the nineteenth century, antiquarian interest in the high-quality medieval building combined with a respect for tradition helped to secure its adoption into Church of England use.

The general conclusion from this experience is that post-Dissolution occupation of monastic sites by country houses has to be thought of as very much the norm, as the documentation of the Henrician reformation suggests. In practice its absence in any specific instance requires special explanation. With careful investigation the vestiges are commonly identifiable on earthwork sites, and the expectation of such evidence is now a commonplace for well-informed field archaeologists. Recognition that this is so goes some way to re-balancing Lincolnshire's dearth of surviving sixteenth-century country houses,

Fig. 2: Samuel Buck's north-west prospect of Barlings Abbey, 1726.

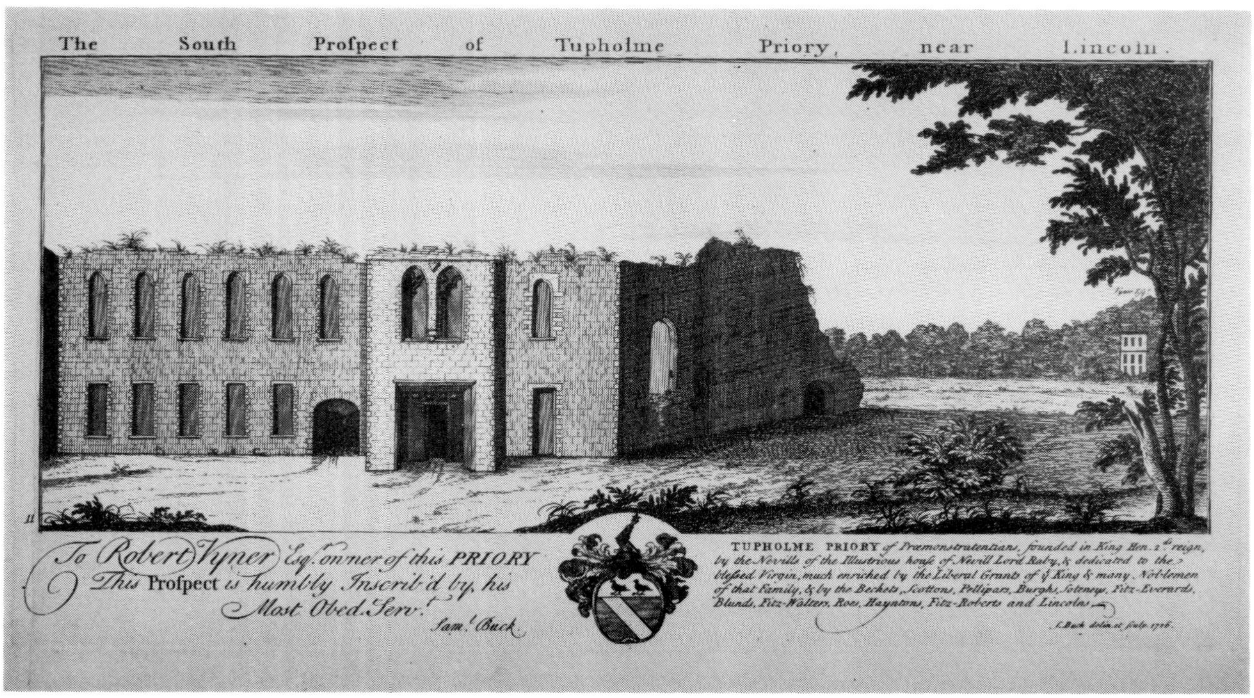

Fig. 3: Samuel Buck's south prospect of Tupholme Abbey, 1726.

and identifies a potential source of information about what is lost.

The resulting earthworks are often intrinsically interesting, particularly when involving large late sixteenth- and seventeenth-century houses with associated formal gardens. So pervasive is this that former monastic sites suggest themselves as a category with especial potential for supplying examples of the earthworks of post-medieval formal gardens, that have themselves recently come under increasing archaeological study.[15] The choices inherent in the adaptation of monastic buildings for continuing but altered use, and the attitudes they may reflect, are of great interest requiring systematic study far beyond this note. At the very least, the influence of the mechanism represented by immediately post-Dissolution country houses in determining what survives on former medieval monastic sites ought to be more routinely part of our thinking than has hitherto been the case.[16]

Notes

1 Rose Graham, 'Excavations on the site of Sempringham Priory', *Jnl. Brit. Archaeol. Assoc.*, 3rd ser., 5 (1940), 73-101; Andrew White, *Sempringham Priory*, Lincolnshire Museums Information Sheet Archaeology Series, 17 (1979).

2 David L. Roberts, 'John Thorpe's drawings for Thornton College, the house of Sir Vincent Skinner', *L.H.A.*, 19 (1984), 57-63.

3 See Paul Everson, 'Lost and found in Lincolnshire', in *From Cornwall to Caithness. Some Aspects of British Field Archaeology*, edited by M. Bowden, D. Mackay and P. Topping, British Archaeological Reports British Series, 209(1989), 55-64.

4 P. L. Everson, C. C. Taylor and C. J. Dunn, *Change and Continuity* (Royal Commission on the Historical Monuments of England/H.M.S.O., 1991), 66-69 (Barlings), 175-78 (Stainfield).

5 Harold Brakspear, 'Bardney Abbey', *Archaeol. Jnl.*, 79 (1922), 1-92, esp. 6-7; Timothy Ambrose, *Nocton Park Priory*, Lincolnshire Museums Information Sheet Archaeology Series, 15 (1979); Neil Loughlin and Keith R. Miller, *A Survey of Archaeological Sites in Humberside* (Humberside Libraries and Amenities, 1979), 181-82; P. J. Hills, *The Priory of the Wood* (Gainsborough, 1961); L.A.O., Yarb. 5/1/1; L.A.O., Yarb. 4/16/2.

6 Maurice Howard, *The Early Tudor Country House. Architecture and Politics 1490-1550* (London, 1987), ch. 7; D. R. Wilson, 'Old gardens from the air' in *Garden Archaeology*, edited by A. E. Brown, C.B.A. Research Report, 78 (1991), 20-35.

7 Richard Muir, *History From the Air* (London, 1983), 248-49; Colin Platt, *Medieval Britain From the Air* (London, 1984), 197.

8 Everson, Taylor and Dunn, *Change and Continuity*, illus. 36.

9 Ibid., 175-77, esp. illus. 24.

10 Ibid., 66-69.

11 National Monuments Record, site reference TF 16 SE 4.

12 David R. Wilson, *Air Photo Interpretation for Archaeologists* (1982), 29.

13 National Monuments Record, site reference TF 16 NW 3; see also Andrew White, *Tupholme Abbey*, Lincolnshire Museums Information Sheet Archaeology Series, 10 (1979).

14 Terence R. Leach and Robert Pacey, *Lost Lincolnshire Country Houses. Volume 4* (Burgh le Marsh, 1993), 45-51.

15 Wilson, 'Old gardens from the air'.

16 See, for example, Paul Everson, 'Post-medieval Essex' in *Archaeology in Essex*, edited by O. Bedwin (Essex County Council, forthcoming).

Artisan Mannerism in North Lincolnshire and East Yorkshire: The Work of William Catlyn (1628-1709) of Hull[1]

David Neave

Dutch influence on both the materials - brick and pantiles - and architectural details - stepped, shaped or tumbled gables - is evident in many seventeenth and eighteenth century buildings in Lincolnshire and east Yorkshire.[2] The influence is particularly marked in a series of buildings erected in the third quarter of the seventeenth century on either side of the Humber estuary. These buildings, three in north Lincolnshire - Worlaby Hospital, near Brigg, Walcot Old Hall, Alkborough and Papist Hall, High Street, Barrow-upon-Humber - and three at Hull - Wilberforce House and Crowle House, High Street and The Olde White Harte, off Silver Street - are in a distinctive local version of a style that has been termed 'Artisan Mannerism'.

Artisan Mannerist detail in the form of decorative brickwork with ornamented pilasters, 'Classical' pediments and strapwork was popular in London at least by the 1630s from where the style spread to country houses. H. J. Louw suggests that where every detail of an Artisan Mannerist facade is executed in brick the likely source is the southern Netherlands but where the decorative detail is picked out in stone it derives from the northern Netherlands.[3] Although the Humberside buildings show influences from both these regions the architectural details strongly suggest that they were all the work of the same architect-builder and documentary evidence indicates that he was from Hull.

Hull's prosperous merchant community had close commercial links with the Low Countries, exporting Yorkshire textiles and corn and importing, among other items, Dutch bricks and pantiles. Dutch craftsmen also appeared in the town, for example in 1644 the Warden and Brotherhood of Bricklayers complained to the Mayor and Aldermen about a bricklayer from Amsterdam accused of deluding the inhabitants of Hull into having their chimneys altered.[4] No direct Dutch connection can be established with any of the Artisan Mannerist buildings on Humberside but many local merchants and gentry are likely to have visited the Low Countries in the mid-seventeenth century and seen buildings of this style.

Wilberforce House, High Street, Hull (Fig. 1), the birthplace in 1759 of the 'emancipator' William Wilberforce and a long-established museum, is perhaps the best known of the group of buildings. Tradition attributes its building to Sir John Lister (d.1640) or to his father John Lister (d. 1617), merchant, and identifies it with the mansion where Sir John Lister, entertained King Charles I in 1639.[5] The present house however was built around 1660 by Hugh Lister (1619-1666), Sir John's fourth son.[6] In his will made 10 February 1664 Hugh Lister bequeathed to his eldest son John:

> the house wherein I now live in Kingston upon Hull... which I built new from the ground... together with my stable on the backside of the said house which I likewise lately built.[7]

In 1709 Lutton Lister, Hugh's grandson, sold the property to the Hull merchant John Thornton,[8] and in 1732 it was purchased by William Wilberforce's grandfather.[9]

Wilberforce House has an impressive two-storey, nine-bay facade with elaborate brick and stone detailing and a prominent three-storey porch. The brick front, rusticated throughout, has Corinthian pilasters at first-floor level between the pairs of windows on either side of the porch. The porch itself has elaborate indented Corinthian pilasters decorated with rectangular and diamond-shaped stone 'jewels', a motif repeated below the sills of the first floor windows.

Within a short distance of Wilberforce House is the remnant of another merchant's house with many similar details. Crowle House is tucked way behind the nineteenth-century frontage of 41 HighStreet. A slightly projecting central bay has a pair of giant jewelled Corinthian pilasters; it is flanked by arched recesses containing decorative stone plaques bearing the initials of the wealthy merchant George Crowle and his wife Ellinor, and the date 1664.[10]

Worlaby Hospital (Fig. 2), eleven miles away in north Lincolnshire, bears a striking resemblance to the Hull buildings. It is dated 1663. Once again giant

Fig. 1 Wilberforce House, High Street, Hull.

Fig. 2 Worlaby Hospital, Worlaby, Lincolnshire.

jewelled pilasters dominate the main elevation, this time four of them dividing the facade into five bays of windows with jewelled brick surrounds. A drawing of 1796 by Nattes (Fig. 3) shows that the almshouse originally had shaped gables with segmental pediments.[11] Worlaby Hospital was built for John, Lord Belasyse (or Bellasis), a leading Royalist commander who in 1662 had been appointed Governor of Hull. As well as founding and erecting the almshouse he built himself a house at Worlaby which John Harris describes as 'bizarre' on account of the bejewelled and pilastered gables and Artisan Mannerist porch.[12]

The distinctive raised brick window surrounds at Worlaby Hospital are also found on the plainer and seemingly much altered seven-bay facade of Papist Hall, Barrow-upon-Humber (Fig. 4). The window heads have decorative keystones and there is a truncated pilaster to the left of the blocked central doorway. Plain pilasters also terminate the facade. Little is known about Papist Hall but it is clearly of mid-late seventeenth century date and it was almost certainly built for William Broxholme (c.1626-1684) who occupied a seven-hearth house in Barrow in 1662, the largest in the village.[13]

Broxholme, who owned the manor of Sutton in Barrow, was a close associate of John, Lord Belasyse. He was a captain in the Hull garrison under Belasyse October 1660 to 1673.[14] In 1663 Belasyse had appointed Broxholme as one of the trustees of Worlaby Hospital. The name Papist Hall suggests that the Barrow house was owned by a Roman Catholic. Although Broxholme is described in the 1670s as 'an indgent Papist' this may be because of his association with Belasyse, a known Catholic, but there is no corroborative evidence of Broxholme's possible recusancy.[15] Indeed the inscription to him in Barrow church describes him as 'a true son of the Church of England, in which faith he died'.[16] The house name was almost certainly acquired in the mid-eighteenth century when the building was owned by John Pannell, a Roman Catholic tallow chandler from Brigg.[17]

Fig. 3 Worlaby Hospital by C. Nattes, 1796. (Lincolnshire County Council, Education and Cultural Services Directorate: Local Studies Collection, Lincoln Central Library)

Fig. 4 Papist Hall, High Street, Barrow-upon-Humber, Lincolnshire. Left half of east front.

Walcot Old Hall (Fig. 5), the third of the north Lincolnshire buildings, also has windows set in raised flat brick surrounds but here there are prominent triangular pediments to the first floor windows. The projecting central porch has a simple pilastered entrance doorway, echoing the remnant at Papist Hall, with triangular pediment above. The eaves cornice is more elaborate. The lack of stone 'jewelling' and the generally more restrained treatment at Walcot suggests a late 1660s or 1670s date. The house was almost certainly built by Thomas Denman, who by 1664 had inherited the Walcot estate from his father Nicholas Denman, merchant and Alderman of Hull. Coincidentally the most prominent of Nicholas Denman's debtors on his death were George Crowle, builder of Crowle House, who owed £400, and William Lister, brother of the builder of Wilberforce House, who owed £100. Crowle was one of the witnesses of Denman's will.[18]

Raised flat brick window surrounds are again a distinctive feature of the Olde White Harte in Hull, but here on the seven-bay facade the surrounds to the second and sixth windows on the first floor are more prominent whilst the other windows have an unusual outer surround. The raised central entrance bay has an open pedimented gable with triangular and segmental pediments to the window and a heavy brick door surround with oval opening. The dentilled moulded brick cornice is very similar to that at Worlaby. This building which was altered in the late nineteenth century is considered to have been the lodgings of Sir John Hotham during his celebrated period as Governor of Hull in April 1642 when he turned Charles I away from the gates of Hull. [19] The facade is at least twenty years later than this date but if tradition is correct and it was the Governor's house then at the time of its building the Governor would have been John, Lord Belasyse.

Drawings and photographs provide evidence of a number of other buildings that once stood in Hull that had similar Artisan Mannerist details to the six surviving buildings discussed above. The merchant George Crowle built a hospital in Sewer Lane in 1668. The five-bay facade was divided up by giant brick pilasters with Doric stone capitals. It had a raised and gabled central bay with pilasters flanking the first floor window. The projecting flat brick surrounds to ground and first floor windows were linked as at Walcot but without the intervening pediments and the dentilled brick eaves cornice was the same as at Worlaby and The Olde White Harte. The main front of the seven-bay Etherington House, 50-51 High Street, demolished around 1870, had the typical raised window surrounds to the first floor, with Corinthian pilasters flanking the end windows. It was dated 1672.[20] The Coach and Horses, Mytongate, only demolished in the 1970s had a row of three linked triangular pediments identical to a feature removed from the Olde White Harte in the 1881 'restoration' and an eaves cornice with pendants similar to the cornice at Walcot.[21] Another post-war loss was the so-called Dutch House, Dagger Lane a most elaborate single-bay building with rusticated brickwork, as at Wilberforce House, segmental and triangular pediments and a shaped gable with segmental pediment as once at Worlaby. One similar shaped gable does survive in Hull on the rebuilt Master's House at the Charterhouse and this provides us with the vital clue to the identification of the probable architect-builder of these Artisan Mannerist buildings, William Catlyn.

The Charterhouse, Hull's leading charitable institution, was largely destroyed in the Civil War and the hospital and master's house were rebuilt in 1663-64. The accounts for this work, which had been carried out by William Catlyn, the town's leading bricklayer, were presented to the Corporation in February 1665 by Alderman George Crowle, who had supplied 8,000 pantiles for the building.[22]

The Catlyn family were responsible for many of the principal building undertakings carried out in Hull in the sixty years from the late 1620s. The founder of the 'firm' John Catlyn I (d.1658) purchased his freedom as a bricklayer in 1621.[23] Before his arrival in Hull he may have been working in Lincolnshire for he can be identified with the John Catlyn, bricklayer who had a child baptised at Barton-on-Humber in 1611.[24] In 1628 Catlyn was Warden of the Bricklayers Company of Hull and in 1633 he was contracted by the corporation to build a new Council House, of brick with windows of free stone.[25] Unusually John Catlyn was also admitted freeman of York in 1651, at the special request of Thomas, 3rd Lord

Fig. 5 Walcot Old Hall by C. Nattes, 1794. (Lincolnshire County Council Education and Cultural Services Directorate: Local Studies Collection, Lincoln Central Library.)

Fairfax. Howard Colvin suggests that this may indicate that Catlyn was involved in the building of Fairfax's houses in Bishophill, York and Nun Appleton, West Riding.[26] Fairfax is likely to have become acquainted with Catlyn's work when he was in Hull during the Civil War, or possibly Catlyn was recommended by the Hull poet Andrew Marvell who lived at Nun Appleton House from late 1650 to mid 1652 as tutor to Fairfax's daughter Mary.[27]

On Catlyn senior's death in 1658 he was succeeded in the business by William Catlyn and his elder brother John Catlyn II (1627-1678). In that year, as well as claiming their freedom by patrimony, the brothers jointly took over the unexpired lease of the family brickyard.[28] It is this second John Catlyn who provides a most significant link with two of the Artisan Mannerist buildings in north Lincolnshire for during the Civil Wars he had served in Belasyse's regiment.[29] He had left Trinity Hall, Cambridge to join the Royalist forces and when in 1661 he decided to abandon bricklaying and return to the scholastic life, Catlyn successfully petititoned for the post of usher of Hull Grammar School, with the help of a testimonial signed by Belasyse and the personal mediation of Captain William Broxholme, then aide to Belasyse.[30] Catlyn went on to be headmaster of the Grammar School (1664-76) and during his turbulent period of office he again sought the support his former commander. When headmaster he continued to exercise his practical skills by executing emblematical paintings, constructing a speaker's platform, and overseeing the restorations of the Grammar School.[31] He left the family business entirely to his brother William and it is he who is the likely candidate for architect of Belasyse's Worlaby Hospital, Crowle House and Wilberforce House.

William Catlyn (1628-1709) was admitted freeman by patrimony on 2 December 1658 and became Warden of the Bricklayers Company in 1667-68.[32] He held a number of public offices. He was a churchwarden of Holy Trinity church in 1674, was chosen as one of the chamberlains of the corporation in 1668-69 and, after refusing the office in 1674, he finally served as sheriff of Hull in 1683.[33] Early in his career he gained the prime building contracts in Hull and the positions to which he was appointed suggest increasing prosperity although when excusing himself from the shrievalty he claimed that his income 'is soe small that I do wonder it comes under publique notice'.[34] William, like his father, found patronage away from Hull and he can be identified with some confidence with the 'surveyor' Cateline who was working for the first Lord Burlington at Londesborough, East Riding in 1661 and 1664.[35]

At Hull in addition to the contract to rebuild Charterhouse Hospital and Master's House in 1663-64, William Catlyn was the chosen architect for the new chapel at the Charterhouse in 1673, and he was engaged in 'beautifying the hall' (Guildhall) for the Corporation in 1680-81.[36] In 1681-82 Catlyn was asked by the Ordnance Board to provide plans and estimates for work on the Henrician defences on the east side of the River Hull, but he was seemingly unwilling to undertake the work on the terms proposed by the Board.[37] Also in 1682 Catlyn oversaw further work at the Charterhouse and the building of the Market Cross, an ambitious structure costing £1,700.[38]

Active though he was, only one surviving building can be ascribed without doubt to William Catlyn and this is in north Lincolnshire. On 4 July 1674 Vincent Amcotts and two other trustees contracted with William Catlyn of Hull to build Brigg Grammar School, established under the will of Sir John Nelthorpe.[39] The building, which comprised a school room and houses for the master and usher, was completed in 1678 and is now used principally as the school library. It is a more restrained building without Mannerist detailing. The slightly projecting pedimented central bay and arched stone entrance flanked by Ionic pilasters suggest that Catlyn had by then 'assimilated the conventions of English Restoration architecture'.[40]

When Catlyn pleaded his inability to take on the onerous office of sheriff in 1674 he stated that it was because of 'my great undertakings in Lincolnshire: the engagement is soe considerable that I know not how to be absent a day scarce without manifest losse and damage'.[41] This could refer solely to Brigg Grammar School but it is possible that his Lincolnshire 'undertakings' were more considerable and included the rebuilding of Harrington Hall, near Spilsby, for the new owner Vincent Amcotts, his employer at Brigg.[42] Amcotts bought the Harrington Hall estate in 1673 and immediately began its remodelling. A detailed examination of the hall following the recent destructive fire revealed that the greater part of the structure is of c.1680. [43] The building has a prominent three-storey porch which although largely of the early sixteenth century is in John Harris's words 'dressed up with an Artisan-Mannerist show face of exceedingly elongated Ionic brick pilasters'.[44] The porch has a sundial dated 1681. In an article on Harrington Hall, in 1974, Marcus Binney compared this porch with that of Wilberforce House without knowing of the Catlyn/Amcotts connection.[45]

Harrington may seem a long way for a Hull bricklayer to travel but other Lincolnshire gentry obtained craftsmen and building materials from the east Yorkshire port. In 1660 the former Parliamentary commander Colonel Edward Rossiter, a close friend and associate of Sir John Nelthorpe, built an ambitious Artisan Mannerist brick house at Somerby, near Brigg (now demolished) and employed Hull craftsmen, including a plumber later employed at South Ormsby by the Massingberd family. At the end of the century Sir William Massingberd obtained bricks, tiles and timber from Hull when building Gunby Hall near Spilsby.[46]

William Catlyn was the archetypeal artisan designer of the mid- to late-seventeenth century as portrayed by Sir John Summerson. He worked himself as a craftsman, contracted for complete buildings, produced plans and elevations of new buildings ('draughts'), oversaw the work of others and not least produced his own materials at brickworks at Trippet and Sutton to the north of Hull.[47] He was linked by marriage to the merchant community of Hull and was an active burgess and office holder in the town. His interest in and knowledge of architecture is evidenced by the fact that on his death in 1709 he left a prize possession, 'A Book of Architecture of Ancient Rome' to the library of Holy Trinity Church Hull.[48] His position, connections, and undoubted ability, point to him as the most likely architect of Wilberforce House, Crowle House and Worlaby Hospital. One final clue was found in Hull Register of Apprentices. In March 1667 Thomas son of Thomas Patten of Worlaby, Lincolnshire, glazier was apprenticed to William Catlyn of Hull, bricklayer.[49] Is this a pure coincidence or does it not suggest that Patten and Catlyn met when they were both working at Worlaby?

Notes

1 This is a revision of an article which first appeared in *East Yorkshire Local History Society Bulletin*, 28 (Autumn 1983), 8-12. I would like to acknowledge the help of Susan Neave and information supplied by John Lawson and Audrey Howes.

2 David Neave, *The Dutch Connection: The Anglo-Dutch Heritage of Hull and Humberside* (Hull, 1988), 11-22.

3 H. J. Louw, 'Anglo-Netherlandish architectural interchange *c.*1600-*c.*1660', *Architectural History,* 14 (1981), 1-23.

4 Kingston-upon-Hull Record Office (K.H.R.O.) M/189.

5 'Procedings of the Summer Meeting of the Royal Archaeological Institute, Hull, 1984' *Archaeol. Jnl*, 141 (1984), 5-6.

6 Humberside County Archive Office (H.C.A.O.) PE 158/1, Holy Trinity, Hull register.

7 Borthwick Institute of Historical Research (B.I.H.R.), University of York, York Wills vol. 58A/277.

8 H.C.A.O. East Riding Deeds Registry A 110/154.

9 Thomas Sheppard, *A Guide to the Wilberforce Museum, High Street, Hull* (Hull, 1907), 20-23.

10 See Nikolaus Pevsner and David Neave, *The Buildings of England: Yorkshire, York and the East Riding* (1995), pls 63 and 64 for comparison of Wilberforce House and Crowle House.

11 Banks Collection, Local Studies Collection, Lincoln Central Library. The drawing of Worlaby Hall is reproduced in Terence R. Leach, *Lincolnshire Country Houses and Their Families*, Part 2 (Dunholme, 1991), 166.

12 *ibid.*; Nikolaus Pevsner and John Harris, rev. Nicholas Antram, *The Buildings of England: Lincolnshire* (1989), 813.

13 P.R.O. E179/190/806.

14 Basil Duke Henning, *The House of Commons 1660-1690* (History of Parliament), 3 vols. (1983), I, 736-37

15 *ibid.* 737.

16 *Lincolnshire Church Notes*, L.R.S., 31 (1936), 19.

17 L.A.O. LCC VI/17d/1, Papists Estates 227.

18 B.I.H.R. York Wills vol.46A/221, will of Nicholas Denman made June 1656, proved Feb 1663/64.

19 Basil N. Reckitt, *Charles the First and Hull 1639-1645* (Hull, 1952), 27.

20 R. A. Alec-Smith 'Two houses of the Etherington family' *Trans. Georgian Society for East Yorkshire*, II (1946-47), 34-45.

21 Ivan and Elisabeth Hall, *Georgian Hull* (York,1979), 11.

22 K.H.R.O. WT/6/114-85. This is the first reference to the use of pantiles in Hull. They would have been imported from Holland by Crowle.

23 John Lawson, *A Town Grammar School Through Six Centuries* (Oxford, 1963), 91.

24 Barton-upon-Humber St Peter parish register.

25 Rosemary Horrox, *The Changing Plan of Hull 1290-1650* (Hull, 1978), 78.

26 Howard Colvin, *A Biographical Dictionary of British Architects 1600-1840*, 3rd edn. (1995), 234.

27 E. S. Donno, ed., *Andrew Marvell: The Complete Poems* (1972) 14, 246-48.

28 *A Town Grammar School*, 92.

29 *ibid.*, 91.

30 *ibid.*, 92

31 One of his emblematical paintings with an inscription in Latin 'To Momus' begins 'Lo, many bricks have I handled', T. Laughlin, 'John Catlyn, 1664-1676' in *The City and The School* (Hull, 1979) [36-37] where examples of Catlyn's paintings are illustrated. In 1676, 'after 13 years slavery' as master of Hull Grammar School, he retired to his living at Burstwick and there painted the large Royal Arms which hangs in the church with a painting of King Charles' execution on the reverse (*A Town Grammar School*, 98).

32 K.H.R.O. Freemen's Book fol. 47; Order Book of the Brotherhood of Bricklayers fol. 56a.

33 K.H.R.O. BRF/3/21, 24-5; M344.

34 *ibid.*

35 T. C. Barnard, ' Land and the limits of loyalty: the second Earl of Cork and first Earl of Burlington (1612-98)', in *Lord Burlington: Architecture, Art and Life*, edited by Toby Barnard and Jane Clark (1995), 194.

36 K.H.R.O. D.897B; BRF/3/25.

37 P.R.O. WO 46.1-2 Information kindly supplied by Audrey Howes.

38 K.H.R.O. BRF/3/25-26.

39 L.A.O. Amcotts 6/C/40/3; F. Henthorn *A History of Brigg Grammar School* (Brigg, 1959), 159-65.

40 Colvin, *Biographical Dictionary*, 235.

41 K.H.R.O. M.344.

42 *Brigg Grammar School*, 22.

43 Ex inf. Naomi Field, Lindsey Archaeology Services. Harrington Hall has undergone an exemplary post-fire reconstruction by Mr and Mrs D. Price.

44 *Buildings of England: Lincolnshire*, 369.

45 Marcus Binney, 'Harrington Hall, Lincolnshire', *Country Life*, 4 July 1974, 18-21.

46 *L.A.O.R.*, 8 (1956-57), 14 and 23 (1971-72), 15.

47 K.H.R.O. M.688, D.923, BRF/3/26; B.I.H.R. York Wills, Dec. 1709.

48 *ibid.*

49 K.H.R.O. BRG/6.

E. J. Willson and the Architectural History of Nocton Old Hall

Carol Bennett

On 7 October 1834, a young man of twenty two and a man old enough to be his father could be seen measuring and sketching the ruins of Nocton Hall. The country seat of the Earl and Countess of Ripon had recently been destroyed by a fire, allegedly started accidentally by workmen who had been fixing iron grates to the tops of the chimneys to keep jackdaws from building their nests there.[1] The fire had first been detected before midnight on the night of 15 July, and despite the fact that the fire engines had arrived shortly after two, the flames were not extinguished until nearly noon the next day. Having taken hold in the centre of the house, the fire spread to the south wing, and then owing to a change of wind, to the north wing, with devastating effect: most of the mansion's contents were destroyed, and all that remained was a shell, with most of the roofs fallen in.[2] The two men recording the building were Edward James Willson (1787-1854), the Lincoln architect and antiquary, and Augustus Welby Northmore Pugin (1812-1852). Pugin, the son of a friend and colleague of Willson's (Augustus Charles Pugin, 1769-1832), was later to achieve international fame as a designer and architect, and as a leading light of the Victorian Gothic Revival.[3] Figures 1 to 5 are a sample of their study, and form part of the Lincoln Cathedral Library Willson Collection. The pencil drawing which is described as being 'from a sketch by the late Mr Pugin' is in the style of E. J. Willson, and is almost certainly based on a drawing by the elder Pugin. A. C. Pugin must have made an earlier visit before his death in 1832, and sketched the old hall while it was still standing (Fig. 1). The plan is unsigned, but the writing on it appears to be Willson's (Fig. 2). Three of the pencil drawings are by A. W. N. Pugin, showing the hall from the east in ruins; a detail of the north wing from the north after the fire; and a detail of the central door on the east side (or garden front) of the west wing (Figs. 3 to 5).[4] In addition there is an annotated draft of the plan and notes by Willson which are in the Society of Antiquaries' collection.[5]

As a friend and collaborator of John Britton, Willson would have been familiar with his account of Nocton Park:

> NOCTON PARK, about two miles and a half north-east from Dunston Pillar, and seven miles south-east of Lincoln, is the handsome seat of the Earl of Buckinghamshire. It is recorded, that in the time of King Stephen, Robert... D'Arci, erected in his park at Nocton a priory of black canons of the Augustine order. At the time of the dissolution, it had five monks, whose annual revenues amounted, according to Speed, to the sum of 57l. 19s. 2d. The site was granted by Henry the VIII to Charles, Duke of Suffolk, and in the time of Elizabeth, it was bestowed by the crown on Sir Henry Stanley, Lord Strange. By the Strange family it was converted into a residence; but the greater part of the old house was afterwards taken down, and the present mansion rebuilt by Sir William Ellys, Bart, in the latter end of the seventeenth century. The house is a handsome building for the period, consisting of a body with two wings, the angles turreted, with cupolas at top; and in the centre rises an octagonal cupola, or lantern. The grounds were planted and laid out agreeably to the formal prevailing taste of the times, but have been much altered and improved by the present and noble proprietor.[6]

There is an ambiguity in Britton's text, allowing for a confusion over whether it was a house made out of the priory that was taken down, and replaced on another site by Sir William Ellys's entirely newly built mansion; or an earlier house on the site of the new one, which was swept away to allow for a late seventeenth-century rebuilding. On closer reading it becomes evident that Britton may be describing two separate houses: a house made out of part of the priory, and a manor house elsewhere in Nocton Park. The d'Arcys were lords of the manor of Nocton from Domesday until the mid-fourteenth century by direct descent, then by indirect descent until the Restoration. Although the d'Arcys held thirty-three manors in Lincolnshire, Nocton seems to have been their principal seat.[7] Clearly, there was a manor house in Nocton which preceded, and then co-existed with, Nocton Park Priory. In 1536 the priory was suppressed; in the following year, the site and some land were leased by the Crown to Thomas Wymbishe, lord of the manor of Nocton, who would have been only about 15 at the time. In 1538 Henry VIII granted the priory and Wymbishe's lease to Charles Brandon, Duke of Suffolk. Nevertheless Thomas Wymbishe and his wife were able to entertain Henry VIII and his fifth Queen, Katharine Howard, at 'Nocton Park' in

Fig. 1: Nocton Hall, detail of a pencil sketch of the north east view, 'from a sketch by the late Mr A Pugin'. (Lincoln Cathedral Library, Willson Collection)

1541, which indicates that there was a house of some size and quality there at that time.[8] If there was any building activity in anticipation of the royal visit on the return from a progress to York, it is far more likely that the priory would have been used as a quarry for modifications to the existing manor house, than that the priory buildings would have been converted into a new manor house.[9] Charles Brandon hastily dismantled Vaudey Abbey in order to enlarge Grimsthorpe Castle in anticipation of royal visits in the course of that same progress to York.[10] At Hainton there was a similar robbing of stone, according to Leland. Sir Thomas Heneage (a cousin of Wymbishe's) 'hath doone much cost ther, yn translating and new building with brike and abbay stone'.[11]

Unfortunately the confusion of a possible house made out of the Nocton Park Priory buildings with the manor house has been repeated, often verbatim from Britton, and persists until the present time, and in recent publications.[12] The aim of this essay is to establish three points: firstly, that there was a manor house which co-existed with the priory at Nocton; secondly, that the old hall on the site of the existing 1841 Hall at Nocton was in origin at least Elizabethan, if not earlier; and thirdly, that Sir William Ellys's late seventeenth-century house was not an entirely new house, but rather a remodelling of the earlier house on the site.

Camden has an equally confusing entry on Nocton, which may be the earliest source for the mix-up between Nocton Park Priory and the manor house in the same park: 'A little distance from Lincoln is Nocton, formerly a religious house where there is a magnificent seat lately built by Sir William Ellys.'[13] Again, the meaning is somewhat ambiguous. But where is the documentary or archaeological evidence for a house of any significance having been fashioned out of Nocton Park Priory ?

The Nocton Park Priory property passed from Charles Brandon to his son, and eventually to his granddaughter, Lady Jane Grey, whence it reverted to the Crown.[14] It seems unlikely that when Elizabeth granted this small priory to the great landowner Sir Henry Stanley, Lord Strange, he fashioned a house

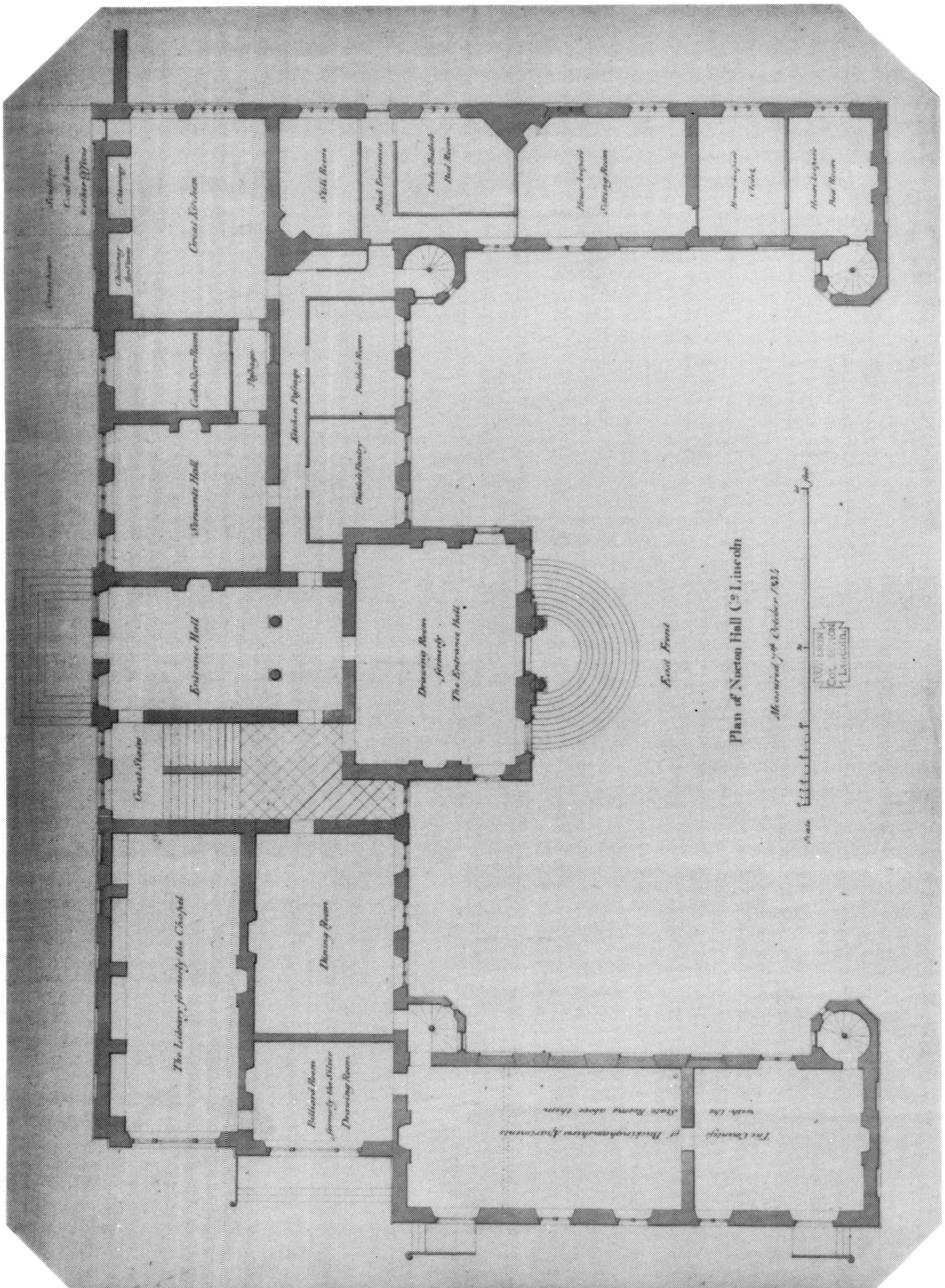

Fig. 2: Plan of Nocton Hall, measured 7 October, 1834. (Lincoln Cathedral Library, Willson Collection)

Fig. 3: A. W. N. Pugin pencil sketch of the ruins of Nocton Hall, 1834. (Lincoln Cathedral Library, Willson Collection)

out of the priory buildings, as Britton states; if he did, it may have been only a farmhouse. There is evidence of a dwelling at the priory in the early seventeenth century, but this was not a large house, which may have been in a surviving range of the priory buildings. By 1628, it is clear that Richard Towneley (the last but three of the lords of the manor of Nocton descended from the d'Arcys), either owned or had a share in the priory, because some of his goods are listed as 'at the Abbey' in the inventory made after his death in that year. Only four rooms are identified there: the great chamber; the chamber over the parlour (and by implication, the parlour); and the buttery. Then the list moves on to 'the inner new Chamber at Nocton', followed by an inventory of a house with more than thirty rooms. Certain features of this larger house can be linked to Willson's plans and drawing, and confirms that this was substantially the same house which was destroyed by fire in 1834.

Aside from the usual hall, parlour, dining chamber and other chambers, Richard Towneley's house had a 'gallerie', a 'sellar', and four chambers in towers (listed as 'the tower','the midle tower', 'the high tower' and 'the Maultley tower').[15] The most convincing evidence that this mansion was indeed Nocton Old Hall is the reference to the 'church-yard chamber', which was presumably a room overlooking the church and its surrounding graveyard. In 1775 when the medieval parish church of St Peter was demolished and replaced by a Georgian church on a site further away from the house, it must have been considered to be inconveniently close to the hall.[16] The oblong shape of the medieval church, marked out in nettles, can still be discerned on a mound immediately to the southwest of the 1841 Nocton Hall (which was built on the site of the old hall). The evidence from Richard Towneley's inventory of the existence of a large manor house with four towers with chambers at their tops, a long gallery and a chamber overlooking the churchyard is overwhelming, and shows that there was a great house on the site sixty years before William Ellys was building there. The material collected by Willson and Pugin reveals that many features of that house survived in Ellys's remodelling. And if some of those features date from the mid to late sixteenth century, there can hardly have been two large manor houses building virtually side by side at the same time in Nocton Park. Nothing remains above ground of the house made out of the priory buildings, and no known illustrations survive. By the time Stukeley visited the site of Nocton Park Priory in 1726, there was nothing there but lumps and bumps on the ground.[17]

The idea that Nocton Old Hall was a remodelling of an even older hall, and not a new house, has hitherto not been investigated in print, but it is clear from Willson's annotated plan that he believed this to be the case. Charles, Lord Stanhope of Harrington in Northamptonshire, bought the Nocton estate from Richard Towneley, who was compelled to sell it after the Civil War owing to sequestrations for recusancy and for loyalty to the Crown. Lord and Lady Stanhope were childless. In 1676 the Nocton estate was acquired by their distant relation by marriage, William Ellys, Kt, of Welbourn, who died a bachelor in 1680. His great nephew, Sir William Ellys, Bart, of Wyham and Nocton, then inherited the Nocton Estate.[18] The young heir's wife Isabella bore twelve children and died in 1686, only six years after her husband acquired the estate, and at a time when he seems to have been carrying out building works.[19] In 1700, Thomas Cox echoes Camden when he describes Nocton Hall as 'The magnificent seat of Sir William Ellys, lately built by him.'[20] Both these descriptions, written in Sir William Ellys's lifetime, indicate to the modern reader an entirely new hall. Bartholomew Howlett, a century later, has a slightly different version of events: 'the greatest part of the old mansion being pulled down [the hall] was rebuilt by Sir William Ellys Baronet in the seventeenth century'.[21] The terms 'lately built' and 'rebuilt' were often used in previous centuries to describe a remodelling, and so these two statements are not necessarily contradictory.

The last owners of Nocton Old Hall, the Earl and Countess of Ripon, believed that their house destroyed by fire dated back to around 1530; and that it was added to in 1680 by William Ellys. They of all people would know that they rebuilt the house on the same site, and they recorded this and other information in an inscription on the north elevation of the main block of the 1841 hall.[22]

It is clear from Willson's notes on the preparatory, annotated plan of Nocton Old Hall that he detected

Fig. 4: A. W. N. Pugin pencil sketch of the north wing of Nocton Hall after the fire of 1834. (Lincoln Cathedral Library, Willson Collection)

Fig. 5: A. W. N. Pugin pencil sketch of the centre of the east front of Nocton Hall, 1834. (Lincoln Cathedral Library, Willson Collection)

evidence of an older house incorporated into it. He records earlier styles of windows, walls and roof features, but he does not engage in speculation as to the date, or indeed, dates, of the building which was re-modelled. Willson evaluates in more detail the characteristics of the 1680s re-modelling, stating in his notes: 'The general style of the house bore a strong resemblance to Belton, but with some inferiority of elevation.' Another of Willson's attempts at interpreting the evidence in his notes concerns the 'neatly wainscotted... *Priest's Study*' at the top of the house, where Willson states the fire started.

> Nocton belonged to J. *Towneley* Esqr. a catholic gentleman but Sir William *Ellys* who rebuilt the house in the reign of Charles IId was a Protestant, and no Catholic inhabited it afterwards. This little room very probably was designed for a private study.

However the fact that Willson believes that this one room in or near the centre of the house (the part which appears to have been the most extensively remodelled), was not the Towneleys' priest hole, does not eliminate the possibility that he may have thought that other parts of Ellys's mansion could date from the time of the Towneleys, or even earlier, to the Wymbishes. These two related families, descendants of the d'Arcys, inhabited a hall at Nocton roughly from the early sixteenth century to the Restoration.[23] Incidentally, the above comment that it was Sir William Ellys who 'rebuilt' the house reveals that Willson believed the earlier hall was not the house made out of the priory, but rather that it was on the site of, or incorporated into, Ellys's hall.

So what were the young Pugin and E. J. Willson looking at? In many ways, they let the house speak for itself, but there is enough in the drawings, plans and notes to enable us to look at it fairly closely, and to evaluate this evidence in the context of other sources. We are told in the report of the fire in the *Stamford Mercury* (18 July 1834) that the house was of brick, although the building material is difficult to ascertain from all the known drawings and engravings, and it is not mentioned in Willson's notes. However the banqueting house still exists west of Nocton Hall, and facing it. Its fine Baroque facade built into the brick east face of a high garden wall is of rubbed brick with stone quoins, and it is tempting to suppose that this front was built of the same materials as the old hall.[24]

The north-east view of Nocton Hall shows an E-shaped house with ogee-capped turrets in the angles of the west wing (Fig. 1). The first impression is that this is a symmetrical house with extruded corners of *c.*1600, like Doddington Hall, and that the central stroke of the 'E' (where there may once have been a smaller two-storeyed porch) was enlarged, given its hipped roof, dormer windows, pediment, dentillated cornice, cross windows, stone quoins, and central doorcase flanked by Corinthian columns and surmounted by a broken pediment, in a late seventeenth-century remodelling (Fig. 5).

Howlett's engraving can supply further information about this central feature. It formerly had a cupola or lantern above, similar to the one at Belton.[25] It shows the cupola positioned on what Willson describes in his notes as a 'platform' over the ridge of the curiously made roof, which is not truly a hipped roof because it has vertical gables with chimneys on its north and south sides. Willson writes that the cupola '...gave light to the middle passage in the centre of the principal rooms'. Howlett's print shows that the cupola had Baroque detailing and was not an example of a Tudor banqueting house or prospect room, of the type which Robert Smythson designed for some of his Midland houses, to which the central cupola at Doddington is related.[26] Willson goes on to note that 'The cupola was taken down by the late Earl of Bucks'.[27]

The plan has north to the right, and shows only the ground floor (Fig. 2). There were two main entrances in the centre of the west wing, on an east to west axis. North of these entrances (i.e., on the right) were the kitchen offices: servants' hall, cook's store room and kitchen on the west side of the west wing; and across the passages on the east side, were the butler's pantry and the butler's room. Moving east from the kitchen was the still room, then on the other side of the back entrance was the under-butler's bedroom. Further east in the north wing was the housekeeper's sitting room — a large room measuring 25'9" by 20'2". Beyond that was the housekeeper's closet, and then the housekeeper's bedroom. This enfilade of rooms, accorded to the housekeeper in the nineteenth century, would have been envied by a guest of the lord of the manor in the seventeenth century. It took up three-quarters of the north wing on the ground floor.

The semi-circular stone steps led to the east entrance in the centre of the west wing, behind which was the 'drawing room formerly the entrance hall'. Beyond that to the west was the 'entrance hall'. Then to the south of the entrance hall was the 'great stairs', and beyond that in the southwest corner, the 'library formerly the chapel'. Also communicating with the great stairs on the south-east side was the 'dining room'. Next came the 'billiard room, formerly the silver drawing room'. Two very large rooms which took up the entire south wing, are described as the 'Countess of Buckinghamshire's apartments with the state rooms above them'.

On closer examination of the Willson Collection drawings of Nocton Old Hall from the east, and both the annotated and the finished plans, it becomes clear that what looks at first sight like extruded corners on the east elevation of the west wing are not rooms as at Doddington, but in fact, polygonal staircase turrets; furthermore, they are staircase turrets which have external openings at ground-floor level (Figs. 1-3). This arrangement has medieval antecedents, and such staircases were meant to serve courtyard-plan buildings; before the innovation of internal passages they facilitated getting from one room to another room by means of crossing the court instead of walking indoors through each room in sequence. Could it be that Nocton Old Hall was once a courtyard-plan house, with either an east range, or a gatehouse and screen wall on that side?

Willson states in the annotated plan that the two northern turrets had stone stairs, and the two southern turrets had wooden stairs. The differing materials of these newel staircases may indicate that the north and south wings were built at different dates. The south wing was offset from the main block southwards by ten feet, which implies that this wing was a later addition, added in order to create a symmetrical front to the house when viewed from the east (Fig. 2). Even if the north and south advancing wings and turrets were built at the same time, the way in which the south wing is offset reveals that there was a pre-existing main block (the west wing) which was not symmetrical. If the main block was originally one room deep, the staircase turrets with external openings would make sense. In fact, there is evidence to suggest that the main block was originally one room deep: the south wall of the library (formerly the chapel) is offset by a little over a foot; but more conclusively, Willson remarks on the annotated plan that there is a chamfered plinth to the east wall of the kitchen, cook's store room and servants' hall. The finished plan shows a blocked two-light window with hollow mouldings in the east wall of the cook's store room. At the bottom of the annotated plan there is a sketch of a double roof and the following description:

> Double Roof over the Kitchen — The west front had been carried up straight with a course of three blank windows. The middle wall appears to have been the west side of the building before the enlargement in the reign of Charles II.

The plan hints at more than one re-modelling of the west side of this block. The three blank window recesses on the west exterior wall of the kitchen (where there were two large fireplaces internally) were probably put there for the sake of symmetry, in order to balance another three blank window recesses on the west exterior wall of the chapel. These were most likely designed as recesses, rather than windows, in order to accommodate panelling behind them, as will be discussed in more detail later. But the kitchen seems older than the chapel. Its west wall juts forward slightly, its fenestration on the north wall is of a different and earlier design, and the blank window recesses have the look of being super-imposed on an older structure, which itself was added on to the former west wall of the house.

A. W. N. Pugin's drawing of a view of the north elevation of the house with the kitchen to the right, shows what looks like Elizabethan or Jacobean fenestration (Fig. 4). The windows of the north wall of the north range were of three and four divisions, with hollow mouldings; these windows were probably not later than the early seventeenth century and could well have been considerably earlier (Fig. 4). They were square-headed windows of two or three mullions each, with transoms. The smaller windows with two mullions had one transom and therefore six lights; two large windows in the north wall of the kitchen had twelve lights, formed by three mullions and two transoms. In the 1680s it was not felt to be necessary to replace all of the windows overlooking the stable yard with modern cross windows of the type which graced the more formal facades of the house, although higher up the building Pugin has sketched in oblong shapes which suggest cross or sash windows.

The north wing of the house was sited on land that sloped away from the house, and was of three storeys, rather than two, for most of its length. The ground floor ceilings were probably somewhat low. This wing reverted to two storeys in the northwest corner, where the lofty kitchen was. Pugin has drawn a line, possibly to indicate a straight join, behind which was the chamfered plinth which Willson noted on the annotated plan.

Who built the older house which hid behind the remodelling of the 1680s onward? It is probably true to say that no single individual built this earlier house, but that rather it was built piecemeal, as is indicated by the offsets and blocked openings already discussed. But the two most likely builders of the greatest proportion of the older house were Thomas Wymbishe (1521-1553) and John and Mary Towneley (1528-1608; and 1541-1606). If Thomas Wymbishe was one of the builders of Nocton Old Hall, it is tempting to connect his work with the visit of Henry VIII and his Queen Katherine Howard in 1541, even though Wymbishe was only about twenty years old at the time, and his wife, Elizabeth Lady Tailboys of Kyme (a baroness in her own right), was about a year younger. There are many stories of lavish overspending in the Tudor period in anticipation of a royal visit. Thomas Wymbishe was a man, according to Leland, 'of many possessions and auncient'.[28] Having curried favour with Henry during his visit to Nocton, he petitioned the King to acquire the barony of Kyme through his wife. His petition failed because he and his wife produced no heirs.[29] It is difficult to say what building, if any, Wymbishe may have carried out at Nocton Hall. It would not be beyond the realms of possibility that he added the south wing, for the sake of symmetry. Symmetrical or nearly symmetrical facades were certainly not unknown in 1541, especially among those with Court connections, such as Henry Daubeny, later Earl of Bridgewater, whose Barrington Court in Somerset was probably built before 1530.[30] Thomas Wymbish spent more than his own income in his lifetime; he died leaving his estate encumbered for fourteen years. He was so hard up that he instructed in his will of 1552 that after his death all his plate, goods and chattels which were not bequeathed as presents were to be sold to pay for his funeral and his debts, but that his wife should have the preferment to buy back whatever she wanted at reasonable prices.[31] This must have been particulary galling for his heiress wife. Had Thomas Wymbishe overspent on building works and entertaining Henry VIII and his entourage? Somehow, the fact that he describes himself as 'Thomas Wymbishe of Kyme' in his will indicates that it is at Kyme, more than his own estate of Nocton, where his ambitions lay. Not enough is known about the additions made to the fourteenth century tower at South Kyme to rule out a building programme by Thomas Wymbish there.

After Thomas Wymbish's death in 1553, the Nocton property passed to his sister Frances, wife of Sir Richard Towneley of Towneley, Lancashire. Once the fourteen-year period was over for the discharge of Thomas Wymbish's debts, in 1568, Frances settled the Nocton property on her only surviving child by Sir Richard Towneley, Mary. Mary had married her father's first cousin John Towneley in 1556; she was heiress to both the Nocton and the Towneley estates.[32] The couple may have begun building work or modifications at Nocton Hall when the estate was settled on Mary Towneley in 1568. Although they also had Towneley Hall in Lancashire, they eventually produced a large family of fourteen children, and they seem to have lived in both houses.[33]

1568 would be a fitting date to ascribe to Nocton Old Hall as it substantially must have looked before the 1680s remodelling. In 1568 the estate would not be encumbered, and the fines and imprisonments for John Towneley's recusancy would only just have begun.[34]

Comparisons can be made with two houses in Long Melford, Suffolk: Melford Hall and Kentwell Hall; also Charlecote Hall in Warwickshire, all begun between *c.*1550 and *c.*1560. The most distinctive feature common to all of these houses is their numerous, lofty turrets, with ogee roofs. They also had centrally-placed entrance porches of more than one storey. Nocton Old Hall originally had a porch of more than one storey, probably centrally placed on the east side of the house, which would have been swept away to be replaced by the pedimented central feature in the remodelling. A 'porch chamber' is listed in the 1628 inventory of John and Mary Towneley's son Richard. Richard Towneley himself (1566-1628) may have added to Nocton Old Hall, especially once he had cleared the charges against the estate for his father's recusancy. His inventory, mentioned earlier, lists an 'inner new chamber' and 'the new chamber'. The Towneley papers in the Lancashire Record Office may one day yield more information about that family's possible building activities at Nocton Old Hall.

In continuing our look at Willson's plan and notes, we return to the chapel, which he describes thus:

> The chapel had a gallery at the northern end on the level with the principal floor. The lower floor was sunk a little below the ground. The pulpit stood in the middle, the south end was raised three steps where the Communion Table stood...
>
> Near to the foot of the great stairs was a door opening into the gallery of the Chapel; and under the half pace [*sic*] a few stone stairs descended to another door of the Chapel, under the gallery, by which the tenantry and servants used to go to prayers. This chapel was commonly used in winter. The chapel in Belton House is still used on Sunday evenings when Lord Brownlow is at home.

This arrangement of access to the chapel on two levels is another similarity with Belton House. The floor of the chapel at Belton is at basement level, where there are windows which are blocked in order to accommodate the panelling, reredos and seating. The windows, on the level of the *piano nobile* (and the Brownlow family's gallery) provide top lighting to the chapel. At Nocton there were two windows at the lower level (later blocked) which look as if they were designed to light the area under the family gallery, which on the annotated plan has been sketched as a broken line running from east to west roughly in alignment with these two windows; then the next three blank (but not blocked) window recesses may have accommodated panelling behind. The south end, where the altar stood, appears to have been altered. According to the annotated plan, the three-light window was 'arched over'. A similar opening in the south wall of the next room, once called the silver drawing room, is described as a 'large arched modern window'.

Reading between the lines, it would appear that the chapel had been converted within living memory to a library when Willson was collating his material; he may have found out about it having been used in the winter months by interviewing the servants, many of whom were probably still resident in the village. Alternatively he may have learned about the chapel on a previous visit, perhaps when A. C. Pugin sketched the old hall. The entrance to the gallery from near the foot of the stairs is not plotted on the Willson plans, and it could be the case that he did not locate it. The chapel evidently underwent modifications on its conversion to a library, including the blocking of the windows under the gallery, in order to accommodate one of the four 'recesses arched for books', of which the bays are visible on the west wall on the plans. It is probable that the door to the gallery from the foot of the stairs was blocked, too, as it does not appear on either plan.

There had been, of course, a famous library of 10,000 books at Nocton Hall, belonging to Sir Richard Ellys, the son of Sir William Ellys who remodelled the hall. He outlived his eleven brothers and sisters and although married twice, died without issue in 1741/42. His widow Sarah was granted a life interest in Nocton and other estates. She later married Sir Francis Dashwood in 1745, and because her husband's appointed heir was the younger son of the first Earl of Buckinghamshire, she had Sir Richard Ellys's library sent to Blickling, where the first Earl of Buckinghamshire furnished the long gallery with bookcases by the time of his death in 1756.[35] In 1766

Lady le Despenser, as Sarah had by then become, relinquished her claim to the Nocton estate in favour of her first husband's cousin and heir, George Hobart.[36]Three inventories of 1766 list the contents of Nocton Hall which were either given or sold to George Hobart or retained by her. These inventories reveal that the chapel was still called the 'chapple' at that date, and not the library.[37] There is no mention of a library, but then if the books were no longer at Nocton the room which housed them may have been empty and so not named in the inventories. Was Sir Richard Ellys's famous library kept in the long gallery at Nocton, as it later was, and is to this day, at Blickling Hall?

The earliest allusion to the existence of a long gallery at Nocton Old Hall is the listing of a 'gallerie' in Richard Towneley's 1628 inventory. The long gallery was not done away with in the late seventeenth century remodelling, as it is mentioned as the setting for the theatricals of the flamboyant Mrs Hobart, George Hobart's wife. On 12 November 1775, Mary Yorke, the wife of the Dean of Lincoln, wrote to her mother-in-law, the Marchioness Grey:

> Mrs Hubbart... is all spirits as usual; and preparing a long gallery at Nockton for a play (the Journey to London which is to be acted in the Christmas holidays; the theatre is plain and neat, indeed very little more than benches set across a long galery; and a little stage raised at one end; no change of scenes, but only two neat ones to let down at the end...[38]

There is another reference to Mrs Hobart's theatre in the Torrington Diaries, where the Hon. John Byng records a visit to 'Norton' on July 15, 1791:

> This is a good old (deserted) hall — with its timber fell'd, and its avenues rooted up; there is a large painted staircase, with several good rooms, and a chapel; also a playhouse fitted up by Mrs H[obart].[39]

Willson expands on Byng's description in his notes on Nocton Hall:

> In my first visit I observed the dates of 1686 and 1687, in the back-plates of some of the fire-places which were of cast iron, large & decorated with ornamental flourishes.
> On the first floor were some large chambers with ceilings richly painted. One in the south wing, represented an eagle flying away with a child.
> Another had a canopy at the upper end of the room where King William III? held his court in... 169 .
> One room had been fitted up as a theatre, and was used about 50 years ago for dramatic exhibitions...

The mythological story of the eagle flying away with the child is that of Ganymede, the Trojan boy whom Jupiter, in the guise of an eagle, snatched and carried up to the heavens in order to make him cup-bearer to the gods. This must have been a Baroque painted ceiling; one can imagine the delight the artist had in depicting figures flying in the sky, probably as seen from below. The throne room may refer to a visit of William III to Lincolnshire in 1695 when it is known he and his retinue visited Belton House and Lincoln.[40] Willson calls the whole of the south wing 'the Countess of Buckinghamshire's apartments' in his finished plan.

Willson describes the three main rooms in the centre of the house on his annotated plan as the 'entrance hall' ('formerly billiard room'), which was approached through the main west entrance to the house. Two columns are plotted near the east end of this hall, which would have framed the door to the drawing room, emphasising the axial alignment of the east (garden front) door in the drawing room with the west (entrance front) door in the hall. Communicating with the entrance hall on its south side was the 'great staircase'. The finished plan shows a dog-leg staircase in a large hall, of which the floor was paved with stone, laid diagonally (Fig. 2). Describing this part of the house, which evidently was completely remodelled from the mid-1680s onwards, Willson writes in his notes:

> The Earl and Countess of Ripon had their private apartments in the centre of the house, over the drawing room, etc.
> The principal staircase consisted of a spacious flight of steps formed of edged beams of oak, wrought with large mouldings. The balustrades were twisted.* The walls were painted with figures in chiaro'scuro,** and the ceiling was painted in rich colours, with Corinthian cornices & rich mouldings, also gilt and painted... There were two windows on the west side below the half-pace & two above it: in each of which there formerly stood a statue of some classic personage (casts... One was Antinous: These were taken down in 180)...
> * The half-pace was supported by a twisted standard of iron, which I saw lying in the ruins, after the fire.
> ** These walls had been painted over with plain colour at the time of a late repair, but that barbarous operation was afterwards removed, & the original painting was restored.

Willson's account of the painted staircase at the old hall at Nocton vividly conveys the splendour and quality of this lost country house. It calls to mind another painted staircase dating from the turn of the seventeenth to the eighteenth century at nearby Culverthorpe Hall. As at Nocton, the wall and ceiling paintings were painted over and are irretrievably lost. The French artist Louis Hauduroy is described as the 'limner' in a 1704 agreement with his employers, the Newton family. The subject of the paintings was the History of Psyche, and as at Nocton, *trompe l'oeil* architecture, gilding and rich colours prevailed, in true Baroque fashion. On the ceiling was the marriage of Psyche with Cupid; and on one windowless side, Psyche with all her lovers. On the other side was a sacrifice by Psyche's father to Apollo, where the architecture was to be coloured marble:

> ... the capitel and basses of the colomnes of the said architecture to be peinted with... goold... under the great pictor is a barelief of psiché... barelief under the windows... and atope att the first story is to be peinted an order of architecture with to nicheches and to Statüe within them with a barelief on the top of the door all being the History of psiché...[41]

The staircase at Culverthorpe survives (Fig. 6). It is made of oak, with panelled risers, and is arranged around a well, with an open string and carved tread-ends. The half-landing is supported by two marble columns of the Ionic order, which is reminiscent of the 'twisted standard of iron' which performed the same function at Nocton. However it would be surprising to find iron construction at such an early date; could this prop have been a nineteenth century replacement of an earlier method of support, perhaps a column made of marble like the two at Culverthorpe?

Typically for the date, the Culverthorpe staircase has twisted balusters, and we know Willson records twisted balusters at Nocton Old Hall. An unusual feature of the design of the Culverthorpe staircase is that it has clusters of four more slender balusters, of the same simple design, where newel posts would be expected, and also in the centres of the half-landing and the top landing, where the bannister is shouldered.[42] In the existing 1841 Nocton Hall there is an oak staircase with an open string, with Gothic newel posts and a bannister which are right for an early Victorian house. Surprisingly, this staircase incorpo-

Fig. 6: Culverthorpe Hall, detail of staircase, c.1700. (Mr G. A. D. Emerson)

rates two designs of early eighteenth-century twisted balusters, and also carved tread ends, all in oak (Fig. 7). These balusters appear to be later in date than the Culverthorpe Hall staircase. The Nocton balusters have more twists. The larger balusters have elaborate vase-shaped plinths, and the curve of these balusters is sharp (rather than rounded) in profile, while the more narrow, simpler balusters have twists which are alternately sharp and rounded. There are not enough twisted balusters for the staircase, and so the numbers have been made up with square-sectioned ones. Were these older balusters and tread ends salvaged from the old hall for reasons of economy? Panels of linen-fold and other designs, and some late sixteenth or early seventeenth century friezes are incorporated into the woodwork of the staircase and its hall. It is tempting to suppose that all of this woodwork was salvaged from the old hall, but of course it could just as easily have come from some other house or houses. Even so, although there are many precedents for moving an entire staircase from one house to another, there is something very puzzling about moving part of one staircase (or possibly two staircases) and incorporating these fragments into another staircase, unless the explanation is that these parts had been retrieved from the previous house on the site and considered to be too good not to be re-used. The balusters and tread-ends are close enough to Willson's description, and if the more slender balusters were originally part of a cluster of four, as at Culverthorpe, this further comparison of these two painted staircases would be an interesting one.

Fig. 7: Nocton Hall, from 1841, detail of staircase incorporating earlier balusters and tread ends.

Turning to A. W. N. Pugin's drawing of a detail of the central feature of the garden front, it is possible to see similarities with the remodelling of the centre of the north front of Culverthorpe Hall, dating from around 1700, and built to accommodate the painted staircase (Fig. 5). Both the Nocton and the Culverthorpe doorcases have columns on either side with banded rustication immediately behind them. At Culverthorpe there are fluted Ionic columns; at Nocton Old Hall there were Corinthian columns supporting a curved, broken pediment. The Culverthorpe door has a straight cornice above it, which gives the appearance of supporting the large staircase window above it. The top of this window touches a carved plaque above it which connects the whole ensemble to the cornice above. Decorative scrollwork, carved in relief, helps to unite a somewhat top-heavy composition. A similar linking of door to window above appears in Pugin's drawing. The sill of the window above the door rests on, or is part of, a plinth-like apron, of which the centre advances slightly. This apron is both behind and above the broken pediment, in a subtle layering of planes. The transition between door and window is softened by the use of scrollwork, as at Culverthorpe. The way in which the doorcase of each house is 'tied on' to the window above so that the two forms merge is typically Baroque, but the Nocton ensemble is less daring. The design of the Nocton Old Hall doorcase and window above is strikingly similar to the south entrance of Uppark in Sussex, a house designed in *c.*1685 to 1690 by William Talman, and like Nocton Old Hall, showing Dutch influence.[43]

Willson repeatedly comments in his notes on comparisons between Nocton Old Hall and Belton House. The similarities of the chapels at both houses have already been noted. The arrangement of a large entrance hall and a saloon beyond, and to one side of the entrance hall the staircase hall, which can be seen at Belton, finds its echo at Nocton. Willson's drawing after A. C. Pugin of the east view of Nocton Old Hall, showing the alterations of *c.*1686 onwards (Fig. 1), compares well with Belton House, built between 1685 and 1688, and with Belton's predecessors, such as Roger Pratt's demolished Clarendon House, Piccadilly, of 1664-67. Pratt's design after all evolved out of the Elizabethan 'E' shape of a main block with advancing wings, so it follows that it is not difficult to dress up a sixteenth century house with Dutch detailing in order to make it look more up-to-date. The comparison between Nocton Old Hall's central block and that of Belton is very strong in the illustrations (for example, Howlett's) which show the central cupola at Nocton, as well as other features common to both houses, such as the advancing wings, hipped roof, dormer windows, dentillated cornice, central pediment and stone quoins.

It is well-documented that William Stanton was the master mason at Belton. It is known that William and his son Edward were master masons at Culverthorpe Hall during the remodelling by Sir John Newton, Bart, when the garden front and staircase were built.[44] William was also the sculptor of the monument commemorating Sir John and Dame Alicia Brownlow (who died in 1679 and 1676) in Belton parish church. Likewise at Heydour the monument of Abigail Newton, who died in 1686, is by William Stanton.[45] In Nocton Church the elaborate tablet to Sir William Ellys's great uncle, Sir William Ellys, who died in 1680, is attributed by John Lord to William Stanton.[46] If that monument is indeed by William Stanton, it would indicate that there is a strong possibility that this London master mason could also have been employed by the Ellys family in the remodelling of Nocton Old Hall, before his own death in 1705. His son Edward Stanton could also conceivably have worked at Nocton, as well as other craftsmen associated with them. Despite Camden's assertion in his *Britannia* that there was a magnificent seat lately built at Nocton by 1695, it simply is not known how long the remodelling of Nocton Old Hall took. The dates on the firebacks are exactly contemporary with the building of Belton Hall in the mid-1680s, a few years after Sir William Ellys acquired the Nocton estate. But the painted staircase at Nocton Old Hall could date from the early eighteenth century, as at Culverthorpe. Sir William Ellys did not die until 1727, and he may have been altering the house over a long period. In the absence of any known building accounts for the remodelling of Nocton Old Hall, the most that can be said is that this vanished house formed part of a group including Belton and the Baroque remodelling of Culverthorpe Hall, but the architect or master mason cannot be identified with any certainty.

After the Fourth Earl of Buckinghamshire died, in 1816, Nocton Old Hall passed to his daughter Sarah Albinia Louisa, who was then in her early twenties and the new bride of Frederick John Robinson, brother of the Third Baron Grantham, later Second Earl de Grey. Frederick was destined to have a long parliamentary career, including a brief spell as Prime Minister. He was created Viscount Goderich of Nocton in 1827 and Earl of Ripon in 1833.[47] The couple seem to have spent more time in London than on their Lincolnshire estates according to an article of 1828 which states that the house has:

> at present a dreary, desolate appearance. Its noble owner, pressed with the cares of state, has no time to spend in this quiet retreat.[48]

However there is a charming letter dating from the early years of the Robinsons' possession of Nocton Hall, which conveys the affection they had for the place. Frederick Robinson writes to his mother on 6 December 1818:

> We have certainly been very alert in all our *improvements*, and notwithstanding the shortness of our stay here, we have contrived to get as many irons into the fire as can well be managed at once... Sarah... is become one of the first rate gardeners; and altho' undoubtedly by no means knowing in the *botanical* part of that science, she directs the proceedings of the gardener with all the airs of lengthened experience. How far this may result from my having recently become a member of the horticultural Society, I cannot pretend to say, but the fact is undeniable, & excites the utmost astonishment in all her ancient friends.[49]

Concerning the gardens, *The Lincoln and Lincolnshire Cabinet* criticizes the 'infant avenue of elms' in front of the house for being old-fashioned, at a time when axial planning in garden design was anathema. No doubt the elms were planted to replace 'the avenues rooted up' which Torrington had observed in 1791. It is likely that the avenue was replaced by the Robinsons.[50] Despite their evident pleasure in Nocton Old Hall, the Stamford Mercury account of the 1834 fire reveals that:

> it is understood a few years since that the Earl contemplated a new erection, and had employed an architect to make plans.

This article also states that Nocton Hall was greatly under-insured:

> The insurance was for 7900l.; the destruction probably is to three times that amount.[51]

In fact, the new hall cost between £40,000 and £50,000. The under-insurance probably accounts for the delay in rebuilding, and the strange re-use of materials of various periods in the staircase. The Ripons decided that the net income of the estate was to be set aside for the house, but they had already set in train other improvements to the estate: in 1833 they built the Poor House, and in 1841, the row of cottages known as the 'Eight Row'. That same year work commenced on the new house and carried on, at a very slow pace, for ten years. The house is of local limestone, dressed with Ancaster stone, in Tudor Gothic style. The architect was not chosen from a well-known London practice, as would be expected from people of their wealth and standing; perhaps it was felt to be more prudent to engage William Shearburn, architect and surveyor of Dorking, who was the son of a joiner on the estate.[52]

There was probably never any doubt that the new house would incorporate the extensive foundations of the old one. In fact the outline of the old hall can still be traced beneath the Victorian one, although the replacement house is a much more compact building. Taking as our starting point the re-instated avenue of elms which appears, with other trees planted later as infill, advancing eastward from the house on the 1905 Ordnance Survey map, it can be seen that although the east and west doors of Nocton Hall are not quite in axial alignment with each other, as they were in the old hall, they still roughly line up with the avenue.[53] We can be fairly sure that these trees formed the 'infant avenue' mentioned in 1828, which, it can be safely assumed, would have lined up exactly with the main entrances in the west wing of the old hall. In fact, Bryant's map of 1825 to 1827 shows two avenues advancing to the northeast: one from the house, the other further south and parallel.

Looking at the exterior of Nocton Hall as it is today, one is struck by the extent of the cellars, which occur even under the terrace to the south of the house (Fig. 8). We know that the old hall had cellars; they are mentioned in the 1628 inventory, and Willson observes that in the principal staircase hall there were steps leading into the cellars which formerly led to the lower part of the chapel. The Stamford Mercury account of the fire notes:

> Some valuable wine, which was protected by the flagged roof over the cellars, was saved: the wine, however, was rendered tolerably warm.

An inspection of the cellars, however, does not yield up any brick or stone construction of either the late sixteenth or the late seventeenth centuries. In any case one would not necessarily expect to find cellars underneath more than a small proportion of the old hall. The ceilings in barrel-vaulted brickwork are remarkably high, and it can only be assumed that with the efficiency of Victorian engineering, the foundations of the old hall were excavated, dug deeper, and then lined with mid-nineteenth century bricks. Nevertheless, using the measurements on Willson's plans, it is possible to trace an outline of Nocton Old Hall.

Assuming from the position of the re-instated avenue that the west door of the Victorian hall is on the site of the west door of the old hall, then the north wall of the north wing matches the line of building of the old hall, measured from the west door of the Victorian house, although the south wall of this wing does not line up with the measurements on Willson's draft survey. The line of the south wall of the south wing of the old hall can be discerned beneath the terrace. Allowing for the way it was offset, the starting point for the south wall of this wing would begin under the south staircase of the terrace on the south side. The south wing would then proceed further east than the existing terrace, to line up approximately with the existing north wing, which advances slightly eastwards from the main planes of the later house (Fig. 8). The foundations of the north west corner of the old hall are now under the car park adjacent to the new main entrance of Nocton Hall on the north side of the building.

In conclusion, with the help of E. J. Willson and A. C. and A. W. N. Pugin, three things are clear: that the manor house at Nocton was distinct from the priory which was founded in its park; that the house which burned down in 1834, where we know extensive building works were carried out from c.1686 onwards, could not have originated from that date, because it had staircase turrets with newel staircases, ogee caps and exterior openings, and also stone-mullioned, hollow-moulded windows, as well as a long gallery, all of which would have been incompatible with a late seventeenth century building inspired by Dutch classicism; and that the outlines of this old hall can still be traced on the site of the present Nocton Hall. When this 'mansion of singular appear-

Fig. 8: Nocton Hall (currently a residential home), viewed from the south east. It was built between 1841 and 1851 for the Earl and Countess of Ripon, by the architect William Shearburn.

ance... which cannot easily be referred to any received order of architecture whatever' burned down in the summer of 1834, it was a great loss to the county.[54] Nocton Old Hall was, indeed, a house of no single period or architectural style, but no less interesting for that.

Acknowledgements

The author wishes to thank Dr Nicholas Bennett, for encouraging the publication of the Nocton material from the Lincoln Cathedral Library Willson Collection; Mr Gary Richardson for making Nocton Hall Residential Home freely available for study; Mrs Sheila Redshaw and Mr Christopher Howard for the loan of village material; and Ms J. Susan Bourne, for guidance on the Towneleys in Lancashire.

Notes

1 Society of Antiquaries, Willson Collection 786/3, fol. 75, 'Local Notes by Parishes and Wapentakes', III.

2 *L.R.S.M.*, 18 July 1834.

3 E. J. Willson was a contemporary of Augustus Charles Pugin, an emigré Frenchman who was a highly skilled architectural draughtsman. As authors, the elder Pugin collaborated with Willson on *Specimens of Gothic Architecture*, 2 vols (1820-1825), in which Willson supplied the descriptions; and *Examples of Gothic Architecture*, 3 vols (1828-1836), for which Willson wrote part of the text. A. C. Pugin's son, Augustus Welby Northmore Pugin (1812-1852), started his training in his father's drawing school in London, and increased his knowledge of architecture by extensive travel, when he sketched buildings and objects, particularly Gothic examples.

4 Lincoln Cathedral Library, Willson Collection album, not numbered. This material is clearly described in the text, and will be given no further footnotes.

5 Soc. Antiqs., Willson.

6 John Britton, *A Topographical and Historical Description of the County of Lincoln, etc* (1818) [a later edition of *The Beauties of England and Wales* (1807)], 756. The Nocton Park entry is accompanied by a Howlett engraving based on a view of the hall by the Louth artist, Thomas Espin. The wording of Britton's text is related to that of the Nocton entry in Bartholomew Howlett, *A Selection of Views in the County of Lincoln* (1805), Nocton (no pagination), which states:

Nocton, the seat of the Earl of Buckinghamshire, is situated seven miles south-east from Lincoln, and formerly belonged to the Darcy's [sic]. The greatest part of the old mansion being pulled down, was rebuilt by Sir William Ellys, Baronet in the seventeenth century. ... In the park stood a monastery of black friars, dissolved by King Henry the Eighth...

The phrase, 'the greatest part of the old mansion being pulled down, was rebuilt by Sir William Ellys' may have been the source of Britton's 'but the greater part of the old house was afterwards taken down'.Unfortunately Britton allied this phrase to Nocton Park Priory by what may arguably be described as a mis-placed semi-colon.

7 Kate Norgate and Maurice Henry Footman, 'Some Notes for a History ofNocton', *A.A.S.R.P*, XXIV, 1 (1898), 349, d'Arcy family tree in 'Lords of the Manor of Nocton', Table 1, opp. 349.

8 *ibid.*, 357-58.

9 *ibid.*, 364, tells of a local tradition that the old hall was built of materials taken out of the priory, and that fragments of Gothic architecture were discovered on demolition after the fire. These were said to have been removed to the vicarage garden.

10 An account of this progress can be found in Gerald A. J. Hodgett, *Tudor Lincolnshire*, History of Lincolnshire, VI (1975), 152.

11 *The Itinerary of John Leland in or about the years 1535 to 1543*, edited by Lucy Toulmin Smith, 5 vols, (1910), V, ix, 37. Heneage, a government official, had been acquiring a number of monastic sites and lands in Lincolnshire from the late 1530s (Hodgett, *Tudor Lincolnshire*, 52-55).

12 J. Saunders, Jr, *The History of the County of Lincoln*, 2 vols, (London and Lincoln, 1833-34), II, 262; Timothy Ambrose, *Nocton Park Priory*, Lincolnshire Museums Information Sheet, Archaeology Series, 15 (1979), 2 ; Charles Kightly, *All Saints Nocton, History & Guide* (n.p., 1991), 2; Terence R. Leach, *Lincolnshire Country Houses & Their Families*, Part 2, (Dunholme, 1991), 191.

13 *Camden's Britannia, newly translated into English; with large additions and improvements*, edited by Edmund Gibson (1695), 478.

14 Norgate & Footman, 358.

15 L.A.O. Inv. 135/167. A different interpretation of the wording of this inventory could be that the whole house was 'at the abbey'. However this would mean that the house had two butteries and two parlors.Although there is no great chamber listed 'at Nocton', there is a 'dyninge chamber' and a 'dininge room next the lowe tower'. This low tower is not listed separately in the inventory.The possibilities are that it was a fifth tower without a chamber;or that it did have a chamber, which was empty; or that it is the same tower as the one described simply as 'the tower' in 'the chamber in the tower'.

16 Norgate & Footman, 367-68. In 1862 work began on the present Victorian Gothic parish church, built on the same site as the Georgian church, at the expense of the Countess of Ripon, in memory of her husband. The architect was Sir George Gilbert Scott.

17 'The remains of Nocton Park Priory... 1727', Bodleian Library, Oxford, reproduced in Ambrose, *Nocton Park Priory*, 1.

18 On 9 November 1676, Lady Chaworth wrote to her brother, Lord Roos, at Belvoir, 'Lady Stanhope hath sold Nocton for 18,000l. to Judge Ellis.' (Historical Manuscripts Commission, *The Manuscripts of the Duke of Rutland*, 4 vols, (1889), II, 31). See also Norgate and Footman, 361-62; 'Lords of the Manor of Nocton', Table II, opp. 362. Sir William Ellys, Bart, was lord of the manor of Nocton from 1680 to 1727.

19 Soc. Anitiqs., Willson. Willson records firebacks of cast iron dated 1686 and 1687 in Nocton Old Hall.

20 Thomas Cox, *Topographical, Ecclesiastical and Natural History* (1700), 1426.

21 Howlett, *Views in the County of Lincoln*, Nocton, no pagination.

22 The plaque reads: 'Hanc villam / anno circiter 1530, regnante Henrico VIII, conditam / amplificavit A.D. 1680 / Eques Gulielmis Ellis / Deinde Georgii Comitis Buckinghamensis factam / A.D. 1780 / excepit denique / Roberti Comitis Buckinghamensis filia uxore ducta / Fredericus Johannes Comes Riponensis / Qui idem consumptam igni A.D. 1830 / eodem situdenuo aedificavit / A.D. 1841.' There is an obvious inaccuracy concerning the date of the fire, which was 1834, not 1830.

23 Norgate & Footman, Table I.

24 The rest of this building (hidden behind large brick-faced garden walls attached to the east facade on the north and south), is of coursed rubble limestone with large limestone quoins. The banqueting house appears to have consisted of one large room, stone paved, with a fireplace centrally placed on the original west wall. There is a later extension to the west, and the building has been substantially re-built in recent years. The buttressed west face of the garden wall to the north of the banqueting house is of stone, and probably dates from the early seventeenth century.

25 Howlett, *Views in the County of Lincoln*, Nocton, plate, no pagination.

26 Mark Girouard, *Robert Smythson and the Architecture of the Elizabethan Era* (1966), 114-15, attributes Doddington Hall, Lincs., to Robert Smythson, and relates its plan with its cupolas to the demolished Worksop Manor (completed 1586).

27 The lantern is mentioned in Britton's *Description of the County of Lincoln* (1818) but it is no longer visible in O. Jewett's view of the east front of Nocton Hall in 'Nocton House', *The Lincoln and Lincolnshire Cabinet* (Spalding, 1828), 7-13.

28 Leland, *Itinerary*, V, ix, 37.

29 Norgate & Footman, 357.

30 John Summerson, *Architecture in Britain, 1530 to 1830* (1969), 41-42.

31 P.R.O. PROB 11/36.

32 Norgate & Footman, 358.

33 Francis Peck, *Desiderata Curiosa* (1732), IV, No. XVIII, 34. In a letter dated 22 February 1582/83, to Henry Stanley, Earl of Derby and William Chadderton, Bishop of Chester, from some friends of John Towneley, a request is made for his release from the New Fleete Prison in Manchester, 'in respect of sondrie great causes & suits for land, a marryage to be made in Lincolnshire for his daughter, &c'. It would also appear from the names of the chambers in the 1628 inventory of Richard Towneley that various family

members resided there, if not permanently, then at least long enough to have a room reserved for them (listed as the chambers of 'Mr Townele', Richard's brother 'Mr Christofer', their sister 'Mrs Plumpton').

34 William R. Trimble, *The Catholic Laity in Elizabethan England, 1558 to 1603* (Cambridge, Mass., 1974), 75-76, 106, 169, 212-13, discusses John Towneley's recusancy, fines and imprisonments from December 1573, when he was a prisoner at York. Norgate and Footman, plate opp. 358, is a reproduction of a painting kept at Towneley Hall, Lancs., of John and Mary Towneley and their family, dated 1601. The painting bears an inscription concerning nine imprisonments for John Towneley's recusancy, which states that his first confinement at Chester Castle dated from about the sixth or seventh year of the reign of Queen Elizabeth I. This would be 1564 or 1565. Then it states he was sent to the Marshalsea, and then to York.

35 Elizabeth Griffiths, ed., *Blickling Hall* (National Trust, 1993), 50.

36 Norgate & Footman, Table II. George Hobart later became the Third Earl of Buckinghamshire in 1793 on the death of his brother.

37 Bodleian Library, Dept. of Western MSS, MS D. D. Dashwood B 19/2, fols. 18, 19a and 19b. I am indebted to Sir Francis Dashwood for permission to consult these documents.

38 Bedfordshire County Record Office, L30/9/111/56. This letter is quoted in Sir Francis Hill, *Georgian Lincoln* (1966), 10.

39 C. Bruyn Andrews, ed., *The Torrington Diaries*, 4 vols, (1935), II, 400-01. 'Norton' is a common variant of 'Nocton', which appears as late as the 1807 map of Lincolnshire which was made to accompany *The Beauties of England and Wales*, engraved by J. Roper from a drawing by G. Cole.

40 Edmund Venables, 'A survey of the houses in the Minster Close of Lincoln, taken by order of Parliament in 1649 and 1651, with explanatory notes and additions', *A.A.S.R.P.*, XIX, 1 (1887), 57.

41 L.A.O. Misc. Dep. 197/118.

42 Gunby Hall, Lincolnshire, has a dog-leg staircase of similar design which is a contemporary of the one at Culverthorpe. It, too, has barley twist balusters, with clusters of four more slender balusters of the same design where newel posts would be expected.

43 Howard Colvin, *A Biographical Dictionary of British Architects, 1600-1840* (1978), 805.

44 *ibid.*, 774-75.

45 Nikolaus Pevsner and John Harris, rev. Nicholas Antram, *Lincolnshire* (1989), 134-35, 381.

46 John Lord, *pers. comm.*

47 Norgate & Footman, Table II; 370-71.

48 *Lincoln and Lincs. Cabinet for 1828*, 9.

49 Bedfordshire County Record Office, L 30/13/20/15. I am indebted to Mr James Collett-White for drawing my attention to this reference.

50 *Lincoln and Lincs. Cabinet for 1828*, 8. The avenue in question does not appear on an estate plan of 1809, in the possession of Mr Christopher Howard, which was prepared in the time of the Fourth Earl of Buckinghamshire (d.1816). It is not plotted on Greenwood's Map of Lincolnshire of 1830 (based on surveys of 1827 to 1828), but it is on Bryant's Map of Lincolnshire of 1825 to 1827.

51 *L.R.S.M.*, 18 July 1834.

52 Annotated version of Norgate and Footman in Lincoln Local Studies Library, notes by M. Footman inserted opp. 27.

53 Ordnance Survey map (1905), 25", plan sheet no. 79.6.

54 *Lincoln and Lincs. Cabinet for 1828*, 8.

Beridges, Benefice and Bricks: An Algarkirk Miscellany

Hilary Healey

Algarkirk is one of the older villages in the Lincolnshire fenland bordering the Wash. The original parish lies on silt, although clay subsoil is encountered at varying depths. The landscape here is characterised by winding lanes which once bordered small, irregular shaped fields (Fig. 1). Unlike its neighbours, however, Algarkirk is not a nucleated village, and has apparently not been so for at least two centuries. The large cruciform church, dating largely from the thirteenth century, testifies to the former presence of a prosperous population and a more substantial settlement than the one which survives today. Slight earthworks marked east of the council houses on the early editions of the Ordnance Survey 6″ map (1888 revised 1906) may relate to medieval crofts. The grass field north and north-west of the church, scheduled as an Ancient Monument, is believed to embrace some of this shrunken settlement; it is one of the few fenland locations where pasture, former parkland, has preserved such a site.

Algarkirk is recorded in Domesday Book as *Alfgare* and there is archaeological evidence of occupation in the form of pottery dating from the seventh to the seventeenth centuries found near the site of the old Rectory in the 1950s and around Rectory Farm in the 1960s.[1] The present buildings in this core area are Sir G. Gilbert Scott's school of 1857 (no longer a school) south of the churchyard, post-war council housing on the opposite side of the road to the east and the former rectory, separated from the north side of the church by the aforementioned scheduled site. This last rectory was built in the mid-1950s in the grounds of the original Hall/Rectory, which was basically of late eighteenth - early nineteenth century apearance, with a twentieth century glass covered verandah on the east front (Fig. 2).

Members of the Beridge or Beveridge family, originally from Leicestershire, were connected with the parish and living of Algarkirk for 240 years, the first Basil Beridge being instituted to the living on 27 February 1637. Six of his descendants were rectors or patrons (and 'squarsons') between that time and

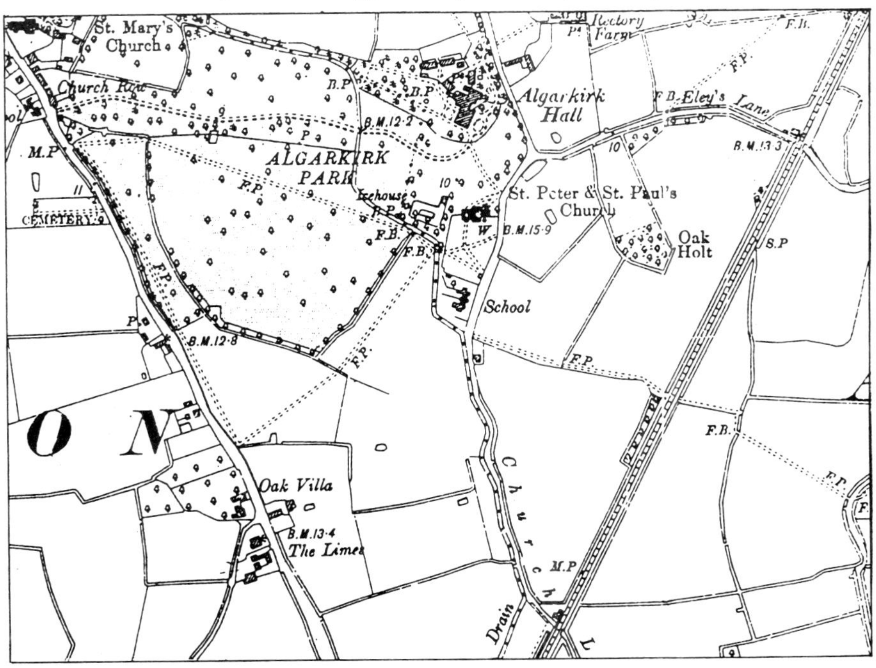

Fig. 1: Part of Agarkirk and Sutterton parishes, showing Algarkirk Rectory and Park. From the Ordnance Survey 6″ to 1 mile map (second edition, 1906), slightly reduced.

Fig. 2: Algarkirk Rectory, early 1950s. The plain glass had replaced an elaborate, almost Art Nouveau style 'verandah' seen in pictures of the early 1900s.

1898. The Rectory or Hall was impropriate. The earliest glebe terrier of 1606 names the 'mansion or parsonage house' and 'two barnes containing eight beies, belonging to the same'. Later, in 1633, there is a 'Faire mansion howse two Faire Barnes a Stable a Garret with one other howse or office adjoyning'. This detail remains the same and there is no change noted until 1693 when only 'A Great Barne' and 'A Stable' are named with the house. In one 1703 terrier the house is given as large, but it is generally simply referred to as 'fair'. In the same year 'Other Edifices ... with an orchard and garden' are included in the list, but none of these terriers give detail of the construction material of the buildings. Traditional timber with mud and stud cannot be assumed, since there were many brick buildings in this part of the fens by the seventeenth century (but see note below).

The long connection of the Beridges with the area enabled them to acquire a good deal of land, which was farmed in addition to 130 acres of glebe. By the 1820s the family had not only acquired considerable property in the district but had also profited from the fen enclosures.

Since the Hall/Rectory was the family's principal residence there would have been regular alterations to the house and buildings over the centuries. It was suggested by K. Healey in 1951 that the pre-eighteenth century house might have been on a different site, but there is some evidence that this is not the case.[2] The plan and appearance of the Rectory together with observations made during its demolition in 1954-55, suggest that parts of the building were at least of seventeenth century date. Varying floor levels and blocked up openings were everywhere and it was clear that many structural changes had taken place. This fact had not a little bearing on the need for demolition!

Several building phases can be established from a study of the twentieth century house plan (Fig. 3). In addition to varying wall thicknesses attention should be drawn to two massive chimney stacks over inglenook fireplaces, features likely to date from at least the seventeenth century. Whether they are contemporary is not clear. The central room (A on plan) with its massive chimney stack at the north end could be interpreted as an original hall. A steep gabled roof was *in situ* beneath the shallower pitch of the eight-

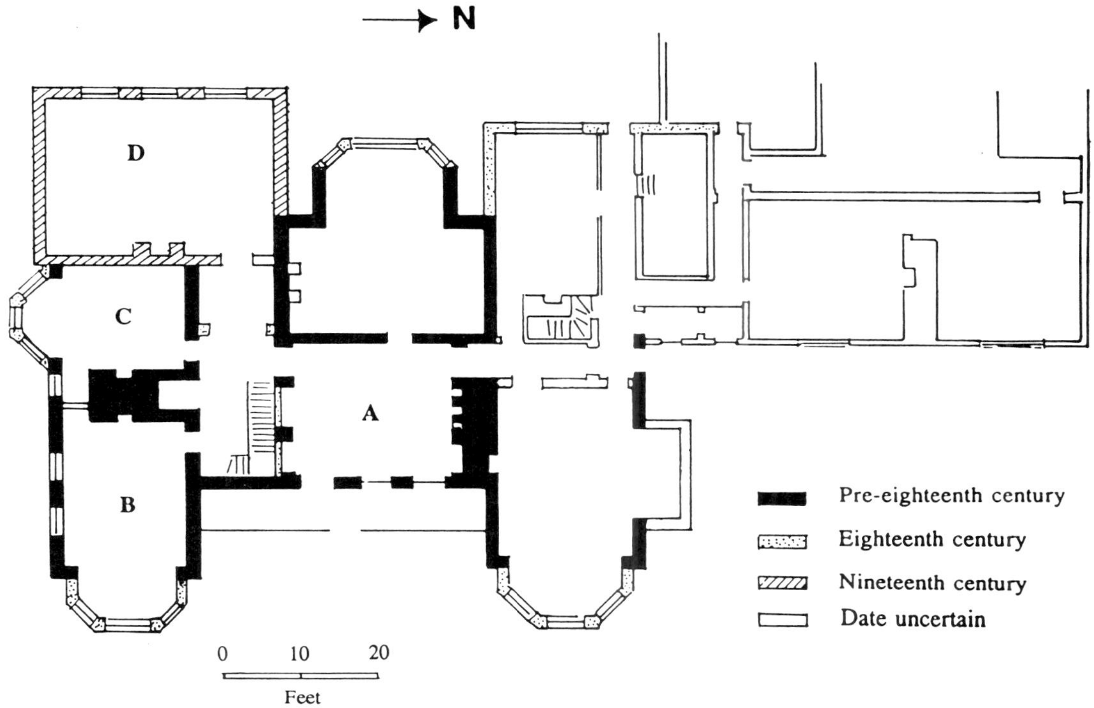

Fig. 3: Algarkirk. Ground Plan of Rectory, based on drawing by L. H. Bond, 1950. The suggested dating is the sole responsibility of the author.

eenth/nineteenth century Westmorland slate roof, and its ceiling, lower than any other in the building, appeared to be an insertion. The chimney surround was partly of seventeenth century date, although not certainly in its original position. The staircase dated to the first half of the eighteenth century, as did most of the interior ground floor (Fig. 4). The block to the south (rooms B and C), at right angles to room A, included another large chimney stack with two large fireplaces backing on to each other. Neither of these was fully revealed during the 1950s occupation of the house, nor was further detail noted during demolition. Beneath the board floor of room B was part of a double row of square padstones, apparently *in situ* for a timber-framed structure. A few photographs were taken during demolition, despite the inadequacies of both camera and photographer. Another set of interior photographs exists from the 1950s, but no other records of the house are known at present.

For the nineteenth century slightly more information on the Rectory/Hall is available. Basil Bury Beridge came to the living in 1782 following the death of his uncle Charles (the second), who had inherited in 1737. He died in 1808, having made his will in 1805. In this he left instructions that

> the Rectory House and all the Outbuildings and appurtenances And also all the Gardens Walks Plantations and Pleasure Grounds thereto belonging shall from time to time be upholden kept and supported in as good Repair and Condition as the same shall be found at the time of my decease'[3]

Although this is fairly standard language in wills it strongly suggests that the 'Garden Walks' etc. in the grounds had been undertaken before 1805, perhaps during his occupancy. The 1791 view by Claude Nattes hints at some of the detail in the grounds (Fig. 5). The sloping roof of a large glasshouse can just be seen to the left of the main house, backing on to the walled kitchen garden. The location of this glasshouse was visible, at least until the 1980s, as a recess in the wall; it has been tentatively identified as the 'Palm House' mentioned in a survey of 1881. The latest surviving terriers, of 1822 and 1864, describe the Rectory as 'slated' and give the overall dimensions of the house as 71 feet by 39 feet, consistent with the twentieth century plan. The stable is given as 35 by 19 feet.

Fig. 4: Algarkirk. Interior view of hall (room A) showing late eighteenth century decor. On the left can be seen the opening to the passage leading to room D. The portrait hanging at the centre of this picture was of the last Basil Beridge, one of a pair with a portrait of his first wife, Bettina Chaplin, painted on ivory. (The late Brian Woodthorpe).

Basil Bury Beridge's son Basil, a minor when his father died, was instituted as rector in 1822 and remained there for almost eighty years. He is probably the best known of the name. He 'added to the estate, and enlarged the house, converting it, he places on record, at great expense to himself, into the Rectory house of the parish'. The source of this last information, quoted by Healey, has not been traced, but it does place emphasis on the house rather than the estate. One of these alterations was probably room D, the large drawing room on the west side of the house, with three full height sash windows opening on to the garden (Fig. 6).

The origins of the small park are unknown. Aerial photographs of 1946 show ridge and furrow at its south-eastern edge, and the boundary looks to have been drawn around the existing edges of furlongs. The western boundary is not wholly clear, since the walled gardens occupy this area. The tithe plan of 1838, the earliest known map,[4] and the Ordnance Survey maps show the southern boundary as a plantation. Despite failed planting schemes and Dutch Elm Disease, a strip of trees and scrub survives, masking remains of a shallow ditch with slight internal bank which can be followed as far as Fourfields School, Sutterton, even where the tree belt no longer exists. The Algarkirk/Sutterton parish boundary crosses the centre of the scheduled site rather than following the course of the Three Towns Drain, or 'old sewer' and this parish boundary line can still be traced from a ditch and some brick bridge fragments. The drain course runs in somewhat straight lengths suggestive of a deliberate re-alignment quite out of character with the drain on its winding course south of the churchyard. Did the Beridges carry out this work to move it further from the house?

As the map (Fig. 1) shows, most of the park lies south of the drain in Sutterton parish, whose records have not been examined in detail. In the 1950s this pasture was ploughed and today part is a housing estate, Fourfields School and playing fields.

One other source of information may throw light on the date of the park improvements, albeit with caution. The Nattes drawing shows features still recognizable in the 1950s, including the bay windows on the east side of the house. The Park is seen to contain a number of small groups of trees. These

Fig. 5: Algarkirk. Drawing by Claude Nattes, 1791, of the 'Seat of the Revd. Basil Beridge' viewed from the south-east, near the church. Three bay windows and the shallow roof with parapet had already been constructed. The wall with two windows seen left of the extreme left hand bay were later to be replaced by the 'drawing room', room D. (Lincolnshire County Council Education and Cultural Services Directorate: Local Studies Collection, Lincoln Central Library)

Fig. 6: Algarkirk Rectory from the west, 1951, showing the early nineteenth century wing (room D) and its three long windows with triple sashes. The statue in imitation stone was one of a number of garden ornaments, thought to be of nineteenth century date. (Lincolnshire Free Press and Spalding Guardian)

may be stylized and not precisely identifiable, but some of them appear from their shape and proportions to be relatively young. Since Nattes's companion drawing of the church illustrates larger and more mature trees one may infer a degree of accuracy in his representations. Two conifers in the Hall drawing may be identified as two which were cut down in the 1950s, of which drawings and photographs still exist. It is tenatively suggested that the younger groups of trees and the 'plantations' are among those mentioned in 1805. In the 1940s there were still a number of very large trees in the Park, including walnut, elm and lime, but most of these have died or been felled within the last thirty years. One of the survivors, a tall plane tree (originally twin trunks, but one is now down) has been calculated at only 100-120 years old, which takes us back to the mid nineteenth century. At the extreme south-east corner of the rectory garden on the edge of the Park, is a huge pollarded small-leaved lime, which may be up to 300 years old. Large mature trees stood in the Park in 1848 when the watercolourist William Callow painted a view of the church and photographs of *c.*1900 record some huge trunks.[5] Some of these trees would have been planted in the eighteenth century. Was the small-leaved lime (a rarity in the fens) planted in the 1600s as 'exotic' planting or an ancient survival?

The latter part of the eighteenth century saw great changes in the Lincolnshire fens as elsewhere in the country; major enclosures had taken place in the 1770s and continued until the 1820s. Developments in livestock improvement and agriculture were paralleled by developments in landscaping of estates and improvements in the management of garden crops for domestic use. The influence of the great landscape gardeners and improvers percolated down to the lesser gentry including townsmen and parsons. On their small estates they found room for a shrubbery, a few specimen trees, a parterre, statuary, perhaps a ha-ha (Fig. 7).

If the initial creation of the modest park was carried out by the seventeenth century Beridges, major improvements on the estate are more likely to belong to the last decades of the century following. A long tree-lined drive with brick bridges swept out across the Park to Sutterton and the main Boston to Kings Lynn road. Here a pair of thatched circular lodges with gothick windows was built, in a style popular either side of 1800. Both lodges, with later

Fig. 7: View of garden looking west, 1958, showing statuary, box hedge parterre and branches of mature cedar tree to left. Wall on right adjoins Palm House site. The finials at the corners of the parterre were originally on the parapet corners of the Rectory. (The author)

Fig. 8: Sutterton. Lodges flanking former entrance to the carriage drive of Algarkirk Rectory, from a 1950s postcard. The further (north) lodge was demolished soon after this picture was taken. (Francis Frith Collection)

alterations, survived until the late 1950s (Fig. 8). Two other structures on the estate are also likely to be of late eighteenth century date. One is the hollow wall around the kitchen garden. Hot or flued walls were in their heyday after about 1750 yet within a hundred years had gone out of fashion again.[6] If it can be assumed that a Lincolnshire country parson (even a wealthy one) was not amongst the most avant garde in his ideas, a date in the late eighteenth century is the time when he might have initiated this work. The same may apply to the ice-house. Ice-houses had become popular in the later 1700s and many were constructed by the rural gentry.[7] A diagram of one is given in the copy of *Chambers Dictionary* (1788) formerly in the Beridge library.

All these works, not to mention outbuildings such as stables and coach house, required bricks, and it was not unusual both to dig and burn these on the premises. The Ice Pond (so named in the tithe award) apparently started life as a clay pit, the bricks being used for the ice-house and other works, since there is a good bed of clay in this area. In 1980-81 the footings of a large eight flued coal-fired brick kiln were excavated near the pond by the Trust for Lincolnshire Archaeology. This was undertaken in advance of proposed cultivation, which in the event did not take place; the site was subsequently scheduled as an Ancient Monument. There was no firm dating for the kiln other than the presence of a few fragments of eighteenth century pottery and there is no documentary evidence. An unsuccessful attempt was made to identify structures where bricks of the same measurements had been used, but the results were inconclusive. A full report of the excavation will appear in a future issue of *Lincolnshire History and Archaeology*.

The lodges had both been extended before 1881. In the 1950s the north one, which had a four-room extension, was bought for a nominal sum by the then Boston Rural District Council and promptly demolished! Quite recently (1980s) a number of bricks stamped with a letter B have been found, although not associated with any particular structure. It is almost certain that B stands for Beridge, even though no stamped bricks were found at the excavated brick kiln.

In conclusion three major development phases under the Beridge family can be suggested. The first, largely conjectural, was in the seventeenth century when the Park was established and a brick house may have replaced a timber-framed one. The house is described as 'large' by 1703. In the incumbency of Charles Beridge (1737-82), both house and grounds underwent their most extensive alterations. Charles himself appears to have spent most of his time in Cambridge, but this might have made it easier for construction work and refurbishment to take place.

Fig. 9: Algarkirk Rectory. Interior of room D, 'drawing room', showing original marble topped gilt console table and stool, with mid-nineteenth century mirror.

The latest alterations included the lavish drawing room (Fig. 9), not present in 1791 but dating to c.1830. Improvements to the kitchen, dairy and outbuildings seem to date from later in the century. In view of his recorded benificence in parish and district the credit for the final flowering must surely go to the last and best known Basil, Canon Beridge of Algarkirk.

Notes

1 Finds from the Rectory gardens and grounds were first reported to the City and County Museum, Lincoln in 1954, and were noted in *L.A.A.S.R.P.*, 6, 1 (1955), 13, note 30. Discoveries from later years are entered in the County Sites and Monuments Record.

2 K. Healey, *Algarkirk.* Booklet produced for an exhibition in 1951 combining centenary celebrations both of the Great Exhibition and the church restoration. Glebe terriers are at L.A.O.: Algakirk terrier bundle; Ter.7/200 and Ter.9/38, also Algakirk Parish 3.

3 L.A.O. Beridge 1/2 copy-will of 1805/1808; Beridge 5/5, dilapidations survey of 1881.

4 Tithe map 1838, L.A.O. M312.

5 Photos L.A.O., Beridge 7/11. Painting by W. Callow in private collection, painted copy in the author's possession.

6 Jean Bolam, 'Hot or flued walls Pt. 2', *The Garden History Society Newsletter,* 22 (Spring 1988).

7 Tim Buxbaum, *Icehouses,* Shire Album, 278 (1992).

Anwick and the Village Picturesque

David L. Roberts

Anwick is a small village four miles north-east from Sleaford. A substantial number of its acres were accumulated into the vast seventeenth century land-holdings of the Carre family which eventually became part of the even larger estates of the Herveys. The Herveys, a Suffolk family seated at Ickworth, became Earls of Bristol and it is the fourth Earl, the Earl-Bishop as he is better known, who concerns us here. During his ownership of Anwick between 1774, when he succeeded to the title, and his death in 1803, three buildings were planned in circular form. These were built of brick under conical roofs and had simple wooden casements in a gothick style. Several architects had experimented with these forms but it is an autograph design of 1799 by John Nash (1752-1835) which comes very close to one of the Earl-Bishop's cottages at Anwick.

During the eighteenth century there were many architectural experiments based on various theories, some aesthetic, some practical and others based on a fusion of both. The Picturesque, as championed by the Rev. William Gilpin's writing, is a term which embraces the analysis of what causes things and places to be picturesque. Gilpin was not keen on cottages in his landscape - only Castles or Gothic ruins were noble enough - and it was left to others to promote the Ornamental Cottage. This fusion of the pretty, the Sublime or the Rustick, Gothick or Antique was a facet of the cultured gentleman's, or lady's, response to landscape. The manner of accenting this ideal landscape with buildings was a source of much scholarly debate. It is impossible to summarize even the work of just one of the host of writers on the theme. Sir Uvedale Price, whose *On the Picturesque* (1794 and 1810) remained the standard work well into the nineteenth century. In an 'Essay on Architecture and Buildings', Price elaborates the essentials needed to build in the countryside. Even this is impossible to summarize without losing nuances essential to a complete understanding. It must suffice to isolate one or two of his remarks to illustrate the present context:

> Architecture is the divinity that raises the porches of cottages, and the rude posts that support them, into porticos and colonnades... There is an idea of rural simplicity annexed to a thatched cottage, which is very much in favour of that covering... it is no less picturesque when mossy, ragged and sunk in among the rafters in decay... Baldness of effect, in all objects, arises from want of shadow...[1]

These and similar observations crowd Price's prose. The Age of Reason produced scholars who tried to identify the undeveloped simplicity of the Primitive House. Men like Abbé Marc-Antoine Laugier were fascinated by notions of the first rude shelter man had built; these had long vanished but fertile imagination rather than archaeology supplied substitutes. Others, like Claude Perrault, searched classical sources to find descriptions of the earliest forms of building. A reconstruction of a Phrygian hut based on Vitruvius's account shows a circular building of turf, its thatched roof supported on a cone of rafters.[2] Sir William Chambers took up the challenge and pronounced 'That the primitive hut was a conic figure... from its being the simplest of solid forms...' Ledoux and several of his French contemporaries, following another route, compiled buildings from elementary geometrical solids. Guislane Joseph Henry, designed Vassale House (Rue Pigalle, Paris) as a '... full cylinder with conical roof. The architect did not worry about the practical disadvantages of the circular plan. He instead made experiments with diversified shapes in the interior...'[3] - its upper floor design is simpler and, although much larger, in many ways anticipates the Nash design. This geometrical theme was taken up by a loosely knit group of English architects towards the end of the eighteenth century. For instance, James Playfair, in his design for Cairness House, Aberdeenshire (1789) included a cylinder and cone pavilion as a motif in the service court.[4] Richard Elsam, writing in 1816, happily summarizes current opinion:

> In the earlier ages we are informed that men lived in woods and inhabited caves; but finding these recesses damp and unwholesome, in imitation of the birds, they built huts to shelter themselves from the intensity of the weather, which they ingeniously contrived by fixing boughs of trees in the ground in a circular form, and binding them together with oziers, and covering the outside with plaster, consisting of reeds, mud and clay. This shape being inconvenient on account of the sloping sides, the square and oblong figures

> were adopted... Sound bricks and good building stones well incorporated with mortar of a good and binding quality, will last for centuries, while those of wood and plaster, mud or clay, are continually out of repair, and therefore ought never to be introduced in countries where better materials can be procured.[5]

Although Elsam only used rectangular forms in planning his cottages, the geometrical theme was further elaborated by the next generation, frequently under a veneer of medievalizing ornament.

In the designs used at Anwick there is a fusion of so many of these elements that it must be assumed their author was aware of British as well as Continental thinking. At the forefront must have been the Earl-Bishop himself. As Jackson-Stops has emphasized,[6] the Earl-Bishop was passionately fond of circular and oval buildings, so much so that he contributed fifty guineas to the building of an oval First Presbyterian church in Belfast erected in 1781! In 1779 Soane designed a circular 'dog-house' for the Earl-Bishop, a miniature rotunda with curving wings (perhaps a loose translation of Gian Lorenzo Bernini's project drawing of the 1660s for the eastern facade of the Louvre)[7] and an oval dining-room for his new house at Downhill, Co. Derry. After the building of another mansion at Ballyscullion in the same county to an elaboration of the rotunda-and-curving-wings theme, this time probably by the Irish architect Shanahan in 1787, the Earl-Bishop spent the winter of 1781-82 on his Suffolk estates for the first time. It was to be ten years before he returned to their 'foggy, ferney' flatness again. 'Capability' Brown was called in to design 'an intire New House' after that first visit but it was never built. A similar fate befell another scheme proposed by C. H. Tatham and it was an Italian, Mario Asprucci, working in concert with the Earl-Bishop and the Sandys brothers, who eventually supplied the draught for the vast rotunda-and-curving wings design for the new Ickworth, six hundred feet wide, begun in 1795. The Earl-Bishop travelled widely, particularly in Italy, forming a circle of acquaintances and collecting works of art. He was, of course, immensely rich, having an income of some £40,000 a year in the 1780s. His acquaintance included the architects, Soane, Brown, Francis and Joseph Sandys, Michael Shanahan, C. H. Tatham and his master, Asprucci, Piranesi, James Wyatt, whom he took up and dropped, often quickly.

It is of interest that an Italian, Pietro Cataneo, was one of the earliest authors to advocate the circular plan as being useful in adding variety to the predominantly rectangular forms of building. Two plates from his *Quattro Libri* of 1554 'Forma di palazzo rotondo fuor dell'uso ordinario' show large houses arranged round central, pillared courts. His recommendation was to start from a rectangular form, cropping its corners and bringing it to an oval or circle. This anticipates the more 'modern' geometrical approach rather than archaeological conjecture. His work was known in eighteenth century England and it is possible that it played some formative role in the Earl-Bishop's obsession.[8]

Against this roll-call, the cottages and forge at Anwick seem very small fry. They are, however, as important in the genesis of their design as they are as representatives of a class of attractive buildings which has largely disappeared. A few years ago, a drawing based on a design by John Nash was published by Nigel Temple,[9] and its close similarity to the Anwick cottages promoted the research for this short account.

Nash lived a few doors away from Soane in London's Regent Street. The two men are now regarded as unfriendly rivals and there may have been a reluctance to discuss architectural matters. Soane however, had a pupil, Joseph Michael Gandy, who published his designs and who may well have taken part in such informal discussions forming the tentative link between exponents of Picturesque architecture. Soane's excursions into the architecture of the Picturesque include a sensitive design for a rustic dairy built at Hammels, Hertfordshire in 1783.[10] Its plan consisted of three conjoined semi-circular apses behind a pedimented Doric portico. Soane noted that 'The Pillars are proposed to be of the Trunks of Elm Trees with the bark on and honeysuckles and woodbines planted at their feet, forming festoons &c. The Roof to be thatched and the ends of the Rafters to appear...'. In 1805 Gandy published a more complex design for 'A Dairy Farm' (Fig. 1).[11] Whilst this is classically detailed, the hub of the scheme is a two story building of circular plan just over twice the diameter of the larger one at Anwick. The division of the circle into rooms is done in much the way Nash used in his design for Mr Pitt (Fig. 2) and in the layout of the vastly larger centrepiece of Ickworth there is a faint suggestion too of the simpler concept seen in the Anwick cottages (Fig. 3).

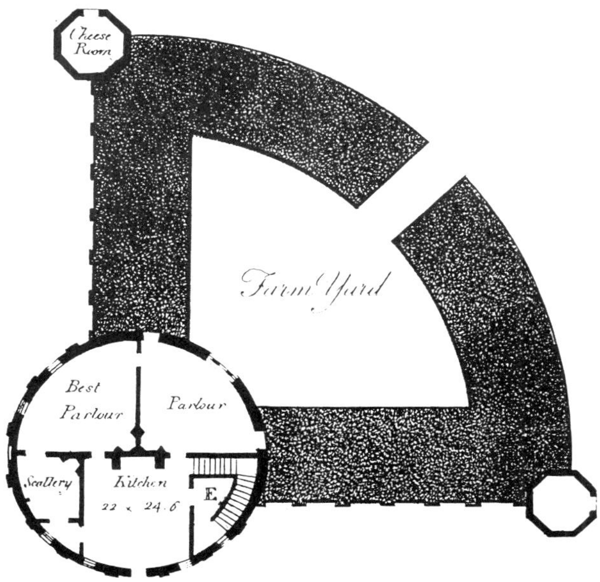

Fig. 1: Plate XXVII, from Gandy's 'Rural Architect' of 1805.

Gandy's design has only one room, the kitchen, of an almost rectangular plan, and the Parlour and Best Parlour are triangular in plan with one curved side. Comparison with the plan of Ickworth demonstrates the Earl-Bishop's choice was to have sub-rectangular rooms, leaving the remaining triangular spaces for lobbies. The same preference seems to have guided the Anwick layout.

John Nash worked in the widest sphere, from Royal Palaces to the humblest cottages - he is perhaps most noted for his work at Blaise Hamlet near Bristol. Early in his career he was associated with Humphry Repton, who worked at Scrivelsby in Lincolnshire for the Dymokes. Later he was to employ Humphry's sons, John Adey and George Stanley Repton, as assistants to whom was added Augustus Charles Pugin, in 1793. Although Pugin's son, Augustus Welby Northmore Pugin, the energetic genius of Gothic, regarded Nash's output with scorn, a considered judgement gives Nash much praise for his command of architectural 'massing' in his lively compositions but is less fulsome about his professional integrity, hasty draughtmanship and impatience with detailing.

The characteristically hasty draught design for Mr Pitt is dated 1799, it is inscribed at the top 'Plan and Elevation of a Cottage at Tunbridge Wells 1799' and has manuscript notes, the first section naming the room functions and then general instructions to the builder. The rooms are lettered on the plan (Fig. 2):

> The Circle 30 ft. in diam. in the inside. A. The kitchen 20 ft. by 15. B. Pantry 4ft 6 [inches] by 10 ft. C. Principal Bed-Room 14ft by 9ft 6. D. Children's Bedroom 10ft by 8. E. Closet 3ft by 2. F. Wash-house 13ft 6 by 7ft. G. Alcove 4Ft by 22ft 8. Six Windows 3ft 6 by 3ft 6 to Transom and 2ft 6 to Peak. A Seat under the Alcove between the Doors. A Lumber Room above the Cieling under the Thatch accessible by a Ladder. Pitch 9ft 6. Chimney 25ft high. Opening of Do. in the Kitchen 3ft. Oven in the Wash-house adjoining the back of the Chimney & projecting into the Principal Bed Room. Chimney square within and round above the Thatch. Length of Rafter that support ye Thatch 20ft. The Cottage built of Lath and Plaster upon a Brick Foundation rising abt. 18 Inches above the Ground. Estimate of Cost about £60.

The Mr Pitt, spelt 'Pit' in Nash's correspondence, was a friend of Mr Legh, one of Nash's more important clients. William Pitt had consulted Nash about works at Holmwood House, Kent, in 1791, but his precise identity and the reason for commissioning the drawing are unknown.[12]

At Anwick, the thatched cottage is of brick rather than the lath and plaster specified. In this context it is interesting to read of the Earl-Bishop's attitude to brick. In reply to his daughter's pleading to have Ickworth built of 'white stone bricks' he wrote:

> What! Child, build my house of a brick that looks like a sick, pale, jaundiced red brick, that would be red brick if it could, and to which I am certain our posterity would give a little rouge as essential to its health... I shall follow dear impeccable Palladio's rule, and as nothing ought to be without a covering in our raw damp climate, I shall cover the house, pillars and pilasters, with Palladio's stucco which has now lasted 270 years... It has resisted the frosts and rains of Vicenza - c'est tout dire - and deceives the most acute eye till within a foot...[13]

Otherwise Nash's specification seems to have been observed.

Although there is, however, no hard evidence that the Nash drawing, or even a copy of it, was in the hands of the Earl-Bishop's builder at Anwick, comparison between the existing house and the Nash drawing shows a similarity beyond contradiction. Only internally are there discrepancies. On the left of the plan axis as built, 'A' the kitchen, has been

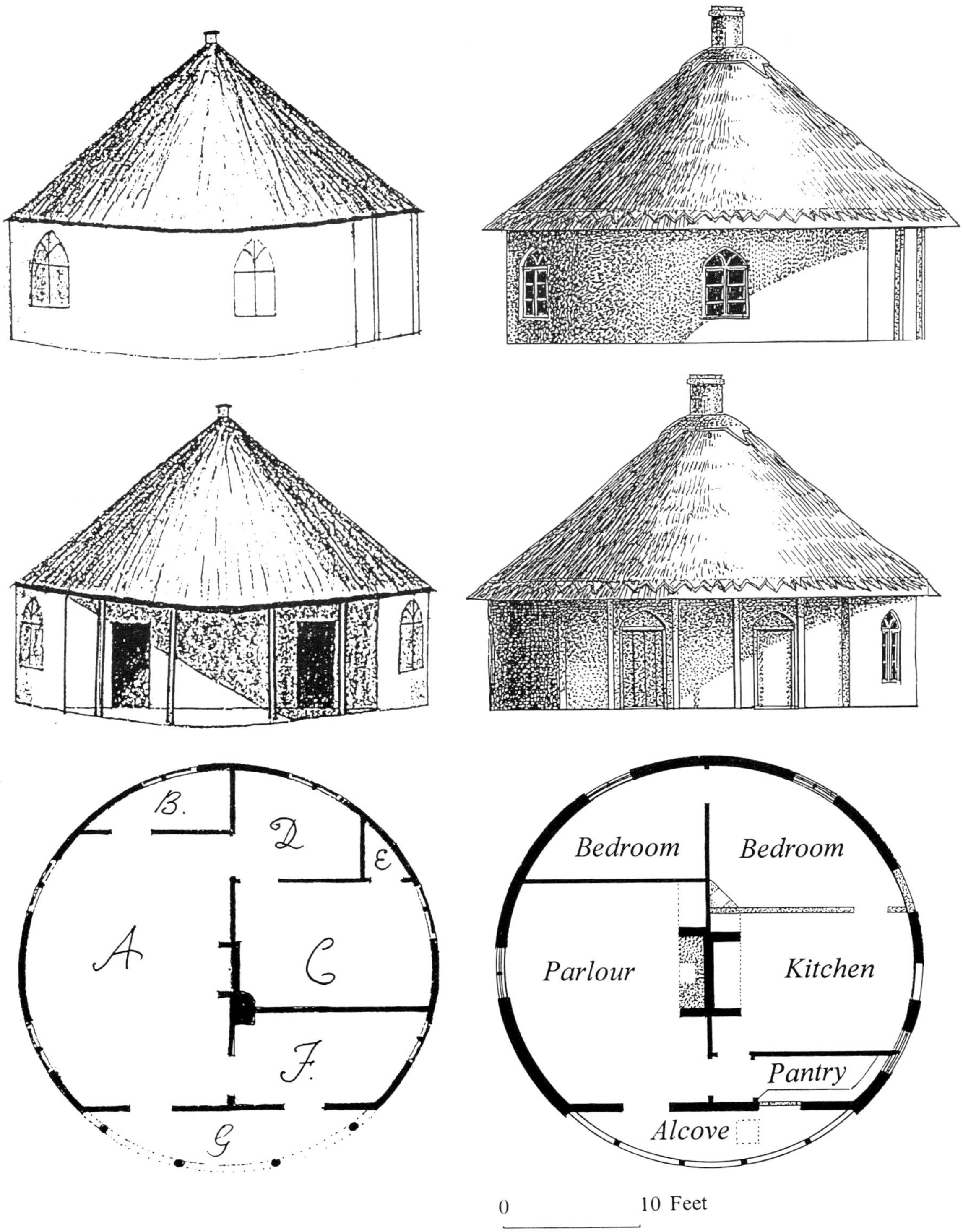

Fig. 2: The left hand column shows the elevations and plan taken from those drawn by John Nash forMr Pit[t] in 1799. The right hand column shows the sketch-plan and elevations from the thatched house at Anwick.

reduced in size and has only one window rather than the two shown in Nash's plan. Oddly, both on the elevation (Fig. 2 upper), and in the building, the single windows lighting 'A' are shown in their 'built' positions. Even allowing for the wobbly drawing of the design, Nash seems either to have made a mistake or allowed for an internal alteration not shown on his plan. On the other side of the axis, as built at Anwick, a later alteration has moved the wall forward to create a larger bedroom. At the same time the window opening obstructed by the new wall was blocked. These alterations are shown stippled on the existing house-plan in Fig. 2.

Alterations were made to the internal arrangement suggested by Nash before building began. His wash-house, 'F', was reduced in size to form the present pantry. His 'B' was enlarged. On the other side of the axis, 'D' and 'E' were perhaps also enlarged before the later alteration. The new intention may have been to light the room by two shared windows along the original lines of the Smithy house. Recently, a new opening with a glazed door has disturbed evidence for an original window at this point. Had there been a window here, the close spacing would echo the road elevation of the Smithy house. It would not have increased the number of windows beyond the six specified by Nash, an important consideration after the third increase in Window Tax on 1 October 1784 levied on houses with upwards of seven windows.

The two original outer doors opening into 'G' are still extant. That intended to open into the wash-house (pantry as built) 'F', has long been disused but seems to have been intended as a 'back door' linking the kitchen through the lobby. This scheme follows the preference shown in many vernacular house-plans in Kesteven where the kitchen and parlour are subject to a genteel social distinction surviving from a very much earlier period. In this context it is important to see the confusion raised by two outer doors of different status standing, undifferentiated, side by side. Status decreed that these should be firmly set apart and the answer was to move the

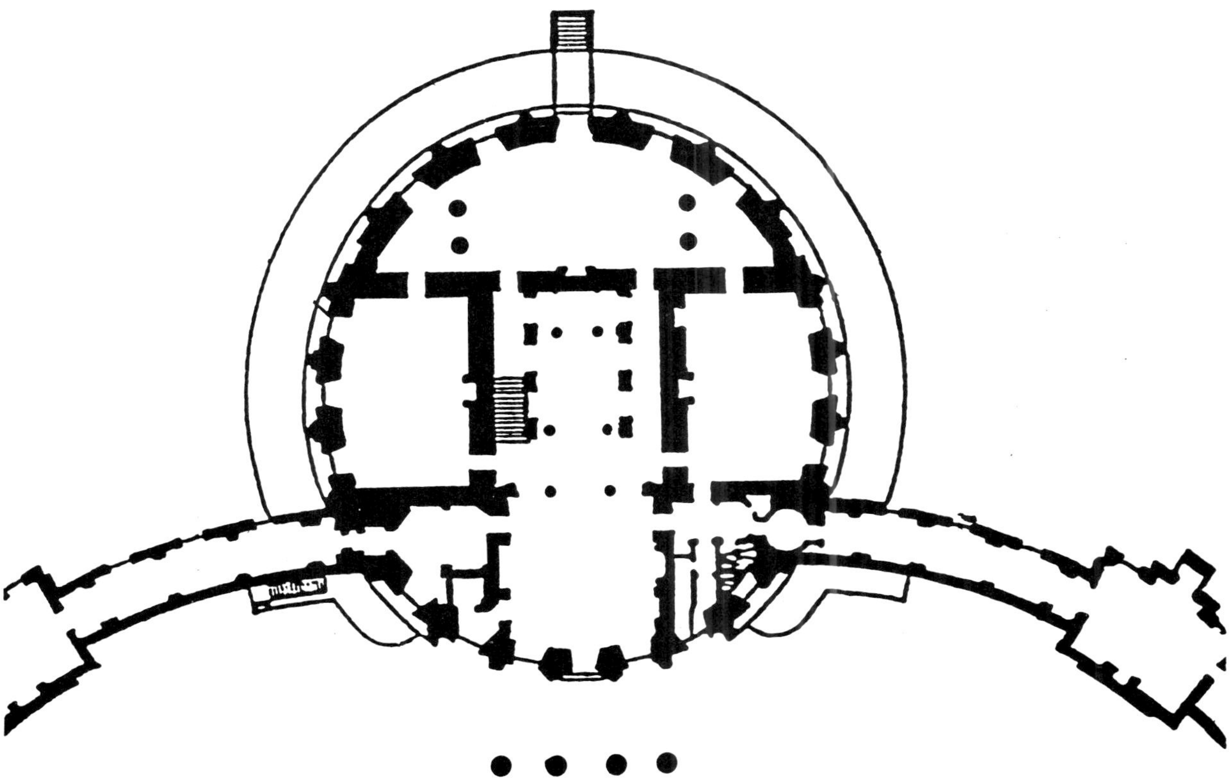

Fig. 3: Part of the ground-plan of Ickworth House, Suffolk, showing the Rotunda, a hundred feet in diameter, and its internal subdivision. (After Jackson-Stops, 'The English Country House in Perspective')

kitchen entrance to the new door at the side.

It might be thought that a smithy, the nineteenth century equivalent of a light industrial unit, could not form part of the Picturesque village. In a letter to G. J. Legh Nash, however, gives intriguing advice on the remodelling of a village in the Picturesque manner. Having discussed the cottages, he goes on to say that they ought to be '...in the most favourable points of view...'. As though to emphasize the relationship of his designs to paintings, Legh was to

> ... make the lodge at High Legh... the termination of the picture when you enter the village... the cross and upper cottage as the foregound... the blacksmith's shop as the next most picturesque object and requiring to be near the road we placed at the other corner & we turned the smiths shop to look up the road so that the fire may illuminate the whole length of road and give a chearfulness at night to the whole village...[14]

Nash obviously saw the smithy as a focus in his 'picture' rather than an embarassment.

The road at Anwick, an eighteenth century turnpike, replaced miry tracks reputed to have been impassable during the winter months or longer, leaving Billinghay, Anwick's neighbour, quite cut off from the outside world. By 1799 the Fens of Anwick, Kyme and Billinghay had all been banked although northwards, from Tattershall Bridge, a traveller saw '... nothing but water and the corn all lost...'[15] The Smithy seems to be a product of that age of improvement. It provided assistance to the traveller on the new road and to the farmers on the newly drained ground as well as a source of income to the landlord on his building investment.

Although Anwick Forge and the Smithy House are overlaid by modern extensions and altered internally, the bones of a composition related to the thatched house are immediately recognizable. Their scale is a reduction by a third of the Nash drawings and the thatched house dimensions. The Smithy has a circular plan just over twenty feet in diameter. The forge

Fig. 4: Photograph c.1930, of the smithy and house at Anwick. From the collection of Richard Powell, the present owner (1994). (Note: a more recent photograph is in NMR together with one of the Thatched House, c.1970, Roberts, Kesteven Record, negs. FY 1402/3, and Museum of Lincolnshire Life Collection.)

hearth retains some traces of original brickwork but is now largely the result of a nineteenth century rebuilding and a reduction in size during the 1950s. The slated roof has heavy softwood framing which helps steady the chimney snaking its way from the off-centre hearth to the roof-cone apex. The doors and windows occupy original positions and may recreate the appearance of the originals but two openings under steel lintels have been cut through part of the western circumference in the 1950s.

The Smithy House is the same size as the Smithy. Its original tri-partite entrance-motif, two (renewed) gothick windows flanking a door to the street, is clearly evident although the door, shown in Fig. 4., has been blocked. Unhappily, the bisecting wall is now all that remains of the original internal plan. Structural and oral evidence confirms that there was a closet at the south-west quadrant sharing a window with the parlour-bedroom on its north side. The chimney brickwork and kitchen-hearth south of the bisecting wall were removed in 1984. Earlier alterations may have removed a similar partition at the south-east angle below the ceiling now stiffened by an inserted beam. This alteration seems to have been effected during the extension of the house eastwards into the rectangular link buildings described below. The only other additions are a clumsy brick porch on the south side of the smithy and an eccentric modern canted bay to the house.

Between the two cylinders of house and smithy was a rectangular building of which only slight traces remain excepting its roof. A brick wall linking the two cylinders supports the centre-spans of framing of the hipped roof. On its north side was an open shoeing shed and workshop later partially boarded in on its west side (Fig. 5). From the photograph, this side of the roof was supported on four wooden uprights. On the south little remains except a stub of walling of

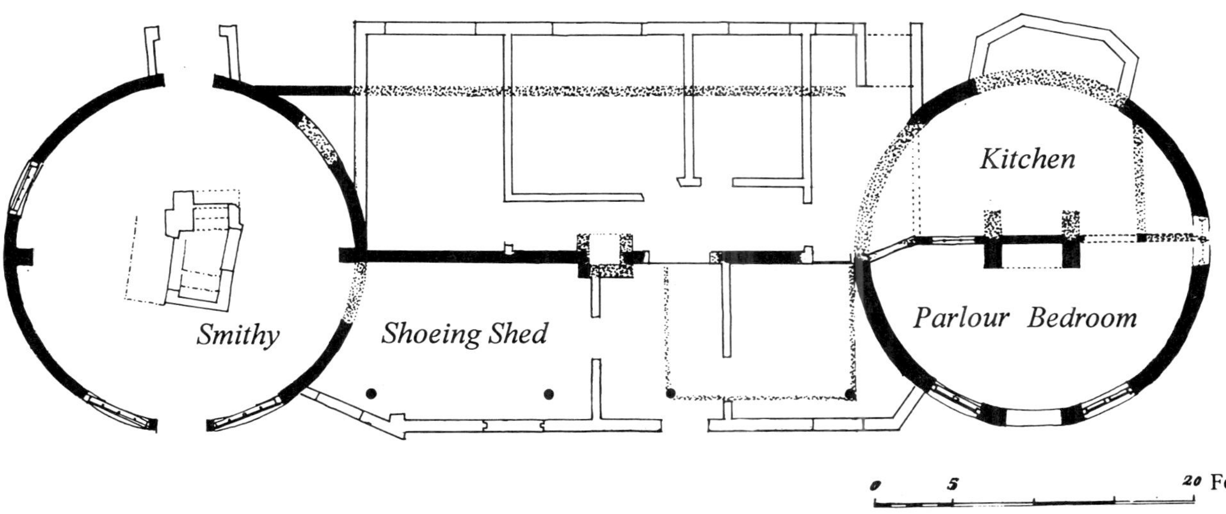

Fig. 5: The ground plan of the Smithy, left, showing the position of the hearth, and the Smithy house, right, with the position of the demolished interior division shown by stippling. Between them lies the large rectangular link-building housing, formerly, the shoeing shed and other working areas. Solid black shows the brickwork of circa. 1800 and stippling indicates the probable extent of the complex before the alterations made since 1950 which are superimposed in outline.

brick laid in the same English Garden Wall Bond, with three intervening courses of stretchers, visible in the unrendered walls of the rest of the complex. It is a matter of debate as to whether this stub of wall is contemporary with the house and smithy. It seems to relate so well to the original brickwork that the rectangular 'link' may be contemporary. If indeed it is, then the problem of roofing the whole complex presented a headache. At present the slated roofs are still part of the work carried out by J. Benjamin of Digby in 1847. What is not clear is whether Benjamin removed thatch and lowered the roof pitches as part of his work. Slate is, after all, a far more sensible, if less picturesque, roof covering for a Smithy with its attendant risk of fire. The evidence of the chimney-stacks suggests he may not have done but it is impossible to compare their patina of age with that of the other brickwork, covered as it is with render or whitewash. As it is, the present pitch is rather too low for thatch and the awkward junction between the circular and rectangular roofs is clumsily but competently done. On the south side of the linking rectangular building the roof has been extended under a still lower pitch to cover the modern extensions providing corridor and bedrooms built in the 1950s. This seems largely to have been a revision of bedrooms attached to the house effected by an earlier scheme which removed part of the house wall. On the north side the wooden uprights of the open shed were removed and a wall erected to provide more living space and an office. It is of interest to note that where the rafter-ends are still visible, these project as butt-ends without soffit-boards. In the specification for the thatched dairy at Hammels of 1783, it was specified '...and the ends of the Rafters to appear...'

The thatched house is now unoccupied and the Smithy and Smithy-house are for sale (1994). It is hoped legislation protecting historic buildings is effective in securing their future. The loss in 1945 of Teapot Hall, Dalderby, an ornamental cottage perhaps associated with the work of the Reptons in the 1790s, has left a sad gap in the surviving body of small houses in Picturesque solid geometry evolved by the architects discussed here. In the case of Tea-Pot Hall, Addy was fooled by the 'primitive' concept into believing it was an early cruck building[16] rather than an essay in solid geometry, a thatched prism - cousin to those cylinders discussed here.[17]

Acknowledgements

The help given by the John Rylands University Library, Manchester, in supplying a copy of the Nash letter from which the left-hand column of Fig. 2 has been adapted, is gratefully acknowledged. Toucan Books have kindly allowed the use of the plan redrawn in Fig. 4.

Notes

1 Sir Uvedale Price, *On the Picturesque with an Essay on the Origin of Taste and much Original Matter by Sir Thomas Dick Lauder* (1842), 393-401.

2 Joseph Rykewert, *On Adam's House in Paradise*, 2nd edn (1981), 57.

3 Emil Kauffmann, *Architecture in the Age of Reason* (1968), 184.

4 J. Mordaunt Crook, *The Greek Revival* (1972), Plate 84.

5 Richard Elsam, *Hints for Improving the Condition of the Peasantry... by Promoting Comfort in their Habitations... Interspersed with... Designs for Cottages...and Embellished with Picturesque Scenery, Elegantly Coloured...* (1816), 15.

6 Gervase Jackson-Stops, *The English Country House in Perspective* (1990), 120.

7 Joseph Rykwert, *The First Moderns: The Architects of the Eighteenth Century* (1980), 32.

8 Pietro Cataneo, *I Quattro Primo Libri di Architettura* (1554), 53 and 54 4 XII reprinted by Gregg Press Inc., N. J., U.S.A. 1964. Inigo Jones had copies of Cataneo's work - see John Harris, et al., *The King's Arcadia* (1973), 64; Batty Langley includes his observations on the Orders in particular - see Eileen Harris, *British Architectural Books and Writers 1556-1785* (Cambridge, 1990), 106, 200, 272.

9 Nigel Temple, *John Nash and the Village Picturesque* (1979), 13.

10 Pierre de la Ruffiniere du Prey, *Catalogues of Architectural Drawings in the Victoria and Albert Museum* (1985), cat.77.

11 Joseph Gandy, *The Rural Architect* (1805), Plate XXVII.

12 Temple, *John Nash and the Village Picturesque,* 125 n 50. citing letter in Cornwall-Legh papers, John Rylands University Library, Manchester.

13 Jackson-Stops, *English Country House in Perspective*, 124.

14 Temple, *John Nash and the Village Picturesque*, 154 citing undated (possibly 17 January 1798) letter in John Rylands University Library.

15 Michael Lloyd, *Portrait of Lincolnshire* (1983), 67; T.W. Beastall, *The Agricultrual Revolution in Lincolnshire*, History of Lincolnshire, VIII (1978), 101.

16 Sidney Oldall Addy, *The Evolution of the English House* (1910), 19-22 (Addy also restates much of the earlier thinking on the round house).

17 There seems to be a gap in the archive material for Anwick. No documents seem to have been recorded in the Suffolk Record Office. There is the map accompanying the enclosure award (L.A.O., Kesteven Awards 2) which shows the plots occupied by the buildings discussed here, but it is just too early to show the houses themselves. The title to the Smithy and Smithy House records their ownership by the Bristol Estate (Mr Powell).

A Country House Inventory: Hagnaby Priory, 1927-1930, Shortly Before Demolition

Nick Lyons

It is no adverse criticism of the Lincolnshire Country Houses booklets which Terence Leach, with Bob Pacey, began to issue not very long before his death, to say that what was planned, was partial; much either could not be recovered, or would have taken too much space and time to record. The field for investigation remains vast. Certain fundamental difficulties facing the researcher in this area are noted in the introduction to Volume 1 of *Lost Lincolnshire Country Houses* - changes in style of life, especially since 1939; lack of illustrations; comparatively early destruction; and the sheer number of lost houses. More can be added to the list. Certainly, anyone who has used estate records will be aware that they rarely include information about the internal arrangements, domestic or economic, of country houses; that architectural archives are especially rare, and pictures of interiors even rarer. True, generalized descriptions of country houses and country house life at different historical times are possible, indeed popular[1], but even a superficial reading of the sources shows how much the appeal of such places lay in their special and peculiar characteristics, dependent in turn upon architecture, domestic facilities (not least their degrees of modernization), and the tastes and proclivities of the family and servants. Given that any large establishment was intended to operate as a distinct social and economic unit, every country house merits an intimate written history of its own; the Lincolnshire pamphlets attempt this for one house, Bayons Manor - admittedly extraordinary for its architecture, literary and political connections, and its demolition - but we are aware that the same may not be done for many others. Something can be done; David Taylor has shown in "*I Remember Normanby*" (Scunthorpe Museum and the Hutton Press, 1994) what may be achieved by exploiting that vital component, the people who made such places work, developing an approach very different to that of Leach and Pacey, although with the advantage that there was already much good documentation relating to Normanby's earlier history. But this cannot be repeated readily for many other big houses, let alone the lesser ones.

In attempting to recover the story of all sorts of houses, not just the largest ones, we are also faced by the acknowledged historiographical irony of probate inventories, which allow us, *ceteris paribus*, a more intimate knowledge of sixteenth and seventeenth century domestic arrangements than is ever likely to be available for the eighteenth and nineteenth centuries. Admittedly imperfect, requiring careful interpretation and references to cognate sources such as wills, parish registers, and taxation returns, whatever their drawbacks probate inventories are hugely better than no inventories at all - which is very nearly the problem facing us once we want to examine the contents of houses from about 1750 - to where? In fact, to the present day. Other sources do appear about the time probate inventories cease - illustration obviously improves, architects' plans survive more often, occasionally inventories were still created in connection with wills and bankruptcies, and auction sale catalogues appear;[2] but there is no comparable required mechanism systematically producing inventories of chattels in large numbers and approximately according to a given pattern. A country house inventory of any date is likely to repay close study, and any from the nineteenth or early twentieth centuries can usually be linked to some sort of illustration or plan, be it no more than an outline ground plan from Ordnance Survey sources.

Hagnaby Priory, near Spilsby, was a double fake. It was given a falsified name and, in the 1830s, became a mock-Tudor mansion, to be extended as such in the 1850s. The place had never had a priory - there was an abbey at Hagnaby near Hannah, well out to the north east in the marsh beyond Alford, but Hagnaby near Spilsby had come before the Dissolution under Revesby Abbey, being served by 'a chaplain and his clerk with a yearly scanty stipend... There was in this parish a ... hermitage at a place called "Segedic" or "Sedgedyke" in Halton Fen which ... became a decoy-farm.'[3] No 'great house' can be traced in the parish before the late eighteenth century, despite much of it being in the hands of powerful and

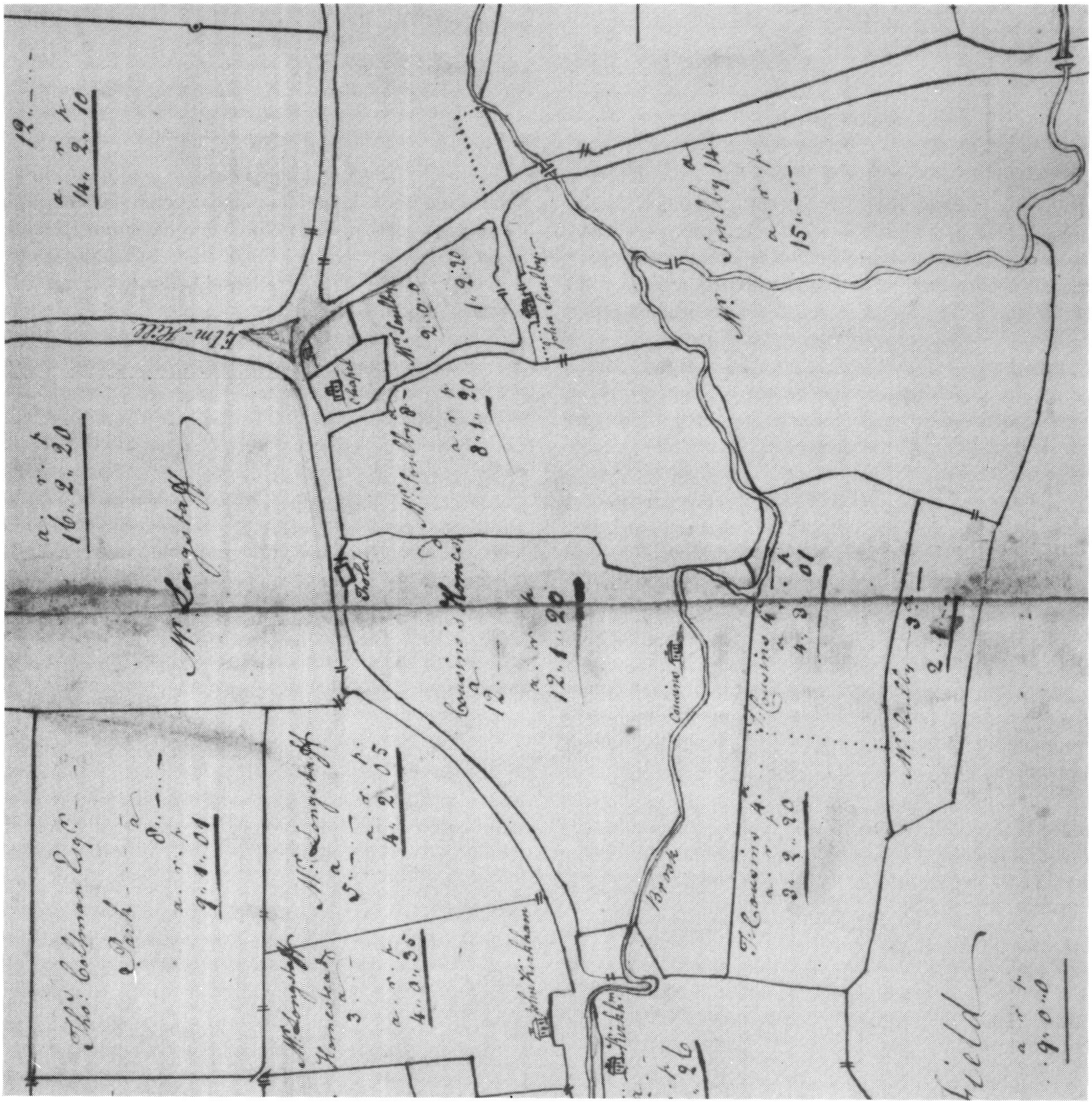

Fig. 1: Part of Thomas Coltman's Hagnaby estate surveyed by French Johnson, 1768. The house shown east of the church appears to be beyond the site of Coltman's new house (Fig. 2), although the marked lanes must have been adapted as the drive around it. (Lincolnshire County Council Education and Cultural Services Directorate: Archives).

well-connected owners during the sixteenth and seventeenth centuries. In 1716 it was purchased by Henry Coltman of Westminster, gentleman, an Exchequer official.[4] In the mid-eighteenth century the family had settled in southern Lindsey, and John Coltman, nephew and heir of Henry, lived in Horncastle. He was associated with the Banks family.[5] His elder son, also called John, died unmarried in 1768, and was succeeded by a younger brother, Thomas Coltman of Derby who immediately had French Johnson survey his estates (Fig. 1)[6]. Thomas lived to 1826, married twice, but had no children; he was responsible for the creation of the first Coltman house at Hagnaby, ownership of which went briefly to his brother George, who died in 1828, and then to George's son, another Thomas. Thomas Coltman (1800-1875)[7] was succeeded by his daughter, who had married Roger Pocklington, taking the name Pocklington-Coltman; but there were no children, the estate passing again through female lines to the Rogers family, which became Coltman-Rogers. Charles Coltman-Rogers may have been preparing to sell the house and estate before his death in 1929, and his heir Julian, having succeeded, completed the process.

The house sold off with the estate was architecturally remarkable, through the work of Thomas Coltman the second, and the Sleaford architects Charles Kirk the elder and Charles Kirk the younger. Thomas Coltman the first (1747-1826) moved to live on his Hagnaby estate between 1775 and 1789,[8] where he created a small park and had built the relatively simple five-bay, three-storeyed Georgian house drawn by Nattes in the 1790s (Fig. 2), and seen by John Cragg of Threekingham in 1799, when he

> went on the side of West Fen about a mile and then entered Hagnaby lordship, which is... enclosed, rode by the side of a very pleasant rivulet as far as Mr. Coltman's new house, it is very handsome of brick and a pleasant piece of land and brook just by. This is only a small village with a chapel [sic] newly built.[9]

Coltman had inherited 'the modest Lincolnshire estate'[10] which, though scattered, offered potential, could the money be found. Hagnaby lay in a line of fen-edge parishes largely enclosed by landlord activity,[11] near to the territories of the Dymokes at Scrivelsby and Banks at Revesby; Thomas Coltman was on good terms with Sir Joseph Banks, and served his interest in county politics and in the county defence scare of the 1790s.[12] His second marriage brought Thomas Coltman money, which seems to have allowed him to build at Hagnaby, redeem the mortgage, and purchase land in adjacent parishes. He was accepted by the landed gentry, and served in appropriate offices in county government.[13]

George Coltman, owner of the Hagnaby estate briefly from Thomas's death in 1826 to his own in 1828, was a doctor in Liverpool, and moved to Hagnaby. His son Thomas had attended Brasenose College, Oxford, from 1819 to 1822, when he took his Bachelor's degree and entered the Inner Temple. Perhaps his bothering to take a degree indicates an expectation that he would need to have a profession, but at the age of twenty-eight he became owner of the estate; possibly he had been engaged in the management already, or even took over when his father succeeded. His late uncle had already adopted the suppositious house name; his obituary in the *Gentleman's Magazine* for November 1826 gives his home as 'Hagnaby Priory'. This name was used in Edward Mogg's revision of *Paterson's Roads* in 1829.[14] Given the times, and the influence of Byron, Scott and a host of other gothic-romantic writers and artists, it is not a surprising adaption, whatever its lack of authenticity. He may have been influenced by the authentic medieval buildings at Scrivelsby, and moved to jealousy of the rather less authentic medieval origins of the great house at Revesby - which, whilst not yet gothicized, stood some distance from the abbey whose name it had usurped. He may even have had to insist on the name 'Hagnaby', since local usage had long been Hawnby or Hornby,[15] but at present no personal papers have come to light to explain precisely his motives in playing with the house's name. Much more was to come. About 1835 the existing house, the late eighteenth century brick box whose elegance had impressed Cragg, was cased in pale brick and given a Tudor-Gothic facade, his architect being Charles Kirk the elder; this was presumably the part of the Priory which survives today, although closer examination is needed to confirm the fact. No plans are known to survive, apart from what can be made out from the estate map of 1839 (Fig. 3);[16] the Priory's grounds are in this developed, but not heavily timbered, and the landscaped or emparked areas do not extend as far as they were later to do. The outline of the house and associated buildings cannot readily be reconciled with Nattes's drawing, so presumably the received date (1835-36) for the first rebuilding - accepted by Pevsner, Harris and Antram, Leach and Pacey, and possibly derived from Hunt[17] - is accurate. Thomas Coltman the younger indulged himself in a great remaking of the house about 1850-51, but scribblings on the 1839 map suggest repeated reference in planning alterations to the grounds; the clearest change

Fig. 2: Hagnaby, the seat of Mr Coltman by Claude Nattes c.1795. Rebuilding of the church accompanied or predated the new house. Close examination of the drawing suggests that there were bay windows extending through all floors of the house on the east. (Lincolnshire County Council Education and Cultural Services Directorate: Local Studies Collection, Lincoln Central Library).

affecting the immediate environment of the Priory is straightening of the village road to the north, and replanting. When all of these changes were accomplished, Thomas Coltman had a huge Tudor-Gothic mansion, set in a well-stocked and developed but secluded walled park (Figs. 4 & 5), with views south across the improved fenlands, sheltered to the north by the wold-edge. Perhaps he did all of this to compete with Banks Stanhope's rebuilding at Revesby.

So far the story has, in the absence of significant archival material, depended on a few facts, put together with extrapolation and surmise; now things get worse. We know who were Thomas Coltman the younger's favoured architects: Charles Kirk the elder (1791-1847) and the younger (1825-1902), both of Sleaford. The names of the Kirks occur repeatedly throughout the nineteenth century records of Sleaford itself, in the annals of Lincolnshire church building and church restoration or 'improvement'; they designed and built municipal structures throughout south Lincolnshire - and very likely beyond - and were ready hands in creating the impressive, anachronistic architecture of the railway age. In terms of church work in Lincolnshire, the period from 1850 to 1890 'is dominated, as might be expected, by James Fowler of Louth and Charles Kirk of Sleaford'.[17] Charles Kirk the younger was also a practical antiquarian, on the committee of the Lincoln Diocesan Architectural Society - of which he was a life member - and presented a paper on 'Kyme and its Tower' to the Society's meeting at Sleaford in 1881.[19] Pevsner, Harris and Antram include nearly fifty references to the Kirks as architects in the second edition of *The Buildings of England: Lincolnshire*; this cannot take account of work outside the county. Yet there seems to be no known collection of their working papers, and neither appears in the *Directory of British Architects 1834-1900* (1990).[20] There is room for a close study of their work, even one which depends upon surviving structures - but that would do nothing to help in this instance. Hagnaby Priory, an impressive creation of its kind, and as honest a fake as ever Victorian capitalist and architect contrived between them, is a lost country house in a very full sense, little recorded information surviving where it might have been expected.

And this brings us to Serendipity. About a year before Terence Leach's untimely death, I purchased from a dealer a small bundle of valuers' inventories, dating from the 1920s to the 1940s, the work of J. Peacock Rayner, Auctioneer and Valuer, then of 37 Silver Street, Lincoln. All were for properties in Lincolnshire; most valued contents, for sale, or prior to leasing houses on furnished tenancy agreements. The most impressive is that for Hagnaby Priory, dated January, 1927; it excludes 'Pictures, Household Linen, Plate and Wines' - and, pencilled in later,

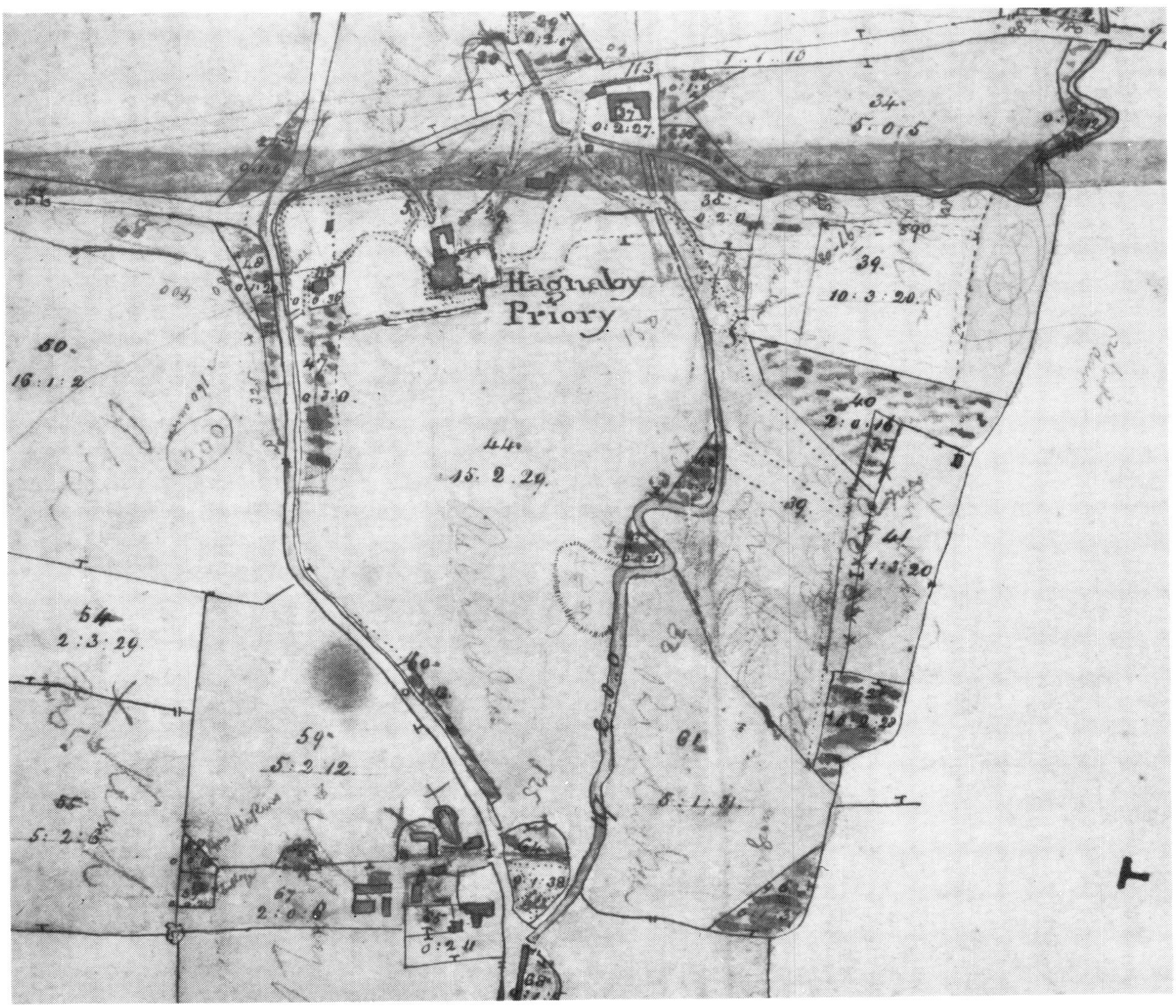

Fig. 3: Hagnaby surveyed by J. S. Padley, 1839, showing development of the Priory grounds, with later pencil notes suggesting further change. (Lincolnshire County Council Education and Cultural Services Directorate: Archives).

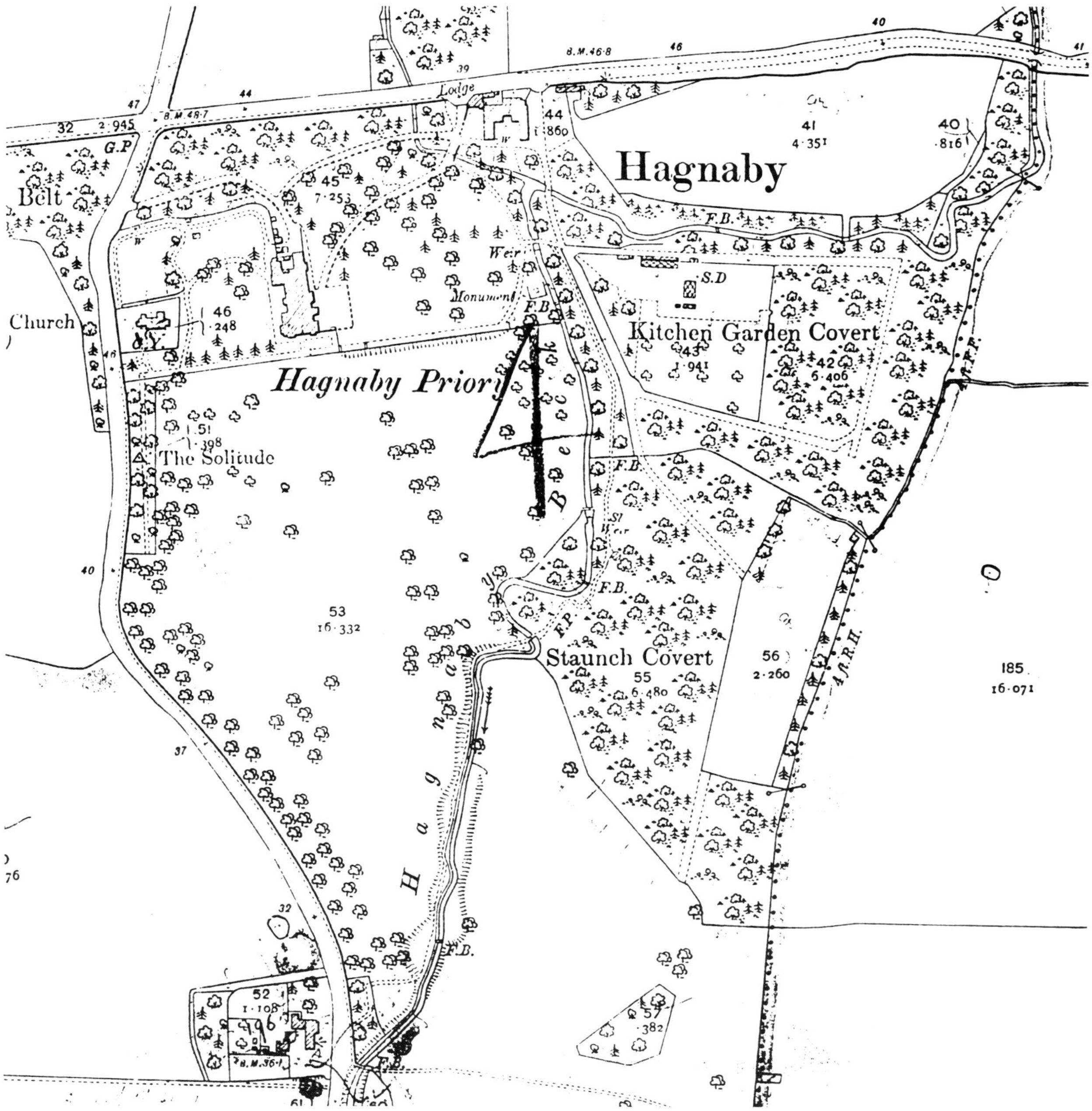

Fig. 4: Hagnaby Priory grounds as shown on the second edition 25 inch Ordnance Survey map 1906.

'& Books' - and all were the property of C. Coltman-Rogers Esq. There are eighty-two foolscap sheets, with the list typed on one side only, in the purple-blue tone so typical of the period. Catalogues for sale of the house itself and estate, and for the contents - as it turns out, residue of the contents - survive.[21] Charles Coltman Rogers died in 1929, the two sales being carried through by his heir, Julian, although the date of the inventory, and notes added to it, suggest that it was compiled with a sale or other break-up of the property in mind. Neither catalogue was well produced; neither carried photographs, nor useful plans - certainly not one of the house - and although the house was commended as a private residence, it inevitably was pronounced suitable as 'a School or Institution'; the 1930s were, after all, to be very much the graveyard-time for large houses and their contents. Exclusion of pictures, plate, wine and books from the inventory - and very much from the sale of contents - suggests that they were either being retained in the family, or sold somewhere more suitable; possibly they went to the Coltman Rogers house at Stanage, near Radnor.

The inventory of 1927 had been drawn up to include all larger objects, down to single pieces of pottery and ornaments. Everyday small-scale detritus was not included; we may guess that cupboards and drawers were not empty, but do not know their contents; however, room by room we can recover some idea of intended or actual use, and suggestible minds draw conclusions about the family's interests and preoccupations. An inventory without an appropriate house-plan is difficult to use; one for a house the size of Hagnaby Priory - scarcely a pattern-book mansion - must be particularly so. The order in which rooms are listed does not allow ready reconstruction of a plan, although dimensions can be recovered from the 1929 sale catalogue. The rooms were named, for the most part sufficiently to record their function, and sometimes to indicate décor, and on which side of the house they lay.

First, the rooms themselves - from published photographic postcards and from the Ordnance Survey maps, we can establish a general geography for the house. The inventory begins at the main entrance, the

Fig. 5: Hagnaby Priory c.1910. (D. N. Robinson Collection)

porch, which lay at the base of the three-storey squared tower. The way leads into the Outer Hall, an inner hall, to the main reception rooms and Library. A main staircase leads to the first floor, where there are four bedrooms, with dressing rooms, and the 'Bachelor's Room'; so far we have been in the 1851 extension, at the south of the whole range, and apparently remain so, descending by another staircase to the Side Entrance, Lavatory, and Gun Room, apparently on the west side of the house. We return to the first floor, to the Centre Landing, to visit more bedrooms; there are four, one apparently directly adjoining the Lower West Sitting Room. Proceeding to the second floor, still in the newer part of the house, we find two lesser bedrooms, and two lumber rooms, one of which seems to be in the Tower.

This completes the formal or family part of the house. Next come the Maid Servants' Quarters, but the route and floor are unclear; probably we are now in the house of the first Thomas Coltman, remodelled in 1835-36. Five separate maids' bedrooms are listed, with a store room, opening off, or otherwise close to, the Back Landing. We now seem to descend one floor, to the housekeeper's room, and through passages to the Butler's Pantry. These are close to the Servants' Hall, near to the Kitchen. Beyond or around are a scullery and two larders. Then we go up again, to the attics, without reference to a staircase or landing, and find five attic rooms, collectively listed as the Men's Quarters. This completes the house, but there remain outside the Wash-house, Laundry, Carriage House, Saddle Room and Summer House.

This rapid, almost blind tour of the house is at least significant of the relationship between architecture and social structure. To the south, i.e. the newly-antique south wing, were the superior rooms, devoted to the family's comfort, amusement, business, social responsibilities, and pretensions. A visitor found the way to the reception rooms guarded by a fake porch in a fake tower, leading into an outer hall which gave way to an inner hall, which was made slightly less imposing only by virtue of being used as a living area. Arrival drew domestic staff from the far depths of the house; like spear-carriers fulfilling minor but impressive parts, they mutely made things work, enhancing the already great figures of the family and their like. Then they retired, workers to their hive, to the kitchens, sculleries, pantries, laundry and further offices, until duty drew them out again, to give function to the form of the south wing; without them, the family's comfort and status were severely diminished, and, hard as a servant's lot might become, their employment in the big house allowed them a kind of security - and greater status - in return. By the time the inventory of 1927 was made, there had probably been no butler in the pantry nor complement of lesser servants for years, yet the archaeology of names had survived in the rooms. Perhaps too the house's relative youth explains why the main bedrooms had no special names - merely the Hall Bedroom, Yellow, Blue, Green and Red bedrooms, and then the Lower East or West Bedrooms. The Victorian age was not a generation away, and it is pre-eminently an house of that period which was seen by J. Rayner Peacock in 1927.

An inventory is primarily a list of chattels, moveable goods, as defined by law - and so far we have merely been playing the historian's game of oblique extrapolation. Because there are no illustrations of the contents, and only brief, single-line descriptions of the furniture, we can put away our guides to the value of antique furniture - this is not Miller's country; impressive, showy, perhaps even unnecessarily vulgar as some of the Priory's contents may have been, we can't play the game of 'Goodness! How much would that be worth today?' But we can consider how the contents room by room bear out their attributed functions, and even if our tentative conclusions appear predictable ones, the example may be important in bearing out reasonable expectations.

The inventory, created in January, 1927, was used at a later date or dates for checking the contents, so there are pencilled notes and amendments. These either confirm presence or condition, note where objects have been moved between rooms, or indicate sale, though whether this was intended or achieved is unclear. Several times the name 'Seaton' appears, which remains at present unexplained. The only dated note, at the front, lists some furniture - largely Chippendale chairs with fixed seats - going 'To Lamming, Spilsby' in June, 1928. G. Lamming appears in contemporary trade directories as builder, joiner, cabinet maker and undertaker. In a few cases additions to the original inventory have been made in manuscript. Inexplicably some pages have been crossed through and the single word 'new' scribbled in pencil; this is found in the cases of the largest and most lavishly furnished rooms, and may refer to the need for a new inventory. Some lesser rooms are struck through, but without comment.

Given the date of the inventory, the death of Charles Coltman Rogers in 1929, the sale of the estate and eventual sale of the contents, there would have been various occasions when reference to the original might have been needed. As it is, the additional notes add somewhat to its value as an historical source, however enigmatical they appear. What survives is a lively reminder that the contents of country houses could change with the means, tastes, and requirements of their occupants. The perfect model of such an house would contain the furnishings acquired when it was first built, and perhaps register signs of later changes in taste, by addition rather than by wholesale refurnishing. Thus at Hagnaby there should have been a relatively small amount of late eighteenth century furniture from the first house, and two similar but distinct collections of Gothickry, Abbotsford oak, and genuine old joined English oak, perhaps with some choice early European imports, from the rebuildings of the 1830s and 1850s. Given the extension of 1850-51, Thomas Coltman the second might well have filled his new-old home with Great Exhibition furniture of the appropriately fantastic sort. From his death in 1875 the house remained in the hands of his only child, Marion Pocklington Coltman (widowed in 1893), until her death about 1920; from her it passed to Charles Coltman Rogers of Stanage. From Thomas Coltman the first to the time of Coltman Rogers the new owners had apparently come to the house, suggesting that the contents would not have been greatly disturbed by extraction, partial sale, or dowry;[22] but changing taste, especially during the time of Marion Pocklington Coltman's ownership, could have seen at least relegation, if not actual removal, of the furniture from the pseudo-Gothic-Tudor periods, and a strong reaction against what was simplistically called Victorianism.

It is not feasible within the scope of this essay to examine minutely the listed contents of every room in the Priory, but an overview should prove at least suggestive. We will progress back through the house from outoffices to the main porch. Outside, the washhouse had become a store by 1927, retaining its wringing machine and small mangle and 'ironbound teak rinsing tub', confused with tennis posts and a canework invalid chair; near it, the laundry remained as it had been intended, with 'iron heating stove' and eleven flat irons, the carriage house contained still a rubber-tyred single brougham and a dogcart, the saddle room held its harnesses, and the summer house its chairs, although a set of bowls was labelled 'give to local Men's Club'. Elsewhere outside, added to the original list, were a water wheel, an Electric Lighting plant, and a 'petrol lawn mower'; only in these last two items had twentieth century technology intruded obviously into the house's domestic economy.

Entering the oldest part of the house - Thomas Coltman the first's house, altered by Thomas the second - we find the Men's Quarters - four attic rooms and the Butler's bedroom. The latter was properly furnished, with single bed, chamberware, chest, a swing glass, Windsor chair and 'stuffed bird in case' - although the heating stove was 'outside door'. Two of the attics were similarly sparsely fitted, but with no aesthetic touches like stuffed birds, and in the First Attic Room only a 'part chair' to sit on. The Far Attic Room contained lumber - trunks, a uniform box, camp chairs, a box of games, and a croquet box; the Middle Attic Room was full of furniture - a hip bath, three mahogany washstands, five damaged chairs and (mysteriously) an 'Antique mahogany framed pulpit, with gallery top, steps enclosed'.

Down in the kitchen area, the larder's contents suggest a transition to twentieth century convenience; amongst the brown ware, dough troughs, box-churn, and other evidence of the sheer hard work needed to keep the household fed, were two refrigerators and an ice-maker. But the Scullery's contents might have dated from the 1850s. So might those of the kitchen: here, a grandfather clock stood, with obvious implications for the servants' timekeeping, overseeing the use of massed copper and pewter and tin-wares, the pans, seven soufflé dishes, ten pie dishes, a dozen small casseroles, a dinner service 'by Goode' of over one hundred pieces, the patty pans, sixteen pie moulds, cleavers and sausage-machine, and much more. Nearby was the servants' hall, well furnished, with seven single chairs, easy chairs, one in mahogany and flowered tapestry, noted as originally belonging in the library - and somehow a child's chair and stool and a 'mahogany framed riding horse, with spring saddle (belongs Nursery)'.[23] But there was another grandfather clock, to help keep the servants' days and hours in proper order.

Approaching the main part of the house was the intermediate zone of Butler's Pantry and Housekeeper's Room. The former still contained trays, the oil lamps, picnic basket and miscellaneous pottery for serving food at table; in a cupboard were decanters, glasses and other fine glassware, but the inventory excluded all plate and wines, so we have to assume that these would have been kept in, or near the butler's pantry. The Housekeeper's Room similarly contained the equipment and furniture appropriate to the station: it was part sitting-room, with 'antique mahogany side table ... mahogany easy chair ... revolving brass newspaper rack on triple supports, claw feet ... antique oak bureau, along with fine china, glassware, teapots, menu tablets and cake stands, the essentials for performance of dignified responsibilities. Linen being excluded from the inventory, we are left to assume the housekeeper's duties in this respect, and the existence somewhere in the house of extensive linen cupboards.

Proceeding still in reverse order to our entry, we go now to the Maid Servants' Quarters, five bedrooms on two landings. Here the listed furniture suggests occupation, current or recent, with seven bedsteads and a spare one on a landing, the rooms having chests of drawers, wardrobes, chamberware and carpets. One room with two beds also had two clocks; another, with bed, a sewing machine, a large painted cupboard, and an inkstand may have been the housekeeper's bedroom. Outside, on the back landing, was the Housemaid's Cupboard, and off the landing a Housemaid's pantry - 'various hot water tins, hot water bottles and slop pails' - and a bathroom, which had presumably made the housemaid's old-fashioned equipment less essential. The evidence of the inventory suggests that the female servants were still, or had quite recently been, resident at the Priory.

Most of the house from here on consisted of accommodation for the family; whatever touches of mere comfort or slight luxury there were in the Servants' quarters had been almost accidental, but as we move into the middle range of bedrooms there is predictable change, rooms being furnished to render wealth ostensible. Even the 'Lumber Room East and Room over [the] Oriel Dressing Room' held items of greater comfort and convenience, such as a collection of folding screens, Chippendale mahogany commode chair, circular music stool on inlaid mahogany triple support, a box of fossils, a bundle of flags, and a mahogany medicine cupboard. On the second floor the East Bay-Window Bedroom contained a large cupboard with an extensive collection of oriental ware, and the complementary West Bedroom, though relatively sparsely furnished, had hangings for six pictures. The Red Bedroom may have been a child's room at some time, containing 'a white enamel and brass mounted single bedstead', jigsaw puzzles, oak framed slates and a box of tiles, although the Pocklington Coltmans are understood to have had no children, and Charles Coltman Rogers' heir had grown-up well before he inherited the estate at Hagnaby. Lower East Bedroom No. 6 had a double bedstead, and rather rich furnishings, including 'a Jacobean Oak writing table, with back of carved panels, inset Oriental plate in colours, fitted carved drawer, on ball frame' - perhaps a nineteenth century fantasy piece. This must have been a large room, since next to it was a Sitting Room, relabelled in pencil as 'Boudoir'; again the furnishings seem rich - antique oak chest with carved freize, double walnut table, three tier dark mahogany whatnot on turned supports, French writing table in rosewood with marquetery border and frieze, ormolu beading, handles and mounts - and a 'circular tin box containing Hussar's head-dress of the olden days'. Bedrooms 7 and 8, whilst less well appointed than 6, had their rosewood, mahogany, Chippendale chairs, brass bedsteads and - still - the chamberwares, although a separate W.C. and bathroom served them. All were carpeted with Brussels or Turkey carpets, and all retained candlesticks and wash-stands for the chamber sets. Picture hangings are listed throughout.

From this set of bedrooms we proceed via the Centre Landing - 'pediment barometer in antique mahogany frame ... by Stampa & Co.', Axminster corridor carpeting, brass stair rods, past warming pans downstairs to the Gun Room. This was renamed in pencil as the Small Dining Room, seemingly appropriately, there being only two Colt revolvers and two flintlock pistols (in cases) to merit what must have been an historic name; otherwise there were chests, chairs, writing-table, a fall-leaved mahogany table - nothing to suggest its function as a dining room either, but nearly all the furniture was marked in pencil as 'moved'; whether 'Small Dining Room' indicates an actual or intended use is not clear. Given its position, and that it had adjacent porch and lavatory, its function as a gunroom would have been well planned, allowing house shooting parties to avoid the main hall.

Beyond the Gun Room formality prevails absolutely. Above are the four main bedrooms, Hall Bedroom with Oriel Dressing Room, Yellow, Blue, and Green, with the Bachelor's Room off the same landing. The Hall Bedroom had predominantly eighteenth century mahogany furniture, an Axminster carpet; in the Oriel Dressing Room the carpet was Brussels, and here the wicker splash guard and sponge basket still survived, as if the hip-bath would be brought again from the back of the house and plumbed bathrooms did not exist. The chamber service was by Minton. The Yellow Bedroom had mahogany furniture on a green carpet with a flowering plant pattern; there were Japanese touches - a bamboo screen with Japanese panels, Japanese toilet pot and cream jug and teapot - but the bed was walnut. In an adjoining bathroom - though the bedroom kept its chamberware - were a bamboo table, an Oriental dish and a Japanese pincushion. The Bachelor's Room had more eighteenth century mahogany on a Brussels floral carpet; in the inventory no bedstead is listed, although one had appeared for the 1930 Sale Catalogue. In the Blue Bedroom was more mahogany on a blue carpet, but with an iron and brass mounted double bedstead with hangings, curtains and vallances. In the Green Bedroom, with more mahogany, was a bedstead in that wood 'with 2 beaded posts at foot, and mahogany canopy, chintz hangings', a Brussels carpet and chintz curtains, and a couch with a chintz cover; the chamber service was painted with flowers. All the main bedrooms had extensive ornaments, hearth furniture, sometimes with pole-screens, many cupboards, bookcases, couches, and side tables. They were appointed almost to the point of ostentation, and in each an attempt had been made to create a comfortable, self-contained and self-regarding world. Whilst not exactly the heart of the house, they could have been equally important private areas, luxurious and cushioned bolt-holes from a naughtier existence outside.

From here we descend to the grandeur of formal rooms below. Most private - if that can be an appropriate word at all at this point of the house - is the library; and we are at a tremendous disadvantage, not knowing what books, or in what quantity, had been here. Those sold in 1930 were predictable, standard authors in sets, some Latin authors, some histories, a few local histories. No bookshelves are listed on the inventory, but it would not have included fittings. There is some incidental evidence of the room being used as a study - ebony inkstand, kneehole writing table, leather blotter, a mahogany writing chair - but the only listed furniture which could have fitted best in a library are two mahogany bookslides and a portfolio stand in oak. An adjustable mahogany music stand, a violin and the bow in a case are reasonably appropriate as well, but scarcely essentials in a working library; but it is not necessary to believe that this was a working library. However, this branch of the Coltmans, whilst it produced no scholars, was far from philistine. Thomas Coltman the younger took his degree at Oxford; Roger Pocklington Coltman subscribed to J. S. Padley's *Fens and Floods of Mid-Lincolnshire* (1882), and Marion Pocklington Coltman, his widow, helped Canon Maddison with the Coltman pedigree.[24]

From the library we move into the most formal rooms, around which the rest of the house's being may be said to centre. Every other part of the house, the outbuildings, the grounds and the estate beyond in principle existed to serve those who lived here; it was, equally, the place where the family's history, accomplishments, and tastes were displayed, much in the manner which has now been deflected into the museum tradition. In the porch at Hagnaby visitors were confronted by a pair of oriental vases on stands, and an 'antique land-measure with wheel and dial by Jonathan Sisson'; entering the Outer Hall (21′ by 16′) they came to a collection of early English oak furniture, a chest, a pair of carved chairs, Queen Anne style chairs, and a 'carved oak Court cupboard in the Jacobean style, finely carved'. Spread around and in the cupboards were the paraphernalia once essential to country house life, but even in 1927 becoming quaint or outmoded - part of a croquet set, a bugle, rainfall guage, bronze gong, umbrella stand, travelling rugs. There was a red Axminster carpet, and much old pewter. Two pairs of flintlock pistols and a cavalry sword hung on the walls. But a softer, more domestic atmosphere pervaded the Lower Hall (22′ by 18′): the same red Axminster, but a grand piano, mahogany furniture, a fine grandfather clock, rosewood furniture, two lances (presumably wall mounted) - and a vacuum cleaner. There was no fireplace, but oak framed seating and a sideboard acted 'to cover heating pipes'.

Off this Lower Hall was the Dining Room, the furniture predominantly eighteenth century mahogany, although the main table was in oak 'on square legs, carved leafage and trefoil ornament'. The carpet had 'crimson ground ... 21′ x 15′9″, with blue ground border, crimson edge, floral design'; the table accommodated twelve Chippendale chairs. Either from the dining room or from the Inner Hall an anteroom led to the main Drawing Room; it contained chairs, bookshelves, a revolving bookcase and a large break-front open cabinet; the predominant wood was walnut, the 'bordered red ground pile carpet 16′9″ x 7′6″' had a leaf pattern, and the curtains were light red silk. Ornaments were largely Oriental, and the room could be illuminated from 'a Chippendale girondole in gilt, with mirrors, fitted electric light branches'. It had also a timepiece 'in bronze and marble on eagle supports, armorial frieze, silvered dial, surmounted [by] old soldiers'. Sumptuous as the whole list is, the Ante Room was less than the large Drawing Room, which may have been the *pièce de résistance*; it was a huge room, 30′ by 25′ overall, with a single Indian carpet 23′ by 14′. There was a great marble mantlepiece, and around the walls were cabinets carrying open and closed shelves, in walnut and ormolu, mahogany, and tulip wood; each was filled with ceramics, largely oriental, much of that Japanese. The most outstanding was 'a Florentine cabinet in various coloured woods, inlaid animals, birds &c. in ivory'. Scattered around were easy chairs, settees, ornamental electric lights, and side tables. Seven pages of the 1927 Inventory were needed to list the contents, out of a total of eighty-two. But the house as planned in 1850-51 needed another, lesser Drawing Room - possibly identified in the Sale Catalogue as the Morning Room, about 18′ by 14′. The carpet was repeated here - 'light ground Indian carpet with green ground border, figured design' - but whereas the larger room had crimson silk tapestry curtains, this had these in old gold tapestry. Otherwise it was similarly furnished.

In terms of the Inventory of 1927 the Priory's fittings and contents seem to have been those of a late Victorian or Edwardian country house, possibly with slightly better heating, it being 'partially heated by radiators', according to the Estate Sale catalogue. Even from the brief descriptions of the Inventory it is apparent that much of the Georgian furniture must have been brought into the new, larger house; the late eighteenth century house could not have accommodated so much; the eighteenth century chairs alone were so numerous that in 1927 they were listed as belonging to sets A through to G, and a pencil note refers to 56 Chippendale chairs being stored in the Dining Room, presumably in 1928 or 1929. As it is listed very little of the furniture can be tied precisely to the 'new' house of the 1830s, and, again as listed, only the Outer Hall in 1927 retained early furniture of oak, imported to lend authenticity to the new Tudor-Gothic house. Although it is not impossible that eighteenth century furniture was brought in after 1851, it is doubtful, and there are sufficient examples of walnut, ormolu, and Japanese wares to suggest a partial refurbishment, perhaps as late as 1900, by which time good 18th century pieces were well back into favour. The Yellow Bedroom was quite aesthetically loaded with Japanese decoration, whilst the quantities of blue and white wares could date from the decades of Chinamania. If there was late Victorian refurbishment, it would have coincided with the period when Roger Pocklington, having married Marion Coltman, took the name Pocklington Coltman and lived at the Priory, as Lord of the Manor, from 1875 to his death in 1893; his widow subsequently took over house and estate, being herself responsible for such local works as church restoration and extension, in 1881, and 1903.

It remains to examine the slight but significant information added to the Inventory of 1927 by unknown hands. Some indicate simply a rechecking of the house contents, recording addition of a few pieces, damage, or deliberate destruction, and pieces missing: a pair of wicker palmstands in the porch had been 'burnt for worm', a leopardskin footmuff in the Outer Hall 'destroyed', a black wool hearth-rug 'gone', as many as thirty pieces of porcelain in the Ante Room were simply 'missing', and four door mats at the bottom of the main staircase were labelled 'removed insanitary'. A needlework settee in the Yellow Bedroom was 'full of worm dust'. A few pieces, mostly of lesser worth, were labelled 'Sale'; the mysterious label 'Seaton' - perhaps indicating sale to a particular dealer - has been previously noted. A very few additions recorded structural damage to the house - a cracked window in the Green Bedroom, damp in the ceiling and damaged wallpaper in the East Bay Window Bedroom. But the most significant notes refer to large scale movement of the furniture within the house, connected to alterations in the functions of certain rooms. The Gun Room, it has been remarked, did not seem to have been used as such when the Inventory was made; most singularly, it held no sporting guns, but much formal furniture. It was renamed, in pencil, as the Small Dining Room, much of the furniture listed as 'moved' to other rooms; other furniture in the Dining Room, Ante Room, both Dining Rooms, and Library, has been labelled similarly, suggesting some considerable reorganisation of the house between the beginning of 1927 and the end of 1929. On the first floor the Red Bedroom appears to have become a Dressing Room and the Lower West Sitting Room a Boudoir, but there are no notes as to the movement of furniture in either case. On the ground floor, the Large Drawing Room went out of use, becoming a store, largely for Chippendale chairs. The Housekeeper's Room had also become the home of several large pieces of furniture; it may have gone out of use, and become a store.

Although the precise occasions when notes were added to the original Inventory cannot be ascertained, their likely sequence tells us a little about the fate of country houses. Perhaps because of Charles Coltman Rogers's relatively advanced age (he was born in 1854) a full Inventory was demanded in 1926; the family pictures and silver - for dynastic reasons, we may suppose - and the better books, wines and linens - were taken elsewhere. For a reason unknown there was subsequently a reorganisation of certain rooms in the Priory, suggestive of some difficulty in running the house perhaps. It may have been at this stage that some surplus furniture was removed or sold off. Allowing that even in 1929 organisation of an estate sale could not have been rapidly achieved, the sales of December 1929 and March 1930 may have been envisaged from the time the Inventory was made; the Coltman line had had its day at Hagnaby, and the owner needed to prepare for the end decently in a time which was especially difficult for landed proprietors.

Notes written in the Estate Sale Catalogue of December 1929 indicate that the bidding for the house itself reached £4,000; it was then 'passed' - not sold - and the remaining contents sold in March,[25] auctioned by J. Peacock Rayner. The better or otherwise more important of them were not included. A few pictures were sold, none well described in the catalogue, but apparently no portraits or larger pieces; nor were any sets of chairs included. It was a bad time to sell houses or their contents; much from the best rooms went only for a few shillings, only the carpets regularly making good prices. The books sold were, as described, mainly standard sets, nothing listed suggesting that the Priory had more than a moderate country house library. Several items of Lincolnshire history and topography were included, as if the family were indeed shrugging off their county connections. Interestingly the pictures included both a coloured print and an engraving of the house itself; I have not yet discovered copies of these. The catalogue contains no clue as to family or estate records being sold.

So Thomas Coltman the elder's little estate was dissolved, and his nephew's great house - first contents, and then the building itself - were sent the same way.[26] The best pieces went elsewhere, the rest were removed, as at any country sale, in pantechnicon, open lorry, cart, by 'bus or just a bit of the way up the road to villagers' homes. Certainly some estate records were dispersed, perhaps at this time, eight plans relating to Coltman properties being sold at Spilsby in 1980, four of them making their way (as is said) to the Lincolnshire Archives Office.[27] Perhaps they got out in 1930 in Lot 342 - 'a walnut portfolio stand with maps', from the Library. Appropriate materials for a closer study of the family and the estate may survive, to help answer the wide range of questions which can appropriately be asked - why did Thomas Coltman choose to build at Hagnaby? Did he demolish an earlier, lesser house? Why was the name 'Priory' assumed? How was it all financed? How could so small a rural estate have supported so pretentious an house? At the local level, there may be people alive who served in the house, grounds or estate; there must be a local oral tradition - *anglicé*, gossip - about house and family, and careful weeding of local newspapers could provide some account of the public faces of both. The Coltmans were, it is true, of no major importance; they made no great mark even as a county family, with their relatively small estate and a succession so interrupted that any close association between the Priory and the county community was likely to have been inhibited. Family ties linked them to the clergy and some minor gentry, but not to the greater families, nor to the older ones; it is no accident that they did not make it into Canon Maddison's idiosyncratic but important statement about 'old' families in *Lincolnshire Wills* (Lincoln, 1888 and 1891) - they were too new, had their roots in trade, professions, and salaried government service. Boasting no major military or clerical tradition, they moved with some success into land; hence, perhaps, the 'antique land measure' inside their great, fake porch in 1927 - a little pretentious, perhaps. It sold for £2 10s. 0d. in 1930.

Notes

1 Cf. the success of Girouard's works.

2 For the particular demands made upon auctioneers and valuers in recent times in preparing lists of property, see W. H. Brown, *Sold: Reminiscences of a Lincolnshire Auctioneer* (Boston, 1986), 26-27.

3 G. Maughan, *L.N.Q.*, *VII* (April 1902), 64. This refers to the ancient parish; Hagnaby's part of the Fen was miles away to the east, Decoy Farm probably being that near Little Steeping railway station. At least one reputable historian has been confused by the name Hagnaby - cf. H. E. Hallam, *Settlement and Society* (Cambridge 1965), 96-97, where the nineteenth century farmstead Hagnaby Grange is identified as having belonged to 'Hagnaby Priory' in the Middle Ages. Less surprisingly, see *The Comprehensive Gazetteer*, 4 vols (n.d., *c.*1901), III, 44, which puts the Praemonstratensian house in the wrong Hagnaby. For a glorious confusion, see Kelly's *Directory* for Lincolnshire (1909 edition). There must be more.

4 For a succinct account of the Estate, see *L.A.O.R.*, 19 (1967-68), 9-11.

5 *The Letters and Papers of the Banks Family of Revesby Abbey* 1704-1760, edited by J. W. F. Hill, L.R.S. (1952), passim.

6 L.A.O. Misc. Don.500/1.

7 See Joseph Foster, *Alumni Oxonienses*, I, 282. Thomas Coltman was first son of George, a doctor, of Liverpool. He was admitted to Brasenose College, Oxford, in January 1819, took his B.A. in 1822, and succeeded to the Hagnaby Estate before he was thirty years old. He was a JP, Deputy Lieutenant, and served as High Sheriff in 1845. He was a student of the Inner Temple in 1822, but does not seem to have gained a legal qualification.

8 *L.A.O.R.*, 19, 11. According to Rev. John Bowyer's *An Account of the ... Society for the Promotion of Industry in the Southern District of... Lindsey* (Louth, n.d., 3rd ed. *c.*1790), 31, 39. Thomas Coltman subscribed to the Society from 1784 to 1789, and Mrs Coltman 1787-89. Their address is merely given as Hagnaby. Thomas Coltman has been publically recognized since 1984 for his close connection with the painter Joseph Wright of Derby; in that year the Coltman heirs sold the portrait of Thomas and Mary Coltman which now hangs in the National Gallery, painted by Wright, with whom Coltman had long been acquainted. The Coltmans owned several other important works by Wright, which presumably were at Hagnaby from the house's construction to the final sale. For this connection see: Benedict Nicolson, *Joseph Wright of Derby, Painter of Light,* 2 vols (1968), I, 189; Allan Braham, *Wright of Derby - Mr & Mrs Coltman*, (National Gallery, 1986); Judy Egerton *Wright of Derby* (Tate Gallery, 1990). These, however, add nothing to our knowledge of the nineteenth century history of the house at Hagnaby.

9 *L.N.Q.*, XI (January 1911), 134.

10 *L.A.O.R.*, 19, 10.

11 Eleanor and Rex C. Russell, *Old and New Landscapes in the Horncastle Area* (Lincoln, 1985), map, p.8. Cf. Bennett Langton to Joseph Banks II, Dec. 1739, in Hill, *Letters and Papers,* 184-85. Cragg recorded that East Kirkby was part open field, part enclosed. (See note 8).

12 Cf. Hill, *Georgian Lincoln* (Cambridge, 1966), *passim*, and Warren R. Dawson, ed., *The Banks Letters* (1958), especially 224-26.

13 *L.A.O.R.*, 19.

14 18th edition, p.300, recording the road from London to Grimsby via Boston and Spilsby - 'Stickford, near at Hagnaby Priory, T. Coltman Esq.' Joseph Noble's *Gazetteer* of 1833 (Hull, Boston, &c.) still calls it Hagnaby Hall.

15 Thomas Allen [& John Saunders], *The History of the County of Lincoln,* 2 vols (Leeds; London & Lincoln, 1834), II, 109 - 'Hagnaby commonly called Hornby'. Cf. Byng's passage on his journey into Lincolnshire in 1791 through 'Honby' - C. Bruyn Andrews, ed., *The Torrington Diaries* 4 vols (1935), II, 374.

16 *L.A.O.* Misc. Don. 505/3.

17 [W. T. Pike, publisher] *Lincolnshire at the Opening of the Twentieth Century* (Brighton, 1907), 19, in Rev. Alfred Hunt, 'Historical Survey of the County', where an illustration and note about Hagnaby Priory bear absolutely no relationship to the main text.

18 *L.A.O.R.*, 9, 50.

19 'Kyme and its tower', *A.A.S.R.P.*, XVI, 1 (1887), 27-31.

20 Compiled by Alison Felstead, Jonathan Franklin, & Leslie Pinfield. I am grateful to Chris Sturman for checking the absence of any reference.

21 Estate Sale, Wednesday 11th December 1929, Boston Assembly Rooms, L.A.O. Martin 4/28/9A; Contents of House, 14th and 15th March 1930, at Hagnaby Priory, L.A.O. Misc. Dep. 572/42. We can assume that the excepted paintings included the Wright of Derby works to which reference is made in note 7 above. For all information relating to Thomas Coltman's relationship with Joseph Wright I am grateful to Chris Sturman.

22 I cannot prove this, yet.

23 Could this in fact have been a later nineteenth century patent exercise horse rather than a child's toy?

24 A. R. Maddison, *Lincolnshire Pedigrees*, 4 vols (1906), IV, Index under Coltman, for references throughout the four volumes.

25 L.A.O. Misc. Dep. 572/42 - Sale of Antique and Modern Furniture, Books, etc. ... at Hagnaby Priory, 14th & 15th March, 1930.

26 I have not found out who eventually was responsible for demolition.

'We Fall to Rise . . . ' : Revesby Abbey from the 1820s to the 1840s

Christopher Sturman

Revesby Abbey, Craven Howard's late-seventeenth century house was remodelled *c.* 1716-18 by John Sherlock of Boston for Joseph Banks I shortly after his purchase of the Revesby estate (1714),[1] and became the Lincolnshire home of his famous great-grandson, Sir Joseph Banks who from the late 1770s visited it annually in the summer and early autumn. However, in the years following his death in 1820 it fell into a state of neglect.

Under the terms of Sir Joseph's will (he had no legitimate children) his Lincolnshire estates were divided between the descendants of two of his father's sisters: his cousin, Sir Henry Hawley, Bt (1745-1826) and his first cousin once removed, Lt.-Col. James Hamilton Stanhope (1788-1825). Neither of these two beneficiaries were to enjoy their inheritance, for Banks left his wife, Lady Dorothea, a life time interest in the estate. John Burcham, land agent of Coningsby (he may well have acted as agent for the estate), writing to the Earl of Mansfield (Stanhope's father-in-law) in March 1823 commented in a forthright manner about Revesby: 'The Estate and Buildings are now in a most dilapidated state... Should Lady Banks survive 4 or 6 years - I am confident it will be in ruin.' The partition took place after Lady Banks's death in June 1828; it was not until 6 September 1831 that the necessary Act of Parliament received its royal assent. Under the scheme (worked out by John Burcham), the Hawley family received Tumby and other estates, whilst Revesby and the remaining Lincolnshire property passed to the Stanhopes.[3]

It was no doubt whilst valuing the estate that Burcham sought the advice of the Boston architect, Jeptha Pacey (his letter to Burcham is dated 8 May 1830):

> In compliance with your direction I have surveyed & examined the Manor House & Offices at Revesby to enable me to give an opinion as to the propriety of repairing the same to make it a good residence.
> I am clearly of opinion that any attempt to repair & make the

Fig. 1 Revesby Abbey c.1800, detail of engraving by Howlett from a drawing by T. Nash after a sketch by W. Brand, from Bartholomew Howlett, 'Views in Lincolnshire' (1805).

present House & Offices a fit residence for a Gentleman would be a waste of money as from the bad state of the Buildings, [and] the ill arrangement of the rooms & offices it would after a large expenditure (the amount of which is impossible to calculate) be at best very incomplete & inconvenient. I therefore recommend the taking down of the present Buildings & to erect a new comfortable House & suitable Offices in another place as in my opinion the Park affords a much better situation than the present, (using such of the old materials as are proper) which I am persuaded will be much to the benefit & comfort of the Proprietor as the increased expence can be no object when compared to the lasting advantage arising to the Estate.[4]

James Hamilton Stanhope's heir, James Banks Stanhope (1821-1904) was a minor; it was not until 13 May 1842 that he obtained his majority, an event celebrated at Revesby. The full report of the festivities in the *Lincolnshire Chronicle* of 20 May 1842 contained a telling comment on the past and the future:

After [Sir Joseph Banks's] death, Revesby soon lost the interest of those who used to be its constant visitors, the blithesome revels that used to take place year to year at its annual fair have gradually declined, and the old abbey, for want of a tenant, was fast going to decay. The furniture, paintings and curiosities which rendered it the resort of the lovers of the fine arts, have been removed, and the splendid park, with its delightful avenues and herds of deer, are the only remnants of its former splendour. Let us hope, however, that another change has come over us, that the gratifying scene which took place on Friday last, will be the prelude to still more lasting benefits which will be conferred upon the neighbourhood, and that the name of Banks, coupled with that of Stanhope, may be raised to its former hospitality and splendour by its present spirited possessor.

The old house, clearly did not tie in with the ambitions of this young country gentleman (he was elected to parliament in 1852) and improving landlord. Within a year, an advertisement appeared in the *Lincoln, Rutland and Stamford Mercury* of 31 March 1843:

REVESBY ABBEY

MR. WEIR respectfully announces that he will SELL by AUCTION, at REVESBY ABBEY, on Monday and Tuesday the 3d and 4th days of April next, the Household FURNITURE, Piano-forte, Paintings, in richly carved wood frames, large folding Indian Screen, Indian Cabinet, pair of Globes, 200 volumes of Books, Dairy Utensils, Brewing Copper and Vessels, Farming Implements, and other Effects of the late Right Honorable Sir JOSEPH BANKS, Baronet: - descriptive catalogues of which may be had of the Auctioneer, and of the booksellers at Horncastle, Boston and Spilsby.

Fortunately, a sale-catalogue is extant.[5] Amongst the household furniture, paintings, books, maps, etc. listed in some detail - there were, for example, four 'four-post' bedsteads, respectively with 'yellow figured plush hangings', 'blue hangings', 'yellow hangings', and 'checked hangings' - the following lots catch the eye:

152 Plaster cast of Sir Joseph Banks, by Garrard, with bracket
153 Transparent paintings exhibited in Soho Square on the recovery of George III
171 Eleven whole length portraits of Indian Chiefs in carved wood frames
*** The above will be divided into lots to suit the convenience of purchasers.

With its contents dispersed, Revesby Abbey was demolished. A further sale was announced in the *Stamford Mercury* of 19 July 1844:

REVESBY ABBEY.
The Residence of the late Sir Joseph Banks Bart., P.R.S.
To be SOLD by AUCTION
By Messrs. WOOD and ROBERTS,
On Thursday and Friday next the 25th and 26th days of July, 1844

THE MATERIALS of the aforesaid ANCIENT EDIFICE, and the extensive Offices thereto belonging, comprising about 16 Tons of Lead, a large quantity of Plain and Pan Tiles, 120 Framed and other Doors, 66 pair of Glazed Sashes and Frames, Staircases, nearly 100 Squares of good Redwood Floors, 9000 Feet superficial of Framed Wainscoting and Dados, Cornices, Architraves, Marble Chimney Pieces & Hearths, Stone Pilasters, Frontispieces, Stable and Carriage-house Fittings, &c., agreeably with catalogue, to be obtained of the Auctioneers at Grantham, and at the Red Lion Inn at Revesby, which is situate about an equal distance from Horncastle, Spilsby, and Tattershall.

The Lead at per cwt.

Credit will be allowed to purchases exceeding in amount 5l., or a liberal discount for prompt payment.

The Sale will commence upon the premises punctually at Twelve o'clock on Thursday the 25th, and at Eleven on Friday the 26th inst.

As a result of this sale there is a fascinating possibility that many unsuspecting Lincolnshire householders may possess materials from Banks's much loved Revesby.

The fact that it was a firm of auctioneers from Grantham who handled this sale, becomes clear from a lengthy account of the laying of the foundation stone (here printed in its entirety as an appendix) in the *Stamford Mercury* of 4 October 1844. Messrs Neale & Wilson of Grantham were employed as contractors - Wilson was the proprietor of the Ancaster-stone quarries at Wilsford. J. B. Stanhope engaged as his architect William Burn (1789-1870), whose work in the county already included Harlaxton Hall (though here he replaced Anthony Salvin as supervising architect), as well as designs for Stoke Rochford House (1841-43) and South Rauceby Hall (1842). Stanhope's new residence (Fig. 2), in the 'manorial style' (today it is described as 'Jacobethan') and completed in 1846 at an estimated cost of £20,000, was located several hundred yards north of the site of the old house.[6]

The building of the new Revesby Abbey was only the beginning of a major scheme of work on the estate: the fine screen and gates on the main road are dated 1848; in the 1850s and early 1860s the village was completely remodelled. Stanhope was a bachelor and he encouraged his heir elect, the Hon. Edward Stanhope, who became MP for Mid Lincolnshire in 1873, to use Revesby. In 1885, no doubt partly in response to losses he had sustained in the agricultural depression of the late 1870s and early 1880s, J. B. Stanhope, who was reported to have commented, 'Revesby has become an intense blister to me',[7] handed the estate to Edward. Sadly, Edward Stanhope died in 1893, and in 1907, following the death of his widow, Revesby passed to the Hon. Richard Philip Stanhope. He married Lady Beryl, daughter of the 5th Earl of Clancart in 1914, but was killed in action in 1916. There were no children to the marriage.

The high hopes which had attended the celebration of James Banks Stanhope's majority in 1842 and the laying of the foundation stone at Revesby Abbey two years later had turned within three generations to dust. There was to be no Stanhope succession, and the succeeding years have been sad ones for Revesby and its collections. In 1918 and 1929, Sir Joseph Banks's Lincolnshire manuscripts (supplemented by Edward Stanhope who made several purchases when another Banksian collection was sold in 1880) were auctioned at Sothebys,[8] and are now scattered across the globe - though as will have been apparent from the earlier part of this note the daispora of Lincolnshire materials had begun many years before in 1843. In 1976, an application was made to demolish Revesby Abbey. In April the following year, Terence Leach was one of the organizers of a special meeting to discuss the future of Revesby held at Horncastle Residential College. Twenty years on Revesby still stands, though its future remains uncertain. To some extent the survival of Burn's house owes much to Terence's early action, a part of his wider and pioneering efforts both to chronicle the history of Lincolnshire houses and their families and to argue passionately for their conservation as an integral part of Lincolnshire's (alas, already much eroded) historical and cultural landscape.[9]

Fig. 2 Revesby Abbey and gardens from the south east, c.1900. (D. N. Robinson Collection)

Appendix: *Lincoln, Rutland and Stamford Mercury*, 4 October 1844

Laying the Foundation-stone at Revesby Abbey, the seat of James Banks Stanhope, Esq. - The interesting ceremony of laying the foundation-stone of the new mansion house about to be erected by James Banks Stanhope, Esq., at Revesby Abbey, took place on Monday last. The arrangements were on a most liberal and extensive scale, and reflect great credit on the worthy proprietor, as well as on the parties who had the superintendence and management of the affair. Shortly before two o'clock, Mr. Stanhope, attended by the Venerable the Archdeacon of Stow, H. V. Bailey, D.D., Lady Mary Vyner, the Hon. Sir Henry Dymoke, Bart., the Rev. Thos. and Mrs. Best, the Rev. John Otter, the Misses Vyner, the Rev. ——— Haymes, Jos. Livesey, Esq., and the Rev. Andrew Veitch, arrived on the grounds, and Lady Mary Vyner having been solicited to lay the foundation-stone, Mr. Stanhope advanced to her Ladyship and presented to her a silver trowel of beautiful workmanship, addressing her in the following words:- "Lady Mary Vyner - You will be pleased to accept from me this trowel, for the purpose of adjusting the mortar prepared for laying the foundation-stone of this my intended residence." The Horncastle band, which had been specially engaged for the occasion, then commenced playing God Save the Queen. Her Ladyship graciously received the trowel from Mr. Stanhope; after which, Mr. John Wilson (of the firm of Neale and Wilson, of Grantham, the builders of the edifice) stepped forward, and handed to her Ladyship an ornamental mallet, expressing himself in the following terms: - "My Lady - It is with pleasure I have the honor, as builder of this mansion, to present to your Ladyship this mallet, in order that you may by using it be fully convinced that the first stone of this building is laid firmly and substantially." The band here resumed the national air, and her Ladyship was again addressed by Mr Mac Leish, the clerk of the works, who handed her a level, and said, "My Lady - As representative of Mr. Burn, the architect, it is my duty to try and adjust all levels and perpendiculars; for which purpose I present to your Ladyship this level, by the application of which you will be enabled to ascertain whether this stone be true in all its points." The band then concluded the national air, and the necessary preparations having been completed, the foundation-stone was lowered into its proper place, and Lady Mary Vyner very adroitly used the trowel, mallet, and level which had been presented to her, and the requisite trials having been made in order to show that the stone had been properly adjusted, the workmen and all present gave three hearty cheers. The Rev. H. Veitch then pronounced the blessing, appealing to the Almighty that he would vouchsafe to prosper the work they had just commenced, and praying that through his divine aid it might in due time be perfected and finished. Underneath the stone was deposited a box bearing a suitable inscription, and containing one of each of the various coins of the present reign. Mr. Stanhope and his immediate friends then retired from the building, the band playing a quick march, and assembled in a tent erected on the grounds, where they partook of a very excellent *dejeûnè a la fourchette* [*sic*] which had been prepared for them. Most of the visitors then withdrew, and the remaining part of the day became a holiday to the workmen. - At five o'clock the various masons and others employed in the works, 140 in number, again assembled near the building, and paraded by the principal approach to the house through the village of Revesby, in an admirable procession of all classes of workmen, with numerous flags and music; and on their return they retired to a spacious barn near the house, which had been very tastefully decorated with a great variety of evergreens, flowers, ribbons, &c., under the direction of Mr. Wilson, the builder, and which had a most imposing effect, the arrangements altogether being very complete. In this building a substantial dinner was prepared for the workmen, and at six o'clock Mr. Stanhope took the chair, supported by the Rev. Hy. Veitch and Mr. Bell, Mr. John Wilson officiating as vice-president. After full justice had been done to the repast, the cloth was drawn, and grace having been said by the Rev. Hy. Veitch, the Chairman gave "The Queen" and the other usual loyal toasts, which were drunk with due respect, the band playing suitable airs. He then proposed the health of Lady Mary Vyner, who had that morning taken so prominent a part in the proceedings of the day: although her Ladyship might not be considered a practical mason, it must have been evident to all present that she possessed considerable skill in the art, and by the manner in which she used the various instruments placed in her hands, that she was fully sensible of the different purposes for which they were applicable. The toast was drunk with great applause - Mr. John Wilson then rose and proposed the health of J. B. Stanhope, Esq., their excellent patron and host, whose liberality and kindness he had no doubt they would all duly appreciate. (Drunk with three times three.) - Mr. Stanhope returned thanks, and observed that it gave him great pleasure to entertain those whom he saw around him. The undertaking which he had lately commenced, he confessed was one of considerable magnitude, and one which had required very mature deliberation before he entered upon it; it would, however, be a source of pleasure to him to reflect that the works in question afforded employment to a large number of artisans and labourers, and he should thereby in some measure be doing good to others. He also considered himself fortunate in possessing the valuable assistance of so eminent an architect as Mr. Burn, of London and Edinburgh, and that of his builders, Messrs. Neale and Wilson of Grantham; independently of which he regarded Mr. McLeish as an active and intelligent clerk of the works. Under the combined superintendence of these gentlemen, he trusted the buildings would be properly carried on, and in due time completed to his satisfaction. Mr. Stanhope concluded by expressing a hope that all would enjoy themselves on the present occasion. - The Chairman next proposed the health of Mr. Burn, and Mr. McLeish returned thanks - He then gave, in a complimentary speech, the health of Messrs. Neale and Wilson, the builders. From what he had hitherto seen of Mr. Wilson, he had no doubt they should proceed satisfactorily with the works they had commenced, and hand in hand until they were completed. - Mr. John Wilson stated it gave him much pleasure to rise and return thanks for the toast; more especially when he considered the very kind, handsome, and liberal manner in which Mr. Stanhope had provided the present treat for the various workmen employed in building his new mansion. He regretted much that his partner, Mr. Neale, should have been absent on that occasion, but he was then in a distant part of the country, and time scarcely permitted a summons to reach him. Had he been one of the party, he would have enjoyed the present scene; and as he was better capable, he would consequently have returned thanks in a more efficient manner for the kind way in which their names had been introduced. As regarded the building they had engaged to execute, he saw no fear, from the straightforward and explicit form in which the drawings were prepared, of performing the works, not only to the satisfaction of the architect, but also of their employer, and to the credit of themselves. After remarking upon the liberal and hospitable manner in which Mr. Stanhope had that day entertained them, he (Mr. Wilson) begged to observe that if there was anything omitted in the day's arrangement (which he could not think would be found to be the case) they must not attribute it to Mr. Stanhope, but to himself: he had received a *carte blanche* from that gentleman, and, with the assistance of his friend, Mr. McLeish, he trusted he had succeeded in carrying out the powers entrusted to him, to the satisfaction of all present. - The party was enlivened during the evening with several appropriate songs and glees, and after some other toasts had been given by the Chairman, the whole of the company about ten o'clock retired to the ball-room, which was an adjoining building tastefully tidied up for the occasion. Here were assembled many who had been invited from the village, and the ball was speedily opened by Mr. Stanhope with Mrs. Bell, the lady of his land-agent. Dancing was kept up with great spirit until two o'clock, when Mr. Stanhope retired, amidst the hearty wishes of all present that he might enjoy long life, prosperity, and happiness. Dancing was again resumed, and the hour of four having arrived, the happy throng were reminded by Mr. Wilson that the time for separation was at hand. The party then retired to their respective homes, each expressing sentiments of satisfaction for the liberal treat they had so fully enjoyed - It is calculated that the building of Revesby Abbey will occupy about three years. It will be a spacious edifice, and the architecture is intended to be of the Elizabethan style. The estate was formerly the property of Sir Joseph Banks, and was left to the present possessor under the will of the deceased Baronet.

Notes

1 For Banks family background and letters detailing building-work at Revesby, see *The Letters and Papers of the Banks Family of Revesby Abbey 1704-1760*, edited by J. W. F. Hill, L.R.S. 45 (1952), esp. xvi and 20-59. John Sherlock's work at Revesby is not noted in Howard Colvin, *A Biographical Dictionary of British Architects 1600-1840* (1978), 733.

2 L.A.O. R.A. 2/C/1/6/5.

3 'An Act to Effect a Partition of certain Freehold, Copyhold, and Leasehold Estates, in the County of Lincoln, late the Property of the Right Honorable Sir Joseph Banks, Baronet deceased', 2 William IV (copy at L.A.O. 2 Hawley/B/64). See L.A.O. Hawley 4/1 for draft schemes of partition.

4 L.A.O. R.A. 2/C/8/4/1.

5 L.A.O. R.A. 2/C/8/4/2.

6 Contemporary details are from *L.R.S.M.* 4 June 1858 (an account of the Lincoln Diocesan Architectural Society's summer excursion). For Burn, whose designs for Revesby are in the Library of The Royal Institute of British Architects, see Colvin, *Biographical Dictionary*, 159-68, and Nikolaus Pevsner and John Harris, rev. N. Antram, *The Buildings of England: Lincolnshire*, (1989), passim.

7 T. Kime, *Some Reminiscences of 'The Stanhopes' of Revesby Abbey about 1855 to 1914* (Horncastle, n.d., but *c.* 1920), 13. See also Aubrey Newman, *The Stanhopes of Chevening. A Family Biography* (1969) and R. J. Olney, Lincolnshire Politics 1832-1885 (Oxford, 1973).

8 For the Banks sales see H. B. Carter, *Sir Joseph Banks (1743-1820). A Guide to Biographical and Bibliographical Sources* (Winchester, 1987), 1-28.

9 Terence's address for the 1993 Brackenbury Memorial Lecture was on the architectural history of Revesby. This article summarizes the results of some of my own work on Revesby and which I communicated to him.

Addendum: Since this article was typeset I have located a good number of Burn's tracings for Revesby Abbey amongst the Sherwin Reynolds plans at L.A.O. (R/11 and especially S/69). This suggests that Neale & Wilson had sub-contracted some of the work to John Stainton, stone and marble mason of Boston, *L.A.O.R.*, 18 (1966-67), 22-24.

James Arundel and Locksley Hall, North Somercotes

John R. Ketteringham

James Arundel was born in Bradford in 1875. His father owned a stone quarry near Bradford and his mother was a member of the Humberstone family, who had their home at the Manor House in North Somercotes.

On leaving school James joined the family firm, which had expanded into contracting for the Railways, the Service Departments and Trinity House which was responsible for maintaining lighthouses throughout the country.

From an early age Arundel had artistic leanings and would often go up on to the Yorkshire moors with his painting materials. He spent as much time as possible at his grandparents' home and many of his paintings have a Lincolnshire theme. The catalogue of an exhibition of his paintings mounted at the Cartwright Memorial Hall, Bradford, in 1958 includes paintings of Torksey Lock, Grimsby Docks, Welton-le-Wold and Locksley Hall. This exhibition was in connection with the conferring on him of the Freedom of Bradford.[1]

Although Arundel had no artistic training, his work became highly regarded and, as well as in his home town, he exhibited in Batley, Hull, Leeds, Liverpool, London, Newcastle-on-Tyne, Paris, Rotherham, Salford, and Wakefield. He travelled widely and spent the five years immediately preceding the First World War in Canada with his family.

After returning to England, Arundel and his family lived for a time in Bradford and Morcambe before moving to Saltfleet in 1918. In 1921 Arundel purchased Old Hall Farm in Warren Lane, North Somercotes (Fig. 1), together with five acres of land for which he paid £875.[2] It seems, from the evidence of Ordnance Survey maps and trade directories, that the house has been known at various times as Old Hall Farm and Locksley Hall. A deed dated 1865 describes the house as The Old Hall Farm or Locksley Hall Farm. Tennyson's poem 'Locksley Hall' was written at some time between 1837 and 1840 and it seems that someone had the idea of naming the house Locksley Hall soon after the poem was published. At the time Tennyson was working on the poem the owner of Old Hall Farm, as the house was known at that time, was a Mr Drury. As Sir Charles Tennyson said in a talk to the members of the Tennyson Society at Locksley Hall in 1961, 'it is clear that the old house was called Locksley Hall after Tennyson's poem and not the poem after the house'.

There is a tradition in North Somercotes that Tennyson wrote part of the poem 'Locksley Hall' whilst visiting the house. It may be that Tennyson had seen the house either when at school in Louth or on his later visits to Mablethorpe but, as Sir Charles says, 'Tennyson very seldom described actual places or people in his poems, generally building up his pictures from innumerable details and reminiscences'. Clearly, naming the house Locksley Hall has caused some confusion to lovers of Tennyson's poetry but there is no evidence of any connection between the house and the poem 'Locksley Hall'. Arundel may have been inspired to use the name Locksley Hall for his newly acquired home after a conversation with his next door neighbour, whose aunt had been a cook for the Tennyson family at Somersby but, even if that was the case, he was not the originator of the name.

The claim that Tennyson wrote part of the poem in the 'ivied casement' of the house was made by John Cuming Walters in his book *In Tennyson Land* which was published in 1890. He gave as his authority 'the late Reverend Doctor Wood'. Dr Albert Wood was rector of North Somercotes from 1883 to 1885 and a Rev. James Wood was rector of nearby Theddlethorpe All Saints from 1830 to 1872. The unfortunate statement made by Walters was repeated by a number of authors and has become an accepted fact in many quarters.[3]

Almost immediately after Arundel acquired the house he commenced extending it and purchased materials from old buildings. Bricks and timber were purchased when the Old Mill House at North Somercotes was demolished and when the bell frame from the parish church of Theddlethorpe St Helen was replaced in 1925 Arundel purchased the timber

Fig. 1: Old Hall Farm, North Somercotes, July 1919.

which was used to make the doors in the 'small sitting room'. Jacobean panelling was bought from Penwortham Priory, Lancashire at a cost of £90 and this was also used in the 'small sitting room'. More oak panelling from the Old Manor at Ardesley, Lancashire was acquired for £10 from the Rev. Perry.[4] Oak beams and rafters came from an old house in Peterborough for £14 and an additional four beams were purchased from Wivenhoe Hall, Colchester for £9.[5] As Pevsner says Arundel 'covered every available surface with riotous wood carving'.[6] The carving was carried out by a local craftsman, Dickie Downs.

Two bells were purchased at the sale of Sudbrooke Holme near Lincoln for £10, and the cost of hanging these in the stairwell was £5. There are actually three bells and Arundel records the purchase of a bell for 17s. 6d. but the origin of this bell is unknown. Three ropes were purchased from Kennington and Sons of Liverpool for £1 17s. 6d. Bells and ropes can still be seen.[7]

Furniture, paintings and ornaments were obtained from a wide area but by far the most interesting group of artefacts purchased by Arundel for the house is the amazing quantity of stained and painted glass (Fig. 2.)

The collecting of stained and stained and painted glass began in the eighteenth century with the most notable example being Horace Walpole at Strawberry Hill. The best example in Lincolnshire was William Stukely at Stamford; sadly, his collection was dispersed after his death in the 1760s. The dispersal of the Tattershall glass provides another good example. In the aftermath of the French Revolution a huge amount of continental glass was imported into England by agents such as J. C. Hampp of Norwich. This formed the basis of important collections such as that of Lord Jerningham at Costessy Hall in Norfolk. In due course many of these collections were dispersed and this process of dispersal was in full spate during the period when Arundel was forming his own collection; indeed, his ledger reveals how many of the Locksley Hall panels came from these sources, such as Viscount Leverhulme's sale at the Bungalow, Rivington (Lancs.) in 1925 and a sale at Coombe Abbey (Warwicks.). The finest collection contemporary with Arundel's was probably that of

Fig. 2: Locksley Hall, staircase window. (Gordon Plumb)

Sir William Burrell who acquired over 600 pieces in the period 1911-37 and installed many of them at Hutton Castle where he lived (they are now of course in the Burrell Collection in Glasgow). Other important collectors included the antiquarian M. R. James, Eric Milner-White, Dean of King's College, Cambridge, and of York, and Philip Nelson, who wrote the first gazetteer of stained glass in Britain, published in 1913; his collection was installed in Speke Hall, now Liverpool Museum. Of course, collecting was not confined to the English; the most famous American example was William Randolph Hearst who began to disperse his collection in 1937. Burrell's glass included pieces acquired from Hearst and from Costessy Hall. This constant selling of older collections obviously provided opportunities to Arundel and his contemporaries.[8]

Christopher Woodforde, curate at St James's, Louth and an authority on stained and painted glass produced a catalogue of the glass, which was published privately in 1932.[9] Arundel's ledger records the purchase of the glass mainly between the years 1925 and 1928 but there are some later acquisitions. The prices paid for the glass, the sources from which it was obtained and its location within the Hall and sometimes the original location are recorded in the ledger. Arundel's inventory has recently been updated and corrected by Dr Penny Hebgin-Barnes and the description of the glass at Locksley Hall which follows is taken from her forthcoming book.[10]

At Locksley Hall seven panels dating from the fourteenth to the sixteenth century which originated in the church of St Peter Mancroft, Norwich, were purchased from the firm of G. King & Son of Norwich. Four of these panels can be identified as those depicting a bishop saint, an angel harpist, the Deity and St Paul. The figure of the Archangel Gabriel came from Buckden (Cambs.) and the small shield of Walkfare from Cantley church (Norfolk). Four composite panels including some sixteenth-century heads of French origin were purchased from Crichton Bros. of London and came from Chertsey Abbey (Surrey). According to Woodforde, the Chertsey panels also included the figure of a youth before a town and the head of an angel trumpeter. All these pieces are now in the staircase window apart from a bishop saint and angel harpist which are in bedroom three.The oval depicting visiting the prisoners and a roundel showing the Prodigal Son feasting were obtained from F. S. Eden's collection. An Adoration of the Magi oval and one of several seventeenth-century armorials came from Adcock of Norwich.Two of the panels in bedroom two were bought at Viscount Leverhulme's sale in 1925.Ten quarries of fifteenth to seventeenth-century date were obtained from Canon R. Gordon Roe of Acle Rectory (Norfolk). Nine of these can be identified as those bearing the arms of England, the city of Norwich, Gardiner, Edgecumbe (?) impaling Park and the Stationers' Company and the badges of Henry VIII, Elizabeth I, Queen Elizabeth of York and Mortimer, all in bedroom three. Three seventeenth-century Swiss panels, an associated coat of arms and two sixteenth-century German panels depicting soldiers were bought at a sale at Coombe Abbey (Warwicks.). From Temple Newsam, Leeds (West Yorks.) came five roundels, including those depicting the departure of the Prodigal Son and a priest blessing a knight. Glass obtained from Thomas & Drake of London included all the pieces in the gallery; two panels of English quarries which came from Sir Hercules Read's collection and are now in bedroom three, fifteen heads now in bedroom one and the Virgin now in the lancet in bedroom three. Kayll and Reed of Leeds supplied the bearded king now in the staircase window, a Last Supper roundel and heraldic fragments. Four square fourteenth-century floral quarries in the staircase window are from Exeter. According to Woodforde, quarries in the drawing room formerly belonged to Sir Augustus Wollaston Franks.

After the installation of the glass recorded above, Arundel turned his attention to the collection of antique furniture and ornaments but in 1937 his Record Book details the purchase of further glass, most of which was to his own design, to complete glazing of the remaining doors and windows. A bill dated 1 June 1937 from Thomas Drake of Holland Park Road, London records the supply of a window designed by Arundel depicting birds of prey and white birds of paradise at a price of £10 10s. 0d. Door panels with a plain background to stained glass bird centres for 4s. 6d.! A further bill dated 24 September 1937, again from Drakes, records the purchase of stained glass medallions and five lights also designed by Arundel, all of bird studies, at a total cost of £71 1s. 8d.[11]

Pevsner considered Locksley Hall to be to be basically sixteenth century though 'much restored'.[12] Although the house may well have originated as the home of a Tudor yeoman farmer, photographs taken before the alterations of the 1920s suggests that it is more likely to date from the late eighteenth century. The use of genuine Tudor material from ancient buildings, which Arundel may well have been able to acquire through his business connections, and the subsequent weathering of this material has led to much confusion and uncertainty as to the exact date of the original building.(The importance of the house, however, is not so much its date but the collection of stained and painted glass contained therein).

Arundel took as much care with the establishment and layout of the garden at Locksley Hall as he had done with the enlargement of the house and the purchase of its furnishings. He employed a gardener named Leak who, from 1 January 1929, was paid £1 1s. 0d. a week, plus a house and garden which he had free of rent and rates. The purchase of trees, shrubs and other plants is recorded in the Ledger Book. During 1926 and 1927 a rosery and lily pond were constructed and the plan for these is reproduced in the Ledger.[13]

Locksley Hall was used by the Coldstream Guards as an Officers' Mess during the Second World War and Mr and Mrs Arundel lived at their house near Bradford. When Locksley Hall was released by the Army the Arundels decided to remain in Bradford and sell their Lincolnshire home. The purchaser in 1945 was Mr H. Taylor, a retired Sheffield dentist, who lived at Locksley Hall until 1970, when the house was sold to Mr David Stanbridge who opened it as a restaurant in 1985. When the Taylors moved from Locksley Hall they took the seventeenth-century Swiss panels, a coat of arms and quarries formerly in the main window of the drawing room to a modern house at the bottom of the drive. In 1988 the house was purchased by its present owners, Mr and Mrs Franklin. Unfortunately in 1991 the bay window of the master bedroom was damaged during violent storms and most of the glass was removed for eventual restoration.

Acknowledgments

I am very grateful indeed to Mrs Maple Bedford, James Arundel's youngest daughter, for lending me the Ledger Book in which her father meticulously recorded his purchases for Locksley Hall. Mrs Bedford also loaned me other papers and spent some time talking to me about her father. References to the Ledger Book below are abbreviated to Arundel Ledger.

I am particularly grateful to Mr and Mrs Franklin for allowing myself and others to look over their house.

Notes

1. This catalogue is in the possession of Mrs Bedford.
2. Arundel Ledger, p. 43.
3. The information about Tennyson's alleged connection with 'Locksley Hall' has been extracted from *Tennyson and Locksley Hall: A Talk by Sir Charles Tennyson on the Occasion of the Visit by the Tennyson Society to Locksley Hall, North Somercotes on August 5th, 1961* (n. d.) 4. Much of this paper was reproduced and expanded by Terence Leach in 'Locksley Hall - 150 years later' in *S.L.H.A. Newsletter*, 58 (October 1988), 27-29.
4. Arundel Ledger, p. 7.
5. *ibid.*, pp. 13 and 29.
6. Nikolaus Pevsner and John Harris, rev. Nicholas Antram, *The Buildings of England : Lincolnshire,* 2nd edn. (1989), 588.
7. Arundel Ledger, pp. 6, 56 and 61.
8. Information from Dr Penny Hebgin-Barnes. There is an interesting chapter on major collectors from the eighteenth century until the present day in Hilary Wayment, *King's College Chapel, Cambridge; The Side Chapel Glass* (1988).
9. C. Woodforde, *The Locksley Hall Collection of Stained and Painted Glass* (Louth, 1932).
10. A full account of the glass including origin and price as recorded in Arundel's Ledger Book together with Dr Penny Hebgin-Barnes' description is given in my booklet *James Arundel and Locksley Hall, North Somercotes* (Lincoln, 1995). I acknowledge permission to quote from Dr Penny Hebgin-Barnes's description of the stained and painted glass in Locksley Hall which is to be published in the forthcoming Lincolnshsire volume of the *Corpus Vitrearum Medii Aevi.*
11. Loose inside the Ledger Book.
12. Pevsner, *Lincolnshsire*, 588.
13. Arundel Ledger, p. 123.

Changing Lifestyles in a Lincolnshire Country House: Brackenborough Hall in the 1950s

Eleanor Bennett

> It is that corner of the world, above all others,
> Which has a smile for me.
>
> Horace[1]

Brackenborough Hall is not one of the great Lincolnshire country houses in the same category as those recorded by Terence Leach in his *Lincolnshire Country Houses and Their Families*, but might better be described as a manor house or 'gentrified' farmhouse. Neither has it been inhabited by titled or 'county' families. True, the medieval de Brakenbergs, men of local standing and education, had their share of knights. Knighthood, however, was not an honour bestowed, but an obligation upon men with land above a certain, variable, annual value, to turn out fully equipped in time of war. It was a case of 'some have greatness thrust upon them', a duty best avoided, rather than a privilege. The Cliffords, a cadet branch of the great family of the north of England, lived at Brackenborough for nearly two hundred years in the sixteenth and seventeenth centuries, and married the daughters of influential Lincolnshire families, but otherwise remained relatively obscure. The Heneage family of Hainton who owned the Brackenborough estate from 1697 to 1868, and built the south-facing wing of the house in the 1730s, apparently never lived there, despite the claims of nineteenth century directories, but leased the property throughout the period to a succession of farming tenants.[2] Later owners have been men who farmed the land conscientiously and played their part in local and county affairs and might be counted among the good rather than the great. Over the centuries brides have come to Brackenborough, children have been born, families brought up, one generation succeeding another. There have been sales and new owners, but the house has remained, changing with the years, altered and developed to meet current needs, soaked in experiences and history.

It was February 1952 when I first visited Brackenborough as a friend of Ralph,[3] the son of the house, who by then had taken over the running of the farm from his father, Christopher, who was a partner in the timber business, Bennetts and Co. of Grimsby. I had come to Louth on the evening train from London. The sheep's eyes shone in the headlights as we drove up the farm road, and the cart-horses stamped and shifted as we opened the drive gate. In the house the panelling in the front hall was dark and impressive and the grandfather clock on the staircase ticked loudly. The electric light, powered from a generator in the stables, wavered every now and then. There was a coal fire in the drawing-room but every time the door was opened an icy blast chilled our feet. There had once been a central heating system in the front of the house. The cast-iron, highly elaborate radiators were still in place, and the coke-fired boiler was in the cellar, but war-time shortages had restricted its use. The wine cellar under the drawing-room had been dug in 1732 when the building of the south-facing wing of the house was begun. During the Second World War it had become the family's air raid shelter and was equipped with wooden benches, and additional access provided from outside.

Dinner was in the panelled dining-room. Sombre brown paint, brown curtains and oak furniture belied the mood of the lively family gathered there. From their heavy gilt frames a nineteenth-century mayor and mayoress of Bideford looked down upon us. She had a glint in the eye which suggested that she was able to manage the servants. At the time of my visit, there were two resident maids at Brackenborough. The house was not so much 'upstairs, downstairs' as 'front and back'. A large room, which earlier had been the farmhouse kitchen, had become the maids' sitting-room. A bell monitor, indicating all the main rooms in the house, was mounted on the wall. Coconut matting covered the brick floor. Bacon joints hung from hooks in the ceiling. An 'Ideal' boiler which heated the water could be opened so that the coke fire within could be enjoyed. It had replaced an earlier kitchen range. In the second half of the nineteenth century a new kitchen had been built adjoining this room, with dairy and pantry beyond, all brick-floored, with back stairs leading to maids' bedrooms. A second range in the new kitchen had backed on to the first, but in the 1930s had been replaced by an Esse, a solid fuel stove, similar to the better-known Aga.

I returned to Brackenborough, newly-married, a year later, in February 1953. Since my parents-in-law had moved to another family house which was already fully-equipped, Brackenborough remained substantially as it was. It is odd, but true, to say that a childhood and youth spent moving every three or four years from one Methodist manse to another was a good preparation for inheriting Brackenborough Hall. In those days *everything* in a manse was provided (and had been used by others before us) - not only carpets and curtains, but all furniture, household linen, crockery and kitchen equipment down to the last teaspoon; and so it was at Brackenborough. Of course there had been the 'special' possessions that made each manse a home, the piano, bureau, nest of tables, best crockery, books and pictures. At Brackenborough we installed our wedding presents. One of the first things I had to do, however, was to buy some smaller saucepans. The previous household had been substantial. I found myself warming milk for two in a six-pint pan, and the frying pans were enormous.

Everything was large (Fig. 1). The house was large. The garden was large, and prolific. Tom Morvinson, the pensioner-gardener, had for many years lived in a cottage on the premises. He had been ill and the doctor told him he should stop work so he had retired to Yarburgh, a village three miles away. He got better and from that time *cycled* daily to work. He brought me one day from the garden a marrow, one of many, about two feet long and of substantial girth. When I looked at it in dismay, 'Can't you stuff it?' said my husband. I was cooking for two. There were other vegetables and much soft, as well as orchard, fruit. I had been used to making jam and bottling at home, and I came armed with a splendid publication, Bulletin No. 21 of the Ministry of Agriculture, Fisheries and Food, *Domestic Preservation of Fruit and Vegetables.*

We had two house cows which were supposed to calve conveniently so that they could give milk for half the year each. Thomas Smart Cram, the foreman,

Fig. 1: 1950s aerial view of Brackenborough Hall and farmyard.

milked the cow twice daily, night and morning. He walked slowly with his bucket to the kitchen door and went to the dairy. One earthenware pancheon was just like a Beatrix Potter drawing. Two others were metal and shallow. I made 'cottager's cheese' which my father-in-law loyally pronounced good, and 'Devonshire' cream, scalding the pans of milk on the Esse. When on special occasions there were big 'chapel teas' we supplied large enamel jugs of milk. In 1970 the foreman, who went off the farm, reluctantly, only when he needed to get his hair cut, and had milked seven days a week, retired. Milk cows were getting more and more expensive. Sometimes calves, like babies, arrived inconsiderately, and for a time we had far too much milk or nearly none. Clifford Gibson, the new foreman, who had worked on the farm since leaving school, was willing to milk, but found it difficult to get a substitute when he wanted to go out, so we decided to give up the house cows. When *bottles* first arrived on the doorstep I felt I no longer lived on a proper farm.

In the years before I arrived Mrs Chapman had come each week to do the laundry in the wash-house, which was part of the range of nineteenth century outbuildings beyond the back door. There was a bread oven in the wash-house as well as the copper. Now, the wash-house was abandoned and the housemaid's pantry in the centre of the house became the utility room. I had brought with me a washing-machine my mother had recently discarded in favour of one of the new electric models. My washing-machine was a squarish zinc tub on legs. Inside were two parallel rows of wooden slats. The washing went in the middle, and a handle, worked rhythmically to and fro, agitated and squeezed the clothes in the soapsuds. A small mangle screwed on to the edge of the tub squeezed out the soapy water. The machine was emptied through a bung-hole in the side and refilled by hose or bucket with fresh water and the clothes were put back to be rinsed and then mangled again. The results were excellent. Earlier models of this type of machine, all of wood, can be seen in Lincoln at the Museum of Lincolnshire Life. I had a basket on wheels and hung out the washing in the field.

The generator supplied electric light, and in earlier days there had been one or two gadgets, but the ancient vacuum cleaner smelt alarmingly of rubber when I tried it, and I regarded the iron with deep suspicion. One of my wedding presents was an Esse iron. This had a metal top with a handle and two detachable stainless steel bases which were warmed on the Esse and interchanged, a modern progression from flat irons.

There is no doubt that the coming of mains electricity in 1955, when all the farm cottages were modernised, made the greatest difference to our lives. By that time I had a year-old baby and up to then had hand-washed baby clothes and nappies. My first purchases were an electric washing-machine, an iron and a vacuum cleaner.

I went round in the afternoons visiting the farmworkers' wives on my bicycle, which I had bought new for £3 19s. 11d. with my life savings in 1936 when I was thirteen. Oil lamps were lit in the cottages only when absolutely necessary. As I sat talking, the face opposite gradually disappeared further and further into the gloom.

'Aren't you lonely', people asked, 'up there, all by yourself ?' In fact all life revolved round the house. Ours was the only telephone, so all messages came to us. If the doctor had to be called someone came to the door, and all farm crises were reported. There was a busy round of business and community life. My mother-in-law had been very good to all the farmworkers' families, a confidante in trouble and a support through illness and loss. The foreman's wife lamented her departure every time she came to my door, until one day it dawned on her that perhaps this was not very tactful. 'But, of course', she added kindly, 'you're better than nothing'. She was a very good friend and taught me how to 'put a pig away'. When I learnt to string sausages I felt I had 'arrived' and was approved.

The maids had departed with my parents-in-law and immediately a new situation arose with regard to the use of rooms and domestic help. The maids' sitting-room was seen as a future nursery-playroom, which in due course it became, and remains to this day. For the previous generation, when nannies were the order of the day, the nursery had been upstairs. Now, the gate, which had prevented wandering toddlers from falling down the back stairs, was moved downstairs to stop crawling babies getting into the kitchen, but allowing for supervision and conversation while the work was going on. My domestic help, for the first year or two, came from one or other of the farm cottages, but from 1955 Mary Gibson cycled out daily from Louth, and was my help and support for six years as the babies arrived and until she herself married. 'I have had experience, you know', she told her health visitor, when discussing her own baby.

Few people who take rubbish to the dustbin have the pleasure of seeing ducks gliding in and out between the reeds and watching moorhens flicking their white tails and calling their chicks, fluffy black balls with tiny red beaks. The dustbins stood on the bank above the moat. In the 1950s there was no visiting dust-cart. Our rubbish was buried. During the war the army had prepared defences at Brackenborough in case of an east coast invasion. The troops left behind dug-out shelters, holes in the ground in the spinney behind the house, and these made useful rubbish pits. Fortunately, the Rural District Council arranged a weekly rubbish collection, just as they were filling up.

By the 1920s the Hall already had piped water, indoor sanitation and baths, with a septic tank to deal with the effluent, a system which was installed in all the cottages in 1955. Water was supplied from a deep borehole, the pump powered by a metal windmill, with a storage tank in the farmyard. When the cattle were inside in the winter they depended on this source also and had first call upon the water. It was the human population who had to economise when the wind dropped.

There was a variety of farm animals in the 1950s, Lincoln Red cattle, sheep, breeding sows and cart-horses. We kept chickens to provide eggs for the house. The children had the experience, denied to most these days, of collecting warm eggs from under the hens and placing them *very gently* in the bucket. There were always surplus eggs to sell. For some years the egg packers' van came weekly from Louth, and then, when the packing-station closed, from Horncastle. Then we were told it was not worth their coming unless we could guarantee thirty dozen eggs each time. We couldn't, so we went back in time and took eggs every week to Louth market.

One of my early jobs was to treat a young pig with a septic toe. I applied bread poultices and it recovered. The stockman brought it to my 'surgery', and I always knew when it was coming because, far off in the farmyard, it squealed hideously as soon as it was picked up, and continued to do so until it was replaced in its pen. 'Cade' (orphaned, hand-reared) lambs and weakly piglets sometimes came to be warmed indoors and the cat had kittens in the nursery cupboard.

Forty years on, a new generation of children is growing up. They have sat in the high-chairs used by their grandfather and great-grandfather. They 'help' make pastry at the kitchen table and their paintings adorn the walls. As others have done before them, they wonder at the Christmas tree in the drawing-room, join in family feasts round the dining-room table, and play games up one staircase and down another, round and round. And the adults? They are guardians, stewards for a time, developing, as did their forebears, new lifestyles with the changing times, but looking out of the same windows, opening the same doors to welcome all-comers to a house with a history. 'It has been truly said that these old buildings do not belong to us only: that they belonged to our fore-fathers as they will belong to our descendants unless we play them false. They are not in any sense our property to do as we like with them. We are only trustees for those that come after us.'[4]

As for Brackenborough, 'Like most old houses, it had a living, perceptible aura of its own; a knowledge of birth and death, of far-off happiness, of time remembered and grief not so much forgotten as folded tranquilly and with acceptance into the pattern of the years.' [5]

Notes

1. *Odes of Horace*, Book 2, Ode VI.
2. Further details and all references are given in my study *Brackenborough, the Story of a Manor* (Louth Naturalists', Antiquarian and Literary Society, 1995).
3. See also Eleanor Bennett, 'Ralph Bennett. A portrait', in *Land, People and Landscapes*, edited by Dinah Tyszka, Keith Miller, Geoffrey Bryant (Lincolnshire County Council, 1991), 237-47.
4. William Morris (1834-1896); from a poster in Gainsborough Old Hall.
5. This quotation appeared, unacknowledged, in an issue of *Period Home* in June 1986. This magazine is now no longer published. Enlightenment as to the original source of the quotation would be appreciated.

Chapel St Leonards and the Flood of 5 October 1570

A. E. B. Owen

In an article some thirty years ago on the upkeep of the Lindsey sea defences between 1550 and 1650 I reviewed contemporary practices in dealing with the threat of coastal flooding.[1] Since this remains as much of a threat as ever, it may be of interest to look in more detail at one such flood mentioned in my article and one of the places affected, Chapel St Leonards or, as it was then known, Mumby Chapel. One good reason for doing so now is that I became only recently aware of an error unwittingly perpetuated in that and an earlier article,[2] by taking on trust what was said by Pishey Thompson in his *History of Boston* (1856). Thompson reprinted the graphic description of the flood given in the contemporary chronicle of Raphael Holinshed, but quoted the year wrongly as 1571, the true year being 1570. The flood affected much more of the east coast than Lincolnshire, but it will be sufficient to quote here what Holinshed says about Chapel (I have modernized the spelling):

> This year [1570] the fifth of October chanced a terrible tempest of wind and rain both by sea and land... Mumby Chapel, the whole town was lost, except three houses. A ship was driven upon a house, the sailors thinking they had been upon a rock committed themselves to God, and three of the mariners leapt out of the ship and chanced to take hold on the house top, and so saved themselves; and the wife of the same lying in childbed, by climbing up into the top of the house was also saved by the mariners, her husband and child being both drowned. Likewise the church was wholly overthrown except the steeple... Many men had great loss, as well of sheep, kine, oxen, ... horses and other cattle innumerable... Master Pelham lost eleven hundred sheep at Mumby Chapel...[3]

The evidence for what follows is to be found in the records, now in the Lincolnshire Archives Office, of the Commissioners of Sewers, responsible alike for land drainage and for the sea defences.[4] They issued instructions for repairs to existing sea banks and for the making of new ones, and received the accounts for such work submitted to them by the parish dikereeves who had to oversee it. The account book of John Markby and Robert Legard, dikereeves for the parish of Mumby and its hamlet of Mumby Chapel, opens with a note recording that by warrants from the commissioners of 9 April and 17 June 1571 they had been authorized to collect rates of three shillings the acre in respect of every acre in Mumby and Chapel, and sixpence for 'every acre within the levy charged to Mumby bank' (i.e. the bank at Chapel). It should be explained that the 'levy towns' of the Marsh were those inland townships deemed liable, in accordance with a scheme drawn up in 1500, to contribute when necessary towards the defences of the 'frontagers', the coastal townships, by reason of being 'within levy and danger of the sea banks'; they were in practice usually assessed at one-fourth the rate levied on the frontagers.[5] The rate, collected by the parish constables, was in 1571 charged on (by the 'long hundred' of six score) 1,415 acres in Mumby parish, 1,228 a. in Orby, 1,044 a. in Willoughby, 348 a. in Welton and Boothby, 369 a. in Bonthorpe, 570½ a. in Cumberworth, 506 a. in Anderby, 442 a. in Farlesthorpe, 894 a. in Hogsthorpe, and 218 a. in Thurlby. Anderby, actually a frontager, may have been included because some part of its land drained, like that of the other townships, through the combined outfall of the Orby Drain and Willoughby High Drain at Chapel. With the added proceeds of a penny rate in Mumby and Chapel for work on the outfall itself, this yielded £426 16s. which almost met the dikereeves' expenditure for the period 2 May - 21 July covered by the accounts.

Having formerly written that 'in 1571' the sea broke in at Chapel while a new bank was still under construction, I must now stress that since the flood actually took place in the previous year, the disaster, instead of interrupting the bank's construction preceded it. So far as I can discover, the only work here prior to 1571 was on the outfall itself, sometimes referred to as 'Willoughby coltrap' (a word seemingly denoting the outfall basin and associated tidal doors), which had been in progress since at least the summer of 1569. Neither in the 1571 accounts for this bank, nor indeed in connection with any other bank, has any mention of the 1570 flood been found so far, but it seems likely that the flood and the new bank may have represented cause and effect. As was customary, the new bank was built behind the old one - just how far behind is not recorded, and we know only that 79½ acres were 'wasted betwixt the old bank and the new'. Compensation for this, and for a further 11 acres behind the new bank, taken for its repair, was paid to eight individuals at three shillings the acre. In the second book of accounts the whole 91 acres (as there calculated) is bleakly described as 'lost to the sea and digged', although it may be wrong to infer from this that the old bank had been completely written off as a first line of defence, since the penny rate mentioned above went in part to making a pair of tidal doors to the new 'goyt' (sluice) 'standing in Mumby old sea bank'.

The body of the accounts consists of labourers' names and wages, arranged by townships: the words 'with horses and sleds' or 'men horses and sleds' appear at the head of the lists of names. The dikereeves used symbols instead of figures to represent the wages of individuals, and their interpretation is uncertain. From other accounts, however, we know the standard pay scales. At Theddlethorpe, where a new bank was under construction that same year, a man with horse and sled bringing clay to the bank received 8d. a day, a boy or woman with horse and sled 6d., a common labourer 5d. until Easter and 6d. thereafter, a carpenter 6d., dikereeves and surveyors (see below) 6d., 'bankmen' or 'spademen' building the bank 6d. The 'levy towns' contributed labour as well as money, providing in aggregate well over half the labour force, although Mumby and Chapel supplied more than any single 'levy town' and on some days almost the entire able-bodied male population of the parish must have been engaged on the work (Fig. 1).

Special measures had to be taken for stopping up a 'gowell' against the new sea bank, a goole (the more usual spelling) being a breach in the bank. This required 'jetty work', protective timbering, for which sixteen trees had to be bought and felled for 36s. 6d. and brought to the site for a further 32s. 4d., haulage being always expensive; two hundred (?bundles) of 'ryes', brushwood, were also bought, and Martin Turner, a carpenter, received 10s. for fifteen days'

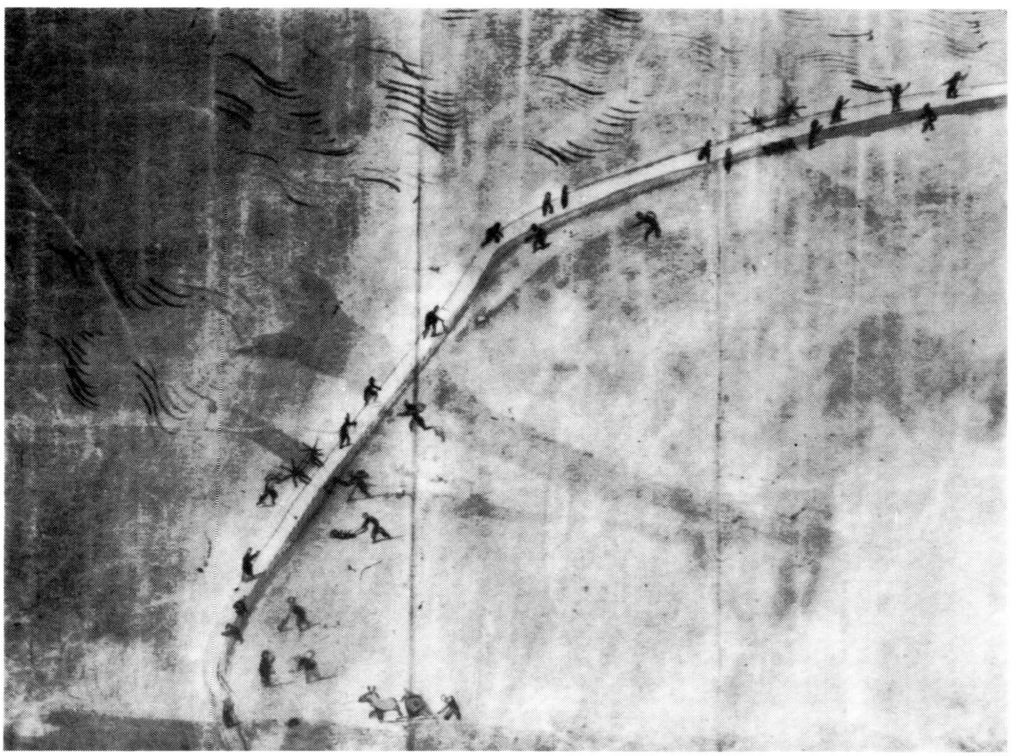

Fig. 1: Construction of a sea bank in the Netherlands, c.1552. Note the hand-operated sluice-gates and (lower left) the wheel barrow and horse-drawn cart used to bring clay to the site. (Detail from a plan attributed to Jan van Scorel showing the projected enclosure of the Zijpe estuary in North Holland province: Algemeen Rijksarchief, the Hague.)

work. For the new sluice already mentioned, a further sixteen trees and more brushwood had to be bought, as well as a hundred nails at 2s.

The dimensions of the new bank are not given but are likely to have been similar to those specified for the new Theddlethorpe bank, itself modelled on a new bank at Sutton. This was to be 13-14 feet high when wet so as to settle to 12 feet, and 6 feet wide on top, with a batter of 30 feet from top to skirt on the seaward side and of 10 feet on the landward side, and thus 46 feet wide altogether at its base. In construction, clay only was to be used; all sand was to be 'clean rid at the foundation, that clay may be laid to clay', and care taken that new work was properly joined to old. No 'manner' (soil) was to be taken within 40 feet of any bank endangered by the sea, nor within 20 feet of any other bank except to fill in a breach against the sea in emergency and the trench to be filled up afterwards; and sleds were to be used in preference to barrows.

After, as we may guess, suspension of work for the harvest, a second book of accounts begins, with work resumed on 10 October. A deleted heading attributes it to the same two dikereeves, acting in accordance with a warrant of 14 August for a rate of 2s. the acre on Mumby and Chapel and 6d. on the levy towns, though this time excluding Anderby and with Hogsthorpe rated at only 4d. (Hogsthorpe, though not reckoned a 'frontager' in 1500, possessed in fact a detached portion of the parish with its own sea bank south of Chapel.) However, instead of this original heading another appears, attributing the accounts to George Metham, esquire, and John Spenluf, 'surveyors and expenditors for the new seabank in Mumby'. The surveyors, it should be explained, acted more or less as clerks of works, mediating between the commissioners, from whom (in east Lindsey at least - the practice in the parts of Holland was somewhat different) they seem to have been recruited, and the dikereeves whose responsibilities did not go beyond those of a modern foreman. Apart from a payment for 'flexes' (hurdles) and piles, these accounts are solely taken up with wages for work on a relatively small scale during 10-29 October, a brief burst of activity 8-10 November, and then in 1572 nothing until May save for two days in late March, perhaps making good damage caused by equinoctial gales. Work was resumed on 5 May and continued, with breaks over Whitsun and on three other days, until 7 June, with a concentration of effort in the final two weeks, a labour force of well over two hundred being employed on 29 May.

We must now look back again to 1570 and ask whether in that autumn the Commissioners of Sewers had been caught unawares, ignorant of the weakness of the local sea defences? To their credit, the evidence is in their favour, if we consider east Lindsey as a whole. Though the details here given are almost certainly incomplete, we may note that in August 1568 orders had been given for the old sea bank at Skegness, 'defective and in decay', to be repaired before next Purification (i.e. 2 February) by the tenants, farmers and occupiers there; and in June 1569 we find mention of a new sea bank there begun the previous year, 14 feet high, 30 feet broad at the base, and 150 falls long. (The 'fall' or perch had different values locally: a bank 800 yards long would result from a 16-foot perch, one of 900 yards from an 18-foot one.) The same month saw orders for the repair of Mablethorpe old bank; from October onwards we have records of work on old and new banks at Theddlethorpe; work on 'Willoughby coltrap' was, as we have seen, in progress; and in June 1570 there is renewed mention of these projects as well as of a new bank at Trusthorpe. Everything points to an energetic programme of repair and renewal of the defences. All that hampered the construction of new banks, then as at other times, was the need for money and labour: a sufficient supply of each could only be found by spreading the work over several years, as the accounts for the new Chapel bank demonstrate.

1570 was in fact a year in which, as historians of climate have made clear, 'a great part of western Europe was troubled with floods'.[6] A particularly disastrous flood in the Netherlands, long famous as the 'All Saints flood' and caused by a tidal surge, occurred on 1-2 November of that year. Events on the Lincolnshire coast are therefore of interest not only for themselves, but as parts of a much wider climatic pattern, and what happened at Chapel and its neighbours makes a modest contribution to the evidence.

Notes

1 A. E. B. Owen, 'The upkeep of the Lindsey sea defences, 1550-1650', *L.H.*, 2, 10 (1963), 23-30.

2 A. E. B. Owen, 'Coastal erosion in East Lincolnshire', *L.H.*, 1, 9 (1952), 330-41.

3 R. Holinshed, *Chronicles of England, Scotland and Ireland*, 4 vols (London, 1808, repr. New York, 1965), IV, 254-55.

4 Records of the Alford and Spilsby Courts of Sewers. Since what is said here derives from the study of a large number of documents, no attempt has been made to give references to individual items.

5 A. E. B. Owen, 'The Levy Book of the Sea: The Lindsey sea defences in 1500', *L.A.A.S.R.P.*, 9, 1 (1961), 35-48.

6 Hubert Lamb and Knud Frydendahl, *Historic Storms of the North Sea, British Isles and Northwest Europe* (Cambridge, 1991), 38.

Andrew Armstrong and the First Survey of Lincolnshire at One Inch to a Mile

R. A. Carroll

Captain Andrew Armstrong was responsible for the first Lincolnshire survey at a scale of one inch to a mile (1: 63,000). As the title on the map makes clear, the work took the three years from 1776 to 1778. In 1779 he surveyed Rutland at the same scale, the map appearing in 1780.

In 1759 the Royal Society of Arts offered 'a sum not exceeding one hundred pounds, as a Gratuity to any Person or Persons, who shall make an accurate actual Survey of any County'. The Society was anxious to promote the large-scale surveying of all counties that had not already been surveyed on that basis. At that time only eight counties had been surveyed at a large scale and using more up-to-date techniques. Additionally, there had not been any national survey since that of Saxton, except for the work undertaken by John Ogilby in association with his road book *Britannia* (1675). Before 1750 Cornwall (Gascoyne, 1700), Sussex (Budgen, 1723), Middlesex (Seller, 1724), Warwickshire (Beighton, 1728), Suffolk (Kirby, 1736), Surrey (Senex, 1729), Huntingdonshire (1731) and Bedfordshire (1736), both by Gordon, were the only counties surveyed at the required scale.[1] The first very large-scale map of all in England was not of a county but of the Fens - mapped by Jonas Moore and published on sixteen sheets at two inches to a mile in 1684.[2]

A scheme for the mapping of Lincolnshire was proposed but never carried through. In 1730 Edmund Weaver wrote to William Stukeley while sending him a copy of his proposals for 'making and publishing, by subscription, an Actual Survey of the County of Lincoln...'[3] The scale suggested was one mile to an inch and the map would be accompanied by an Index Villaris, coats of arms and explanatory notes. The intended price was to be five shillings on taking out a subscription and a further five shillings on receipt of the whole map pasted down on canvas, or a final half a crown if supplied in sheet form. Noblemen who wished to have their coats of arms engraved around the edge would make an initial payment of one guinea and a similar final payment. Blome in the seventeenth century was an enthusiastic supporter of this method of raising funds for his mapping projects. Nothing much seems to have come of his idea, but Weaver was still printing his proposals through the 1730s and 1740s in his annual almanac entitled *The British Telescope: Being an Ephemeris... with an Almanack....* Weaver was a licensed physician at Frieston, near Grantham, who made barometers, undertook surveying work and, from 1737, taught in the school at Caythorpe.[4] After the activity of the 1720s and 1730s there is a gap largely because of the heavy financial outlay involved. The map of Sussex by Thomas Yeakell and William Gardner only covered half of that county before work stopped through shortage of subscriptions. Kingsley quotes their prospectus in which they estimated that the whole undertaking 'will employ us, from first to last, six years, and cost more than 2,400£ for Surveying, Drawing and engraving...'[5] The estimate they made was that 400 subscribers would defray the costs; only 250 were forthcoming in the event. That proposal was made in June, 1778. Further evidence of the costs of county surveys is provided by Armstrong's own submission to the Royal Society of Arts of the more modest costs he incurred in his Northumberland survey. The account shows:

> Expenses of survey (September 1766-March, 1769) for himself, one assistant, two labourers and horses: £350; 9 copper plates, each 24" by 18": £14.10.0; For Engineers, by agreement: £90; Paper for 500 maps: £27; Printing copper plates: £20; Printing the Index, 500 copies: £10; Printing and advertising the Proposals, etc: £5. Total: £516.10.0.[6]

However, the financial offer of the Royal Society of Arts led to an upsurge of work in this field. Jefferys was particularly prominent and worked on a number of projects, which included surveying Bedfordshire (at 2 inches to a mile), Buckinghamshire, Huntingdonshire, Northamptonshire (with T. Eyre), Westmoreland and Yorkshire (on 20 sheets); in some of these cases he acted as engraver. Before the Royal Society of Arts' offer he had made a survey of Staffordshire. He bankrupted himself in the process.

Andrew Armstrong and his son, Mostyn John, became almost as active in the field. The first county surveyed by Andrew Armstrong was Durham, engraved on four sheets and published in 1768, the engraver being Thomas Jefferys. Three versions exist for 1768, issued by three different publishers. John Cary and J. Christopher produced a new edition in 1791. Between 1766 and 1769 Armstrong was joined by his son, Mostyn John, in a survey of Northumberland, which was published on nine sheets in 1769. A single sheet reduction came out in 1770 and went through a further three editions between 1781 and 1796. The pair next turned their attention to a survey of Berwickshire, which appeared on four sheets in 1771, with a reduced single-sheet version the following year. This concentration on three Border counties has led to the suggestion, for lack of other biographical facts, that Andrew Armstrong came from a Borders family.[7] By 1773 their six-sheet mapping of the Lothians had been engraved by Thomas Kitchin and, in 1774, their final work of collaboration appeared - the mapping of Ayrshire. In this case the reduced single-sheet edition appeared first in 1774 and the fuller edition in 6 sheets a year later. The engraver of the large Ayrshire sheets was Stephen Pyle, who later engraved the Lincolnshire sheets.[8] Pyle also engraved in 1779 *A MAP of the Great LEVEL of the / FENS,/...* which included parts of Lincolnshire as far west as Stamford and north to Tattershall. This map was drawn by Kinderley and 'corrected by M. J. A.' - surely the initials of Armstrong's son.[9]

After 1774 the Armstrongs do not appear to have worked together again, although they advertised together, and Strawhorn feels forced to conclude that by then the father was convinced that his son was not a very good surveyor and that they should go their separate ways. Mostyn John moved to Peebles and produced a county survey in 1775, which Pyle engraved on two sheets. The son issued proposals for mapping Norfolk and Cambridgeshire but settled in Norfolk, married there and was made a Lieutenant in the Norfolk Militia by Lord Orford, who was intended to be the dedicatee of the Norfolk map, which was never prepared. Later he was described as County Surveyor for Norfolk and died in 1791.[10]

Andrew Armstrong moved south after the completion of the map of Ayrshire, commencing his work on Lincolnshire in 1776. When the eight sheets were published in 1779 they were followed the year after by the single sheet required to cover Rutland. No more map work is recorded after these two projects. Curiously, no estate surveys or other mapping activity by father or son are known before the maps of Durham and Northumberland; Andrew seems only to have surveyed whole counties.

Biographical details about Andrew Armstrong are so few that he has always seemed a very shadowy figure. In 1934, W. King-Fane asked his readers for details about Armstrong.[11] Two years later J. B. King gave the only reply; namely that Captain Andrew Armstrong was buried at St Michael's in Stamford on 6 January, 1784.[12] Further detail is added, citing Harrod, that he was buried at the eastern end of the church-yard, but no stone marked the grave.[13] St Michael's parish register also records that Armstrong was 72 at the time of his death. Of his early life we have few facts. Moir says he joined the 32nd Foot as a Lieutenant as from 31 August, 1756, that when the regiment was reduced in numbers he went on to the half-pay list in 1763 and is entered thus in the Army Lists up to 1796.[14] When Armstrong applied to the Royal Society of Arts for a reward for the Northumberland map he described himself as 'a Lieutenant on half pay from the 32nd Regiment'.[15] The 32nd Regiment had expanded with the raising of a second battalion in Scotland to cope with French incursions being made in Minorca, the same that led to the execution of Admiral Byng for his campaign's failure. In 1763 the 2nd Battalion, which never served abroad, was disbanded and Armstrong was entered in the half-pay list.[16] It seems likely that he stayed in Scotland or the Borders and by 1766 began his first surveying works, the maps of Durham and then Northumberland. After the map of Northumberland came out Armstrong always described himself as Captain, and it is possible that he was promoted captain in one of the many militia regiments of the time, although evidence is lacking. When Armstrong applied to the Royal Society of Arts for their bounty his Northumberland map was hung in the Society's Great Room for a month and he was finally rewarded with £50, the only sum he ever received from that body.

We know nothing of his surveying training. The map of Lincolnshire is, of course, a great achievement but there is a lack of detail and there is a sufficient degree of error to suggest that he had become somewhat casual in his approach; certainly there is far more detail in, for instance, his map of Northumberland. Stukeley's large-scale map of the Fens of 1723 provides us with much more information and set a standard, based on close local knowledge, that is not found in Armstrong's work. To achieve the detail that Stukeley shows over the whole county area would imply much greater care and accuracy than Armstrong brought to bear. Of Armstrong's detailed methods we can only make informed guesses. In the Companion to the map of Peebles his son says the textbook used as a model by himself and his father was Murdoch Mackenzie's book on maritime surveying. They would have practised a form of triangulation as their map of Durham with its triangulation diagram proves they were familiar with the system. In the case of his Lincolnshire survey, unfortunately, no clues have been left as to the location of the triangulation points he used.

The first proposals issued by Andrew Armstrong for his Lincolnshire map may have appeared in the early months of 1776; he had, by then, already waited on Sir Joseph Banks hoping for his approval of the mapping proposals. In a letter of 24 January, 1776 he reminds Banks of this, presumably, abortive attempt at an interview and submits with his letter 'a proposal from my son at Edinburgh setting forth the Conditions and Manner of Survey which if they are thought proper, may be printed...' In his reply two days later, Banks upbraided Armstrong for failing to wait for an opinion on the surveys before sending proposals. Sir Joseph went on to regret that he found the surveys deficient and that he needed to know more of the mode of survey and to see the instruments used in the mapping process: 'I should not chuse to encourage any Survey, which is not grounded upon several large Triangles, which can only be accurately measured by instruments of the best Construction.' [17] One may only presume that Armstrong did provide Sir Joseph with the necessary assurances since Banks finally ordered two sets of the finished product. Nevertheless, one may sympathize with Armstrong, who had by then already surveyed five counties in ten years!

The following eighteen months must have been spent in the surveying work, including the establishment of the triangulation points on which Banks set so much store. At that point two advertisements appeared in the Lincoln, Rutland and Stamford Mercury in the issues for 19 and 26 June, 1777. The words used were:

> Proposals for publishing by Subscription, Accurate Maps of the Counties of Lincoln and Norfolk, to be taken from actual Surveys, and laid on a Scale of one Inch to a Mile. By Captain Armstrong, and Son. Each Map will be elegantly engraved and printed on eight sheets of Imperial Paper. Price to Subscribers Two Guineas. Subscriptions are taken by the Surveyors now in Lincolnshire and Norfolk, by the Printer of this Paper and Mr. Nott, in Stamford, where Proposals at large may be seen...

Armstrong was not given to spending too much money on advertising, but the subscriptions that came in must have been sufficient for him to progress with his surveying in Lincolnshire. When Armstrong's son wrote from Edinburgh in January, 1776 he must have been near the end of his own survey of the Great North Road from London to Edinburgh, since that work appeared in the June following. This road book must have been well received since it was revised for an issue in August; in a further issue an advertisement (dated 1 January, 1777) listed all the works of father and son, including the forthcoming Lincolnshire on eight sheets at two guineas.

That Armstrong's methods were at fault can be deduced from some of the errors that appear. He seems, for instance, to have gone astray in the area south of Horncastle (Fig. 1); Langton is badly misplaced in a position due west of Martin and due south of Horsington; further errors occur further east, with the positions of East Kirkby, Hagnaby and Stickford, where *inter alia* he places the village of East Kirkby where the church and house are and invents 'South Kirkby' south of the church. A mistake that was copied by Cary and many of those who copied him was the inclusion of Hughington; this spurious place is near Heighington, which is also marked; the closeness of the two names is clearly the result of some confusion in the surveyor's notes. It is instructive to lay the Ordnance Survey one inch to a mile map over Armstrong's map. In many cases Armstrong's accuracy is all that one could expect; in others there is a difference of as much as 50% (for instance, between Mareham on the Hill and Hameringham). Error in the siting of Anderby and Hogsthorpe has been noted; at the same time, however, the depiction of the coastal detail accords with the documentary evidence.[18] Hachure is used to suggest high ground; the 'Cliff' is

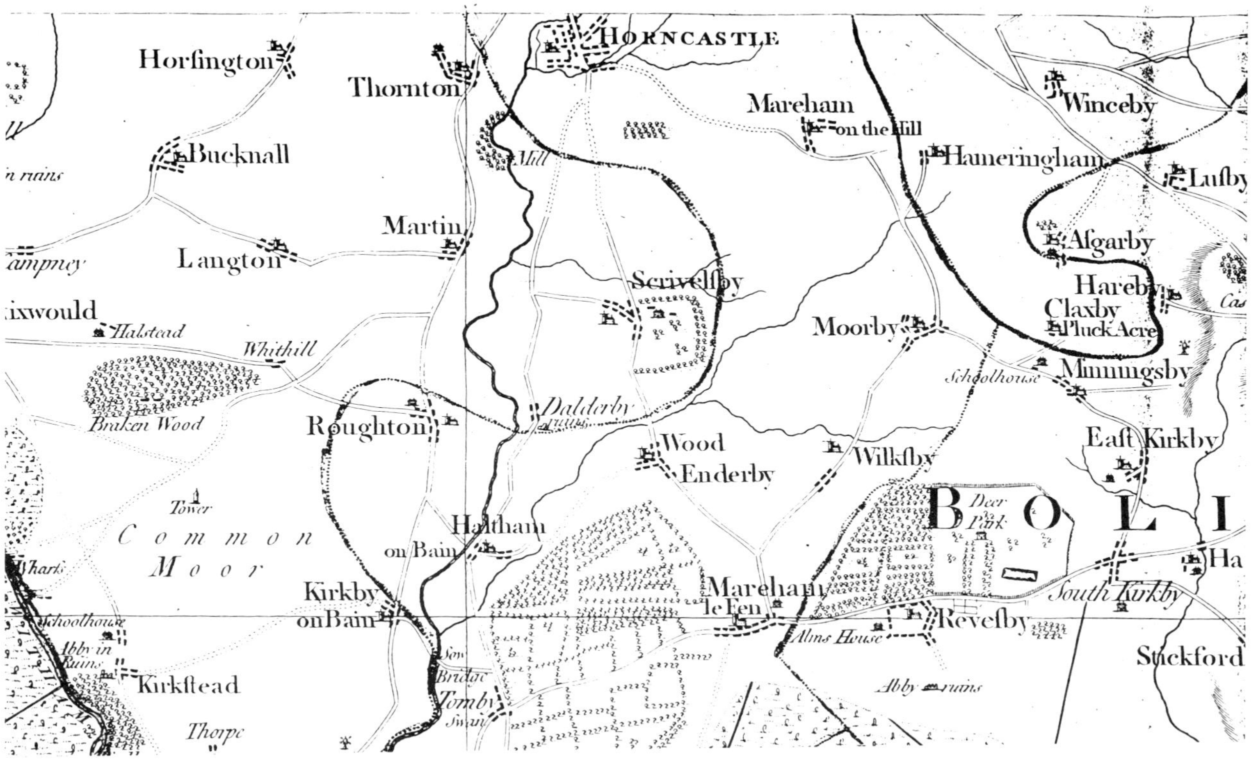

Fig. 1: A section of Armstrong's map showing the area south of Horncastle (sheet VI).

thus indicated, but in the Wolds its use adds little to one's understanding of the land's profile; its use in a line from Wainfleet almost to Boston and, as a 'flattened' oval, enclosing the land between Spalding to a point east of Gedney leads one to distrust the map, since these are hardly hilly parts of the county. Such examples should not be exaggerated for the general standard is acceptable for its time; Mack describes Armstrong as 'the learned Andrew Armstrong' and, while he was was sorry that Armstrong had not seen fit to record the names of the old fields and other features in his Berwick map, he still points out in his discussion of the Northumberland map how much that has come down was due to Armstrong's diligence in noting otherwise unrecorded names.[19] The Lincolnshire map suggests that corners were cut in his later work. He was after all in his mid sixties when he began to survey Lincolnshire.

In 1778 was published 'An Index to Captain Armstrong's Map of Lincolnshire...' to be given free to subscribers to the final work, due for issue in January, 1779. The index listed all the villages on the map, their respective wapontakes and a grid reference. A further subscription list was published separately and probably much nearer the final time of publication since this version ran to thirty nine pages (as opposed to the nine-page section in the village index); again the names of the subscribers, their addresses and how many copies they had ordered are listed. There are 294 names and the total number of copies was close to 400; in the earlier example there were 236 names and the number of copies ordered totalled 281. Many prominent Lincolnshire names are included, headed by The Duke of Ancaster, to whom the map is dedicated. Sir Cecil Wray, M.P. and Charles Pelham, M.P. were the largest private subscribers with ten copies each, but the Board of Customs wanted twelve copies. Two sets were ordered by Sir Joseph Banks; Louth Corporation ordered three. Other interesting names among the subscribers are George Tennyson (of Market Rasen), John Grundy and Guy's Hospital, whose ownership of land near the modern Sutton Bridge is marked on the map.

The map was issued on eight sheets, which are

numbered in their outer margins with large roman figures. Nearly the whole of the second sheet (the upper north-east section) contains the title, with an engraving of a hunting scene at Dunston Pillar (Fig. 2); the seventh sheet (the lower south-west section) contains the dedication and address to the dedicatee, Robert Bertie, Duke of Ancaster and Kesteven, Marquis and Earl of Lindsey, etc. etc. Besides the delineation of the county there are inset plans of Louth (sheet four), above an engraved view of the ruins of 'Louth Abby', Grimsby (sheet two), Spalding (sheet eight) and Boston (sheet six). The plans of Grimsby and Louth are the first of those towns in the public domain. The date in the map's imprint is 20 January, 1779. Only one announcement appeared in the *Lincoln, Rutland and Stamford Mercury*, that for 25 February, 1779:

> London, Jan 30, 1779. Just published, Price Two Guineas. The Map of Lincolnshire, on eight Sheets:- 6F. 8I. by 4F. 8I. With each Map is given a Useful Index, Distances, Tide-Tables, &c Sold, and delivered to Subscribers, (on Payment of the second Part of the Subscription) by Captain Armstrong, at Mr. Wolf's, Copper-Plate Printer, Exeter-Street, Strand, and by no-one else in London. Captain Armstrong has now brought down a Number of the Maps; and Subscribers, or others, may have them at the principal Booksellers in Stamford, Boston, Grantham, and Lincoln where different Ways of fitting them up may be seen.

The Lincolnshire map was submitted to the Royal Society of Arts for a grant but this was turned down in December, 1779. Armstrong may have been strapped for cash later since he offered to sell the plates for the Northumberland map but the Royal Society of Arts refused his price of £20.[20] It is perhaps worth recording that by the time of the final disbursement in 1809 that body had awarded only £460 for work on thirteen different county maps and that only Donn (Devon) and Burdett (Derbyshire) received the full sum of £100.

There is no documentary evidence to suggest how well Armstrong's work was received. The plates were never used again, although the plates for other counties at this scale were quite often used more than once. For instance, Faden re-issued in 1804 the four sheets covering Huntingdonshire that Jefferys had prepared in 1768. However, a single sheet version

Fig. 2: The title of Armstrong's map, with an engraving of Dunston Pillar (sheet II).

appeared in 1781 and there were three further issues with the last appearing with the imprint of Laurie and Whittle in 1794.

When Lord Brownlow wrote to Lord Mulgrave, Master General of the Ordnance in 1817 on behalf of the gentry of the county who wanted to make a case to the Ordnance Survey to survey Lincolnshire out of turn he wrote how it was necessary 'to obtain a good Map of this county, inasmuch as the only work of the kind that exists is a Map, executed about 60 years ago by Armstrong very incorrectly done at the time and now from the number of changes occasioned by enclosures, drainages, &c become positively useless'.[21] The map was, in fact, only thirty-eight years old and allowance must be made for Lord Brownlow's desire to see his scheme succeed. The map did undoubtedly fill a gap; perhaps it did quickly become dated as suggested, but, the bulk of the drainage work (in Wildmore, East and West Fens) did not affect hunting, which was the prime reason for the gentry's wish for a new and better map. In the event, the Ordnance Survey map was not as great an improvement as the gentry had hoped, a fact that was, at least tacitly, acknowledged in the adoption of new methods of surveying, engraving and presentation by the time of the issue of sheets covering Cambridgeshire in 1830.

Notes

1 J. B. Harley,'The re-mapping of England', *Imago Mundi*, XIX (1965), 57; W. Ravenhill, 'The Honourable Robert Edward Clifford, 1767-1817: a cartographer's response to Napoleon', *Geographical Journal*, 160 (1994), 159-72 discusses the background to mapmaking at the end of the eighteenth century, prior to the creation of the Ordnance Survey and (pp. 162-63) contrasts the French approach to national mapping with the county by county approach adopted in England; Elizabeth M. Rodger, *The Large Scale County Maps of the British Isles, 1596-1850* (1972), v-vii.

2 E. Lynam, 'Early maps of the Fen district', *Geographical Journal*, 84 (1934), 420-23; E. Lynam, Maps of the Fenland', *The Victoria County History of... Huntingdon, III* (1936), 291-306; Rodger, *Large Scale County Maps*, 8.

3 The letter and proposal are printed in: *Stukeley's Diaries and Letters, III*, Surtees Society, XXXI (1888), 266-67.

4 Bernard Capp, *Astrology and the Popular Press* (1979), 52, 242-43 and 336; L.A.O. Sub. VIII/49. I am grateful to Miss Weaver of East Bridgford, who provided me with certain details of Weaver's life.

5 David Kingsley, *Printed Maps of Sussex, 1575-1900* (1982), 93 quotes the annotated copy of Richard Gough's *British Topography* (1780), 475 held in the Bodleian Library.

6 J. B. Harley and C. W. Phillips, 'The Society of Arts and the surveys of the English counties', *Journal of the Royal Society of Arts*, CXII (1963-64), 43-46, 119-24, 269-75, 538-43. Armstrong's account is illustrated on p. 271.

7 J. Strawhorn, 'An introduction to Armstrong's map [of Ayrshire]', *Ayrshire Archaeological and Natural History Society*, 2nd Ser., 5 (1959), 232-55.

8 Pyle is recorded as active between 1770 and 1780. His last work appears to have been the 4 sheets of Co. Antrim of 1780; Rodger, *Large Scale County Maps*, 40.

9 The map appears in Vol. 5 of the enlarged edition, issued in parts from May, 1778, of Blomefield's originally uncompleted *History and Antiquities of... Norfolk*. Armstrong's son had a large hand in the revision.

10 Betty Chambers, 'M. J. Armstrong in Norfolk', *Geographical Journal*, 130 (1964), 426-31; *Norwich City Directory*, (1783).

11 W. King-Fane, 'Pre-Ordnance maps of Lincolnshire', *L.N.Q.*, XXII (1934), 37-46, 57-61 and 71-77; the request for details of Armstrong's life and parentage is on p. 48.

12 *L.N.Q.*, XXIII (1936), 104, citing *Lincolnshire Parish Registers*, V, 274 under St Michael's, Stamford.

13 W. Harrod, *History of Stamford*, 2 vols (1785), II, 315; the second edition of 1822 says that no stone had been erected. Armstrong's death was not noted in *Gentleman's Magazine* and the relevant issues of *Lincoln, Rutland and Stamford Mercury* have not survived.

14 D. G. Moir, *The Early Maps of Scotland to 1850*, 2 vols, (1973), I, 136. Moir also states (p. 120) that Capt. Armstrong died in 1794 (he cites Mrs Chambers' 1964 article, which does not refer to Capt. Armstrong's death anywhere).

15 Royal Society of Arts, GB. A,83.

16 G. C. Swiney, *Historical Records of the 32nd (Cornwall) Lt. Infantry* (1893), 45.

17 John Rylands University Library, Eng. Ms. 700.2 and 700.3.

18 A. E. B. Owen, 'Beyond the sea bank: sheep on the Huttoft outmarsh in the early thirteenth century', *L.H.A.*, 28 (1993), 39.

19 J. L. Mack, *The Border Line from the Solway Firth to the North Sea* (1926), 65-66 for discussion of the Berwickshire map and pp.50-63 for discussion of the Northumberland map.

20 Royal Society of Arts, Min. 6 February, 1782.

21 L.A.O. 4 BNL 14

Sir Joseph Banks and the East Fen

David N. Robinson

Where Dirtmouth joins to Gowples filthy meer
And Eweholmes Reeds by Starlings broke...
Has barbarous Banks prevaild while worthy Walls
In vain to rouse the tardy Sokemen calls...
Sure Rennie, aided by infernal Bower
Are come my muddy Dykes & Sykes to scour
To starve my Geese, banish my water fowls
And seize my Fishes in their native holes
Rip up the bosom of my favourite Slough
With the fell Harrow & detested Plough...
I feel my Waters ebbing fast away
Symptom too sure of following decay
Soon will my Mud too, unobstructed roll
Through the wide Orifice of dire Hobhole...
While you're away, Goodwin will let for Woad
Mattlode & Cowmouth break up vastly good,
Roger will grow both Barley Beans & Oats
And Dobbin pasture Oxen Sheep & Goats...
Let not this Rennie meddle with your Drains,
He'll empty all those pretty little tracts
Where Pikes now prey on Eels & Eels on Jacks...

These lines, part of 'The Mire Nymph', a poem addressed to the Proprietors of the East, West and Wildmore Fens, were conceived by Sir Joseph Banks and written down by his faithful clerk William Cartlich. The manuscript, which is in the University of Wisconsin Library, is dated January 1807, when Banks would have been in his London residence, 32 Soho Square. Written, it would seem, in a gloomy mood of self-condemnatory nostalgia, the lines summarize the conflicts over the drainage of the East Fen in the first two decades of the nineteenth century.

The names Dirtmouth, Gowple, Eweholme, Goodwin, Mattlode, Cowmouth, Roger and Dobbin are those of former meres in the East Fen, the result of medieval peat digging. They can be found, among some fifty others, on William Dugdale's map of 1662 and in modified form on J.S. Padley's map of 1810 (Fig. 1), with variations in spelling. Gowple becomes Goop Hole, Eweholme was Emholme and changed to Henholme (close by the present Henholme Bridge over the Bellwater Drain north of New Leake), Goodwin was Great Goodin, Mattlode was Matlade and later part of Gasswater, Roger was always Rogger, and both Cowmouth and Dobbin became part of Middle Water.

That Dirtmouth (Durtmouth) joined Gowple to Eweholme, Banks knew from personal knowledge. When Arthur Young of the Board of Agriculture visited Lincolnshire in 1799, he reported that 'Sir Joseph Banks had the goodness to order a boat, and accompanied me into the heart of this [East] Fen which... had the appearance of a chain of lakes, bordered by great crops of reed... It is in general three to four feet deep in water, and in one place, a channel between two lakes, five to six feet.' In fact, Banks had known the lakes and meres from his youth.

He was two years old when he first came to Revesby (in 1745), where he spent his formative years. By the time he was in his early teens he was big and strong for his age, and during holidays from Eton would take a servant and a boat into the East Fen where the lakes abounded in pike, perch, bream, tench and eels, and the water so clear he could spear large fish with a hay fork. Moreover it was a veritable aviary, from garganies and great crested grebes to teals and terns, with beautiful butterflies, and a botanical paradise with near two hundred species. There he became familiar with the distinctively coloured and textured natterjack toad (the Jacks mentioned in the poem), which he was later to describe as a new British species. And beyond the lakes and meres lay some three hundred acres of mossberry or cranberry fen.

William Banks, Joseph's father, had a keen interest in questions of drainage, not least because tenants of his farms had stock on the intercommoned East, West and Wildmore Fens. The key to improving the lowlying lands on either side of the Witham lay in straightening the meandering course of the tidal river from Dogdyke to the sea. John Grundy of Spalding produced his first scheme in 1744, including a sea sluice, but there was little discussions until 1753 when he prepared a further report, amended again in 1757 to locate the sluice at Boston. Three years later Langley Edwards of King's Lynn and John Smeaton were brought in to advise on the best scheme to achieve both land drainage and improvement of navigation of the river. Agreement was finally reached

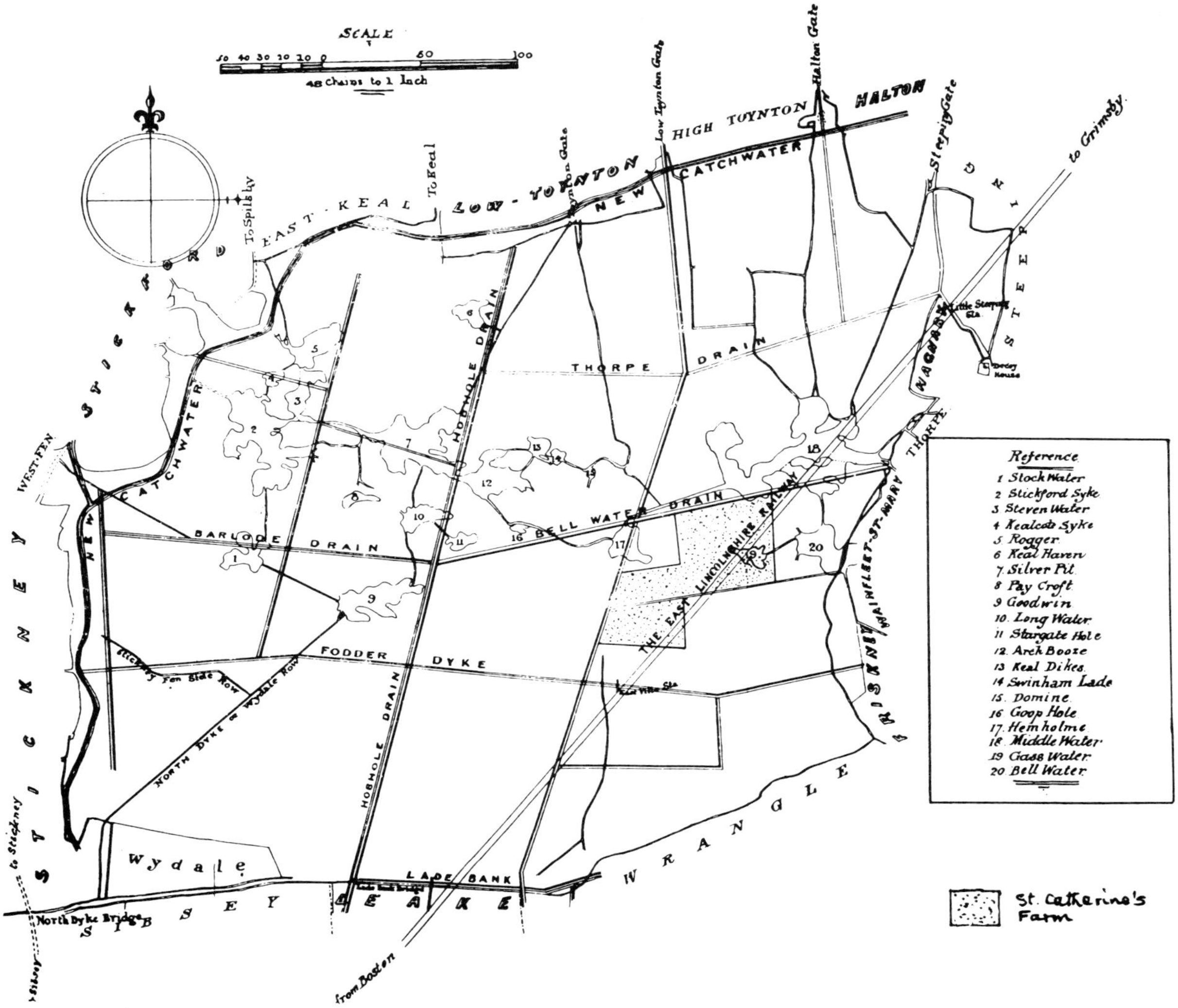

Fig. 1: The East Fen in 1810, showing the old deeps and new drains, and the location of St Catherine's Farm. (Adapted from J. S. Padley, 'The Fens and Floods of Mid-Lincolnshire')

in 1761, just after William died, and Joseph (then 18) subscribed £23 towards the expenses of obtaining an Act of Parliament. This received Royal Assent the following year: 'An Act for Draining and Preserving certain Low Lands, called the Fens, lying on both Sides of the River Witham... and for Restoring and Maintaining the Navigation of the said River, from the High Bridge in the City of Lincoln, through the Borough of Boston, to the Sea.' When the work was complete, with new cuts for the Witham from Chapel Hill to Langrick, thence to Anton's Gowt and to Boston, and the Grand Sluice there opened in October 1766, Banks was away exploring Newfoundland and Labrador.

The Act made provision for the election of Commissioners for each District; the Fourth District which included the East, West and Wildmore Fens had a Commissioner for each parish with rights of common. The Commissioner for East Kirkby was Richard Codd, grazier, the father of Edward (1739-1815), later the Rev. Edward Walls who was referred to in the poem. The Act also provided for the Commissioners of the Fourth District to elect eight General Commissioners every three years; among those elected at the first meeting in 1762 was Robert Banks-Hodgkinson of Overton Hall in Derbyshire, then the guardian of Joseph Banks. He was followed in 1769 by Benjamin Stephenson of Mareham-le-Fen, steward of the Banks Lincolnshire estates. In 1775, his exploring days done, Banks himself was elected a General Commissioner and became chairman, a position he held until his death. The same year the Rev. Edward Codd of Spilsby was also elected a General Commissioner; he served six years. He was the cousin and heir of Joseph Walls of East Kirkby (he was High Sheriff of the county in 1768) and changed his name to Walls under the terms of the inheritance (*c.*1780).

The Witham Act was beneficial to the West and Wildmore Fens, but had little effect on the East Fen where some 2,000 acres were always under water (the Deeps). Highland water flowed into the lakes which issued through the White Cross Clough (sluice) to the Steeping River at Wainfleet and thence to the sea at Gibraltar Point. A survey of the East Fen in August 1773 found about eighteen inches of water on the surface and the White Cross Clough 'in a ruinous condition'. The following year the landowners met in London and Spilsby, and John Grundy proposed improving the drainage through Wainfleet Haven, while the southern part would drain via Hill Dike to the Maud Foster Drain and into the Witham at Skirbeck. No action was taken.

Ten years later some proprietors took matters into their own hands, deepening the Mill Drain from Nordyke Bridge (between Stickney and Sibsey) to Cherry Tree Corner on the Medlam Drain, and thence to Anton's Gowt. This produced a partial drainage of the East Fen and lowered the water in the Deeps, but it also destroyed herbage on the fen and hindered navigation of the pools and dykes. The fenmen commoners erected a dam across the drain and 105 of them signed a petition:

> It is well known that the temperate and industrious of the poor inhabitants of the Soke of Bolingbroke has, for a long time, supported themselves and their families comfortably with the produce of the East Fen, by fishing and getting coarse and fine thatch. Many of us, by the blessing of God and our own industry, has procured a cow or two, which we used to graze in the said fen in the summer, and get fodder for their support in the winter, but, alas, of these privileges we are in great measure deprived by a set of men called Commissioners, who hath imbibed such a rage for drainage, that exceeds both utility and justice. Utility, because it destroys the grass and herbage, and is hurtful both to farmers and poor men, because it deprives the poor of their privileges - for the fishery is ruined, the thatch is destroyed, the fodder is very scarce.

Another product of the fen was fuel: in the late 1780s the overseers of the poor in Bolingbroke were buying between 10 and 23 loads a year of East Fen sods.

In the 1780s and 1790s Edward Walls was apparently on cordial terms with Banks, writing on one occasion that he hoped to breakfast with him before he left Revesby, making his winter grazing available for Banks's sheep, and with his wife and daughter joining the famous Banks fishing parties on the Witham. In one letter (17 May 1794) he commented that 'the Fens are prosperous', but others saw the fens as 'waste' and capable of cultivation and a higher output.[2] In 1793 it was estimated that 40,000 sheep rotted on the three fens, and that 'the number stole is incredible: they are taken off by whole flocks'. The problem was not so much the mechanics of drainage as how to divide the land inclosed amongst those who claimed to have rights on the different fens.

When Arthur Young met Banks in 1799 he found that

> he had the most liberal ideas upon the subject of reclaiming the fens. No man can be more desirous that it should be effected; but knowing that there will arise difficulties, if the parties concerned do not concur in the design... he has desisted from coming forward himself, at a time when the scarcity of money might render the attempt questionable.

Two things were to change matters, and rapidly. Harvests were poor in 1799 and 1800, bread prices were high and there was famine, coupled with the threat of invasion by Napoleon. Secondly, the decision of the proprietors of Wildmore Fen, of whom Banks was the most prominent, meeting at Horncastle in 1799, to employ the Scottish engineer John Rennie to undertake a survey and determine a scheme for draining the three fens. Banks already knew Rennie (then aged thirty-eight) who had been elected a Fellow of the Royal Society (Banks was President) the previous year.

Surveys were undertaken by Anthony Bower, resident engineer at Lincoln, and his assistant James Murray, and Rennie made his reports in April and September 1800. His plan had three elements: to intercept the highland water by catchwater drains, to create a proper network of drains to deal with water falling on the fens themselves; and to increase the dimensions of the outfall sluices. For the Wildmore and West Fans it mainly involved enlarging and extending existing drains, but the solution proposed for the East Fen was much more radical: it meant abandoning the White Cross Clough and creating new drains to a central fourteen-miles long drain south through the highlands at Fishtoft to the aptly named Hob Hole (devil's hole) in the then winding Witham estuary. This was the part of the plan which was to generate the greatest controversy.

Thomas Stone strongly advocated the claims of Wainfleet Haven on the grounds that the drain to Hobhole would not completely drain the pits in the East Fen, and that 'the Proprietors must be prepared to endure many and expensive calls upon their pockets' - prophetic words indeed. William Pocklinton of Sibsey (he had been a drainage commissioner) on the other hand was of the opinion that it was practicable to drain the three fens through Maud Foster. He proposed leaving the deeps of the East Fen as they were 'on the ground that this would save a large amount of expense, and that they would be much more useful left, as affording a basin for the reception of water in violent floods, and as a reservoir for water for the use of the country in dry seasons; and also as a nursery for fish and fowl, and for the production of reeds for thatching and bumbles' (rushes for chair bottoms). It is an interesting speculation that this course of action (or inaction) would have given us one of the best wetland nature reserves in the country.

There were also differences about the amount of land claimed by the Duchy of Lancaster in lieu of manorial rights. This was finally agreed at one twentieth of the land after deduction of land to be sold to pay for the works and the land taken up for drains and roads. A further one tenth went to tithe owners. The Special Commissioners then had to divide the residue into parochial allotments, half to owners of houses (proprietors) and half to those with rights of common (commoners). In other words all common rights were to be extinguished. The fifteen parishes with rights in the East Fen were East and West Keal, Spilsby, Stickford, Stickney, Toynton All Saints and Toynton St Peter, Thorpe, Halton Holegate and Little Steeping in the Soke of Bolingbroke, and Benington, Leverton, Boston East, Butterwick and Leake in the East Holland Towns.

It was a highly complex undertaking and Banks was extremely busy taking the chair at meetings in Spilsby, Horncastle and Boston to agree the heads of Bills to be prepared for presentation to Parliament and to raise subscriptions to meet those costs. At a meeting of proprietors (not commoners, be it noted) at the Bull Inn, Horncastle in December 1800, there was unanimous agreement to proceed, and they resolved 'That the Thanks of the meeting be given to the Chairman for his unremitting care and attention in promoting this most beneficial work'. However, Banks was not without his critics and, it would appear, enemies. In September 1799 the Witham Fourth Commissioners issued an order for Banks to scour out the Outring Dyke along his Revesby frontage to the West Fen. In a letter to the Commissioners he argued that the fence ditch in question was not within their jurisdiction, and complained that not only was the order issued 'in the middle of one of the most calamitous Autumns ever remembered' when all hands were necessary to get in the harvest, but that his parish had 'been selected from amongst many others under similar circumstances to be the sole object of this unprecedented Order'. This he lay 'to the charge of a Personal enmity against me which has of late arisen in the minds of a few of my Neighbours'. Was he perhaps referring to Edward Walls ('worthy Walls')?

Walls had been elected a Witham Commissioner for East Kirkby in March 1799. He attended all the remaining meetings that year, but not again until April 1802 when Banks was re-elected a General Commissioner, when the minutes record that 'It was Ordered that the Clerk do write a Letter to the same effect as the one now drawn by Messrs Walls and Parkinson to such of the General Commissioners as have not attended at the several meetings since their last election [1799].' However, Walls could not claim a satisfactory attendance record for himself: he did so only twice more, in April 1811 and November 1814 (he died in 1815). His criticisms both of the drainage and of Banks did not extend to being present at the meeting of Commissioners in May 1801 when they signed their consent to three Bills for draining and dividing and allotting the three fens. Those Bills passed through Parliament with remarkable speed, receiving Royal Assent on 2 July 1801.

The two Acts which applied to the East Fen were for 'The better and more effectually Draining certain Tracts of land, called Wildmore Fen, and The West and East Fens... and also the Low Lands and Grounds in the several Parishes, Townships, and Places, having Right of Common on the said Fens, and other Lands and Grounds lying contiguous or adjoining thereto'; and for 'Dividing and Allotting certain Fens, called the East and West Fens' (into parochial allotments). The Special Commissioners appointed for the daunting task of transforming a complete landscape were John Renshaw of Owthorpe (Notts.), William Whitelock of Brotherton (Yorks.) and Joseph Outram of Alfreton (Derbys.), who were allowed three guineas a day including travel time and expenses. Renshaw died the following year and was replaced by Charles Wedge; the other two died in 1810 and were replaced by Samuel Dickinson and Joseph Truslove. Three Lincolnshire graziers were appointed Quality Men, at two guineas a day, for valuing the land to be divided and allotted: Robert Millington of Gedney, William Thacker of Langrett (Langrick) Ferry and Thomas Rockliffe of Fulletby. Appointed Clerks to the Commissioners were Samuel Tunnard of Boston and Joseph Brackenbury of Spilsby. The works were carried out under the direction of John Rennie, with Anthony Bower as resident engineer. The contractor for the largest works was John Pinkerton of Boston.

Notices soon appeared in the *Stamford Mercury* from March 1802 for canal cutters, the main job being the Hobhole and side drains to it. The first cut was from Hobhole to Benington Bridge (seven miles), from there to Lade Bank (three miles, started in 1805), and then through the East Fen Deeps (three miles, 1806 to 1808). The last was the most difficult because it was through patchy peat. The men were

Fig. 2: The barrow and plank method used to dig the main drains in the East Fen, and still in use a century later. (D. N. Robinson Collection)

1st. JANUARY, 1810.

LINCOLNSHIRE.

East, West, and Wildmore Fens Drainage.

TO BE

Sold by Auction,

AT THE PEACOCK INN, IN BOSTON,

In the County of Lincoln,

On THURSDAY the 1st. and FRIDAY the 2nd. Days of FEBRUARY next,

BEFORE the Special Commissioners, acting under and by Virtue of certain Acts of Parliament, passed in the 41st. and 43d. Years of the Reign of His present Majesty, for the Drainage of the said East, West, and Wildmore Fens, at their adjourned Meeting then to be holden, pursuant to the Directions of the said Acts.

IN LOTS,

SUBJECT TO SUCH CONDITIONS OF SALE AS SHALL BE THEN AND THERE PRODUCED;

SIX HUNDRED AND THIRTY-SEVEN ACRES THREE ROODS AND TWENTY-TWO PERCHES, OF

PASTURE GROUND,

IN THE EAST FEN,

Between Fodder Dyke and White Cross Clough Drain, and adjoining the Parish of Wainfleet.

AND ALSO

SIX HUNDRED AND NINETY-EIGHT ACRES, ONE ROOD, AND THIRTY-NINE PERCHES, OF

PASTURE GROUND,

IN THE WEST FEN,

On the North Side of Frith Bank, between Newham Drain and Whistley Bridge, and on the East and West Sides of the Common Fendyke, adjoining Medlam Inclosures.

TYTHE FREE.

Fig. 3: Handbill for the sale of land in the East Fen, 1810. (J. O. Dodds)

paid 6s. or 7s. a day, 3s. or 4s. a day as a weekly subsist with the balance on satisfactory completion of their job. The method of working used was barrow and plank (Fig. 2). A steam engine was built at Hobhole to pump water from the advancing cut. The Hobhole Sluice was built between March 1805 and September 1806. Then followed the Lade Bank and Fodder Dyke drains (1807), the East Fen Catchwater in two stages (1807 and 1808), and finally the White Cross, now Bellwater, Drain (1808). Large quantities of bricks were required, a total of 13,700,000, of which 6,300,000 were used in the East Fen, for sluices and bridges, together with 26,000 cubic feet of freestone and 4,000 cubic feet of timber. Coal was brought in by water to burn the bricks in clamps, the clay being taken from the drains being dug.

Clearly it was going to be a costly operation. Banks had estimated the cost at not less than £400,000. By mid-1805 it appeared that £100,000 had been spent on the Hobhole drainage alone, and there had to be two amending Acts (in 1802 and 1803), with a further one in 1810. To pay for it all, auction sales of land in West and Wildmore Fens started in 1802. The first sales realised £40 an acre, increasing to £50-£65 in 1805; by the end of that year some 7,000 acres had been sold for £286,400. Sales in the East Fen, where the land was worth much less, did not commence until the drains were nearly complete. There were three main sales, in lots not exceeding 100 acres and tithe free, held at the Peacock Inn, Boston in October 1807 (1,806 acres), September 1808 (1,689 acres) and February 1810 (637 acres; Fig. 3), the latter selling at only £33-£34 an acre. Some was re-sold in smaller lots by private contract almost immediately afterwards.

There was increasing concern about the rising costs and the amount of common land being sold, to the benefit of proprietors and speculators, but not the commoners, and from 1803 a series of letters appeared in the *Stamford Mercury*. Although signed 'A Commoner', it seems certain that everyone knew the writer was Edward Walls, and from 1810 he did put his name to them. He repeatedly called for a meeting of commoners, particularly of those in the Soke of Bolingbroke, at which proper accounts of expenditure could be seen. In the latter respect he was no more successful than the Witham Commissioners, and Walls continued to blame the Chairman of the undertaking (Banks). In fact, a general abstract of accounts was published for 1802, 1803 and 1804, but this did not satisfy Walls. Writing in November 1806 he complained about the unfinished state of the works, and noted that the value of land sold had risen to £363,290, and he published a notice requesting Banks to call a meeting of commoners. No such meeting had been held when Banks composed the poem and included his fiercest critic 'worthy' Walls. So the flow of letters continued in 1808. That published on

25 November is the most detailed exposition of Walls's case, and is here given in full:

To the Commoners having a Right in
EAST, WEST and WILDMORE FENS.
Gentlemen,

Having received from the Treasurer a statement of the lands you have sold, and the monies you have raised, I think every Commoner is entitled to such information; and I am mistaken if many of the following statements are not wholly unknown to more than nine-tenths of the Commoners having a Right in these Fens.

From a meeting of land-owners at the St. Alban's Tavern in London on 16th April, 1774, and from another meeting at Spilsby on 7th June following, Mr Grundy, the Engineer, was employed to make a Report of the practicability of draining the East Fen.

Mr Grundy demonstrated the practicability of *an effectual Drainage* of that Fen from levels and from an engraved plan; and there is every reason to believe that all the Fens would have been drained about that time if the measure had met with the approbation of the present Chairman.

Whether this great and good work has been reserved for a more fortunate period is left to your decision. Mr Grundy's estimate of the expense was £37,314 14s. 0d. and you will observe, Gentlemen, what proportion it bears to present expenditure. 12,577 acres have already, and more must soon, be sold. The sales of your land have raised £500,075 and £2,397 12s. 2d. have been paid to the Treasurer from other sources; you have got considerably beyond the half million of MONEY and the works you see in a very unfinished state.

Put an average estimate on 8,740 acres of very valuable land sold in the West and Wildmore Fens, and put an average estimate of the value of the remainder of the lands in those two Fens, and you will at once clearly see how your property is curtailed. After, Gentlemen, making these comparative statements it must raise your indignation to have your ears stunned with vociferous eulogisms on the present *proceedings only* BY THE NUMEROUS HIRELINGS, who are basking in the sunshine of your prosperity.

It is observed that public works cannot be carried on without great abuse. If the position be a truism, it is particularly to be lamented in this great and good work, where so many humble Commoners are materially interested. But surely, Gentlemen, the abuses which have crept into the present undertaking might have been very much lessened.

If the Chairman, when so repeatedly requested, had called a public meeting; if he had attended to the Act of Parliament, and directed the Treasurer to produce, *annually*, a just, fair, intelligible account; the abuses would never have arisen to the present pitch. And why the Chairman would not have *those public accounts* so settled and adjusted as, *in his private concerns* he settles and adjusts his own, seems to require some explanation; for the Chairman to do *in his own case* what he would NOT do *in others*, appears to be bordering upon a false philosophy. After a lapse of 8 years no fair account can be produced; for as I observe in a private letter to the Treasurer, 'If the Commoners expect a fair, just, intelligible account of the ITEMS constituting the expenditure of their monies, you and I, Sir, can tell them, and tell them truly, they may as soon expect the sky to fall to give them an opportunity of catching larks.'

The numerous, expensive, and extensive drains that are made and making, the Chairman must acknowledge, cannot have a due supply of water. You will ask, how then are they to be kept in a proper state for drainage? There is a fund for a perpetual job. Exclusive of 1/- per acre, charged by the Witham Act, 1/- per acre will be payable from ALL THE FENS (when inclosed) and the contiguous low lands, to go in aid of keeping in repair superfluous drains.

Calculate, Gentlemen, the annual amount and you will be stricken with the enormity of the sum entailed upon your property.

If the Chairman had *only* directed a fair annual account, if he had properly called public meetings £200,000 of the Commoners' money would have been saved, and all the Fens (at the latest) would have been in a state of cultivation at Lady Day 1807. By adding the loss of £200,000 to the loss from the Fens *not* being in a state of cultivation at Lady Day 1807, it will be difficult to estimate THE INJURY THE COMMONERS AND THE COUNTRY have sustained.

I am, Gentlemen,
with real regard to your true interest
Your most humble Servant
A COMMONER

In 1810 and 1811, Walls was writing at length about the question of chapels and also the problem of extra-parochial lands. The Special Commissioners were required to allot lands for chapels for divine worship 'according to the law ecclesiastical of the realm'; lands had been allotted but no chapels were built until 1816: St Peter, Wildmore and St. Paul, Carrington. It took the amending Act of 1818, because of increasing population, before the East Fen chapels were built: St Peter, midville (1819 by Jeptha Pacey) and St Paul, Eastville (1840 by C. J. Carter[3]). What, it seems, had not been realized was that the lands sold were extra-parochial and thus, according to Walls, 'a place of refuge for all disorderly persons - for vagrants, cheats, whores and thieves - living by plunder, terrifying the inhabitants and destroying the peace and security of the whole neighbourhood'. In another letter he specifically takes Banks to task for not ensuring the parochialising of all the fens in the first Acts. He was also still pressing (January 1811) for the publication of costs, which had by then risen to £570,512, well over even Banks's estimate. Yet Walls was at the Witham Commissioners meeting in April 1811 when Banks was re-elected; did he vote against?

When Walls was writing there was in fact a Bill in preparation, which was passed in June 1812 as 'An Act for Forming into Townships, certain Extra-parochial lands in Wildmore Fen and in the West and East Fens...'. In the East Fen the new parishes of Eastville and Midville were created, totalling 5,138 acres which represented 40% of the total area drained (12,664 acres). Over the three fens the land sold to pay for drains, roads, dividing and allotting and other expenses made up one third of the total area.

Among the land which went to be part of Eastville parish was that sold by auction on 1 and 2 February 1810 in Boston. The sale attracted the attention of John Trotter of Coutts Bank in London, and during January he consulted John Rennie who had bought 400 acres nearby and just south of the Fodder Dike two years before (named as Rennie's House on Bryant's map of 1828 and now called Slates Farm). Rennie said there was no difficulty in finding a tenant if farm buildings were provided, that he was making a 6% return on his investment, and that the best profit was to be obtained from 'land which is pared and burnt which is of course the worst' (at £25-£35 an acre). Through his agent Henry de Bruyn of King's Lynn, Trotter bought five lots totalling 408 acres 2 roods 2 perches for £14,108 including duty and commission (£34 11s. 7d. an acre).[4]

Later in February Trotter and his wife took a boat from Boston (the new fen roads were not made up until 1813) and was taken aback to find that he had bought more mere than moor, although Mrs Trotter was fascinated by the adjacent cranberry fen. De Bruyn described the land purchased as 'like a sponge for the quantity of aquatic hollow roots which abound and reach down for nearly three feet'. The land was located south of the White Cross Clough (Bellwater) Drain and east of Henholme Bridge, and included the former Gasswater (the Mattlode of Banks's poem). De Bruyn reported that in the south-west corner there was 'a great deal of low boggy ground into which I had the comfort of getting up to my knees and had it not been for the assistance of one of the labourers I might have gone up to my chin' (this would have been the former Faire Fishes mere), and also that 'several fodder stacks and a mud hut belonging to the commoners' would have to be removed. A present day aerial photograph still shows a mass of former peaty creeks across the farm, called St Catherine's.

Only a fortnight after purchase it was advertized to let for 14 years, tithe free and subject to a drainage tax of 1s. per acre, 'with the advantage of navigation leading to Boston'. Following the advice of Rennie, the notice stated that

> the whole of these lands must be pared, burnt, and then sown with cole-seed for sheep feed, and afterwards sown with corn. The tenant will be allowed to take two crops a year and a fallow. The landlord will erect necessary farming offices, and dyke, fence and plant with quick all the outside fences. The internal dykes and fences are to be done by and at the expense of the tenant, and made into inclosures of about 20 acres each.

Meanwhile Trotter wrote for advice from Anthony Bower; he had been the resident engineer and when the main work finished became a works contractor, though remaining on call to the Commissioners. Trotter also went to see Banks at Soho Square for advice, and found him 'in gouty good health'. Finding a new tenant was not easy, but a lease was taken by Thomas Clater, who already farmed at Butterwick, for a rent of £900 a year. The landlord was to erect the buildings (taken down in the 1960s) and the tenant was to be allowed up to £600 against vouchers for paring and burning. Bower quickly organised the dyking, hedging and fencing through a sub-contractor, John Walker, at a cost of £568, and the work was finished by early April.

Immediately Clater brought in a gang of twenty men to pare and burn: cutting off the matted turf using a breast plough with horizontal share, or by spade in the wetter parts, stubbing out wire roots, digging out hassocks, and heaping and burning. By the end of April 140 acres had been done and a further 200 acres in May, but some areas had to be worked over twice; the cost was £298. The ground was not firm enough to use horses, and ploughing was also a manual operation using a breast plough. Seed was broadcast by hand and bush harrowed to bury the seed - 256 acres of cole, 105 acres of oats and 16 acres of lintins (tares). The remaining wet and reedy 32 acres on the site of Gasswater had not yet been pared and burnt. The oats did well and found a ready sale as the Napoleonic war kept prices up.

The following year, 1811, Clater's income was £1,752, including £1,415 for oats, £237 for cole-seed and £46 for agistment of sheep on green cole. By 1812 he had introduced stock, some land had sunk a foot by treading of cows and horses, and the number of sheep were gradually increased. He also began claying or marling, spreading the clay from deepening the ditches in winter. Good clay was found at four feet and trenches were cut across the fields and the clay spread out from them. By 1813 the claying had cost nearly £280 and the 'marled crops looked well', but prices were falling, with oats returning less than £3 an acre compared with over £10 an acre two years earlier.

In 1815 crops of onions and carrots failed entirely, and more land was put down to grass. But the land was difficult and the depression was running against Clater who was falling behind with the rent. Trotter sought the opinion of John Brown, a prominent famer at Swineshead, who reported that the farm was in 'a proper state of husbandry' but that 'without claying the land is not worth occupying'. Even as late as 1831 the tenant, then Samuel Tusting, was complaining of the land being 'so low' and 'so moist'. This contrasts with Anthony Bower's confident report of 1814 in which he stated 'the East Fen Deeps are so perfectly drained, and so confident are the proprietors of this, that part of them now forms a considerable farm-yard'.

During heavy rainfall in April 1816 'some evil-disposed persons... cut through the bank of the East Fen Catchwater Drain' near Halton, 'whereby the floodwaters caused great damage to the low grounds in the East Fen'. Under a further amending Act of 1818 the low grounds of Great Steeping, Thorpe, Irby, Firsby, Bratoft, Croft and Wainfleet All Saints (the Five Thousand Acres) were incorporated into the Witham Fourth District, the River Steeping straightened and other improvements made for the better protection of the East Fen. John Burcham, a well known and very experienced inclosure commissioner, was appointed sole Commissioner to carry out the works. In April 1820, Banks was re-elected a General Commissioner, although his last visit to Revesby had been in autumn 1817. On 9 June the waters of the East Fen drains were run off in order to clean them out. And on 30 June the Award for dividing and allotting the East Fen was read at a meeting at the Peacock Inn, Boston, but Banks did not live to see the final act of his endeavours; he died on 19 June.

Unfortunately however the satisfactory condition of the drainage was not permanent. This was due to shrinkage of the spongy peat as it dried out and, with consolidation by working, the surface was lowered by up to two feet; and also silting in the Witham estuary at the Hobhole Sluice. During the winter of 1866-67 there was continuous heavy rainfall and a large part of the East Fen was under water for weeks. Viewed from Keal Hill, where Banks himself must have stood on more than one occasion contemplating those East Fen meres, the whole area had the appearance of one extensive lake. Rennie had relied on gravity drainage, and not until the opening of steam pumps at Lade Bank on the Hobhole Drain in September 1867 could the lowlying parts of the East Fen, including St Catherine's Farm, be said to be well-drained.

Notes

1 For general background to the draining of the East Fen see, in particular, W. H. Wheeler, *A History of the Fens of South Lincolnshire* (Boston, 1896). J. S. Padley, *The Fens and Floods of Mid-Lincolnshire* (Lincoln, 1882) and James Dear and T. Taylor *Aspects of Yellowbelly History; The Development and Settlement of the East West and Wildmore Fens* (Spalding, 1988) also contains valuable material. For Banks, see especially, H. B. Carter, *Sir Joseph Banks* (1988). Arthur Young, *General View of the Agriculture of the County of Lincoln* (1799) has been invaluable, and, to a lesser extent, Thomas Stone's, earlier, but similarly titled work (1794). In addition to other relevant (printed) materials mentioned in the text, I have had access to the manuscript Minute Books of the Witham Fourth Drainage District (1762-1854).

2 For the Witham fishing parties see Carter, *Sir Joseph Banks*, 348-50, 583. Some of Walls's letters to Banks are calendared in Warren R. Dawson, ed., *The Banks Letters* (1958), 853-54.

3 The information in Pevsner is erroneous: the architect was not J. C. Carter but C. J. Carter of Louth (I am grateful to Christopher Sturman for this point of detail).

4 Here I am indebted to J. O. Dodds of Sudbury, for allowing me to use his unpublished ms. 'Genesis of St Catherine's Farm, Eastville'.

[For the full text of Banks's 'The Mire Nymph', see p. 108]

Sir Joseph Banks as a Writer of Topical Verse

H. B. Carter and Christopher Sturman

In his more truly domestic moments Sir Joseph Banks was occasionally inspired to pen a few affectionate lines to Dorothea, his wife, as the devoted husband he certainly was. Of these a few survive to remind us that in this pleasant habit he was as many other men are, and no more distinguished in the quality of his verse than the general run. Apart from this domestic verse he also, from time to time, took part in the social exchanges of rhymed felicities, in which both his wife and his sister, Sarah Sophia, were apt to indulge with their friends. These were evidently born of the quick impromptu in a moment of inspiration by the evening fireside, or the garden tea table on a summer day at Spring Grove or Revesby Abbey. There were, however, other occasions to elicit this form of expression not so light-hearted nor so pleasant in their undertones. Of this kind, most of the examples of which we know (and containing much of Lincolnshire interest) belong to a collection dating from the years 1806 to 1807,[1] a stressful period for Banks in private and for the nation at large.

For the country there was the series of political changes which followed the death of William Pitt in January 1806 and culminated in the fall of the Grenville administration in March 1807, and the election which followed. For Banks at this time these events had their bearing on his county interests and, more than usually, on his concern for its representation at Westminster. At the same time, as a man of property in the Fourth District along the River Witham, he was deeply engaged in the contentious and difficult issues of fen drainage in his neighbourhood, and the enclosures to follow. He was also now facing his own very personal crisis, as he took stock of his growing incapacities and the evident need for him to retire, in effect, from many commitments in a free-ranging life that otherwise had no retirement imperative. All these factors conspire together, and shed some light on why Banks, in the shackles of gout, should at this time have exploded briefly into polemic verse.

Of political intent the collection contains 'A bundle of fools' caps: worked up from tatters of oratory, scraps of patriotism, rags of democracy & remnants of common sense, picked up in the Castle Hall at Lincoln, 11 November 1806, the day of the General Election intended for the use of those whom they may fit; and for the amusement of those who may choose to try them on upon their neighbour's heads' and the ten sets of verse under the blanket title 'The Goldsmith's Garland or The Banker's Delight: being a selection from the songs intended to have been sung and the verses intended to have been distributed at Lincoln during the memorable contest for the representation of the County, between the landed & the Mercantile interest', the latter directed explicitly against Colonel Richard Ellison MP, the banker of Ellison & Co. Of these, only the first two pieces in 'The Goldsmith's Garland' seem to have been published. Printed by Weir of Horncastle, whom Banks often used for his local purposes, they appeared anonymously, but as electoral grapeshot, they fulfilled their intention. Ellison lost the county but retained the city.[2] The collection also contains the manuscript draft of Banks's 'An Elegy on the Demolition of the Spires of Lincoln Minster', printed for him by William Bulmer (1807) as a Christmas appeal for their restoration and diocesan support against the Dean and Chapter, who had ordered their removal from the western towers. Almost alone in his strong feeling on the case, his lay defense of Gothic aesthetics failed before the legal despotism of the Church.[3] This was evidently a cathartic experience for, thereafter, Banks seems to have remained a man of simple prose.

Of local interest to Revesby, is Banks's 'Anthem' intended for the annual meeting of the Horncastle Dispensary, of which he was its president, but it is three items, two relating to fen drainage and one directed against the current incumbent of Scrivelsby Court, which are here printed in their entirety.

Of some modern relevance in the unending debates about the proprieties of land use is Bank's complicated self-flagellatory satire 'The Mire Nymph: A Poem Addressed to the Proprietors of the East, West and Wildmore Fens', under the pseudonym 'Martin Mudlark Tide Waiter' - in its way a masterly summary of the burning issues of fen reclamation and enclosure set in the geography of the Fourth District, one of whose Commissioners was the Rev. Edward Walls (formerly Codd, 1739-1815), of Boothby, an implacable opponent of John Rennie's plans for the Hobhole Drain among others. [See David Robinson's account, pp 97-105]. Walls's opposition to Rennie, and the work of the resident engineer, Anthony Bower of Lincoln, was but part of a long-standing disagreement with Banks, the genesis of which was outlined by Walls himself in a printed letter to Dr Edward Harrison of Horncastle in October 1804:

> In his Correspondence with the Bishop of Lincoln, relating to the building of Chapels in Wildmore Fen, Sir Joseph Banks, so far back as the 15th of September, 1799, endeavours to hold me up to my Diocesan, as a character unworthy of His Lordship's regard.
>
> Then a sham Prosecution for a Libel (for I afterwards found it was to be nothing more) commenced under the Direction (as my Solicitor too late told me) of Sir Joseph Banks.
>
> Trusting from his Letters to me that Sir Joseph Banks was (at that time) my most cordial Friend, I readily submitted the Matter to his sole Arbitration. When the conditions of his own Arbitration were, most shamefully, broken, I earnestly entreated Sir Joseph Banks only to see, whether they had been duly observed. This request was by Sir Joseph Banks, in my opinion, very dishonourably and unjustly denied to me.
>
> Afterwards Sir Joseph Banks endeavoured to inflict a much deeper wound. He circulated a printed Paper, accusing me of cheating my Ward.
>
> What I required after all these repeated Attacks, I must require now - "That Sir Joseph Banks shall prove his Statements or make to me a proper Apology." Does Christianity enjoin from me more than this?[4]

Walls, whom Banks isolated in the agonized musings of 'The Mire Nymph' as 'the Genius of the teeming pen', mounted his attack on Banks in a number of pamphlets printed by Sheardown of Louth[5] and in letters, signed 'A Commoner', to the *Stamford Mercury*. On 31 December 1804 Banks wrote to Harrison from Soho Square:

> I see he [Walls] has printed his Lucubrations on the Fen accounts, he is made of stuff too impenetrable to feel anything mental or your Letter which is a wise answer to a foolish adress would have stopd his hand, till I have seen this new production it would be idle to give an opinion on it but unless he has muched improvd his stile & matter it must prove a *telum imbelle et sine ictu* like all the rest of the Arrows shot out of his Fools Quiver.[6]

Walls continued to shoot his arrows; Banks at the same time as composing 'The Mire Nymph' (January 1807) impaled the pamphleteering prelate on his nib in 'Parson Printapace: A Satyre', a blistering tirade heated perhaps to an unusual extreme by his winter gout (though as Banks's epigraph suggests he may have been influenced by the satires of Alexander Pope and his fellow 'Scriblerians').

The philippic tendency in this odd outcrop of verse-making was also to be found in the 'Lines designed for the Proprietor of the Manor of Scrivelsby' which derided the pretensions of his litigious neighbour Lewis Dymoke (1763-1820), the King's Champion. The manuscript is dated October 1806, a time when Lewis's (ultimately unsuccessful[7]) intention to petition for the revival of the barony of Marmion might have become common knowledge. Banks soon returned to this issue drafting, in December 1806 another work in the collection, the 'Established anecdotes and unestablished opinions concerning the Marmion family and the tenure of grand seargentry by which the Manor of Scrivelsby in the County of Lincoln is said to be held'.[8]

All three poems printed here reproduce the transcriptions of Banks's original drafts made by his secretary, William Cartlich, who copied faithfully Banks's (notoriously inconsistent) use of capitals, spelling and punctuation. Alterations made by Banks have been included though no attempt has been made to indicate the nature or extent of these emendations.

The Mire Nymph
A Poem
Adressd to the Proprietors of the East West
and Wildmore Fens
By Martin Mudlark Tide Waiter.

Where[1] Dirtmouth joins to Gowples filthy meer
And Eweholmes Reeds by Starlings broke, appear
From easy Couch of soft alluvial Mud
Unmovd since Noah landed from the flood.
Uprose the Murky Naiid of the Fen
Seldom before beheld by honest Men
Her head was crownd with Sedge, her bosom bare
Eeels crawld like Lice among her clotted hair.
Deep were her Eye balls sunk, her aguish cheek
Shone deadly pale, above her Peat staind neck,
Why will ye, shreikd she, torture my repose,
Am I a prisoner to my deadly foes
Has barbarous Banks prevaild while worthy Walls
In vain to rouse the tardy Sokemen calls,
Patron of Mire, whose economic lore
My Geese my Ducks my Dabchicks all adore
Sure Rennie, aided by infernal Bower
Are come my muddy Dykes & Sykes to scour
To starve my Geese, banish my Water fowls
And seize my Fishes in their native holes
Rip up the bosom of my favorite Slough
With the fell Harrow & detested Plough
They'll steal my Bell[b] & give me no redress
All the metallic treasure I possess.
I feel my Waters ebbing fast away
symptom too sure of following decay
Soon will my Mud too, unobstructed roll
Through the wide Orifice of dire Hobhole
Smutching fair Neptune's face with Peaty brown
And murdering all the Fish for five miles down.
Where wert thou Genius of the teeming pen
When I was sacrificd to these vile men
Was you at Louth or Spilsbys Justice seat
Crownd with your ancient triple cornerd hat
or was you Counting up the Present yeild
of Rotten Boothbys Tithe Commuted Field
or on the orphans well allotted Share
Planning the ways & means of Future War
perhaps inspecting all the Neighbors holes
To find who pilferd Hobhole Engines Coals
Or measuring how much Revesby Bridge exceeds
The just proportion of the public Needs.
Perhaps on Skegness Sand encircled shore
Woeing [*sic*] a Sea Nymph at the Ale house door
While you're away, Goodwin will let for Woad
Mattlode & Cowmouth break up vastly good,
Roger will grow both Barley Beans & Oats,
And Dobbin pasture Oxen Sheep & Goats.
Curse on your prattling persevering pen,
You should have raisd a Mob of Fishermen,
Folks fit to cope with syllogistic foes,
And answer knock down arguments with blows.
Alas! Alas! my dreadful fate I feel,
I shall no more have pasture for an Eel,
While you my friend still more distressd than I
Must chuse another theme when Goodwin's dry.
Borough of Boston moderate my woe
Twas you who savd me forty Years ago
Beat down Hobs Sluice, choak up Maud Forsters throat,
And force all Drainage up to Antens [*sic*] Gout
So shall my pretty deeps unbroachd remain,
Wildmore & West Fen be o'erflowd again;
All purchasters of Land be driven away,
And drowning made the order of the day.
Ye Nymphs of Wainfleet listen to my strains
Let not this Rennie meddle with your Drains,
He'll empty all those pretty little tracts
Where Pikes now prey on Eels & Eels on Jacks
Till not a Stickleback alive is seen
And cheerful Browns exchangd for fulsome Green,
He'll make the Dust fly, all your Parish o'er,
Where never Dust flew, since the flood before,
And when your Gout's decayd & Haven foul;
He'll carry Partney River to Hobhole,
Serving your Parish, & th'adjoining Fen,
With water run to waste by Firsby men
To Croft to Thorpe to Braytoft I appeal,
Is it consistent with the public weal,
The Goose, fair Learnings prop, whose usefull Quil
Dear Parson Walls can brandish with such skill
Should be expelld & in the place be seen
Fat Oxen lounging on the deep hued green
And Sheep, whose Wool fit nor for Verse nor prose,
Is only suitable for Leicester Hose
If the Geese go, Learning will disappear
And Parson Walls scarce publish thrice a Year.
Tird with her prate the Nymph reclind her head
And sunk exhausted to her Miry Bed.

([1]) Pits or Meres in the Fen that are never dry.

([b]) Tradition says that the men of Sibsey lost their Bell in Bell Water or that the Churchwarden sold it & spent the Money the truth will appear

Parson Printapace: a Satyre

Alas how much tis easier to succeed
in writing than in getting folks to read.
Mart. Scrib. Book 1. line 19.

Traind up to guide the Plough & break the Clod
And not till ripe in years transferrd to God,
Whom no learnd Bishop duly could ordain
had he not read Laerticus in vain
You, who in Robes of holy Office dressd
Art Farmer, Steward, Tithingman & Priest,
if your seard Conscience, callous cold & dry
retains the least abhorrence of a lie,
if shame, fair virtue's friend, still holds a part
in any nook of thy case-hardend heart
Review with coolness what in truth appears
to have been the business of your last ten years;
Like an old Toad, in black attire arrayd,
half buried in the filth your spleen hath made,
Swoln up with rancorous spite & pride accurs'd,
till like a bloated Corpse you all but burst
you have sat, distilling from your vapid pen
foul words designd to injure honest men.
For years you toild with unabating pains
and rackd incessantly your fruitless brains
to give to honest deeds, of these our times,
the guises & semblance of atrocious crimes
till tird & sick with the disgusting sight
Men ceasd to read & made you cease to write.
Since then you have howld as cur dogs howl in vain
gainst the projected size of the Hobhole Drain
Exerting all the cunning you posess
to impede its course & baffle its success.
One year you write, the Deeps nere draind can be
The next that all things moist will glide to Sea
till the parchd Soil will crack & rift & burst
And all the Creatures on it, die of thirst.
Presumptuous man who midst the public sneer
profess yourself a Civil Engineer,
Censuring with arrogance what Rennie plannd
and what your poor head nere well understand
Your unread Pamphlets pild in order due
Will make a heap at least as tall as you,
A Mass composd of substitutes unfit,
for wisdom cunning, impudence for wit,
for candor malice, and for truth exact
Wilfull mistatement of each leading fact.
Devoid of talent & of manly sense.
Replete with folly & with insolence.
Take then the Bards advice, 'twill do no harm
Resign your Stewardship & let your Farm,
Silence for ever your pert prating Pen
& try to live a life like other men
Anxious by goodly acts in time t'attone
for all the uncharitable deeds you've done
Do thus & of these Lines you'l hear no more
if not expect the Bishops Paritor.

Lines designed for the Proprietor of the Manor of Scrivelsby, who, because he claims to hold the Manor by the Tenure of Grand Sergeantry, expects to be Styled, as the Sons of the Nobility are, Honorable, declines all Friendship & even Acquaintance with the Gentry of his Neighborhood, oppresses his Tenants beyond all example in the County, enters with alacrity into every litigious dispute he can contrive to raise, & seldom ends them but in a Court of Justice; never fails to prosecute all Persons whatever their description may be, who trespasses on his Game, & has servd some Gentlemen with discharges, because their Dogs have in passing along the Road, ran through his Hedges.

Champion methinks you look too high,
because by ancient Sergeantry,
an Office is your due,
The Title should not make you proud,
for till your Claim has been allowd,[1]
it dont belong to you.

Your Ancestors, as Heralds write,
were steel-clad Barons, traind to fight,
& Knights, of high degree,
Folks, who nere mingled with the herd,
Nor ere by action, thought, or word,
debasd Nobility.

But all who care about the Matter,
know that your Grandsire was a Hatter,
who near to Newgate dwelt,
An aprond Cockney, vastly willing,
to earn a sixpence or a shilling,
Or scour a greasy felt.

(1) The King has an acknowledged right to dispence with the Service due from any of his Subjects, The silly & expensive Service of a Champion of England at a Coronation, is surely in constant danger of being thus dispensd with.

They know, that when at Hogsdons Balls,
Midst Belles & Beaux from City Halls,
Your Father wishd to shine,
That those who knew his Father's Shop,
their Precedence refusd to drop,
if in the wholesale Line.

Your Ancestors were Barons bold,
in Courage not to be controlld,
Regardless of the Foe;
When ere they sought to Tented Field,
Each bore this Motto on a Shield,
Pro rege dimice.

But our Militia men declare,
that tho of hardyhood in War,
his Son assumes the name;
Yet naked Pistols, urgd in season,
have coold his Choler down to reason
& made him wondrous tame.

Since then as all the Children prattle,
the [Champion] dares not wager Battle,
May he by Heavens kind grace;
Learn, that his Masquerading Station,
in Armor at the Coronation,
gives neither Rank nor Place.

That his unwarrantable claim,
to fix a Style before his name,
must for the future cease;
It springs not from bright honors fount,
but from the blundering account [(1)]
of some old Clerk o' the Peace.

That all his Neighbors are inclind,
as equals to be frank & kind,
& past affronts forgive,
If on his part he'l lay aside,
his most intolerable pride,
& as their equal live.

([1]) he is Stiled Honorable in the Commission of the Peace for the Division of Lindsey.

Acknowlegement

Banks's poems are printed by courtesy of the Department of Special Collections, Memorial Library, University of Wisconsin - Madison.

Notes

1 These are now at the University of Wisconsin - Madison. Banks's extant verse is described in H. B. Carter, *Sir Joseph Banks (1743-1820). A Guide to Biographical and Bibliographical Sources* (Winchester, 1987), 215-19.

2 For particulars of these elections, and a specimen of the verse printed by Weir, see Sir Francis Hill, *Georgian Lincoln* (Cambridge, 1966), 220-23.

3 *ibid.*, 271.

4 British Library Add. MS. 52, 281, fols 75-76. In a further copy (fols 77-78), a manuscript alteration to the penultimate paragraph concludes the final sentence after the word cheating 'and (according to my Letter) of robbing my Ward'.

5 e.g. *Statements Submitted to the Right Honourable Sir Joseph Banks, President of the Royal Society of London* (Louth, 1803); *A Letter to the Right Honourable Sir Joseph Banks*, 2nd edn. (Louth, 1804); *An Address to the Ninety Commoners Having Rights in the East, West and Wildmore Fens* ... (Louth, 1807).

6 British Library Add. MS. 52, 281, fol. 92.

7 T. R. Leach, 'Champion of Champions: Samuel Lodge and the history of Scrivelsby', in *A Prospect of Lincolnshire*, edited by Naomi Field and Andrew White (Lincoln, 1984), 103 note 21.

8 Printed in Samuel Lodge, *Scrivelsby, The Home of the Champions...*(London and Horncastle, 1893), 176-81. Lodge notes that the 'ballad' was 'found at Revesby among the many valuable manuscripts of the late Sir Joseph Banks, although there is no reason for thinking that he composed them'. Lodge expands considerably Banks's notes - the original slips containing historical extracts utilized by Banks are at L.A.O. R.A. 4/E. T. C. Banks, the author of the *History of the Ancient Noble Family of Marmyan* (1816) included an account of the Marmion barony in his *Dormant and Extinct Baronage*, 3 vols (1807-09), I, 129-35. The correspondence between Lewis and John Dymoke with T. C. Banks, about their claim to the barony, 1806-24, is in a private collection (L.A.O. microfilm 2/8).

Tithe and Tithe Owners: Problems and Solutions[1]

Rex C. Russell

From before 1760 until after the passing of the Tithe Commutation Act in 1836 tithes were bitterly unpopular, and the payment of them was increasingly resented. Tithe payers, time and time again, struck local bargains with local tithe owners to abolish tithes; before 1836 the tithe owners gained much in these unequal bargaining negotiations.

What were some of the reasons for the unpopularity of tithes? If one was a nonconformist (a Congregationalist, a Quaker, a Baptist, a Methodist), one supported one's own church voluntarily and gladly, and naturally resented aiding the Established Church and the wider establishment by paying tithe. The members of the Society of Friends (the Quakers) had long resisted paying tithes. Their publication *A Collection of the Sufferings of the People called Quakers for the Testimony of a Good Conscience...* printed in 1753 contains very many accounts of imprisonment for the non-payment of tithes. For example:

> *Anno 1658 Arnold Trueblook* was committed to *Lincoln Gaol* for Tithes, and after many Weeks Confinement died there...In the same year *John Pidd* of *Beckingham*, was again imprisoned six Months...*Hezekiah Croft*, of *Eagle*, for a Demand of £6. 13s. 4d. for Tithes, was imprisoned seventeen Weeks, and after his release...had his cattle taken away to the value of £40. Also *John Wressel, James Hutchinson & John Johnson*, were kept in Prison till some of their Relations, for Demands of £1. 15s. 10d. for Tithes, paid their Prosecutors £6. 10s...

It is not difficult to understand nonconformist resentment, but why did farmers and landowners detest the payment of tithes?

The period under consideration was one of increasing agricultural productivity: more land was coming under regular cultivation: more crops were grown: landlord and tenant capital was being invested in farming. As production increased so tithe increased. It was felt that, as Lord Ernle wrote in 1912,

> Tithe-owners were sleeping partners in the cultivation of the soil. They contributed neither capital nor labour to the... farm; they risked nothing in the venture. But they shared the profits derived from increased productiveness.[2]

The writers of the reports on the agriculture of the counties of England, reports published by the old Board of Agriculture in the 1790s and early 1800s, condemned tithe as a major obstacle to agricultural improvement. Bailey and Culley on Northumberland, for example:

> In our journey through this county, whenever we enquired what was the chief obstacle to improvement? the answer was universally 'Tithes'! — An imposition so pregnant with mischief, and so often the source of violent dissensions betwixt the clergy and their parishioners, should if possible be removed, either by purchase, commutation, or any other means by which a *fair equivalent* shall be rendered for them; for so long as they exist, it is impossible to expect that agricultural improvements will be carried on to the extent of which they are capable...
>
> It is surprising that a grievance of such magnitude should have evaded the revision and regulation of the legislature; and that it should be always so strenuously opposed by the clergy their having no wish to take anything from them, but to enter a *fair equivalent* for what is their due.[3]

This hostility to tithes was expressed in vivid terms in The Oxford Encyclopaedia, published in 1833. The entry on Tithe reads (Vol. 4, 864):

> It is universally acknowledged that the payment of tithes in kind is a great discouragement to agriculture. They are inconvenient and vexatious to the husbandman, and operate as an impolitic tax upon industry. The clergyman, too, frequently finds them troublesome and precarious... and his just rights are with difficulty secured: he is too often obliged to submit to imposition, or is embroiled with his parishioners in disputes and litigations, no less irksome to his feelings than prejudicial to his interest, and tending to prevent those good effects which his precepts should produce.
>
> It is therefore of the utmost importance to parochial tranquility, and even to religion, that some just and reasonable standard of composition could be fixed.

The vicar of Broxbourne and Hoddesdon, in Hertfordshire, wrote

> I am confident that I am defrauded by many of my parishioners of Vicarial dues and rights to which the laws of Heaven and earth entitle me... for the very word 'tithe' has ever been... unpleasing and odious to farmers... Those who pay them, pay them very partially and... grudgingly and of necessity.[4]

There are, from this period, many broadsheets and ballads which attack tithes. The following verses were printed in *Drakard's Stamford News*, in January 1831:

REVOLUTION IN A FARM-YARD

There's not a joy the Parson gives like that he takes away,
When he eyes the tenth of all the land and claims it for his prey.
There's not a pig the Parson takes from out the farmer's sty,
But grunts to leave his native home and heaves a bitter sigh.
There's not a cow the farmer hath that grazes in the field,
That doth not low and swing her tail whene'er the pig is killed.
There's not a turkey in the yard that gobbles more and more,
Whene'er he sees the Parson enter at the farm-house door.
There's not a goose the farmer hath that swims upon the pond,
That doth not stretch his neck and hiss to see his master wronged.
There's not a duck upon the farm but gives an extra quack,
Whene'er he finds his master glad to see the Parson's back.
There's not a cock that struts around but crows more loud and gay,
When he sees the Parson mount his horse and proudly ride away.
There's not a thing upon the farm but shows some kind of fear
Whene'er he hears the name of Tithes or finds the Parson near;
But nothing shows resentment more than doth the patient ass,
Who always brays and turns its rump whene'er the Parson pass.
Now, ducks and geese that swim the pond, call help from all around;
When next you meet him drag him in; - tis but a Parson drowned.
The horse will scamper o'er the mead more briskly than before,
The cocks and hens will sleep in peace, the pigs more soundly snore;
The ass shall sing his song of joy, the bull shall toll the knell,
To let the geese and turkeys know the Parson's gone to H-LL.

The chorus of a popular drinking song rejoiced in hostility to tithes: 'We've cheated the Parson, / We'll cheat him again, / For why should the Parson have one in ten...' Several Staffordshire pottery figures portray a farmer's wife thrusting her tenth child at the parson ('You've had a tenth of all our crops and stock, now have and maintain our tenth child'):

The *Parson* comes, the *Pig* he claims,
And the Good Wife with taunts inflames;
But she, quite arch, bow'd low and smil'd,
Kept back the Pig, held out the Child:
The Priest looked gruff, the Wife looked big,
Zounds Sir! quoth she, no *Child*, no *Pig*.

A song entitled 'The Sucking Pig' glories in the discomfiture of the tithe-collecting parson who has refused the tenth piglet chosen for him by the farmer

O then, replied the farmer
Since my offer you refuse,
I pray, sir, walk into the sty,
There you may pick and choose.
Then in the sty he ventured
Without any more ado;
The old sow ran with open mouth
And at the parson flew.
O then she caught him by the coat
And took off both his shirts,
Then ran her head between his legs
And threw him in the dirt.
The little pigs his waistcoat tore,
His stocking and his shoes;
The farmer cried, 'You're welcome, sir,
I hope you'll pick and choose...[5]

The first reason why farmers and landowners resented tithes has already been made clear. They considered tithe an imposition on increased productivity: the tithe-owners gained without contributing anything. The second reason why tithe was bitterly unpopular was its great complexity. For this, the example of Barton on Humber will suffice. Details of Barton tithes appear in a copy of the Terrier 'for the better preservation of the rights of the Church of St. Peter's and St. Mary's... made in the Year 1730':

The Glebe Lands belong to the Impropriator who has tyth Corn and Hay in both Parishes, except in the Ings; for the Meadow there he has two Pence an Acre, in lieu of tyth, according to an Ancient Custome.

The Incumbant is a Vicar, his Tythes are paid as followeth (viz) for every Score of Weather Sheep sold at or after Easter is paid to him two shillings and sixpence, for every Score of Ews then sold one shilling and eightpence. Every tenth Lamb or the value of it. If there be only six Lambs the Vicar to have one, giving the owner four pence. If the owner have but four Lambs, he is to pay the Vicar four Pence. The tenth of Wool or the value thereof, for every Mort from Martinmass to Candlemass is paid one halfpenny, and after Candlemass one Penny, if six Piggs the Vicar is to have one, paying the owner two pence. If four the owner pays the Vicar two pence, for every Hen Turkey or Duck at Easter two Eggs. If ten Chickens the Vicar is to have one or two pence. If four Chickens the Vicar is to have four eggs. If five the owner pays One penny, If six the Vicar pays the owner four Eggs and has one chicken or two pence. The Tenth Swarme of Bees, the tenth Pint of Honey, the tenth of Wax or the tenth penny [if] the wax was sold. For every new bared Cow the Vicar is to have at Easter three pence: for every Stripe Milk Cow three half Pence; for every Dove coat Mill or Kilne or Malthhouse the Vicar is to have at Easter two Shillings. All Fruits and Roots pays the tenth, for every Garden and every House each for Smoak the Vicar is to have at Easter One Penny... All Hemp, Flax, Willows, and Thorns pays the tenth to the Vicar...[6]

The complexity was a problem both for the tithe-payer and the tithe-receiver. Long before 1760 the tithe-payers especially were looking for solutions to this problem. A solution by national legislation had to wait until 1836 when the Tithe Commutation Act was passed and implemented locally. Local solutions were possible long before that Act.

Local Acts for the enclosure of a parish presented an opportunity for solution. Between *c.*1760 and 1836, in hundreds of Lincolnshire parishes, open field agriculture was swept away by hundreds of separate Acts of Parliament. The majority of these Acts contained provisions for the commutation of tithes — if the tithe-owners agreed, of course, but *only* if they agreed. Therefore, before enclosure Bills were drafted, negotiations took place between tithe-payers and tithe-receivers. Such negotiations could be both lengthy and complex, especially if there was more than one tithe-owner in the parish.

How many people had to be consulted before paragraphs relating to tithes could be included in the draft Bill? If the local incumbent was a rector then normally one person (but the rector would be in touch with his bishop). Where the local incumbent was a vicar at least two tithe-owners had to be consulted - the vicar and the rector - the rector could be a layman, or the Dean and Chapter of Lincoln, or one of the colleges of Oxford or Cambridge. In several parishes more persons or institutions had to be consulted. In Middle Rasen, for example, there were five - the Vicar, the Bishop of Lincoln, and three lay tithe-owners, Dame Ann Cust, Catherine James and Marmaduke Dixon. In Tetney there were twelve tithe-owners to be consulted, the Vicar, the Bishop and ten lay tithe-owners. When the proposed enclosure of Caistor Moor was under discussion eight tithe-owners were involved in those proceedings; they were the vicars of Caistor, Grasby, Searby and North Kelsey, the Prebendary of Caistor, Matthew Burkinshaw of Grasby (lay rector), the Dean and Chapter of Lincoln and the Prebendary of North Kelsey.

The question under discussion during these negotiations was, in brief, 'How much land do you want in lieu of tithes? How many acres will you accept to rid us of tithes once and for all?'

In these negotiations the tithe-owners, the vicars and the rectors, were in a dominant position. They knew that tithe-payers were determined to get rid of tithes, but that they could not do so without compensation to the tithe-owners. They knew that farmers and landowners confidently expected greater production of titheable crops from intended agricultural changes. The tithe-owners knew that if they did nothing, increased productivity in crops would certainly mean greater value in their tithes. The tithe-owners held the whip hand.

Some tithe-owners could and did delay intended enclosures until they were promised the proportion of land they asked for in lieu of future tithes. For example, the intended enclosure of Wrawby cum Brigg was held up from 1794 until 1800 because Clare Hall, Cambridge, (the rector) would not agree to the terms proposed to them by the rest of the landowners and the vicar of Wrawby.[7]

The normal agreement to grant land in lieu of tithe at Enclosure was as follows. The owners of titheable land would give to the tithe-owners, in lieu of future tithes, one-fifth of the arable lands, one seventh of the commons and one-ninth of the old enclosures. In some cases, as at Barton on Humber in 1793-96, tithe-payers agreed to the award of land in lieu of future tithes to the lay tithe-owner (George Uppleby of Barrow on Humber) and to the award of a Corn Rent to the vicar. The total value of the vicarial tithe for the year 1789 to 1790 was as follows:

	£	s	d
Pigs	7	11	8
Lambs and Wool	44	1	10
Orchards	5	1	10
Turnips	1	10	6
Agistment tithe		15	0
Rents	14	9	0
TOTAL	73	9	10

The value of tithe to the vicar of Barton was £73 9s. 10d. in the year 1789-90. The total value of the living for that year was £116 9s. 5½d. During the negotiations preceding enclosure it was agreed to offer the vicar, in lieu of future tithes from the open lands, a corn-rent of £150 a year. The vicar was, as normal, to benefit considerably from enclosure and it was estimated that the whole annual value of the living would increase by nearly £100. The average annual value of the living over the three years 1790, 1791 and 1792 was shown to have been £123 16s.

5½d. The value of the living immediately after enclosure was estimated as £222 9s. 7d. This total was made up as follows:

	£	s	d
Corn Rent	150	0	0
Tithe Tents on Homesteads, etc.	30	0	0
Rent of Glebe allotment and House, etc.	20	0	0
Surplice Fees	17	4	7
Easter Dues	5	5	0
TOTAL	222	9	7

The lay tithe-owner here agreed to the enclosure of Barton on condition that he was awarded 900 acres in lieu of tithes. These were to be in one block adjoining his lands in the adjacent parish of Barrow on Humber. Uppleby stipulated too that there was to be only one highway between Barton and Barrow and that there was to be no pit for digging road making material adjoining the road. George Uppleby got his way and benefited greatly by this enclosure.[8]

One solution to the tithe problem, before 1836, was the award of land in lieu of tithes at enclosure. In 116 Lincolnshire parishes in which land was awarded in lieu of tithes, some 37,380 acres were awarded - a substantial figure, revealing something of the extent of the tithe problems.[9] This total acreage was divided as follows:

16,811 acres	awarded to local incumbents
6,472 acres	to other Church Institutions
14,097 acres	to Lay landowners

Table 1 summarizes, for twenty-two parishes in Lindsey, this solution to the tithe problem.

Table 1: Land Awarded in Lieu of Tithes

Parish	Acreage to be Enclosed	Total Acreage awarded in lieu of Tithe	Area of Tithe Allotments as a percentage of the land to be enclosed
Alvingham	1302	392	30.1%
Faldingworth	2007	311	16.9%
Fulstow	1980	329*	16.6%
Hackthorn	2698	424	15.7%
Heapham	1095	176	16.0%
Hemswell	2414	466	19.3%
Ingham	1921	349*	18.2%
Kirkby cum Osgodby	1346	353	26.2%
Ludford	2167	199+	9.2%
Market Rasen	730	94	12.9%
Middle Rasen	2678	389	14.5%
N. & S. Cockerington	1219	385	31.6%
Rothwell	2553	364	14.2%
Spridlington	2088	325	15.5%
Thoresway	2787	480	17.2%
Tetney	*c.* 4000	696	17.4%
Upton & Kexby	3097	676*	21.8%
Waithe	701	134	19.1%
West Rasen	1281	420	32.8%
Yarburgh	940	216	22.9%

* In Parishes indicated thus these totals include small acreages allotted for glebe.

\+ In Ludford Corn Rents were to be paid to the Church after enclosure.

The table shows the *total* acreages awarded in lieu of tithes. Some of such awarded acres went to enrich lay tithe-owners, as we have seen. The total acreages of many landed estates were greatly increased by land awarded in lieu of tithes. Here are but three examples of this.

1. The estate of the Earl of Yarborough
   2372 acres were added to this from six parishes

Cabourne	341 acres	Habrough	158 acres
East Halton	502 acres	Kirmington	190 acres
N.&S. Killingholme	709 acres	Swallow	472 acres

2. The estate of Charles Winn, Esq.
   657 acres from three parishes

Frodingham & Scunthorpe	535 acres
Santon	122 acres

3. The estate of John Charles Crowle, Esq.
   833 acres from two parishes

Goxhill	582 acres
Wootton	251 acres

In several hundred of those parishes enclosed by act of parliament the tithe problem was solved - to the great advantage of the tithe-owners, both clerical and lay. W. R. Ward, amongst others, has stressed that the terms of commutation were remarkably generous to the clergy. He suggests that what was obvious in these rural parishes was the sudden rise in the affluence and social standing of many of the parsons and he believes that this new wealth often divided the parson from his people in the most literal sense.

> The clergy seemed to be profiting... there is not much doubt that while the commutation of tithe greatly reduced the friction between the clergy and the farmers, it helped to alienate them from the small free-holders and labourers.[10]

The awarding of land in lieu of tithes at enclosure was *one* solution of the tithe problem. What was the solution in those parishes (or rather in *some* of those parishes) which did not undergo parliamentary enclosure, in those parishes in which tithes remained both a burden and a problem?

The passing of the Tithe Commutation Act was the solution.

The burden and the problem to be removed and solved can be clearly seen in the following newspaper report about a parish in Cambridgeshire. (This report, which purports to record the increase in the annual value of tithes, I find difficult to accept at face value.) It is from the *Lincoln, Stamford and Rutland Mercury* dated 24 December 1830.

> *Cambridge*. At a vestry meeting at Leverton, in the Isle of Ely, on the 9th inst. a petition for the abolition of the tithe system was unanimously adopted: it contains the following statement:- That the tithes of this parish and hamlet, which originally supported the poor as well as the clergy, are double the poor-rates, and have risen progressively on the change of Rectors, viz., 1774 to 1795, from about £300 to £900 pounds; 1795 to 1808, from £900 to £1200; 1808 to 1811, from £1200 to £1900; 1811 to 1830, from £1900 to £2600 per annum; and from their £1200 per annum (for a period of more than 22 years) your petitioners have had no resident Rector, not even one day in a year; and your petitioners most humbly submit for the consideration of your honourable house, that this non-residence has arisen from the system of pluralities and not from the 'dampness and unhealthiness of the parish' or the want of a suitable residence.'

How was the Tithe Commutation Act implemented locally? The Tithe Commissioners, appointed under the act, expected local tithe-payers and tithe-receivers to reach local agreements about commutation. When such agreements had been reached they were confirmed and made legally binding by the Tithe Commissioners. Only if agreement could not be reached locally did the Commissioners themselves intervene to decide on the parish terms of commutation.

The act was implemented locally mainly between 1836 and 1848. Hundreds of tithe commutation notices appear on the pages of the Lincoln, Rutland and Stamford Mercury, and these provide details about who called the meetings to discuss tithe commutation, where these meeting were held, and the progress of the discussions.[11] The resultant tithe award gave details of the annual money rent to be paid to the tithe-owners. This was a corn rent fluctuating in value according to a seven-year average of the market prices of wheat, barley and oats. The amounts of the local tithe-rents varied greatly from parish to parish, according to the acreages liable to this rent, the sizes of the parishes, the previous values of the tithes and the proportions within parishes of arable, meadow and pasture and woodland. Here are a few examples of annual tithe rents, in figures of the later 1830s and of the 1840s.

Bigby	£739	Linwood	£395
Walesby	£570	Legsby	£270
Normanby le Wold	£551	Thornton Curtis	£234
Edlington	£469	Scrafield	£143
Roxby cum Risby	£425		

Who called the meetings to discuss and decide upon the terms of tithe commutation? And where were such meetings held? Notices in the county newspaper show that, almost invariably, it was laymen and not the clergy who initiated these decisive discussions. The most favoured place for such meetings was the parish church: next in favour were the local inns and lastly came private houses and parish schools. The present writer knows of no minutes kept of such meetings: if such existed they would be of great historical value.

In the considered opinion of Professor Eric E. James the tithe commutation was carried out with remarkable smoothness and lack of local ill-feeling. The reason for this was because the Commissioners were wise enough to trust the localities to know their own situations. Professor Evans sums up:

> For the first time after Commutation, the landowner knew clearly and in advance what he must pay, and the tithe owner what he might expect. The advantage was overwhelming.[12]

The issues raised in this essay suggest two lines of research which could supplement some of the work of Terence Leach. One of Terence's many interests was landed families, their estates and their houses. The present writer wishes to suggest that (as far as he knows) little work has been done to ascertain how much landed estates grew in consequence of land awarded in lieu of tithes. He suggests that this could be a most useful area of enquiry. Secondly, still in connection with this theme, he believes that work needs to be done on how well, or how badly, lay rectors carried out their obligation to keep in repair the chancel of their parish church.

The best way in which we can honour Terence is to attempt to develop the work he carried so far. Let us carry it further in his memory.

Notes

1 Revised version of the first Terence Leach Memorial Lecture, given at St Andrew Hall, Lincoln, 29 October 1994.

2 *English Farming Past and Present* (London 1912), 332.

3 J. Bailey and G. Culley, *General View of the Agriculture of the County of Northumberland* (Newcastle, 1797), 156-57.

4 Quoted in Eric J. Evans, *Tithes, Maps, Apportionments and the 1836 Act* (Chichester 1993), 7; see also his *The Contentious Tithe* (1976).

5 Reprinted in Roy Palmer, ed. *The Painful Plough* (Cambridge 1973), 20-21.

6 L.A.O. Barton glebe terriers.

7 For full details of this, see Rex C. Russell, *The Enclosures of Market Rasen 1779-1781 and of Wrawby cum Brigg 1800-1805* (Barton on Humber, 1969).

8 Full details of Barton enclosure are in Rex C. Russell, *The Enclosure of Barton-upon-Humber 1793-96* (Barton, 1968).

9 For details of each of these parishes see these four books by Eleanor and Rex. C. Russell: *Landscape Changes in South Humberside* (Hull, 1982); *Making New Landscapes in Lincolnshire* (Lincoln, 1983); *Old and New Landscapes in the Horncastle Area* (Lincoln, 1985); *Parliamentary Enclosure and New Lincolnshire Landscapes* (Lincoln, 1987).

10 W. R. Ward, 'Church and society in the first half of the nineteenth century', in *A History of the Methodist Church in Great Britain*, Vol.2, edited by R. Davies, A. R. George and G. Rupp (1978), 20-27.

11 Rex C. Russell, 'Tithe awards, their value to local historians', *Lincolnshire Past & Present*, 17 (Autumn 1994), 3-11, and 18 (Winter 1994/95), 8-11.

12 Evans, *Tithes, Maps, Apportionments and the 1836 Act*, 30.

The Youngs at Kingerby: The Making, Unmaking and Re-Making of a Lincolnshire Estate

Richard Olney

In the eighteenth and nineteenth centuries parishes in Lincolnshire - and indeed many other English counties - could be characterised in terms of their patterns of landownership. Some, the close parishes, were in single, or virtually single, ownership; others, the open parishes, had numerous small estates; and others were a mixture, containing large and small properties. Whatever its configuration, a parish tended to retain it throughout the period *c.*1650-1900. The individual owners changed, but the pattern of ownership did not significantly alter. There were, however, occasional exceptions. A close parish might be sold in lots by its proprietor, and become an open one; or, conversely, a large estate might be built up by the piecemeal absorption of small properties - as at Tealby with the Bayons Manor estate. At Holton-le-Moor, near Caistor, the parish was in single ownership in the early seventeenth century. It was disposed of piecemeal by the Bestoe family from 1649 onwards, but was later re-assembled by the Dixon family, who by the late nineteenth century owned the whole parish. The farm that had been the first to leave the estate in 1649 was the last to rejoin it in 1875.

The Kingerby estate, near Market Rasen, is perhaps unique, at least in north Lincolnshire, in that between 1650 and 1911 it underwent this process of deconstruction and reconstruction not once but twice. As with Holton-le-Moor, the history of the parish is bound up with that of a prominent and successful local farming family. But, unlike the Dixons of Holton, the Youngs of Kingerby were Roman Catholic, and their connection with the Market Rasen and Kingerby neighbourhood was closely intertwined with the family's Catholic tradition.

Kingerby is a small parish of some 1,430 acres, bounded on the east by the parish of Kirkby-cum-Osgodby, on the south by the road from Bishop Bridge, on the west by the river Ancholme and on the north by the Kingerby Beck, which divides it from Owersby. Somewhat secluded, it lies off the main highways: the lane from Kirkby runs west past Kingerby church and Hall, and after a mile turns south to join the Bishop Bridge road. At this point it divides the lower ground near the Ancholme, which was meadow and marsh in the eighteenth century, from the slightly higher ground in the more easterly section of the parish, which was mostly pasture at the same period.

In 1651 a Londoner, Edward Grosvenor, bought the parish (apart from Kingerby Wood, which went with West Rasen) from the Puckering family. He did not retain the whole estate for long. Six years later he sold the lower ground near the Ancholme, about 400 acres, to John Lodington of Snarford and William Tourney of London. (This land was still outside the Young estate in the early twentieth century: by the mid-nineteenth it had passed partly to the owners of estates in adjoining parishes, the Angersteins of Owersby and the Cholmeleys of Bishop Norton (on the other side of the Ancholme).) In 1660 Grosvenor sold two more portions of the estate. The manor house and the land near it was bought by Peter Richier of Lincoln, and land in the north of the parish by Sir Edward Rossiter of Somerby, near Brigg. This left about 300 acres, to the west of the Richier property, which Grosvenor settled on his daughter on her marriage to Thomas Blount, the property (which included the lordship and advowson) later passing to the Oxfordshire Catholic family of Perrott. During much of the eighteenth century the greater part of Kingerby remained divided into these three portions, of a little over 300 acres each. But between 1785 and 1798 they were reunited in the hands of the Young family.[1]

The Youngs, originally a Welsh recusant family, had been living in the Kingerby neighbourhood, though not at Kingerby itself, since just after the Restoration. The first John Yonge known to Lincolnshire history settled at West Rasen, where in 1673 he is recorded as a servant to the Catholic Constable family.[2] During the eighteenth century the Youngs farmed not only at West Rasen but also at Claxby-by-Normanby and Normanby-le-Wold, some four miles east-north-east of Kingerby, where in the early part of the century the Catholic family of Markham was settled. (There were also links, though less persistent ones, with the Heneage estates.) David Young (1701-1793), a grandson of the original John Young of West Rasen, farmed at Normanby-le-Wold. David's second son Isaac (1731-1792) married Ann Champney of West Rasen and farmed in that parish, but Isaac's youngest brother Edward (1734-1829) eventually succeeded to the principal family farm at Normanby. By the early 1790s the main landowner in Claxby and Normanby was Charles Pelham (created Baron Yarborough in 1794): he had bought out the Markhams around 1770, but was tolerant of dissenters on his estates.[3] It was with the descendants first of Isaac and then of Edward that the Kingerby estate was destined to be involved throughout the nineteenth century and beyond. (Fig. 1).

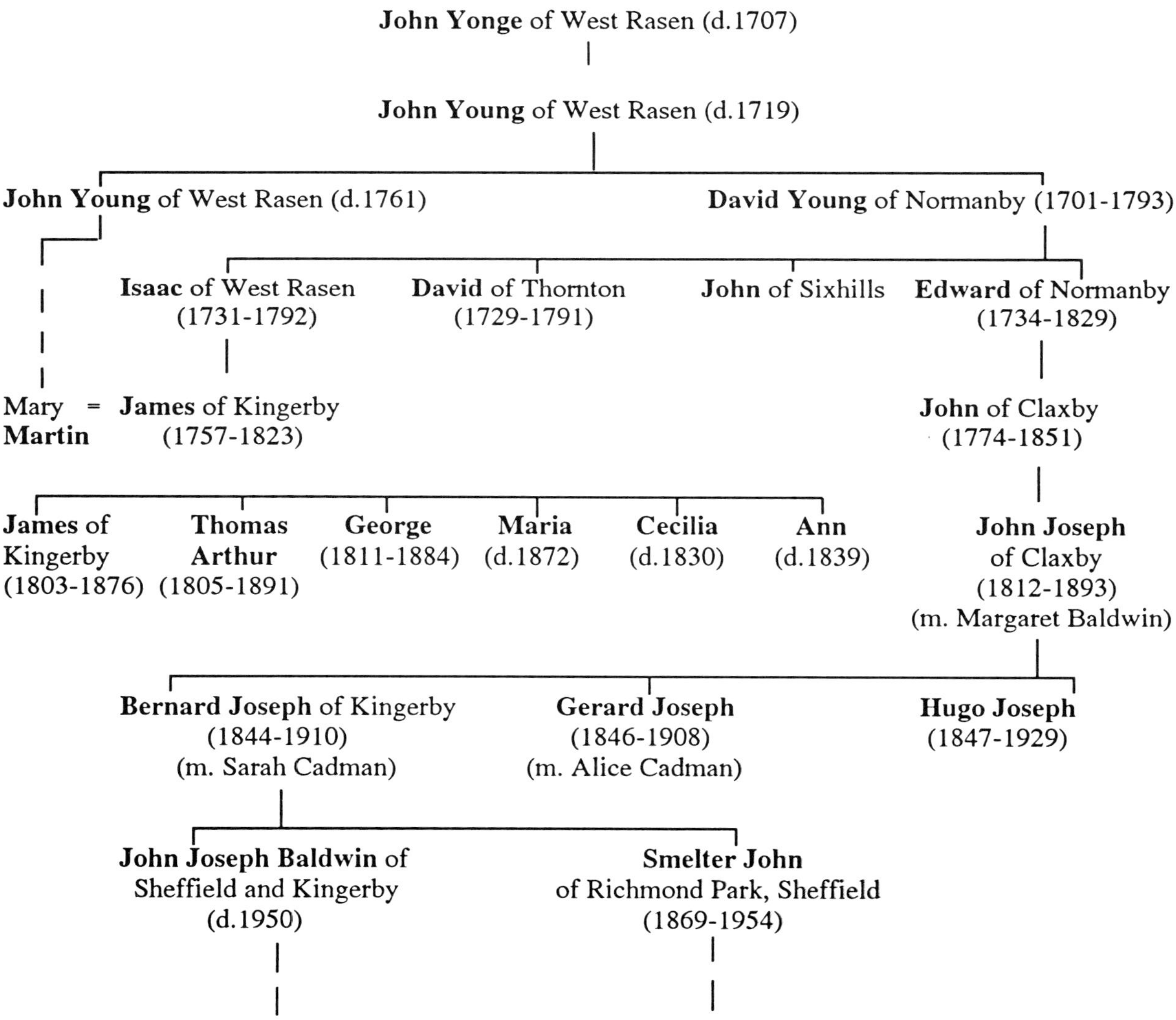

Fig. 1: Simplified pedigree.

Isaac Young was clearly a successful farmer, and following the Catholic Relief Act of 1778 he was able to invest some of his agricultural profits in land. In 1785 the Kingerby Hall estate, the former Richier property, came on the market, and Isaac purchased it for £6,000.[4] He would have been very familiar with the property, which lay conveniently close to his other business interests. But it also had a religious significance. From 1702 it had been leased by the Knight family, which had strong local and Catholic connections, and until 1782, when a new chapel was built in Market Rasen, there had been a place of worship attached to the Hall.[5] In 1788 Isaac's son James (1757-1823) was able to buy the former Rossiter property for £5,000, acting on behalf of his father. Finally, in 1798, when James had succeeded his father in these two properties, the former Perrott property, 325 acres of mainly breeding and grazing land, was purchased by him for £8,800. He now had a ring-fenced estate of about 936 acres, which he continued to farm during the prosperous years of the Napoleonic War. In 1798 he married Mary Martin, the daughter of a Marylebone builder and developer but a descendant, through her mother, of the West Rasen Youngs. In 1812, with a rapidly-growing family, he completely rebuilt Kingerby Hall as a modern three-stored gentleman's residence, with a Tuscan Doric porch.[6]

It was at James's death in 1823 that the troubles of the Kingerby Youngs began. Like many farmers of the period he wished to leave the farm intact to his eldest son, but he also wished to provide for his younger children. In his will, therefore, he left the Kingerby estate to his son James (1803-1876), but with the responsibility for paying his brothers an income and for maintaining his sisters. Thomas Arthur (1805-1891) and George (1811-1884) were left sums of £10,000 each, charged on the estate, the interest on which James had to pay them out of his income. Had he been an efficient farmer, farming in favourable times, he might have managed this and still made a good living, but he did not turn out very satisfactorily, and got behind with the payments to his brothers. In 1838, after much disputation, Thomas Arthur and George agreed to relinquish their financial claims in return for the equivalent in land. The estate was valued and partitioned, 236 acres in the north of the parish (later Jesmond Farm) being allotted to Thomas Arthur, and 274 in the south-west part of the estate (Grange or Lodge Farm, later known as Spa Farm) to George. This left James with 426 acres in Kingerby, around the Hall, and some unsettled property in Kirkby-cum-Osgodby.[7] Thus by 1840 the estate was again divided much as it had been in the mid-eighteenth century, though not along precisely the same boundaries.

More trouble followed the death of James Young junior in 1876. He had never married, but had a family of three natural children, and under his will he left about 226 acres in Kingerby and Kirkby-cum-Osgodby in trust for them. Part of this land was sold in 1877, and the rest, following a deed of partition, in 1884. The remaining land in Kingerby, however, including the Hall, had been intended for the support of James's sister Maria. She had died in 1872, before her brother, but not before she had fallen under the influence of a priest, Father Dolman, who had a scheme for a seminary at Kingerby Hall, and whom Maria made her heir. The Kingerby Hall estate, of some 200 acres, was eventually sold by Dolman's mortgagees in 1893, thus completing the break-up of the Young family property. Meanwhile Thomas Arthur had sold Jesmond Farm, to a cousin, in 1875; and he later devised the lordship and advowson, inherited from James, to the same cousin before his death, without issue, in 1891. George also died without issue, in 1884, leaving Grange Farm to another cousin.[8]

The tribulations of the Kingerby Youngs, however, had not gone unobserved or unlamented by their Claxby cousins. To follow this branch of the family we must revert to Edward Young of Normanby, the brother of Isaac. Edward's son John (1774-1851) became the leading Yarborough tenant at Claxby, and was succeeded at Claxby House by his son John Joseph (1812-1893). Unlike the Kingerby branch in the late eighteenth century, these Normanby and Claxby Youngs in the early and mid-nineteenth century showed little interest in the purchase of land. But they did increase their substance by marrying brides from well-to-do families outside the county. J. J. Young married Margaret Baldwin, from a Manchester mercantile family, and his eldest son Bernard Joseph Young (1844-1910) married Sarah Cadman, heir to a small estate at Handsworth, on the outskirts of Sheffield. Bernard had two brothers, Gerard Joseph

(1846-1908), who married Sarah Cadman's sister Alice, and Hugo Joseph Young (1847-1929), who inherited a good part of his mother's (Baldwin) money and became a successful barrister.

It was these three brothers, Bernard, Gerard and Hugo, who among them rescued the Kingerby estate. It was to Hugo that Thomas Arthur conveyed Jesmond Farm in 1875, followed by the lordship and advowson of Kingerby in 1889. Hugo also acquired some — perhaps eventually all — the land sold off for the benefit of James's natural children. When Kingerby Hall came on the market in 1893 Bernard bid for it. He was unsuccessful, but at a second attempt, in 1902-3, he secured it and the surrounding land, restoring it once more to family ownership. He himself continued to live at Richmond Park, his Victorian house near Sheffield, but he let Kingerby Hall to Gerard, who already farmed in the neighbourhood. When Gerard died in 1908 he bequeathed Grange Farm, inherited from his cousin George, to his elder brother Bernard, and when the latter died two years later it passed to Bernard's son John Joseph Baldwin Young (d.1950), a Sheffield solicitor. The following year Hugo, by then Recorder of Lincoln, sold his Kingerby interests to his nephew J. J. B. Young, who thus achieved the reunification of the estate as it had existed between 1798 and 1838.[9]

The economic circumstances in which Isaac and James Young senior acquired the Kingerby estate in 1785-98 were thus rather different from those of their collateral descendants in the period 1875-1911. At the earlier period it was a case of local agricultural profits being invested in a local agricultural business. In the last quarter of the nineteenth century there were no such profits to be made, and few thought it worthwhile to invest profits of any kind in agricultural land. The brothers Bernard, Gerard and Hugo were motivated more by a sense of family tradition, and the money for the purchases came mostly if not entirely from outside the county. But, as we have seen, the Catholicism of the Youngs was a key element in their family identity, an identity that to some extent set them apart from their Protestant farming neighbours; and it was this identity that reinforced their ties with the Kingerby neighbourhood over the generations. In the first three-quarters of the nineteenth century the owners of Kingerby Hall were less staunch, but the religious tradition was maintained especially by Thomas Arthur Young. It was a tradition that he seems to have passed on, along with many family papers, to his young cousin Hugo.

J. J. B. Young did not regularly reside at Kingerby, but he looked after the estate through the years of depression and two World Wars, and was succeeded in 1950 by his son Michael, who came to live at Kingerby in 1947 and proceeded to modernise and expand the estate. In 1970, he was obliged to sell it, the purchaser being Mr J. Dickinson of Blyborough. Both Michael Young and his successor bought in land near the Ancholme, nearly restoring the estate to its 1650 boundaries. (It was again advertized for sale, at 1,362 acres, in 1974.) Since 1970, then, there has been no Young presence in Kingerby, but the family and its Catholic tradition continues.

Acknowlegements

I am most grateful to Mr J. M. B. Young, of Oxford, who not only allowed me access to his family papers, without which this article could not have been written, but also elucidated many points for me from his own knowledge of the family's history. Dr Mary Finch was also most generous with information, advice and encouragement.

Notes

1. L. A. O. Bates and Mountain deposit, 4 B.M. 4/1.
2. Hull University Library, Constable-Maxwell MSS, DDEV/ 39/73.
3. L.A.O. Yarborough MSS, deeds, rentals and accounts; L.A.O. Lindsey land tax records; Humberside Record Office, Beverley, Chichester-Constable MSS, DDCC/151.
4. Young family papers; L.A.O. 4 B.M. 4/1/61.
5. Philip Bailey SCJ, *The Roman Catholic Mission and Chapel, Osgodby, Lincolnshire* (1993), 16.
6. Nikolaus Pevsner and John Harris, rev. Nicholas Antram, *The Buildings of England, Lincolnshire* (1989), 415.
7. Young family papers; L.A.O. 4 B.M. 4/1/70.
8. Young family papers; L.A.O. 4 B.M. 4/1/71.
9. Young family papers.

Christopher Turnor (1809-1886) and His Buildings

Catherine M. Wilson

In 1978 Terence Leach delivered the Kitching Memorial Lecture in Bardney on the subject 'The Turnors and Their Wragby Estates'.[1] Not long after that, I became interested in a set of farm buildings at Kirmond-le-Mire. They had a date - 1868 - and the initials C.T. on a stone over the barn door. Driving around the county, I started noticing other buildings bearing the initials C.T., particularly on farm cottages around Panton and Stixwould, and in the Kirmond and Binbrook area. I quickly discovered that the initials belonged to Christopher Turnor (1809-1886) of Stoke Rochford and Panton, whose family were major landowners in the county from the seventeenth to the early twentieth century. Terence's article was invaluable as a starting point for information about the family and their estates. Like so many other people, I owe him a real debt, not only for his tremendous knowledge, so readily shared, but for his warm friendship through the years.

Christopher Turnor was born at Stoke Rochford, near Grantham in 1809, the son of Edmund Turnor, a local gentleman and well-known antiquary. The family had moved to Lincolnshire in the 1650s and had, over the years amassed a vast estate in the county. When Edmund died in 1829, the young Christopher inherited over 20,000 acres, virtually all of which was in Lincolnshire. In 1873, he owned 20,664 ac. 3r. 14p. in the county with an annual value of £27,513.[2] He controlled this estate for more than fifty years until his death in 1886. He is an enigmatic character. He was the third largest landowner in the county but apparently held no public office, other than a year as High Sheriff in 1833 and five years as MP for South Lincolnshire from 1841 to 1847. He married into the peerage as did his son, and yet he features hardly at all in the county's social calendar. He built a stately home at Stoke Rochford, worthy of any duke, but remained a commoner throughout his life. As far as is known virtually no records survive of his management of this huge estate but, because of his massive building programme, he has probably left more of a physical mark on the county than any other single person.

He owned a great swathe of land through the middle of the county from the limestone uplands of South Kesteven, through the fen edge and clay soils of the Wragby area to the high land of the chalk Wolds; from Stoke Rochford in the south to Binbrook in the north. The holdings included virtually the entire soil of seven parishes: Kirmond, Panton, Stixwould, Little Ponton, Stoke Rochford, Wispington and Wragby. He was Lord of the Manor of six more, patron of the living of ten parish churches and owned land altogether in thirty-three different parishes.

His main seat was at Stoke Rochford, but he owned another major house at Panton in the centre of the estates. The house at Panton was built in 1720 and rebuilt in the 1770s. It has now been completely demolished, though the outline of the foundations are still visible, and the magnificent stable block survives. Also surviving are the impressive buildings of Warren Farm, designed either by Carr of York or William Legg. This is one of very few sets of farm buildings on his estate that Christopher Turnor did not rebuild. His investment in new buildings on his estate was considerable though unquantifiable, in the absence of estate records.[3]

The earliest dated building I have found is the new gate lodge at Stoke Rochford, dated 1834, just five years after he inherited. By 1840 he had started on a new house at Stoke Rochford - a vast and imposing affair, designed by William Burn, one of the best known architects of the day, which still stands - though now used as a conference centre. In the ensuing years Turnor helped to build or rebuild churches, schools and other public buildings all over his estate, such as the church at Stixwould, rebuilt in 1831 and enlarged in 1864, the school at Stixwould built in 1851 and the church at Kirmond-le-Mire, designed by the Lincoln architect W. A. Nicholson in 1847. He also carried out a massive rebuilding programme on his farms, including farmhouses and cottages.

Christopher Turnor's tenure of his estates coincided almost exactly with the period known as 'High Farming' in England. Confidence in agriculture was

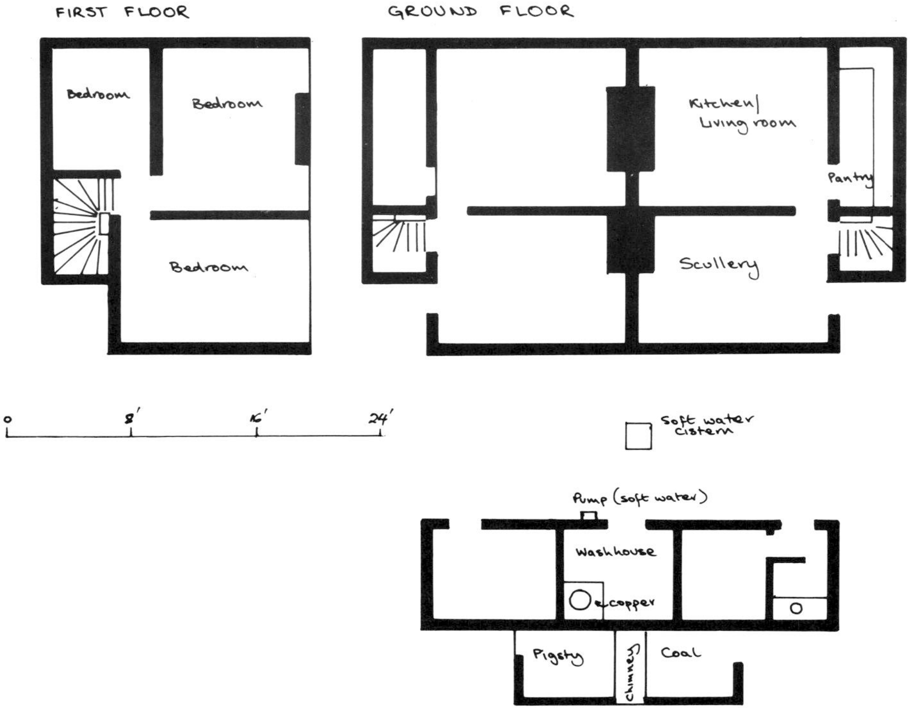

Fig. 1: Manor Farm Cottages, Barlings.

high and progressive landowners across the country were investing in new crops and new buildings to accommodate the changes in husbandry techniques and the new, more scientific, approach to farming. The establishment of the Royal Agricultural Society in 1838, and the publication of its journal from 1839 onwards, provided a focus for information and new ideas. The journal contained articles not only on best husbandry practice and new machinery but also advice on the layout of farm buildings and the design of labourers cottages. Whilst there is no evidence that Turnor was actively involved in the Society, he was certainly very much part of the 'High Farming' movement, which has been described as 'not simply a method of farming; it was a state of mind'.[4] It is against this background that Turnor started improvements on his estate.

Following the Turnor trail is both fascinating and frustrating. Whilst he was actively building for nearly forty years, there is little consistency and no apparent pattern. Most of his buildings have a Turnor 'hallmark', one distinctive feature being the window design, and most have a date stone with his initials, but there is no single design for his cottages or his farm buildings. He did not start on one part of the estate and work through systematically, but seems to have worked in several areas at the same time. So for example there are two pairs of cottages in Stixwould both dated 1836, but built to completely different designs. Other cottages in Stixwould are dated 1855, 1857, 1858 and 1862, but are all to different designs again. Two sets of farm buildings, Manor Farm at Barlings and Newstead Farm at Stixwould are both dated 1847 but are built to completely different designs. And yet the farm buildings at Little Ponton are virtually identical to those at Manor Farm, Kirmond-le-Mire, although they are separated by seventy miles, and one is built of stone whilst the other is brick!

The building materials used vary considerably, with yellow brick at Barlings, where the brick works were close by, sandstone at Kirmond, limestone at Little Ponton, and red brick elsewhere. Turnor owned at least one brickworks at Panton, and as the other materials are all very local it is likely that most of the building materials came from within the estate.

The absence of plans or estate correspondence

means that observation 'in the field' is really the only way to discover the extent of Turnor's works, though a good guide of where to look for at least some of the buildings is the sale catalogue for the Panton Estate (Wragby, Panton, Langton, East Barkwith, East Torrington and Lissington) on August 15 and 16 1917.[5] This gives considerable detail of the 6,260 acres comprising twenty farms and small holdings that were to be auctioned on that occasion. Some buildings have of course been demolished in the intervening years, and many more have been altered, but enough remains to give an insight into the tremendous endeavour of this little known Lincolnshire gentleman.

'If the right construction of our barns, and stables, and cattle-sheds, is a matter of no small importance, that of the dwellings of our labouring population must claim to be so in still higher degree...' So wrote John Grey in an essay 'On the building of cottages for farm- labourers'.[6] In 1856, T. W. P. Isaac was recommending that cottages should be built in detached pairs which were both cheaper and warmer than building them singly, and there should be one-quarter of an acre of garden with each pair.[7] Both authors published detailed specifications for typical cottages that landowners were recommended to adher to. Good housing was seen as vital for the 'moral character' of the work force, as well as encouraging them to work harder. Christopher Turnor certainly took notice of this advice.

Across his estates, and certainly in parishes where Turnor was the major landowner, he built new cottages for his farm workers. I have counted over seventy that still survive and the search has been by no means exhaustive. Most of the cottages are in pairs, with a few groups of three or four. Externally they are quite plain with no unnecessary decoration and as indicated, they are built to different patterns so even where they exist in groups they do not give the appearance of being part of an 'estate village' as for example at Denton, on the Welby Estates, or Blankney, laid out by W. A. Nicholson in the 1830s and 1840s, where all the cottages are built to a standard design.

Descriptions exist of some of the cottages in the catalogue for the sale of the Panton Estate in 1917. For the most part they had two or, more usually three bedrooms upstairs, two rooms downstairs, with wash-house, coal-house , pigsty and privy outside. The three bedrooms were considered essential to 'preserve decency and morality' enabling boys, girls and parents to be separated for sleeping purposes.[8] It is also known that, in Stixwould at least, all the cottages had the use of an allotment and access to land to graze a cow.

Of those cottages that survive, most have been inevitably been altered internally to provide modern accommodation, but I did record one pair at Barlings before they were converted to a single dwelling (Fig. 1). They are, at 1875, the latest dated cottages I have found, but they are adjacent to an earlier farm building (1847). Interesting features are that they were provided with a cistern to collect rainwater for washing clothes, conveniently situated just outside the wash house, and a well with pump for other use. The wash-house was equipped with a copper for heating the water. There was a range and a sink in the scullery, whilst the pantry had low level stone shelving to keep food cool.

Most cottages have also been altered externally, particularly with the insertion of new windows, but a pair at Strubby dated 1873 does survive in its original form to give a good idea of a 'typical' pair of Turnor cottages (Fig. 2). A similar pair at Kirmond-le-Mire is dated 1868 (Fig. 3), whilst a parallel at Woodnook is dated 1872 (Fig. 4). A different design was employed at Warren Farm, Panton in 1870 (Fig. 5), whilst gabled versions exist at Panton (Fig. 6) and elsewhere.

It is not known how much Turnor's cottages cost to build, but Henry Goddard, a Lincoln architect, writing in 1849 quotes just over £230 for a pair of cottages.[9] For perhaps a hundred cottages, this represents a considerable investment over the years, though it is nothing compared to the £60,000 Christopher Turnor spent building his own house at Stoke Rochford!

Turnor built substantial farmhouses for his tenants, many of whom stayed on the Turnor estates for several generations, and indeed bought their farms when the estate was broken up. As with the cottages, the farmhouses were well-built, but without ostenta-

Fig. 2: Pair of yellow brick cottages surviving in near original condition, 1873, Strubby, TF159774.

Fig. 3: Pair of sandstone cottages,1868, Kirmond-le-Mire, TF 184926.

Fig. 4: Pair of limestone cottages, 1872, Woodnook, SK 943325.

Fig. 5: Pair of brick cottages, converted to one dwelling but retaining original window type, 1870, Warren Farm, Panton, TF 181798.

Fig. 6: Pair of brick cottages, 1858, Panton, TF 172789.

Fig. 7: The Hollies, Lissington, TF 109837.

tion, they were built to different styles, of different materials and at different dates, and yet have a Turnor 'hallmark'. There was sufficient accommodation without being over large so that they still make good family homes today.

The Hollies at Lissington is a good example (Fig. 7). When I visited the house a few years ago it had apparently changed hardly at all since it was described 1917, so it is probably safe to assume that it had not changed much in the period between 1860 and 1917. The entry in the sale catalogue is as follows:

> The residence is brick built and slated and contains front entrance with staircase, drawing room with bay window, pantry in hall, dining room, morning room, milk dairy from hall with entrance from backyard, passage room or office,landing with WC, six bedrooms, servants bedroom and groom's bedroom over the back stairs, kitchen and dairy. There is a brick paved yard with wash house , apple house and other buildings, a large kitchen garden and good orchard.

Other examples of Turnor farm houses can be seen at Newstead Farm, Stixwould, where the house is still complete with its paved yard and wash house, the Chestnuts at Binbrook, Hall Farm at Strubby, Ivy House Farm (now known as Manor Farm), at East Torrington, and Grange Farm at East Barkwith.

Enclosures paved the way for great agricultural changes in Lincolnshire, as elsewhere. The planned farms of the mid-nineteenth century, particularly noticeable on the Wolds and the Heath, were a response to changes in the thinking behind, and practice of husbandry, both for crops and livestock. The mixed farming 'self-sufficiency' of the late eighteenth and early nineteenth centuries began to change after 1830 with the increasing understanding of the science behind farming, and with the increasing importance of cattle rearing for meat production. These changes had a significant effect on the design of farm buildings. In 1851, G. A. Dean commented:

> A compact and well-arranged steading is of immense importance to the farmer; it is there his livestock are sheltered and fed a great proportion of the year, it is there the produce of his farm is manufactured and consumed, and it is there he collected the means of enriching his lands and increasing the quantity and improving the quality of his crops.[10]

The invention of the threshing machine in 1786 made obsolete the threshing barn so important in the eighteenth century. Instead only storage for the threshed grain, root crops and other feed stuffs was required. A particular development was the introduction of enclosed yards or 'crews' where cattle could be kept and fattened, with the resulting manure being used as fertiliser for the arable crops. Good quality stables with associated tack rooms improved the housing of the horses that had, in Lincolnshire at least, replaced cattle as the common draught animal. Open sided sheds were needed to house the new and improved machinery - the iron ploughs, seed drills, fertiliser spreaders and threshing drums, and the large wagons to transport the increasing yield of the cereal crops at harvest time. The buildings needed to accommodate grist mills, root choppers and chaff cutters as close as possible to where the animals were fed to economise on labour.

In 1850 the Royal Agricultural Society ran a competition for a design for a set of farm buildings. There were many entries, with the winning design being submitted by Sir Thomas Tancred. His buildings, which were designed to be flexible to suit individual circumstances, covered two and a half roods, or just over half an acre, and cost £1,060 15s. 5d. This and other designs were published in the Society's Journal in 1850.[11]

The farmsteads built by Christopher Turnor, whilst not copying the published designs, are excellent examples of planned farms, which incorporate all the recommended features and more. They are well-built and laid out for maximum efficiency for both livestock and labour force. The larger ones are self-sufficient entities, incorporating piggeries and hen houses, coach-houses and dovecotes, blacksmiths and wheelwrights shops, brew-houses and even a privy for the farm-workers. The buildings are mostly E-shaped in plan and invariably have the barn and wagon shed facing north, with the crew yards facing south so the cattle got the benefit of any sun whilst the carts and wagons avoided it, thus preventing the timber drying out and shrinking.

I have found about twenty sites where the buildings survive in whole or in part. Not all are dated, but those that are range in date from 1847 to 1870. The size varies considerably, obviously depending on the size of the farm they were serving. The smallest, at Manor Farm, Barlings, is an exception to the rule, being rectangular in shape with a cattle yard in the

Fig. 8: South range, Woodnook Farm, Little Ponton, SK 943325.

Fig. 9: South range, Grange Farm, Little Ponton, SK 917322.

Fig. 10: North range, Grange Farm, Little Ponton, SK 917322.

Fig. 11: Hurst frame and line-shafting, Grange Farm, Little Ponton, SK 917322.

middle. The larger ones are all E-shaped in plan, with two crew yards, and they are very substantial, over 2,888 square yards in area. Most have stabling for about a dozen farm horses, indicating a farm size of 200 to 250 acres.[12] Ivy House Farm (now known as Manor Farm) at East Torrington, however, has a separate stable block with accommodation for 18 horses. It also had the following accommodation:

> ...Saddle Room, Small Barn, Nag Stable and Loose Box, three Crew... seven Loose Boxes Coach House opening out into the Courtyard... Chaff House and lean-to Store Place, and the remaining side of the Block is taken up with a six-bay Wagon Shed, Barn and Cake Granary. A block of brick and tiled Blacksmiths' Shop, Trap House and Cart Shed, tiled Cow House for six adjoining same and lean-to Poultry Houses, two brick and tiled Pigstyes.

Two substantial farms survive in Little Ponton parish in the south of the county - Woodnook Farm (Fig. 8) and Grange Farm (Figs. 9-12). The hamlet of Woodnook is one of the most attractive Turnor sites and is little changed since Turnor's day. A fine set of farm buildings lies on the high ground immediately west of Ermine Street. Local limestone is used for all external walls, whilst the internal walls are of brick. The farmhouse, dated 1869, is adjacent. Nearby Grange Farm, Little Ponton, is equally attractive, and similarly built of stone externally and brick internally. It is dated 1866 and has a pulley wheel on the outside of the building, indicating the use of a portable steam engine for driving barn machinery. In fact a grist mill and the line shafting to it still survives inside the building (Fig. 11). Grange Farm is larger than Woodnook and slightly more ornamental and is complete with dovecote (Fig. 9). These two sets of buildings are paralleled by buildings the Chestnuts, Binbrook and Manor Farm, Kirmond-le-Mire, at the opposite end of the county. Although they are not identical, there are many similarities, particularly between Woodnook and Binbrook, and between Little Ponton and Kirmond (Figs. 13 and 14). These buildings all date from the 1860s and show Turnor at his best. They would all repay further study, both for their own sakes and for what they can tell us about Lincolnshire farming at this interesting period.

Fig. 12: Interior of barn, Grange Farm, Little Ponton, SK 917322.

Fig. 13: South range, Manor Farm, Kirmond-le-Mire, TF 188926.

Fig. 14: View from north, Manor Farm, Kirmond-le-Mire, TF 188926.

Perhaps fortunately, Christopher Turnor did not live to see the full impact of the slump, particularly in grain prices which took place in the 1880s and 1890s, leading to great difficulties for landowners and tenants alike. Only thirty years after his death, the break-up of his estate began, with the sale of the Panton Estate in 1917. His massive building programme carried out at a period of great agricultural prosperity must have absorbed most of the estate income, leaving little in reserve as a buffer against falling prices, but many other estates were in a similar position, with the period 1890-1920 seeing many farm sales and considerable hardship. But over a century after his death, many of Turnor's buildings survive to enhance the Lincolnshire countryside, and provide a source of fascination for agricultural historians. I hope that this article will stimulate others to follow the 'Turnor Trail' and find out more about this interesting Lincolnshire character.

Acknowledgements

This article was written almost entirely from field observation of surviving buildings on what used to be the Turnor Estates and from what I have gleaned from discussions with current owners. I would like to thank those owners for allowing me access to their property, also Chris Johnson of the Lincolnshire Archives Office for his help with documentary sources, to colleagues on the Industrial Archaeology Committee for their help with some survey work, and to my husband Peter for taking and printing the photographs.

Notes

1 This lecture was published by the Association of Friends of Bardney Abbey, and the Bardney Branch of the Workers' Educational Association.

2 *Return of Owners of Land*, 1873 (1875)

3 Shirley Brooks has brought to my attention the fact that Turnor could have received loans from the Inclosure Commissioners, who were authorized to administer loans under the various Land Improvement acts of the mid-nineteenth century. This is referred to in A. D. M. Phillips 'Landlord investment in farm buildings in the English Midlands in the mid nineteenth century', in *Land, Labour and Agriculture, 1700- 1920: Essays for Gordon Mingay*, edited by B. A.Holderness and Michael Turner, (1991), 191-210.

4 Susanna Wade-Martins, *Historic Farm Buildings* (1991), 62

5 L.A.O. T.S.J. 9/(c)/109

6 *Jnl. Royal Agric. Soc. England* (hereafter J.R.A.S.E.), 5 (1845), 237-44.

7 T. W. Isaac, 'On the construction of labourers' cottages', J.R.A.S.E., 17 (1856), 494-512.

8 *Ibid.*

9 'On the construction of a pair of cottages for agricultural labourers', *J.R.A.S.E.* 10(1849), 230-46.

10 *The Land Steward* (1851).

11 H. S. Thompson, 'Farm-buildings', *J.R.A.S.E.*, 11(1850), 186-92.

12 It is estimated that roughly one horse was needed for every twenty acres of land - Wade-Martins, *Historic Farm Buildings*, 104.

Amiable Dreamers.
A View of Late Nineteenth Century Village Schools Through Parish Magazines

Ruth Tinley

The value of parish magazines as a source of the history of the latter part of the nineteenth century is often underestimated. These informative monthly magazines began to appear in the Lincoln area from about 1867 and some continued into the twentieth century. Copies were kept by individuals who had them bound into volumes which increased the chances of survival. Country parishes grouped together and this study concerns the *Deanery of Graffoe Parish Magazine*, first issued in July 1872, covering sixteen parishes to the south west of Lincoln (Fig. 1).[1] It was meant, among other things, to serve as a means of communication between clergymen and parishioners, and to be a record of parish and family life as connected with the church. For those parishes which sent in a regular contribution, this purpose was fulfilled. Views expressed were obviously biased towards the church. A wide range of topics appeared including reports of entertainments, self-help organisations such as friendly societies and pig clubs, church news and accounts, obituaries and historical notes. The subject receiving the most attention however, was schools and education.

October. 1874.

THE

DEANERY of GRAFFOE PARISH MAGAZINE,

FOR

Aubourn,	South Hykeham,
Bassingham,	Norton Disney,
Carlton-le-Moorland,	North Scarle,
Stapleford,	Skellingthorpe,
Doddington,	Thorpe-on-the-Hill,
North Hykeham,	Thurlby.

"For my brethren and companions' sakes: I will wish thee prosperity, Yea because of the House of the Lord our God: I will seek to do thee good."

PRICE THREE-HALF-PENCE.

LINCOLN:
JAMES WILLIAMSON (LATE W. & B. BROOKE).

Fig. 1: Title page from an early issue of 'The Deanery of Graffoe Parish Magazine'. (Writer's collection)

Forster's Education Act of 1870 had changed the concept of education and attention was drawn to the various amendments and related Acts. In January 1877 the editor reminded readers that the new Education Act came into operation on the 1st January. This Act was a matter of deep concern for many years. A 'Soiree' was held at Swinderby so that the requirements of the Act could be explained to mothers and fathers. Letters from the Rev. J. J. Reynolds, rector of South Hykeham, were published. In June 1877 he wrote:

> Although not an advocate for the new educational law, which contains such stringent rules on compulsory education, yet it is of great consequence that its requirements should now be understood. I will at present only mention what is required in order to enable children to be employed by their parents or others in renumerative labour. This year a child of 9 years old may be so employed provided that a certificate, signed by the teacher of an elementary school under Government inspection, can be produced;
> 1st. That the child has attended school during the preceding year not less than 250 times.
> 2nd. Or that it has passed an examination before Her Majesty's Inspector in the 2nd. Standard.
> Next year (1878) the child must produce a certificate of having attended school 250 times this year, or of having passed a 3rd. Standard examination.
> But though a child of 9 may now be employed if he has either of the before named certificates, yet he must also make 250 attendances this year, or he will not be able to be employed next year.
> Next year (1878) no child under 10 can be employed, but any child above 10 may, provided he has an attendance certificate that he has been at school 250 times each year for 2 years or he has passed the 3rd. Standard examination.
> In 1879 a 3 years attendance certificate will be required, or the examination certificate.

> In 1880 a four years attendance certificate; and in 1881 a five years certificate, or the 4th. Standard examination.
> All children therefore now between 5 and 10 years must be kept at school every year till 10 years old or they will not be able to be employed between 10 and 14 years of age, unless they can get the 4th. Standard examination, which few children who have not been regularly at school will be likely to be able to do. Parents had better trust to the attendance certificate than the examination, because the attendance certificate may be *secured* by half a year's - 25 weeks - *regular* attendance, but a child may fail the examination. But let parents remember to secure the attendance certificate *as early as possible in the year* for many things may interrupt attendance...

Mr Reynolds adds a postscript saying that the Act applies to all ranks and classes and that his own son, now seven, will not be able to be employed without obtaining the 4th Standard certificate!

From 1878 the 'Child's School Book' was compulsory. This is referred to in August 1878 as 'the vexed subject'. It was a document which recorded the child's date of birth, number of attendances, and Standards passed, so that the Labour certificate could be issued (Fig. 2). There was a lot of hair-splitting about the details of how evidence of date of birth was to be procured. Since civil registration of births was not *compulsory* until 1875, not every child would have a birth certificate.

The July 1885 issue carried the following 'Lincoln Union, Elementary Education Act. Notice to Parents and Employers.' This referred to part time employment Labour certificates granted on passing the 3rd Standard in reading, writing and arithmetic, if the Attendance committee were satisfied that family circumstances rendered the child's employment necessary.

Another aspect which was frequently aired was funding. Some parishes published annual school accounts. The main income was from the 'Government grant' awarded by attendance and efficiency defined by the Government Inspectors' reports, and from childrens' payments, or 'School pence' (a system whereby parents paid a small fee for the first, and less for each subsequent child), plus subscriptions from the better off parishioners. In December 1890

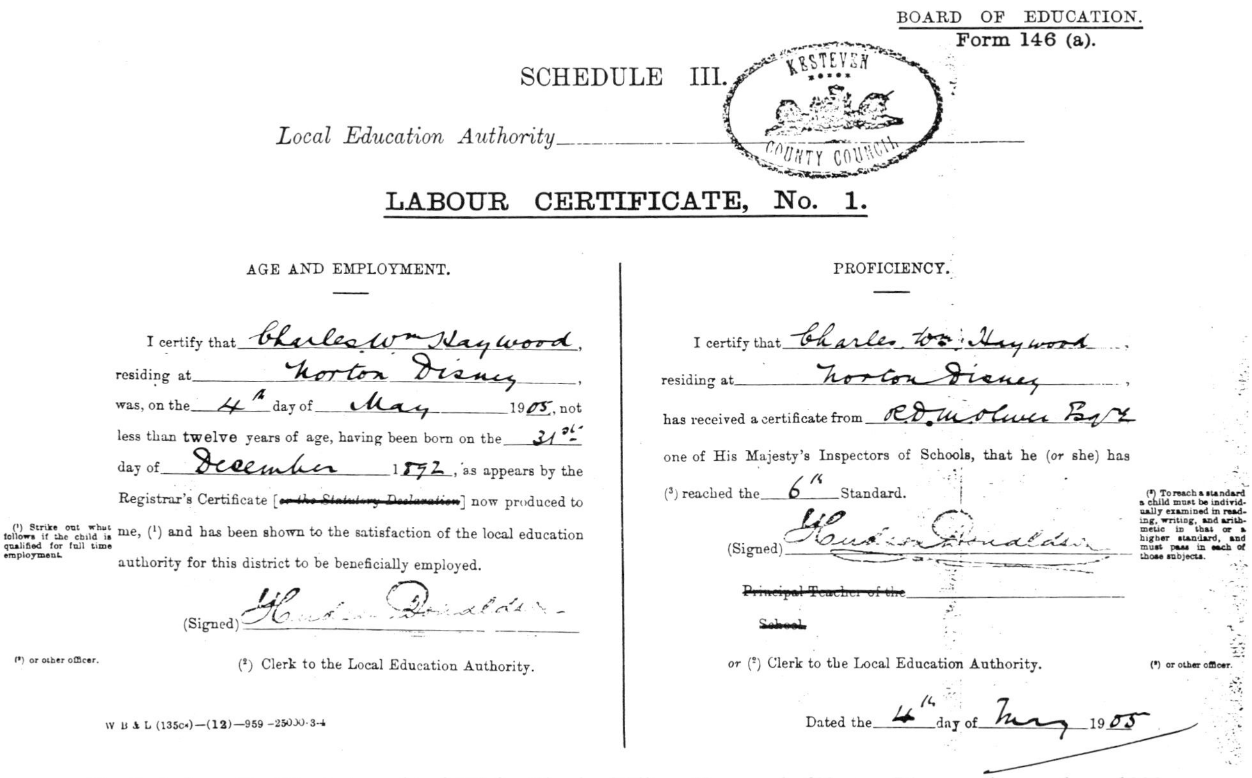

BOARD OF EDUCATION.
Form 146 (a).

SCHEDULE III.

KESTEVEN COUNTY COUNCIL

*Local Education Authority*________

LABOUR CERTIFICATE, No. 1.

AGE AND EMPLOYMENT.

I certify that Charles Wm Haywood, residing at Norton Disney, was, on the 4th day of May 1905, not less than twelve years of age, having been born on the 31st day of December 1892, as appears by the Registrar's Certificate [~~or the Statutory Declaration~~] now produced to me, (1) and has been shown to the satisfaction of the local education authority for this district to be beneficially employed.

(1) Strike out what follows if the child is qualified for full time employment.

(Signed) [illegible]

(2) Clerk to the Local Education Authority.

(2) or other officer.

W B & L (135c)—(12)—959 -25000-3-4

PROFICIENCY.

I certify that Charles Wm Haywood, residing at Norton Disney, has received a certificate from R. D. M. Oliver Esq. one of His Majesty's Inspectors of Schools, that he (*or* she) has (3) reached the 6th Standard.

(3) To reach a standard a child must be individually examined in reading, writing, and arithmetic in that or a higher standard, and must pass in each of those subjects.

(Signed) [illegible]

~~Principal Teacher of the~~ ________ ~~School.~~

or (2) Clerk to the Local Education Authority.

(2) or other officer.

Dated the 4th day of May 1905

Fig. 2: Labour Certificate issued in 1905 for Charles William Haywood of Norton Disney, who was born 1892 (Mrs C. M. Hardy)

the Deanery had ten Church schools, one Wesleyan school (at Bassingham), and two Board schools. At Eagle, where there was a strong non-conformist presence detailed accounts for the Board school were published in 1879, with the following comment 'The Board incurred extra expense as there were elections to be paid for... Elections were held because of the perverseness of the managers. Happy the parish which has no Board.' In 1878 the Inspector responsible for the Lincoln District reported 'School Boards are not popular in the country, either with churchmen or dissenters, once the *cost* is fully understood. Shrewd farmers usually prefer to subscribe liberally to ward off a Board.' A Board had to be formed where voluntary funds were not available and it was often difficult to find the five suitable men required; some of those elected, however worthy, were totally illiterate.

In September 1891 the editor attempted to summarize the Elementary Education Act of 1891. This was to promote free education, and offered a further grant in lieu of School Pence, payable per child, on average attendance figures. This was optional, and the school managers at North Hykeham at first decided against it, but changed their minds when they realised all the other local schools were accepting!

Much space is given to the reports of the Government Inspectors, both specific and general. For Stapleford in July 1883:

> The little school in this parish was examined on March 30th. The report of Mr Oliver, H M Inspector, is as follows: The order is good. Reading fair. Writing very fair, but Arithmetic very poor. Needlework is successful but Grammar fails, being satisfactory in the 3rd Standard only, and Geography is of no value. The specimens are good and abundant, the singing pleasing. The infants are in good order, fairly taught, but the elder children should improve in reading... My Lords will look for improvement in arithmetic next year as a condition of an unreduced grant.

At Bassingham in April 1885, the Inspector reported 'Unquestionably the Attendance committee and their Officer have been culpably negligent in the manner of enforcing regularity of attendance... and the effect is most unjust and injurious to all concerned...' The presence of two schools in Bassingham was probably the trouble. In July 1893 it was reported that the managers of the two schools had met and decided to amalgamate and form one Board school, because:

> a) the existence of two schools in a small village with decreasing population seems superfluous, and also creates unhealthy rivalry and antagonism.
> b) the 'dual system' interferes with due control. Scholars have been taken from one school and sent to the other on the mere caprice of the parents.
> c) the ever present difficulty of raising funds.

There were long reports of a general nature by the various Inspectors discussing topics such as attendance, teaching methods, problems peculiar to agricultural areas, and other matters relating to education and schools. One Inspector, writing on the causes of want of intelligence in children, blamed it on three causes, 'drink, intermarriage, and epidemics', adding 'it is commonly said that the poor do not mind these little ailments. Very probably they do not dislike or dread them so much as the rich, but that does not follow that they are not equally *injured* by them'!

Staffing is also mentioned. In most of the village schools the teachers were single women, and there are frequent reports of changes. In May and June 1877 an advertisement appeared for a Certificated mistress for North Hykeham:

> Salary £30 [per annum], half the Pence and half the Government grant; with Furnished rooms next door to the school. £50 guaranteed for the first twelve months. Apply to the Vicar.

A similar advertisement in the same year for South Hykeham adds 'children nice'! There were most changes at North Hykeham; this may have been due to the fact that the Vicar, being a Diocesan Inspector of schools for Nottinghamshire, was not easy to work under. Towards the latter part of the period mention was made of teachers passing further examinations themselves.

Certain pupils, mainly girls, became 'monitors' and helped with the teaching. On passing an examination they became pupil teachers. The progress of Emma Clark of South Hykeham was followed - monitor, pupil teacher, in 1894 Certificated teacher, and in 1895 attending Lincoln Training College.

Premises and equipment did not figure very often. In December 1877 North Hykeham reported that the money from the sale of parish property 'will fulfill all the conditions required in pursuance of the Elementary Education Act of 1870'. On 19 March 1878, 'the scholars were back in proper quarters after the enlargement of the school, and gained in comfort'. The project had been a large undertaking including also the erection of a teacher's house, and accounts were published. In October 1883 it was said that when the children returned after the harvest holiday 'the school had been whitewashed, painted and thoroughly cleaned, and a cupboard put up to keep the books and needlework in'. In 1894 plans were made at North Hykeham for more alterations in accordance with the new requirements. The plans were returned as unsatisfactory, but sent again, almost identical, with a challenge to the Department to show how else the alteration could be effected, and they were passed.

At Carlton-le-Moorland the school was 'beautifully restored' in 1893, to meet the requirements of the Act. Work commenced on 28 August and 'many have shown a warm interest in the work, as was proved by the fact that bricks and lime, and sand were readily brought in carts to the spot. Owing to the drought there was some anxiety about providing water for the builder, but this was soon dispelled'. Other schools were noted making required alterations at the same time.

There is little mention of equipment. At Thorpe-on-the-Hill there was a report of buying new desks; at South Hykeham (Figs. 3 and 4) a 'tortoise' stove was installed; a cracked school bell at Swinderby was lamented; and a clock was procured at Eagle. The accounts show the purchase of books (some being sold to the pupils). In 1882 £4 18s. 6½d. had been spent on books, registers, maps, slates, apparatus and stationery, and 10s. 9d. on 'working materials' at South Hykeham.

This was a view of schools in the deanery between 1872 and 1895 as presented by the churchmen. They were less than enthusiastic, (and possibly afraid of loss of control), though they recognised the need to keep abreast of the legislation, which they found difficult to explain. The economy of these villages depended on Agriculture. The employers were not landowners, but tenant farmers and smallholders, and associated tradesmen. The labourers were mostly illiterate; they needed the earnings their children brought and few saw any need for the amount of

Fig. 3: Pupils at South Hykeham School 22 May 1895. Mrs Reynolds, widow of the late rector, the Rev. J. J. Reynolds, with her son and three daughters making their farewell visit. Teacher believed to be Miss Layne. (Writer's collection)

Fig. 4: South Hykeham School, built 1870, opened 2 January 1871 (Miss C. Mumby)

schooling advocated. Many of the children would far rather thave been out working in the fields than sitting in school. They were not being shut up in factories and forced to work long hours continually. An Inspector's report in 1878 lists the kind of work country children were doing, 'bean and potato planting, bird scaring, cattle tenting [preventing from straying], carrot weeding, haymaking, potato gathering, helping with the harvest...', all seasonal occupations. At the time J. J. Reynolds wrote his letter to the magazine, British Agriculture was at an all-time low. Throughout 1877 comments such as 'this peculiar summer' and 'to have a harvest *Thanksgiving* seems a mockery in these inclement times', indicate the uneasiness which was widespread.

The parish magazines present a one-sided view. Other contemporary sources would give a different view. Later historians, with the benefit of hindsight, would give a broader analysis. New ideas meet with suspicion, and new legislation often causes bewilderment; it is useful to remember the feelings surrounding the beginnings of universal education. It is not surprising that many of the people, including the parents, could not catch the vision suggested by the Eagle correspondent, following the 1891 Act, who thought that the changed situation (with regard to education) such as a few years ago would have been 'the idea of amiable dreamers'.

Note

1 The only source used is the *Deanery of Graffoe Parish Magazine* (1872-95). The sixteen parishes were: Aubourn, Bassingham, Boultham*, Carlton-le-Moor land, Doddington, Eagle, North Hykeham, South Hykeham, Norton Disney, North Scarle*, Skellingthorpe, Skinnand*, Stapleford, Swinderby, Thorpe-on-the-Hill and Thurlby* (* these parishes are rarely mentioned).

I published an article based on the same source, 'Village entertainments in the 1870s' in *Lincolnshire Life*, 19, 12 (March 1980).

The Changing Face of the Marsh Village

Betty Kirkham

A glance at a map of Lincolnshire shows the most easterly part is bordered by a string of villages mostly from two to four miles apart. Passing through some of them on the A52 today one may be forgiven for thinking they have changed little during the last hundred years.

Hogsthorpe for example lies on the main road between the well known holiday resorts of Skegness and Mablethorpe. The narrow main street today forms an annoying bottleneck and causes hold ups for the thousands of cars and lorries which have to pass through it.

The little houses lining both sides of the main road are closely packed and show few signs of their former importance. Many of them were built in the late-eighteenth and early-nineteenth centuries and look like simple artisan's cottages. A talk to octogenarians who have lived here all their lives shows this simple appearance to be far from the full story. Hogsthorpe hugs to its breast a faded glory as an impoverished dowager clings to her last few jewels.

At present there are only two shops in the main street, a garage in South End, a hairdressers in Thames Street and a Craft Centre in West End. Yet the village was once of great importance locally as attested by unpublished poetry written by a local business man in 1871 and local folklore and the numerous trades listed in early directories. Even during the nineteenth century the church and streets and houses were lit with gas from Hogsthorpe Gas Works in Mill Lane. The only remaining sign of the Gas Works today is part of an old headstone from over the doorway bearing the carved lettering 'GAS W'. This is built into a garden pond feature on the site of the old Gas Works premises. During modern road works old gas pipes are sometimes unearthed and oddly enough they still smell of gas. In 1885 the Hogsthorpe Gas Company Limited was managed by the aptly named Mr J.W. Sparks. Later a man named Richardson took over and then a Mr Wright from Yorkshire bought it. In a few years he was bankrupt. It appears to have ceased production sometime between 1885 and 1900. The last lamplighter was Charlie Hall.

In 1868 there were two mills in the village. One mill was situated on the highest piece of land between Sea Road and Mill Lane. Mill Lane was then only a grass track. The entrance to the mill and buildings was off Sea Road. The mill was owned by John Sivill. He died in 1907 and by 1913 the milling was done by William Sivill. In 1916 Mr Jack Lake was there. The mill was later taken over by the Topliss family. Soon after the first world war the mill was taken down. The house was demolished in 1994 and all that remains now of this thriving business are some of the buildings (Fig. 1).

Fig. 1: Hogsthorpe mill which was situated between Sea Road and Mill Lane.

The other mill in the village was called High Mill and was situated on the opposite side of the road to the church and a hundred metres to the west, and at the time of building it was on the highest point of land in the village and open to all the prevailing winds.

In 1868 John Rogers was miller and baker at High Mill. By 1885 Jonathan Cheales and his brothers were millers and bakers and farmers there. By 1913 Fred Blanchard took over as miller and baker. In 1954 the sails and top were removed and an engine installed which powered the mill for a few more years. By 1970 the Wing family had taken over the premises and did only baking. The mill was reduced in height to about eight feet which is all that remains of it today. The bakehouse and buildings are now the Craft Centre.

There was also a local brickworks. In 1885 J.W. Sparks was the owner, perhaps the same J.W. Sparks who managed the Gas Works. The old brick pits down Langham Lane are now used for fishing. The brickworks went out of production in 1895. The Methodist Chapel and many of the houses were built from these local bricks.

Apart from these important trades the village in 1885 had four shopkeepers, three bakers, two brewers, three publicans, six shoemakers, a plumber, a glazier, a sadler, a Lloyd's Agent, two butchers, a land measurer, five grocers, five drapers, two carriers, two bricklayers, a blacksmith, a coach builder, a wheelwright, a joiner, a stonemason, three tailors, two dressmakers, at least twenty farmers, a cattle dealer, a tin-ware dealer, a surgeon, a schoolteacher, a druggist, an oil cake dealer, an insurance agent, a hairdresser, a stay-maker, a gardner, a tile maker, a cabinet maker, two carriers, an auctioneer, a post office and finally an undertaker. Many of these tradespeople carried on a second trade.[1]

Only careful examination of the architecture of the houses in the main street will reveal clues to their former use. For instance the wooden slatted ventilator, measuring three feet (just under one metre) square, in a passage to the rear of a onetime butchers shop, and the unusually large windows to some properties are clues. Strange bricked up doorways, odd patches of concrete coming right to the pavement show where once bay windows of a shop extended further out, old roof lines still showing on remaining properties, all these tell a tale.

Older residents still refer to the village as a town. They can remember the time when on a Saturday night the main street was lined with stalls lit by paraffin flares and pots were sold from straw hampers in the grounds of the Victora Tavern.

Practically every house in the main street was at one time or another a shop. As can be seen from the list of trades the villagers had no need to leave the village as every necessity was catered for.

A glance at the day book of Mr Raynor a former grocer in High Street dated 1819 shows just some of the goods he stocked. Nitre, salt, currants, bread, broom heads, whale oil, lace, sheets, nankeen, thread, pins, tincture of rhubarb, tallow, sheep salve, red ocre, nails, brimstone, turpentine, feathers, rush lights, locks, brass pots, cinder sifters, tobacco, bed cord and tick, beaver hats, hemp traces and yeast and many more and varied goods. What a large stock he had to carry. People came from the surrounding villages to shop here and Hogsthorpe was known as the metropolis of the marsh.

This position as a trading post in the marsh was sustained for many years. The horse drawn carrier's cart and the pony and trap maintained contact with the outside world until the coming of the motor car to the village. The first two tradesmen to have motorised vehicles in Hogsthorpe, were the grocer G. Stow and the butcher W. Wright. They invested in Model T Fords, though this was not until 1922.

In 1871 the population of Hogsthorpe is recorded as 878 while that of Skegness is given as 349 these figures reflect the importance of Hogsthorpe as against that of Skegness. By 1991 the cencus gives a figure of 797 for Hogsthorpe, but that of Skegness has risen to 16,346. Though the population of Hogsthorpe has not changed so dramatically as that of Skegness there has been a significant if fluctuating decline in the population of Hogsthorpe commencing immediately after the coming of the railway to Skegness and continuing until the building of more houses in Hogsthorpe by developers during 1980 to 1990. More significant are the changes which have occurred in the lifestyle of the villagers. Where once a great deal of the employment was to be found within the village now almost all employed people commute to work, many to Skegness. Most people have to go into Skegness or Alford to do the main part of their shopping. From being a vibrant and important trading post Hogsthorpe is now a village of mainly retired people with large houses turned into nursing homes and flats.

Great changes in character have also occurred in other nearby villages along the coast also brought about by the popularity of the holiday trade spreading from Skegness northward. Travelling from Hogsthorpe to Skegness the next village we come to was once called Mumby Chapel, now called Chapel St Leonards. Here in 1881 there was a population of 262 with only one shopkeeper listed in 1885. The majority of the men earned their living by farming, the rich grass of the marshland has long been famed for fattening sheep.[2] A little fishing was done and some people supplemented their living by breaking up boats.

As late as 1928 disused boats were towed from Grimsby and beached at Chapel St Leonards at high tide. They were quickly broken up and the timbers pulled by horses to the village green where they were sold to farmers and builders. A roof timber in a building on the site of Hogsthorpe Gas Works has strange writing carved into it, I suspect Russian and most probably from such timbers.

Even before the turn of the century the benefits of sea bathing and the health giving sea air began to be publicized. People with money began to pay summer visits to Chapel St Leonards. They came especially from the midland towns. Some of the larger houses were built by Nottingham business people.

By 1920 old railway carriages and small caravans and tents began to be placed on farmers fields to accommodate the holiday makers. Householders opened their doors to accommodate families for bed and board. Thus grew up a type of business which was to become more profitable than farming or fishing or boat breaking.

So many people from Nottingham came and built houses and settled here permanently that the village came to be known locally as 'Nottingham by the sea'. The resident population grew until in 1991 it had reached 2,884. Numerous organized caravan camps now cover many acres of the former grazing land. Chapel St Leonards too has changed in character completely.

The next village south on the A52 is Ingoldmells which in 1911 had a population of only 208 persons. Travelling through here today on the main road it appears to have changed little from the turn of the century, but to go down Sea Lane to the Roman Bank the transformation is amazing. Where here in 1920 all was green fields grazed by Lincoln Red cattle and Lincoln Longwool sheep, with just the odd farm around, today houses and shops and amusement arcades line the road with every available other space covered by thousands of caravans.

Standing on the sea bank today and looking west the white roofs of the closely packed caravans stretch out like a rolling sea. It is said to be the greatest concentration of caravans in the country (Fig. 2). The caravans are empty in the winter but occupied in the summer by thousands of holiday makers, many from the midlands, who flock to the seaside. The population changes from just under two thousand in the winter to many thousands in the summer. This influx of people weighs heavily on the services of sewerage, water and electricity which have to adjust to accommodate their needs from Easter to the end of October.

At the eastern end of Sea Lane the Blue Anchor firm have built a tourist attraction called Phantasy Island which it is said is somewhat akin to Disneyland. It has a glass pyramid weighing 300 tonnes and towering 100 feet into the air and is a landmark for miles around. The biggest crane in the world was brought in to help in the erection.

A little further on the Roman Bank, but still in the Ingoldmells Parish, is the holiday camp built by Billy Butlin in 1936. This expands yearly and is filling the surrounding landscape with ever more caravans. Oh yes, Ingoldmells too has changed in character.

Travelling along the Roman Bank towards Skegness are ever more caravans and chalets uniting Ingoldmells and Winthorpe and stretching on to join up with Skegness. Where at the turn of the century it was possible to travel from Hogsthorpe to Skegness and look to the east and enjoy the sight of low rolling sand dunes, almost unbroken by buildings, it is now only possible to get a brief glimpse of them when nearing Anchor Lane at Ingoldmells. Sadly development here is soon to wipe out this pleasure.

Of all the marsh villages Skegness has changed most of all. It may sound strange today to refer to

Fig. 2: Caravans by Sea Lane Ingoldmells in June 1973. (Potato Marketing Board)

Skegness as a village but in 1868 it was indeed only a village having a population of just 322. Today it is a thriving town with a population of 16,346. This is not the place to go into minute detail of why and how these changes in Skegness have come about. The subject has been ably documented by others.[3] Suffice it to say that due to the coming of the railway to Skegness in 1873 and the foresighted planning of the town by the Earl of Scarbrough and his agent J. H. Tippet, Skegness grew to be an important holiday resort. It is this growth of Skegness which has gradually brought about the great changes in the other villages mentioned (Fig. 3).

Fig. 3. Population Figures 1801 to 1991

	Hogsthorpe	*Ingoldmells*	*Skegness*
1801	451	137	134
1811	515	137	132
1821	591	155	150
1831	698	206	185
1841	790	259	316
1851	832	286	366
1861	874	319	322
1871	878	301	349
1881	719	241	1,338
1891	651	204	1,488
1901	557	163	2,140
1911	590	208	3,775
1921	511	262	9,246
1931	531	292	9,122
1951	599	669	12,539
1961	494	790	12,847
1971	543	1,278	13,578
1981	683	1,526	14,590
1991	797	1,623	16,346

No census was taken in 1941.

The coming of the motorised transport meant that as Skegness became more crowded holiday makers could choose the quieter beaches of Winthorpe, Ingoldmells and Chapel St Leonards and so on along the coast towards Mablethorpe. Thus though many of these places have remained fairly constant in their winter population the summer population has increased tremendously and the lifestyle of the coastal residents has changed also.

The income of most of the tradespeople is dependent on satisfying the summer visitors. The shops and houses and amusements are geared to accommodate their needs to such an extent it is sometimes difficult in the height of the season to obtain common everyday household objects. The shops seem full of souvenirs and bright holiday clothes.

The main roads have been widened and straightened out in several places to accommodate the vast increase in traffic. Even so they are now totally inadequate during the peak holiday season with traffic jams occurring frequently in Skegness and movement between Skegness and Ingoldmells is reduced to a crawl.

So while the immediate coastal villages continue to thrive on tourism places like Hogsthorpe the onetime 'metropolis of the marsh' lying a little inland, sleep quietly away with only older residents knowing of the enormous changes which have taken place in the last hundred years. All that remains in Hogsthorpe today of an important trading place is a narrow main street with two visible shops and people passing through having no idea of its former glory.

Acknowledgements

I am indebted to the late Mr J. E. Farnsworth for the gift of the 1819 day book from the village grocery shop. Thanks are due to my husband for much information on the early state of the villages. I am indebted to Chris Sturman for suggestions on my first draft.

Notes

1 Throughout this article I have relied on the following: Lincolnshire *Directories*: White's 1842 and 1856 and Kelly's 1868 to 1933.
For the 1991 census figures I am grateful to Lincolnshire County Council for permission to quote from their '1991 Census Profiles'. (Department of Highways and Planning, 1994). Source of census figures 1801 to 1901: Census Reports summarized in the *Victoria County History, Lincolnshire*, II, edited by Walter Page, (1906), 368.
Source of other census figures: Office of Population Censuses and Surveys, supplied by Technical Services Group, Dept. of Highways and Planning, Lincolnshire County Council.

2 A. E. B. Owen, 'Beyond the sea bank: sheep on the Huttoft outmarsh in the early thirteenth century', *L.H.A.*, 28 (1993), 39-41.

3 See for example Winston Kime's, *Skeggy, The Story of an East Coast Town* (Skegness: Seashell Books, 1969); *Skegness in the 1920s and '30s* (Skegness: C. H. Major & Co. Ltd 1988); *Victorian and Edwardian Skegness*, (Skegness: C. H. Major & Co. Ltd, 1989); *Around Skegness in Old Photographs* (Alan Sutton, 1994). Also Richard Gurnham, 'The creation of Skegness as a resort town by the 9th Earl of Scarbrough', *L.H.A.*, 7 (1972), 63-76; Julie E. Hewson, 'Who were the Skegness pioneers? A study of the people who settled in the new town of Skegness. 1871-1881', *L.H.A.*, 21 (1986), 63-65. Geo. H. J. Dutton, *Ancient and Modern Skegness and District* (Skegness: Dutton Cash Stores; London: H. Marshall and Son, 1922) remains of interest.

William Hallgarth: Local Historian

Janet Tierney

Born in 1909, the son of a well-known Grimsby chemist, William Evrington Ray Hallgarth started his working life as a shop assistant, until the Second World War swept him away from the shop counter. He was destined never to return to it, deciding after demobilization to take advantage of the post-war emergency training scheme and took up schoolmastering instead. Having qualified, he taught at junior schools at Humberston, Binbrook, and latterly, Edward Street School in Grimsby.

William Hallgarth was, by all accounts, an inspirational teacher, and, subsequently, an entertaining lecturer. During the early 1950s, he had begun to develop an interest in local history, alongside his more athletic pursuits. His young pupils were taken out at every opportunity on historical excursions, visiting windmills, farms and churches, and investigating the old buildings and street patterns of Grimsby before the demolition work of the 1960s got underway. In addition, he had begun to build up a collection of what might be termed the bric à brac of the past - the Victorian and Edwardian knick-knackery of kitchen implements, ornaments, old-fashioned underclothes and baby garments, cameras, lantern slides - in fact, all the material beloved of local history museums up and down the country. His methodology was purely nostalgic; he collected what interested him, and what he felt, rightly, would interest others, rather than what was academically representative.

Hallgarth's academic interest in local history manifested itself principally in a long series of articles in Lincolnshire Life magazine. He was a regular contributor throughout the 1960s and early 1970s, to the extent that he could be advertized by Pinchbeck Lawn Tennis Club as 'Mr. W.E.R. Hallgarth of *Lincolnshire Life*', when in October 1965 he gave them a 'very interesting and exciting evening's entertainment on the subject of *Life in the Gay Nineties*'.[1] The articles were mainly potted histories of villages, appearing under such titles as 'Old Bolingbroke - birthplace of Henry the Fourth';[2] 'Wragby - a Lincolnshire "village" with a Danish origin';[3] or 'Old and New Friskney - a Lincolnshire village between Marsh and Fen'.[4] They all followed the same basic pattern, beginning with the Domesday Book and moving more or less swiftly through the centuries until reaching the nineteenth and twentieth, where he might dwell on a few local characters unearthed by his trawls through trade directories, local histories and original documents, many of these already a part of his burgeoning collections. Copious notes on each village or topic were kept in a series of exercise books, and, as his articles and lectures multiplied, he maintained a correspondence with a growing number of Lincolnshire contacts as well as academic specialists such as Rex Wailes, with whom he shared a passion for windmills. The exercise books appear to have been taken with him on his lecturing excursions around Lincolnshire, since many of them carry hurried entries obviously relating to people coming to him at the end of a lecture to add some interesting snippet of their own to his subject.

Lecturing and writing were also a means of helping Hallgarth to augment his already voluminous collection of historic photographs. It is not known exactly when he began building up this collection. Certainly, like most people before the war, he had access to at least a basic camera. He had always been a keen sportsman - an avid footballer, he played table-tennis to a high standard, and was a keen cyclist, both as a leisure pursuit and competitively. Many of the photographs he took himself in the 1930s relate to sporting excursions throughout the County with the Cyclists Touring Club, sporting socials in Grimsby and events in which he and fellow club members participated, such as the 'Biggest Ever' Hospital Carnivals in the town. Later, particularly in the early 1960s, he was to undertake some specific recording projects. During 1962 and 1963, for example, he spent the spring and autumn months recording existing windmill sites, in many cases where no historic photographs of the working mill have survived providing the only evidence of a structure before demolition or adaptation to new uses. Hallgarth was also very interested in rural dissent, and took many photographs of the small rural Primitive Methodist chapels which in the 1960s were falling into disuse and decay. Rather curiously, given that a substantial proportion of his collection of old Grimsby photographs related to the old commercial quarter of the town around St James's Church, there are very few of that area taken after the Second World War, and no recording whatsoever by him of the extensive demolition work and rebuilding in the Old Market Place and the Bull Ring. This work appears to have been left to other photographers.

At his death in June 1979, William Hallgarth left a collection of slightly over 17,500 photographs, together with approximately 15,000 negatives and several thousand glass 'magic lantern' slides, which he used for illustrating his various talks. He had also built up a substantial collection of picture postcards, all of which he copied and occasionally transferred to lantern slide format. The collection covered not only the historic county of Lincolnshire, but included also photographs from other parts of the country relating to subjects of particular interest to him - most specifically, windmills. He identified, and acquired copies from, most if not all the existing public photographic collections in the county, and several of the major private ones. The Museum of Lincolnshire Life, for example, allowed Hallgarth to take contact prints of many of the negatives from the important Parkinson Collection for his own collection, as well the Exley Lincolnshire windmill photographs. Although he retained the copyright to them, it would appear that some of his prints from the Nainby Hoard were given in return to the museum. Hallgarth does, however, appear also to have collected a number of glass lantern slides by Parkinson, showing a series of views of the Welland gripped by ice and snow.

Frank Parkinson (1873-1956) was a gifted amateur photographer, born at Spalding and resident from 1910 at Pinchbeck. Working with a half-plate camera, Parkinson was responsible for a remarkable series of pictures of agricultural workers and rural life in the neighbourhood of Pinchbeck in the two decades before the First World War. He portrayed men and women working at harvest, children and old women gleaning in the fields around Pinchbeck, and the plover-catchers in Cowbit Wash. One of the most interesting of these photographs illustrates the very differing attitudes to death and its portrayal possessed by nineteenth century society. Parkinson's son died in infancy, and the photograph taken by himself shows the family group of father, mother, grandmother and small daughter looking dejectedly at the baby laid out, with the coffin lid and his bonnet and shoes prominently displayed in front of the child. While the Hallgarth collection contains many graveside portraits (Fig.1), funeral processions (of the great and good) and tombstones, and family portraits with symbolic empty chairs and large photographs, this is the only picture that actually shows a dead body, despite the fact that post-mortem photography was widely advertised by Victorian photographers.

Among the private collections which Bill Hallgarth acquired was that made by his friend Will Phillips of Fulstow. Mr Phillips's father had taken over the village shop and sub-post office in 1880, and on his retirement, his son took it over and continued to run it until 1964. Will Phillips himself was an excellent photographer, and a large number of his pictures showing life in Fulstow during the first forty years of this century - including such gems as the crowded interior of his village store, taken in 1910 - subsequently became part of Hallgarth's own collection.

Hallgarth told many stories during his lectures regarding his acquisitional triumphs over the years. With the collecting instincts of a magpie, he discovered discarded glass negatives being recycled as cucumber frames, cloches and hen-house windows, and begged them from their owners. The 'hen-house' story specifically is related to the Nainby Hoard, where, having asked for the negatives and provided suitable replacements, he was shown a hundred or so more awaiting use, and acquired those as well. Certainly, there are many whole-plate glass negatives surviving in the Hallgarth Collection showing scratches, ancient mould growth and water damage consistent with such abuse!

Edwin Nainby was born at Gedney, married and moved to Long Sutton, where his two eldest children were born, and finally to Alford, probably arriving there in 1872, shortly after the birth of his second son, Arthur. He set up his photographic business at West Street, with his wife Jane employed as his assistant, later opening additional premises at Spilsby, and remained there until his fourth son, Alfred, took over after the First World War. Unlike Parkinson, who photographed purely for pleasure, Nainby, as a professional photographer, was commissioned to pro-

Fig. 1: Frank Parkinson and family, with dead infant.
(W. E. R. Hallgarth Collection, Grimsby Museum and Heritage Service)

duce a wide range of subject matter - Christmas displays of poultry, wheelwrights shops, bank frontages, sunday school treats, Band of Hope rallies, weddings, funerals, even the local newspaper vendor with placards on his cart advertising the declaration of war in August 1914. As well as recording events in the town of Alford itself, Nainby, as the only professional photographer in the area, went out to most of the villages around the town (Fig. 2), as far as Sutton-on-Sea and up into the Tennyson country around Somersby, leaving a substantial record of country life at the turn of the century.

The Nainby Hoard (as Hallgarth referred to the collection) because of its wide variety of subject matter, is probably the most significant part of the Hallgarth Collection because it provides the fullest picture of country life. As with his collecting of ephemera, Hallgarth collected basically what interested him, and it would be fair to say that what actually interested him was the quaint, the archaic, the picturesque and the nostalgic. He was not, and did not set out to be, an academic collector, systematically attempting to provide a complete and contextual record of county life from the middle of the nineteenth century onwards. In providing a record of rural activities - agriculture, rural crafts, rural celebrations - the collection is magnificent (Fig. 3), as in the record that it gives of the topography of small market towns, such as Alford and Spilsby, Brigg, Barton and so on. Where it is deficient, however, is in its holdings of images of the non-picturesque and of industrial activity. There are group portraits of the industrial workforce of small companies, for example, but very few images of work actually taking place in a factory context. Of the ninety or so photographs of Gainsborough, for example, only one shows the exterior of a factory, together with four pictures of traction engines standing outside Marshall's works; there is only one of a works interior - that of Marshall's, turned over for the production of Bristol fighter planes during the First World War. There are, however, a great many very

Fig. 2: Belleau, near Alford, photographed by Edwin Nainby in the late 1890s.
(W. E. R. Hallgarth Collection, Grimsby Museum and Heritage Service)

Fig. 3: Cutting barley by sail reaper at Nettleton, near Caistor, in 1898. The original photograph was lent to William Hallgarth in 1971, by Tom Harrison, the small boy in the foreground, who was the last survivor of the group.
(W. E. R. Hallgarth Collection, Grimsby Museum and Heritage Service)

interesting photographs of the town, the shops and the waterfront, although surprisingly few of the Old Hall. It is a similar story for Lincoln (Fig. 4). In his home town of Grimsby, apart from several prints of Red Hill and Chantry Lane, the working part of the town is virtually unrepresented. While there are many charming views of the Riverhead and sailing ships in the Royal Dock, there is surprisingly little photographic evidence of the fishing industry, and that relating primarily to the late nineteenth and early twentieth century. It is difficult to know whether this apparent lack of interest with the contemporary and with unromantic industry reflects Hallgarth's own collecting preferences, or whether those from whom he collected felt that such photographs, reflecting the utilitarian, would not be of interest.

When Bill Hallgarth died suddenly in 1979, Peter Chapman, writing an obituary mused: 'I wonder how many thousands of people he has given pleasure to over the years, how many young minds he has stimulated, how many eyes opened... ?'[5] Pleasure and stimulation Hallgarth certainly provided during his lifetime; but the immense quantity of information to be gained by historians and others from the visual resource that he created will be of more lasting significance.

Fig. 4: Traffic on the River Witham at Lincoln, looking east from Thorne Bridge. (W. E. R. Hallgarth Collection, Grimsby Museum and Heritage Service)

Acknowledgements

I am most grateful to Andrew Davies of the Museum of Lincolnshire Life for information relating to Edwin Nainby and Frank Parkinson.

Notes

1 The information was taken from a poster advertizing the event, which was photographed by William Hallgarth. It is included in the collection of his photographs held by Great Grimsby Museum and Heritage Service at the Welholme Museum Store.

2 *Lincolnshire Life* 16, 3 (May 1976), 28-34, 36-37.

3 *ibid.*, 16, 5 (July 1976), 20-27.

4 *ibid.*, 15, 12 (February 1976), 24-31.

5 'Odd Man Out', *Grimsby Evening Telegraph*, 27 June 1979.

'I Came to be a Wanderer Upon the Earth'

David Kaye

So wrote John Wesley in his famous Journal on 3 July 1788, when he was eighty-five years old. By then the travelling scene had changed greatly from what it had been when he first embarked upon his itinerant ministry half a century earlier. When he had felt his 'heart strangely warmed' in that evening meeting in a chapel in London's Aldersgate in May 1738 there were virtually no turnpikes in Lincolnshire, the exception was that section of the Great North Road between Grantham and Newark, although work was progressing on two other stretches of main road, viz. Grantham to Stamford, and Lincoln to Baumber (where it joined the prehistoric ridgeway known as Caistor High Street into Horncastle).

But no matter how fine a new turnpike might be it could not prevent snow blocking it, and in February 1747 Wesley experienced this hazard on Witham Heath. He had set out on horseback on Tuesday, the 17th from Stamford for Grantham, taking no heed of warnings by the local Methodist society, assuring them that he could make it through to his destination. He didn't, and rather than face his Stamfordian friends, he returned only as far as Great Casterton to spend the night, before successfully completing his scheduled journey next day.

His native Epworth, like the rest of the Isle of Axholme, was not joined up to the turnpike network, and so at certain times of the year its roads became impassable. For example, on 15 April 1752 he wrote in his Journal:

> I rode on to Epworth. But I was nigh shipwrecked in sight of that port. Attempting to ride over the Common, the nearest way, my mare was quickly imbogged; but being lively and strong, she made a shift to set out, and I was glad to round by Torne-Beck.

On the other hand, although the highway between Louth and Grimsby was not turnpiked until 1803 — twelve years after Wesley's death — he managed this journey on 10 May 1851, although 'it rained incessantly as we rode to Grimsby.'

When he was elderly he still cut across unturnpiked territory to visit two of his favourite, isolated places. Firstly there was the farming hamlet of Langham Row, near Hogsthorpe, where he sought peace and fellowship with farmer George Robinson and his sixteen children! His second refuge was with Robert Carr Brackenbury of Raithby-by-Spilsby, one of the few members of the squirearchy to befriend the preacher. (Brackenbury built for Wesley a small chapel over his stable block, and it was here that Terrence established the Brackenbury Memorial Lectures each summer.)

Occasionally, very occasionally Wesley walked to an appointment, as he did to Burnham, near Epworth, on 16 April 1752, and as he wrote, 'I had no thought of preaching there, doubting if my strength would allow of preaching always thrice a day... But finding a house full of people, I could not refrain.'

His stamina seems to have been phenomenal. For instance, on Tuesday, 29 August 1745, he set out from near London to ride to Lincoln in order to meet with a group of Grimbarians. As he explained, 'we set out an hour before day, and rode with only an hour or two intermission, till about an hour after Sunset', and then adds ruefully, 'but we could reach no further than Cold-Harbour' (along High Dyke, near Grantham), having to complete the ride to Lincoln the next morning.

His entry for Wednesday, 17 December 1777 noted that highway robbery was very prevalent, but added, 'but I had a good Protector still. I have travelled all roads, by day and by night, for these forty years, and never was intercepted yet.' We can be sure that had a highwayman tackled the fiery little preacher, he would have been verbally cut down to size!

Not only did he have to contend with poor roads, but also with a lack of bridges. When he began his 'field preaching' there was no bridge across the Trent downstream from Newark. In 1756 one was opened at Newton-on-Trent (the Dunham bridge), but that at Gainsborough was only erected in his final year. Likewise Tattershall Bridge post-dated him by four years. Thus we find him on Saturday, 7 July 1789 having to cross the Witham by other means:

> Here I met with such a ferry as I never saw before. The boat was managed by an honest country man, who knew nothing of the matter, and a young woman equally skilful. However, though the river was fifty yards broad, we got over it in an hour and a half.

What biting sarcasm from a man who expected efficiency!

Some forty-five years previous to that incident he had a similar experience whilst attempting to cross the much wider Trent at Owston Ferry. On Saturday, 22 October 1743 he was riding 'en route' to Grimsby. By the riverside he found other would-be passengers (six men, two women and two horses). He described the scene:

> Many stood looking after us on the river-side, in the middle of which we were, when, in an instant, the side of the boat was under water, and the horses and men rolling one over another. We expected our boat to sink every moment; but I did not doubt of being able to swim ashore. The boatmen were amazed as well as the rest, but they quickly recovered and rowed for their lives. And soon after, our horses leaping overboard, lightened the boat, and we all came unhurt to land.

Probably in those conditions the ferry would not have attempted the dangerous crossing but for Wesley's insistence. Incidentally he remarks that one of the horses pinned him to the deck, so that he would not have been able to swim to safety after all.

Then there were the equally notoriously treacherous washes to cross too in the South of the county. On Monday, 2 April 1755 he tackled the Cross Keys Wash (near to where Sutton Bridge now stands), and on the following day the equally daunting Fossdyke Wash. Guides were necessary to escort travellers at both sites. It was not to be until 1830 and 1815 respectively that causeways and bridges were completed at these two places on the lower reaches of the Nene and the Welland.

So how did Wesley keep so fit that regularly he covered up to 5,000 miles per annum on horseback until advanced old age caught up with him? From time to time he committed to his Journal his recipes for good health. On his seventy-third birthday (28 June 1776) he included in his list:

1. Continual exercise and change of air;
2. constant rising at four;
3. the ability, if ever I want to, sleep immediately;
4. the never losing a night's sleep in my life.

No wonder that just before his seventy-seventh birthday he climbed Boston 'Stump'!

The Builders of Boston Centenary Wesleyan Methodist Chapel, 1839/40

Neil R. Wright

One of the largest and finest Methodist chapels in Lincolnshire is Centenary in central Boston, just north of the Market Place. It was originally built in 1839/40 (Fig. 1) and was so called because it was a century earlier, in 1739, that John Wesley had established the first Methodist societies. Centenary, which is the direct successor of the first Methodist chapel in the town, was gutted by fire in 1909 but was quickly rebuilt and is still in use today. There was a Methodist society in Boston by 1759 and they built their first chapel in 1764 but the centre of their circuit was at distant Grimsby and, as Leary says,

> on the whole Boston Methodism during the eighteenth century was rather weak, sustained by a few women, inspired on occasions by the few visits of [John] Wesley and the sporadic calls of the travelling preachers from Grimsby or Horncastle.[1]

In 1800 Boston Methodism scarcely existed, but in 1808 the congregation moved to a larger chapel and in 1812 had 125 members. In 1819 and 1827 societies of the Methodist New Connexion and Primitive Methodists were formed in the town, those remaining in the original society thereafter being known as Wesleyans. Their 1764 chapel was in Wormgate at its junction with Fountain Lane (Fig. 2) and it could only accommodate about 170. The second Methodist chapel was in a new residential development close by, at the junction of Red Lion Street and a minor street later named Chapel Street. This chapel was west of the junction, next to the Blue Coat School (Fig. 2). It was extended in 1818 and by 1829 a Sunday School had been built on the opposite corner. Robert Carr Brackenbury, the Squire of Raithby, preached at the opening of the chapel in 1808. After Centenary was built the previous chapel at the corner of Chapel Street was 'converted' into two houses, though the two houses which still remain look as if they were newly built *c.*1841 after the site was cleared. On occasions these houses were occupied by Wesleyan ministers

Fig. 1: Wesleyan Methodist Centenary Chapel, Boston (built 1839/40), from Pishey Thompson, 'History and Antiquities of Boston' (Boston, 1856), 208.

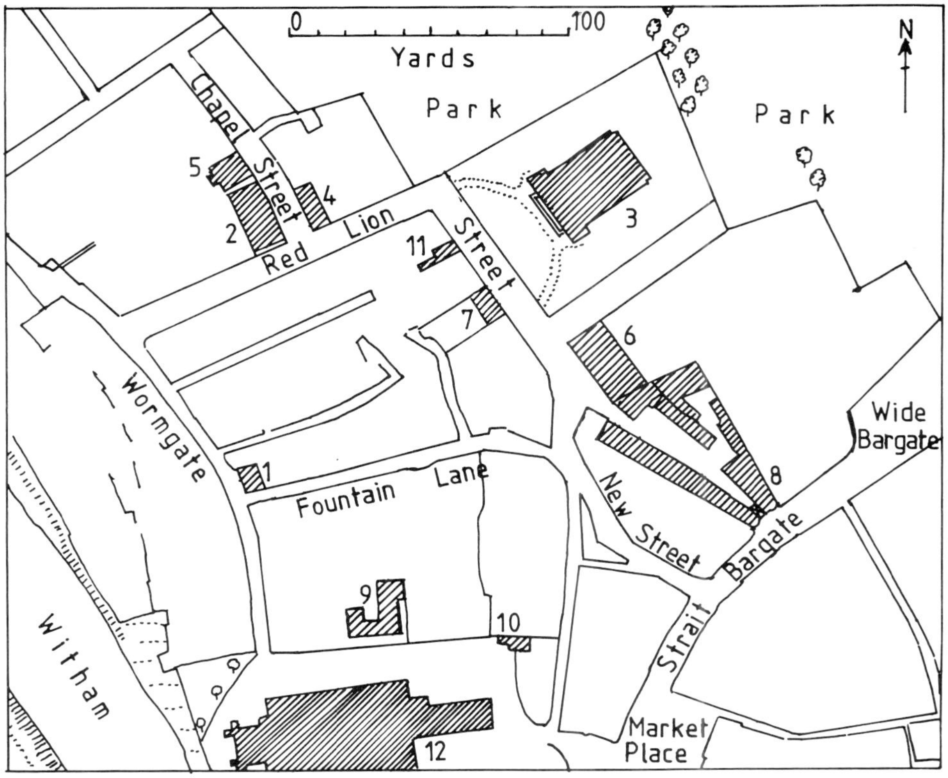

Fig. 2: Red Lion Street area of Boston, 1841.
1: First Methodist Chapel (built 1764). 2: Second Methodist Chapel (built 1808, extended 1818). 3: Centenary Wesleyan Methodist Chapel (built 1839/40). 4: Methodist Sunday School (next to Second Chapel). 5: Blue Coat School (built 1805). 6: Theatre (built 1806). 7: 7 Red Lion Street - Matthew Case's beerhouse. 8: Red Lion Inn. 9: Vicarage. 10: Dr William Small's house in Church Close. 11: 11 Red Lion Street - home of Mrs Mary Wilson (built after 1829). 12: St Botolph's Church.

and sometimes Primitive Methodist ministers.

Within thirty years the Wesleyan Methodists had outgrown their extended second chapel and they looked for another site. Adjoining Red Lion Street was a large private park attached to a house in Wide Bargate and in March 1839 they paid £1,800 for a plot covering over one acre on the edge of the park (Fig. 2). The foundation stone of their new chapel was laid in the middle of the plot on 27 September 1839 and it was opened on 1 October 1840. The inside dimensions were 100ft by 70ft and 43ft high, and it could accommodate 2,300 people. This was a vast increase on their previous provision. The front of the chapel was a colonnade of four massive pillars between two towers which stood forward of the main body of the chapel (Fig. 1). In these towers were the main staircases to the gallery, and in the tops of the towers were small classrooms. In 1849 a day school and a separate house for the master were built at the back of the plot, behind the chapel. Even before the chapel was completed the first Wesleyan burials had taken place on the northern part of the plot, which was used as a cemetery until 1856. The new chapel cost about £11,000 and £3,000 had been raised on the opening day but the debt was not finally cleared until 1856. Methodism continued to grow and by the mid-nineteenth century Methodists outnumbered all other Dissenters in Boston and rivalled the Anglicans for the number of regular Sunday worshippers.

Clearly something happened in the early years of the nineteenth century to lead to this phenomenal growth, but unfortunately we lack direct evidence as to what that was. However a collection of verses by William Small, first published in 1840 when Centenary Chapel was opened, do give us a clue.[2] They describe in primitive doggerel the early history of

Methodism in the town, and in particular list those involved in the building of Centenary whether as leaders of the church or as craftsmen or professional advisers. Eventually 5,000 copies of the verses were printed and sold to help defray the costs of the chapel.

There were two William Smalls in Boston in 1841, distantly related to each other - one was an unmarried retired draper living in London Road and the other was a doctor living and working in the Church Close. One William Small had his children baptized in the Methodist Chapel and was a preacher of two years standing in 1840, so it must have been Dr William Small (1796/1801-1860) as he was the only one with a family, and he lived not far from the Chapel (Fig. 2). Dr William Small left Boston in 1843 and later emigrated to Australia where he died.

The enumerator's returns for the 1841 census give details of many of the people listed in the verses; further information can be found in the more detailed records of the 1851 census, as well as in county directories published in 1830 (Pigot), 1842 (White) and other years. There are also references to some individuals in the *Stamford Mercury*, which was the main newspaper serving Boston at that time. From these sources details have been collected on sixteen of the seventeen trustees in whom the site of Centenary was vested in March 1839 and on most of the other people listed in the verses in connection with the building or opening of the chapel.[3]

Most of the seventeen trustees were respectable shopkeepers and craftsmen, with one farmer and one market gardener, as well as a solicitor and one who combined the roles of shipowner, wharfinger and coal merchant. Five of them had premises in the Market Place, with one down Dolphin Lane nearby. Most of the shopkeepers still lived above their premises, although some had prospered sufficiently to live in suburban houses in West Street Road (now part of Sleaford Road) and Spilsby Road. Several of the seventeen were linked to each other by family or business connections. Morris Cooper (1809-1887) from Norfolk was a tailor and draper in business with Simpson Goy Pape (1799-1844/45) from Alford in the Market Place and in 1837 married Sarah Pape; Cooper and Pape were both trustees. Henry Danby Pocklington (1799-1867) from Sutterton was a builder who owned land in West Street on both sides of the junction with Bond Street. Pocklington lived in one house there, and rented the house next door to young Thomas Taylor (1816-1889/92), a currier, leather seller and boot maker; both Pocklington and Taylor were trustees.

The evident leader of the Wesleyan Methodists in Boston at this time was Robert Houlden Hubbert (1799-1873), who was born in St Mary-le-Wigford parish, Lincoln and became a draper with premises in Boston Market Place. At one time he was in partnership with Joseph Harpham Small (1794-1862) whose sister, Maria (b.1798), he had married about 1820. Joseph H. Small was not a trustee in 1839, but he or (more likely) his son of the same name (1821-1895) were later trustees of other Wesleyan premises established in 1859, 1870 and 1875. Dr William Small who wrote the verses on the occasion of the opening of Centenary was apparently Joseph's brother, and hence brother-in-law of Robert Hubbert. On 27 September 1839 the foundation stone of Centenary Chapel 'O 'Twas laid by one with honours due, / and *Hubbert* is his name', and as treasurer of the building fund Hubbert started it off with a personal donation of 300 guineas.

The drainage and reclamation of the fens around Boston had started in the late eighteenth century and had led to the rising prosperity of the town as agricultural produce from the fens was shipped through the port of Boston. The trade of the port grew, commerce prospered, and as emigrants were attracted to take up new jobs and seek their fortune so the population increased. New warehouses and business premises were built, and then new houses for workers and masters. In turn this brought prosperity to tradesmen established to meet the needs of the inhabitants of the growing town. The occupations of the seventeen trustees were just such businesses as would prosper in this situation. They included a shipowner, a solicitor, a grocer, a hardware dealer, three tailors and drapers, two leather workers (a currier and a cordwainer), a hairdresser, a dyer, two chemists, a builder, a stonemason, a [market] gardener and a farmer.

From the 1851 census and other genealogical sources it is possible to establish the place and date of birth of all the trustees except William Temple. Of the remaining sixteen only three were born in Boston or Skirbeck, and these included young Thomas Taylor (born 1816) whose father's place of birth is not known. Ten were born elsewhere in Lincolnshire and three came from outside the county. Three were born nearby (Brothertoft, Sibsey, Sutterton) but others came from further afield (Lincoln (2), Alford, Brigg, Faldingworth, Stamford and Tattershall). The three born outside Lincolnshire were Morris Cooper from Swaffham (Norfolk), Henry Marshall (1799-1856/61) the solicitor from St Pancras (Middlesex) and Edward Thompson (1786-1866/68) the shipowner from Misterton (Nottinghamshire). The average age of the trustees seems comparatively young - only 38 years and 9 months - and itself suggests a young and dynamic church. Two were aged 52, one 49, one 48, six were 40, one 38, one 32, and four 30 or less.

Some of the trustees also gave practical help with the design and construction of Centenary Chapel. Henry Marshall of Witham Place was by profession a solicitor and was Clerk to the Boston Paving Commissioners (responsible for street improvement and maintenance) but, according to the verses, was 'also famed for *architectural* skill' and drew up the 'grand design' for the new church. He also exhibited his faith by christening his daughter born in 1839 'Wesleyana'. Marshall's plans for the chapel were then 'a little modified by *Pocklington* & Co.', that is the building firm of Henry D. Pocklington who was also a trustee. Pocklington was also involved in the construction and, according to the verses, 'he'll have to *live by loss*' rather than have it said 'that he had fill'd his pockets full, and meant to run away.' Another trustee who contributed was Edward Thompson the shipowner and wharfinger:

> For good Foundations, *Thompson* praise
> Who Yorkshire Landings got,
> Of which three tons & upwards, some
> Did weigh upon the spot.

Thomas Smith (1789-1867) was a trustee and a builder in the firm of Slight and Smith but the verses do not indicate that he was professionally involved in the construction, which seems surprising.

Many of the other trustees were businessmen in or near the Market Place. John Robert Briggs (1799-1884) was a chemist with a shop in the Market Place and a home in Spilsby Road; apart from young Thomas Taylor he was the only one to be born in Boston. Just outside Boston was Skirbeck parish which was the birthplace of James Lilley Hildred (1786-1852), one of the oldest trustees who was a hairdresser with premises now covered by Marks and Spencers. Another chemist was John Field Smyth (1811-1864) who had been born in the parish of St Mary Magdalene in Lincoln and who at this time lived above his premises in High Street, at the corner of Bridge Street. Henry Strawson (1801-after 1849) came from Faldingworth and was a grocer at Bargate End, while William Woodcock (1791-1882) born in Stamford St Martin was a hardware dealer in Dolphin Lane. William Warwick (1799-1872/81) had been born in Tattershall and was a cordwainer (shoe-maker) living and working in Red Lion Street almost opposite the previous Wesleyan chapel. One of the youngest trustees was John Jackson (1807-after 1851) who was a dyer in Field Street, just to the south of Bargate End; he apparently went out of business in the early 1840s but his premises were taken over and continued as a laundry for several more years. The other trustees were William Temple the farmer whose premises were apparently either in Boton West or on the south bank of Cowbridge Drain, and Edward Willson (1809-after 1863) a market gardener born in Sibsey who shared a site with his father in Wyberton Low Road, Skirbeck Quarter.

The verses also give details of the suppliers and craftsmen on the project, and other people who supported or were in some way connected with it. Most of those involved in the construction were aged between *42* and *53* and had been born outside Boston; only the younger ones had been born in the town. Several had premises in Wide Bargate, Wormgate or Union Street which, like the chapel, were in the north-east quarter of the town. The job was not awarded to a single contractor, as it would be now, but each craftsman or supplier was engaged to undertake their particular task. It was therefore necessary to have a skilled person in overall charge, to supervise and co-ordinate the work. For this purpose they engaged William Lewin (1795-1863) who was surveyor to the Witham Drainage Commissioners at their office in Bridge Street. He had been born in Farnham, Surrey and had come to work for the Commissioners in Boston in the mid-1830s; his sons founded the timber business now known as Harrison & Lewin. The verses described him as 'skill'd in all designs, of Buildings, ev'ry sort' and gave him 'the praise, the *pilot* claims/ Who steers his ship to port.'

The main builders were apparently Stainton & Son who had a yard at Bargate End; in 1842 they were described as bricklayers and stone and marble masons. The principals were John Stainton (1789-1878) who had been born in Spilsby, and his son William (1815-85) born in Boston. The 1851 census recorded William as a builder employing 55 men; one of these was Samuel Sherwin, a young apprentice architect, and eventually the firm became Sherwin, Reynolds & Co. 'The ground [on which Centenary was built] contain'd a bed of clay, / Which soon to bricks was turn'd', and Small said a million were used in the building. On the Witham bank about half a mile north of Centenary chapel was William Howden & Son's Grand Sluice Ironworks, and the verses indicate that

> *Howden and Son* have Pillars cast
> Most beautiful and round;
> To prop the Gallery is their task,
> And there they will be found.

William Howden (1774-1860) from Cleish in Kinross, Scotland, had founded the first ironworks in Boston at the start of the century and later produced the first steam engine to be made in Lincolnshire.

> For rearing up the wide-spann'd Roof,
> Let *Willshire's* name resound.

This was evidently Thomas Willshire (1786/91-after 1841) who in 1841 was a carpenter lodging with Matthew Case in Red Lion Street, opposite Centenary (Fig. 2). We know very little about Willshire except that he and his wife Alice had a son Thomas christened in Boston in June 1821 and that another Thomas Willshire, presumably his father, died in December 1816 and was buried in St John's churchyard. The plaster ceiling, consisting of 'doubly sunk panels with ventilating bosses',[4] was 'wrought by *Robinson*' but we have not been able to identify him in any of the sources so far used. The roof was covered by 'John Marshall... who put the slates so neatly on the Roof'; Boston-born John Marshall, jun. (1797-1848) was a slater and slate merchant in Union Street as well as a bricklayer, brickmaker and builder.

> The varied Colours of the place
> So rich and well applied,
> Display a debt of credit due
> To *Smith* of Bargate Wide.

This would appear to be Boston-born James Smith (1806-1875) of Pen Street, off Wide Bargate, listed under 'plumbers, painters and glaziers' in 1842 and described as a 'painter employing 9 men' in 1851.

> But when you through Transparent Glass
> The distant prospect view,
> Reflect, to *William Henry Smith*,
> A meed of praise is due!

The 1841 census indicates William Henry Smith of Wormgate was born between 1811 and 1816 but nothing more is known as he is not listed again after 1842.

The verses also mention a few other people in connection with the project. The first of these is Mrs Mary Wilson (1771/81-1846), the only woman in the verses. Small says, after listing the trustees:

> Our Sister Mary Wilson's name
> To these would added be,
> Did not her sex alone prevent
> What all would gladly see.

Her husband Robert, who died in 1821, had been a Baptist but Mary was evidently an independant minded and active Methodist as early as 1810 when she registered her home for meetings. By 1841 she was living with one servant at 11 Red Lion Street, directly opposite Centenary (Fig. 2), and when she died in June 1846 she left the balance of her estate towards the liquidation of the debt on the chapel.

The verses also indicate that two of the guests at the laying of the foundation stone in September 1839 subsequently addressed the crowd from the balcony of John Noble's shop in the Market Place. One was the Rev. George Cubitt (1791-1850) an eminent minister who had served in Boston in 1820/21 and the other was the aged Rev. John Kershaw (1766-1855) who entered the ministry in 1788 and had served one year in Boston in 1789. He could talk of Methodism in Boston fifty years earlier, before most of his hearers were born. John Noble (1788-1866) was a self-made bookseller and printer and a General Baptist but was very liberal in his religious views and radical in his politics. He allowed the use of his balcony for these speaches, and in 1840 published the verses which are the basis of this article. The other distinguished contemporary Methodist was Dr Robert Newton (1780-1854) who was President of the Wesleyan Conference in 1840. The verses indicate Newton gave his support soon after the fund raising had started, and Leary says he gave the evening sermon at the opening of Centenary on 1 October 1840. Newton regarded Kershaw as his 'spiritual father', according to Kershaw's obituary, and this might go partly to explain Kershaw's attendance in Boston after such a long interval. The morning sermon on the opening day was given by the Rev. Thomas Jackson of London who had been in Boston in 1804 and was President of Conference in 1839, but for some reason he was not included in the verses.

Matthew Case (1786/91-after 1842) is mentioned because he played a crucial role in a fund raising effort soon after the site for Centenary had been acquired and before construction started:

The *Booth Tea Party*, which was held,
Direct upon the spot,
Presented to admiring eyes,
A scene not soon forgot.

For seven and twenty hundred friends
Did sit in comfort down;
Within one vast & *Giant* Tent,
The wonder of the town.

The water which they drank at Tea,
Came boiling o'er the street,
From *Case's*, through a metal tube,
Just to the waiters' feet.

Some dozens kept outside, because
They could not get within;
(Necessity obeys no laws)
They feasted at an Inn.

The tent on the site was 130ft by 70ft. Matthew Case married his wife Elizabeth in Boston in 1817 but the only directory in which he is listed is that of 1842, when he was a brewer and beer retailer, living above his beerhouse in Red Lion Street (Fig. 2); similar information was given in the 1841 census which also showed Thomas Willshire, 50+, and his son Thomas, 20+, lodging there. The verses refer to 'Some dozens' who could not get in and were 'feasted at an Inn' despite the general Methodist abhorrence of drink. The nearest Inn was the Red Lion which gave its name to the street, but since Case was already supplying the tea perhaps his beerhouse was the 'inn' referred to.

This study of Wesleyan Methodists in Boston in 1839/40 shows that many of the leaders were prosperous shopkeepers and businessmen. This in itself is not surprising as this class continued to be a mainstay of Wesleyan Methodism for another century or more. Were the leaders of Centenary in 1839/40 differed from those of fifty or one hundred years later is their youth, with an average age below forty, and the fact that nearly all had been born outside the town. Later leaders were predominantly local born and often had parents who had been active in Centenary. Some families such as the Smalls and the Hubberts were involved with this chapel for several generations extending into the twentieth century. Never since the early nineteenth century has the church been dominated by newcomers to the town, so this does seem to point to the fact that the growth of Methodism to become a major factor in the spiritual life of Boston was led by people who were Methodists before they arrived there, rather than by the conversion of people already in the town.

Notes

1 The general history of Methodism in Boston is dealt with in William Leary, *Methodism in the Town of Boston*, History of Boston, 6 (Boston, 1972), see particularly 5-7 and 27-39.

2 The verses are published in full in Leary, 46-49.

3 The one trustee not found in the 1841 census was William Temple, listed as a farmer in 1839. This failure to find him suggests that he had either died or left the area by 1841. In 1817 a William and Ann Temple had a son Thomas who was born in Thornton [le-Fen?] and christened in Boston - these might be William who was a trustee of Centenary in 1839 and Thomas who was a trustee of the Wesleyan's Town Mission in Lincoln Lane in 1859. The Methodist circuit based on Boston included Thornton-le-Fen in the West Fen north of the town. Even if this is the case, the birth of Thomas in 1817 does not tell us where William was born, as the fens north of Boston had not been settled until after 1800.

4 Pishey Thompson, *History and Antiquities of Boston* (Boston, 1856), 208.

Billy Paddison (1839-1916): Methodist and Farmer

Linda Crust

William Paddison, farmer, coal-merchant and Methodist was born at Lissinglea, near Market Rasen, in 1839. His parents moved to the long triple-parish village of Saltfleetby in the Lincolnshire marsh when he was seven years old and he spent the remainder of his life, until 1916, in that parish. This paper intends to discuss the effects of Victorian Methodism on him in the rural setting both in his personal and business life. The evidence is taken mainly from his own diaries, written between 1860 and 1916, some of which are deposited at the Lincolnshire Archives Office.[1]

Wesleyan Methodism came to Saltfleetby about 1807. The first small chapel building was taken over by the Primitive Methodists about twenty years later when a new Wesleyan chapel was built. There were soon two Wesleyan chapels known as the East End and the West End (in the parishes of Saltfleetby All Saints and St Peter respectively).

Paddison was not a typical Methodist as, after his early thirties, he never again attended chapel due to a nervousness in crowds which nowadays might be called agoraphobia. Using a biblical metaphor, Paddison referred to his nervous affliction as his 'thorn'. His diaries are heavy with agonising over his trials - mental, emotional, spiritual and financial. His search for God is described in non-conformist language of the day, often with a liberal dose of self-pity:

> I feel myself a sinner and Oh how often I grieve the good Spirit. But I can trust more in Jesus Christ than I once could. I have a little more courage to speak a word for him who has done so much for me. I do love him a little more and, I hope I am not deceiving myself when I say, I believe he loves me in return.[2]

His rather solitary battle for faith and 'salvation', or justification through that faith, continued to the end of his life. He was not cut off from religious life in spite of his inability to go to chapel as he read newspapers, Methodist magazines and religious books and 'enjoyed a conversation' with various acquaintances and visiting ministers. Titles that survive from his reading list include Cardinal Manning's, *England and Christendom*, *The Life of Cardinal Wolsey* by Mandel Creighton, *John Wesley's Diary* and a paper on tithe in the *Edinburgh Review* of January 1888.

Paddison's mother was a Wesleyan, indeed her Aunt Clapham had had the privilege of being the Chapel Keeper at City Road Chapel in London and had been honoured to hold a bowl of water in which 'Mr Wesley washed his hands'. Elements of idolatary tinged early nineteenth century Methodism in a way that nowadays is reserved for pop-stars: a hat peg from Good George Robinson's chapel at Langham Row was mentioned, a slip of ticking once belonging to the mattress of a missionary was treasured by Paddison's mother as if it were a medieval relic of a saint.[3] William Paddison, senior, was less sentimental than his wife and son and more concerned with 'scratting and saving, saving and scratting'. He generally attended the Primitive Methodist Chapel in Saltfleetby. Paddison senior actually had the good fortune to die, at the age of seventy eight, in a state of grace at a Love Feast in the Primitive chapel in 1878, having just given his testimony. This seems a little unfair as he appeared, at least to his son, to be a rather harsh, untrusting man, neither kind nor sympathetic to his wife. Paddison regarded his mother, on the other hand, as an angel.

Christianity, in the Methodist style, was early instilled into the young, shy, nervous, child through the medium of bible stories and the Methodist children's magazine which Mrs Paddison bought for Billy and his sister. In this way, using the rhymes and improving stories as primers, the children learnt to read. Christianity and literacy were mixed in their Sunday School life at Saltfleetby too. A new Primitive Methodist Chapel was built in 1847 which soon had about 100 scholars. Paddison recalled the superintendent standing with a bible in one hand and a long cane in the other: 'at the slightest provocation down came the cane like a flash of lightning on the deliquent's head.'[4] He wrote of feast days and processions with flags and brass bands and tea with plum bread afterwards. The hymns carolled by the infant Methodists told of the joy of Sunday School, 'our homes with joy forsaking, we join the Sabbath school'.[5] There was a strong presentiment of the cold world outside the safety of the chapel:

> There sheltered from the wolves and cold,
> Dear little lambs within the fold...

and a golden promise of reward after a virtuous life:

> A beautiful land by faith I see -
> A land of rest, from sorrow free.[6]

The fact of death was with a child from the beginning:

> The angel vanished, and a cloud
> Came with a coffin and a shroud.[7]

Life was harsh; God was good; reward would come after a life of faith but death was inevitable.

For a few years, from 1851 when it was built, Billy also attended the National day school in the village where his attendance was sporadic according to his father's needs on the farm. Attendance at this Church of England school also involved some Anglican church going on a Sunday but chapel attendance was constant. His father, although possibly crude and almost unlettered, was a Class Leader for a time and chapel was the social and religious centre of life. It was also the theate and symbol of respectability - the passport to an aspiring life - a measuring stick of good intention.[8] In 1851 the Religious Census figures show that nearly three-quarters of those who attended a place of worship in Saltfleetby attended a Methodist Chapel. 123 attended various services at the three Anglican churches but 306 attended a Methodist chapel; figures for Sunday School attendance are: Anglican 65; Methodist 102.

Amongst Paddison's papers is an undated booklet *Rules of the Society of the People Called Methodists* based on guidelines laid down by John and Charles Wesley in 1743.[9] This sets out the tenets by which he aspired to live. As one would expect, it was forbidden to swear, fight, quarrel or brawl or defile the Sabbath. Paddison recorded in his diary that he was glad that he owned no railway shares when the trains started to pass through Saltfleetby station on Sundays. Slightly less expected is the proscription against 'using many words in buying and selling'. Paddison was a successful farmer and tradesman. He was a wheeler-dealer in many commodities. He aggravated many less successful people in the village - but his business letters were always clear and straight-forward. This was doubtless partially due to his intelligence and self-taught business skills (perhaps he had one of the many Victorian guides to letter-writing) but could also have been due to an aim to stick to the 'buying and selling' tenet.

The medieval sin of usury was also in the Methodist rule book. Money lending and borrowing was common amongst businessmen and there are instances of Paddison pointing out to debtors that interest should be charged and asking them to contribute a sum to chapel funds.[10] Sometimes this was 'unkindly received' and it is easy to imagine that he had a reputation as a skinflint - a reputation that has passed down three generations in the village to this day. He certainly pursued debtors with some vigour - once through Falkner & Son, solicitors, of Louth, when a young man 'flitted' leaving a debt of £8 which was the annual rent of a three acre field used for market gardening.[11]

Another rule or tenet was the banning of 'uncharitable or unprofitable conversation; particularly speaking evil of Magistrates or of Ministers'. Magistracy was above Paddison's social class so he was naturally respectful to such as William Robert Emeris, esquire, and William Grant, esquire, the chief landowners of the area; but when Mr Grant died and his daughter Mrs Pahud inherited land tenanted by Paddison he did not hesitate to speak uncharitably about her when he felt himself wrongly deprived of his tenancy without compensation.[12] Ministers of the Methodist Church were generally not spoken ill of on the evidence of his diary - but Ministers of God in the Established Church were another matter.

Henry Usher, rector of Saltfleetby St Clement, was a man whose 'besetment' was servant girls and there could be no excuse for him. Rather surprisingly, but impressively, and a measure of Paddison's good name and discretion, Mr Usher called him in to give counsel in the matter. One feels that Paddison, who occasionally had a little besetment himself, would have urged the gentleman to look to his soul. On Mr Usher's death, Paddison recorded a terse judgement in his diary 'a dishonist man and a livertine [sic]'.[13]

Paddison's encounters with Church of England clergy were frequent. Of another Saltfleetby rector, Paddison was more generous, 'Although a [Church of England] clergyman, I believe he was a Christian.'[14] The Church of England appeared to be synonymous in Paddison's mind with general ungodliness and specific wrong-thinking over the trust in the sacrament as a means of salvation, but he did not spurn trade with its clergy. J. Swithenbank, a later rector of St Clement's, was a customer and sometime debtor to Paddison. He bought coal, newspapers, bacon and vegetables from the Methodist farmer and even borrowed money from him - on which Paddison charged a reasonable 5% interest![15]

Both Wesleyans and Primitives were strong in confidence by the second half of the nineteenth century and although they were reasonably outwardly respectful to the clergy of the Church, in areas of many freeholders, such as Saltfleetby and Sturton-by-Stow, deference to such clergy was thin and obsequious behaviour either a rarity or a hypocrisy.[16] Paddison indulged in some newspaper correspondence (unfortunately the paper has not been traced) on the Church of England, which he referred to as 'that withered up fig tree'. He went on to state that, in his opinion, 'the only true Church on earth are these who have felt themselves defiled by sin and have come to the Saviour and are now washed in his cleansing blood'.[17]

Another of Paddison's bones of contention against the Church of England was the commutation of tithes to a yearly rent-charge in 1839. This he referred to as a 'tithe' all his life. In fact in Saltfleetby only half the rent-charge went to the incumbent; the other half went to the current impropriator.[18] This arrangement, in equal proportions, was very rare - no other Lincolnshire example is known.

Although Paddison's status (he owned and rented about 120 acres by the turn of the century) made him respected as he emerged to become a member of the rural middle class, he was not a candidate to be a member of the Bench. He was, however, a dikereeve for a few years and he also became a Guardian of the Louth workhouse. In this capacity another Methodist tenet raised its head to the disadvantage of the workhouse inmates. Alcoholic drink was not forbidden by Methodists but the rule book which Paddison held restricted 'spirituous liquors' to cases of extreme necessity. Paddison, who had seen many come to ruin through drink translated this freely and voted strongly against the inmates' allowance of beer on Christmas day.[19] He agonised a little over the rightness of a Methodist farmer growing malting barley but his final decision on the matter is not known.

Some rules must have posed no threat of temptation to a naturally temperate Paddison, such as the avoidance of the wearing of gold and costly apparel. He was very much against vaingloriousness and quick to point out a moral when a showy family, who had once displayed their earthly teasure in the form of a pony and trap, came to financial grief.[20] The only person I have been able to speak to who could remember Paddison was a very old man who described the farmer as looking like 'nothing on earth'. Vanity over appearance certainly did not show in any of his writing.

The laying up of treasure on earth he was patently guilty of but did not see it as incompatible with the laying up of treasure in heaven:

> Well I must confess that I have an aspiring nature, the seeds of pride in my heart, and a natural desire to rise in the world and for this I have struggled hard and long, but I hope I can say with a clear conscience that it has not been my desire to encroach on anyone else or gain one penny in a dishonest way.[21]

After a harsh, poverty-stricken childhood, and given his nature, it was not difficult for him to abide by the rule for avoiding 'softness and needless self-indulgence'.

Living in Saltfleetby and with no taste for alcohol, the 'taking of such diversions as cannot be used in the name of the Lord Jesus' was not too difficult if one presupposes adherence to the ten commandments. There is one surprising episode, however, in Paddison's younger life - date unspecified as 'some years ago' - when he went to Smithfield Cattle Show and was lured to a London Music Hall: 'I thought the music sweet and bewitching, there were wonderful sights, abundance of tobacco smoke, and a strong smell of all kinds of intoxicating drink.' After enjoying himself Paddison then had the wit to condemn the evil nature in himself and commented that 'nothing but the grace of God and the instructions of a Godly mother could have saved me from being overwhelmed with the evil influence and finally ruined'.[22] Saved, Paddison returned to the village.

Paddison's reading was more catholic than might be expected, it included books on church history and general history besides Methodist writings. He possessed Freeman's *History of the Norman Conquest* in five volumes together with at least one volume of Buckle's *Civilisation of England.* There is no evidence that he sinned against the rule forbidding the 'singing of songs or reading of books which do not tend to the knowledge or love of God'. Nor is there reason to suppose that he avoided the vaguer exhortations of the rule book to do good and be merciful. In all his doings he was honest - if rather careful. The Christian duty of clothing the naked was not very relevant to his life and times, but he did buy an 'oil smock' for a boy working in the coalyard.[23] He also deducted ten shillings for the smock from the lad's annual wage of £8. He did promise a penny to poor old Neddy North who was ninety one, a brick burner and a beggar, every time he came to the door, provided that he did not come more than once a week, and he lent him several 'Joyful Newsis'.[24]

Bankruptcy was a commonplace in the agricultural depression of the late nineteenth century and the Methodist rules had a procedure for investigation of any member who became bankrupt or compounded his creditors. Paddison was not without pity for hard-working men who failed through no fault of their own and he recorded seeing an old man in Louth market who had lost everything to his creditors. He shook hands with the poor fellow and cheered him up with the words, 'Whom the Lord loveth, he chastiseth.'[25]

In spite of the Wesley brothers commanding members to give honour to the King and Government, through Paddison's Methodist eyes Queen Victoria was a sinner as she consorted with such people as Sir Henry Irving and Miss Ellen Terry amongst other 'theatricals'. Paddison's view was that even St Peter could not be induced to admit her.[26] Paradoxically, he saw Edward VII as the 'best king that England ever had'.[27]

Paddison always maintained that his non-attendance at chapel was not of his choice but imposed upon him by his somewhat reclusive nature. In 1901 he bought a little cottage next door to the Primitive Chapel and had a dream of fixing a telephone line from the chapel to the cottage: 'I think if I had a tellephone fixed from my ear to the Chapel I should be able to hear with them and worship God.'[28] Nothing came of this scheme.

Not only did Paddison portray his own life but the lives of the villagers were examined post-mortem and their suitability for salvation is assessed in the diaries. They range from Mrs Drury who was 'a wonderful woman to pray' swooning and leaping over pews,[29] to the miller's sister who was a fast and dressy girl who married a rich old man then lived in sin with a younger one after the old one's death. The latter was luckily converted on her deathbed by a dissenting minister and her soul was saved.[30]

Paddison was a man of his time,[31] extraordinary in many aspects, yet in some ways he typified the Victorian country boy, striving hard, living by Christian principles in essentials and failing to maintain the absolute letter of his chosen laws at times. He paid lip service to humility but would advise the rector and the Catholic priest of Louth, Father A. J. Rowley, on theology. 'He was a Roman Catholic but I believe sincer[e]ly trying to be a Christian.'[32] His faults were all human but his thoughts were divine. Billy Paddison is an endearing example of Victorian Lincolnshire Methodism.

Notes

1 L.A.O. Misc. Dep. 730.
2 Hymn sheet from Primitive Methodist Sunday School Saltfleetby, L.A.O. Paddison 6/1/79.
3 Paddison diary, privately owned, 16 December 1888.
4 'History of Sollaby' by Paddison, unpublished ms., L.A.O. Misc. Dep. 731/2.
5 Hymn sheet from Primitive Methodist Sunday School Saltfleetby, L.A.O. Paddison 6/1/79.
6 *ibid.*
7 *ibid.*
8 *Lincolnshire Returns of the Census of Religious Worship 1851* edited by R.W. Ambler, L.R.S., 72 (1979), 190-91, 194-95.
9 L.A.O. Paddison 5/6.
10 L.A.O. Misc. Dep. 730, 27 December 1907.
11 L.A.O. Paddison 6/2/139.
12 L.A.O. Misc. Dep. 730, 20 July 1899.
13 *ibid.*, 3 January 1897.
14 *ibid.*, 19 September 1897.
15 L.A.O. Paddison 1/1, Rough ledger 1888-1897.
16 *Stow Church Restored 1846-1866*, edited by Mark Spurrell, L.R.S., 75 (1984), *passim*.
17 Paddison diary, privately owned, 3 April 1892.
18 *Kelly's Directory of Lincolnshire and Hull* (1905).
19 L.A.O. Paddison 6/2/97.
20 L.A.O. Misc. Dep. 730, 29 May 1894.
21 *ibid.*, 16 July 1889.
22 L.A.O. Paddison 6/2/1.
23 L.A.O. Paddison 2/2, ledger 1886-1892.
24 Paddison diary, privately owned, 22 February 1891 - Paddison's plural form of the Methodist magazine Joyful News.
25 L.A.O. Misc. Dep. 730, 8 March 1895.
26 *ibid.*, 24 January 1901.
27 *ibid.*, 20 May 1910.
28 *ibid.*, 18 January 1901.
29 *ibid.*, 29 May 1894.
30 *ibid.*, 12 March 1893.
31 See also Linda Cust, 'William Paddison: Marsh Farmer and survivor of the agricultural depression, 1873-96', *Agricultural History Review*, 43, 2 (1995), 193-204.
32 *L.A.O.* Misc. Dep. 730, 5 June 1904.

Some Fitzwilliam Family Portraits

R. W. Pacey

In the first volume of what was to be his unfinished survey of county houses and their families, Terence noted:

> Some local houses and estates were impoverished by religious and political issues. Such may have been the case with that of the Fitzwilliam family, who probably once had a substantial house at Clixby, where, in the very early 18th century, it was said 'At Clixby is the seat of Sir John Fitzwilliams, a Popish gentleman of about £200 per annum; he has a chapel in his house, to which many Papist resort'. These Fitzwilliams originated from Yorkshire and one had married a William Dalyson of Laughton. William Fitzwilliam (d.1634) of Clixby married Elizabeth daughter of John Wytherwick of Clixby [Claxby], being the daughter of William Fitzwilliam of Mablethorpe. John Fitzwilliam was not, I believe knighted. He died in 1718. The history of his family is annoyingly obscure. The Mablethorpe Fitzwilliams had large estates in Withern and the Mablethorpe region in the 15th century and later. A.R. Maddison thought that the family died out in the eighteenth century but this may be incorrect.

Although Terence was not aware at the time he wrote, the Fitzwilliams did in fact survive, through the female line and their last member was Mrs E. H. Rudkin (Fig. 1). I first met Terence at Mrs Rudkin's house in Willoughton and our common interest in Lincolnshire houses and families led eventually to us jointly writing four volumes of *Lost Lincolnshire Country Houses*. The combination of these circumstances and Terence's interest in portraits of local families has prompted me to write something on a group of portraits which once belonged to Mrs Rudkin and were of several ladies of the Fitzwilliam family, of which she was the last member.

The Fitzwilliams lived at Clixby near Caistor from the early 1600s. They were Roman Catholics and so were not involved in public life, and married only into other local Catholic families, such as the Withernwicks of Claxby and the Monsons of Northorpe. The male line of the family died out with Charles Fitzwilliam in tragic circumstances in 1802. His wife was Mary Benton, the daughter of William Benton a surgeon of Barton. She was evidently a great beauty. The first of the portraits (Fig. 2) is a pastel drawing of her a girl of about twelve, probably by Russell, who drew members of the Royal family and several of the Tennysons, during the time that he lived in Hull. The portrait is now at Normanby Hall. The second portrait of her (Fig. 3) is a miniature now at the Usher Gallery, probably by Thomas Corregio Smith. She is shown with her hair tied in a ribbon looking upwards against the trunk of a tree. The back of the frame has some of her hair braided into it. It was obviously a mourning piece. She died after giving birth to a daughter in 1800 and it is easy to imagine the young Charles Fitzwilliam looking at it in his grief. He did not survive her for long and died in 1802. He clearly knew that he was dying as he left a detailed will[2] appointing trustees to bring up the daughter Frances Mary. Charles was buried alongside his wife Mary under a black marble slab in the centre of the aisle of Clixby church.

The daughter Frances was under the care of Mrs Mellish of Hodsock Hall near Retford until she came of age and inherited the Clixby estate. While in that area she met Richard Hannam and eventually married him. They had a large family but few of them lived to any age. The eldest son Charles married Mary Henrietta Porter the daughter of another surgeon. The parents must have disapproved of the match as they eloped and married at the chapel of St Cross in Winchester. Mary Henrietta seems to have been a spirited girl and in her younger days had had an involvement with a curate of Corringham. It is not quite clear who he was, but he was evidently an accomplished painter and painted a miniature of her eye (Fig. 4). The first of these eye portraits was painted by Richard Cosway (1740-1821) who was commissioned by Mrs Fitzherbert to paint her right eye as a present for her lover, the Prince Regent. The Prince then had his eye painted and the picture set into a ring which he gave to Mrs Fitzherbert as a birthday present. These miniatures were often painted as the relationship was disapproved of, because the lady could not definitely be identified. The later photograph of Mary Henrietta (Fig. 5) is clearly a much less idealised representation.

Richard Hannam seems to have been a spendthrift and by 1853 the Clixby estate was sold by the

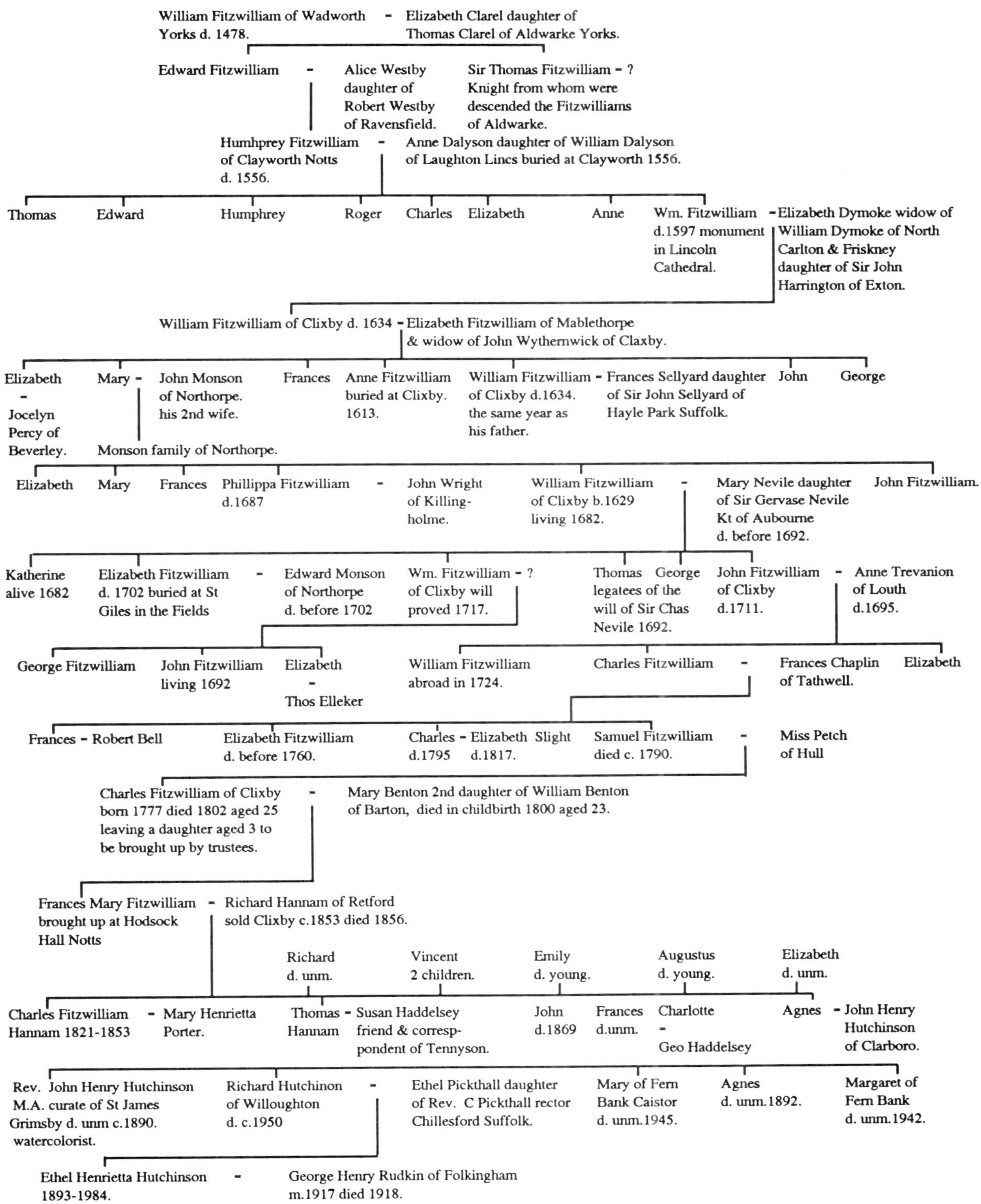

Fig. 1: Pedigree of the Fitzwilliam family of Clixby.

Fig. 2: Mary Benton, probably by John Russell.

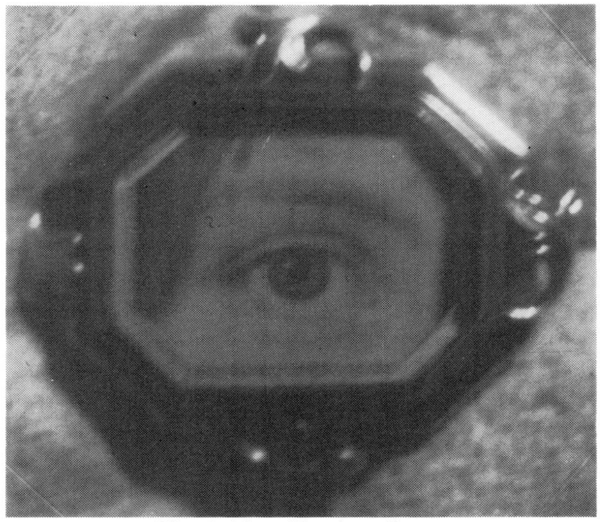

*Fig. 4: Mary Henrietta Porter.
Eye portrait by the curate of Corringham.*

Fig. 3: Mary Benton, probably by Thomas Corregio Smith.

Fig. 5: Mary Henrietta Hannam (nee Porter).

Fig. 6: Frances Hannam (née Fitzwilliam) in old age.

mortgagees. Frances was Mrs Rudkin's great grandmother and her portrait in old age hung at the side of the fireplace at Willoughton (Fig. 6). Some of her diaries from her old age survive and give a picture of a lonely widow interested and concerned for her family who lived around her in the Retford area. Her daughter Agnes married John Henry Hutchinson of Clarborough Hall near Retford. Their eldest son John Henry was educated at Cambridge and taught at Bloxham school. He was eventually ordained and was curate of St James's church Grimsby. He was a very fine watercolourist and painted mainly seascapes. He died while at Grimsby in 1890. The second son Richard was Mrs Rudkin's father. After his father's death his mother moved to Fern Bank, Caistor with his two spinster sisters. Richard married Ethel Pickthall, daughter of the rector of Chillesford, Suffolk, who had come to Lincolnshire as governess to the Nicholson family of Grayingham Grange. Mrs Rudkin lived on at Willoughton after her parents' death and eventually moved to Toynton All Saints and at her death the Fitzwilliam family came to an end.

Notes

1. *Lincolnshire Country Houses and Their Families. Part 1.* (Dunholme, 1990), 47.
2. Author's collection.

The Fawssetts of Lincolnshire and the Development of the Medical Profession

Dennis R. Mills

One of the most notable features of their family history is that the Fawssetts (pronounced Fossett) managed to maintain themselves for long periods at very nearly the same level in society. From before 1500 until about 1620 they were minor gentry, after which follows a sketchier period in Cambridgeshire and Norfolk, until they return to Lincolnshire in the 1760s with the first of the medical men, Richard Fawsett of Holbeach, and Fawssett doctors practised in the county from that point for the next two centuries. Such continuity is not unusual and affords the historian an opportunity to illustrate the development of the medical profession using evidence from a single family. It shows how the role of the 'general practitioner' was enhanced through better and more formalized training and there is also some indication of the wealth and social standing of the Fawssett medical men. This memorial volume is an appropriate place for the essay, given Terence's interest in Lincolnshire families and the help he gave me with some of the research.

In the care of the present Fawssett family is a family tree 'prepared about 1850 to the order of Frederick Fawssett the elder and from the detailed researches of one who signs herself C. Fawssett the younger'. Wherever it has been possible to cross-check C. Fawssett's work it has proved to be very substantially correct.[1] It shows that the family originated in the county with John Forsett of Bilsby, near Alford, who is said to have come out of Northumberland before 1500. In the sixteenth century they were marrying into such well-known county families as the Heneages of Hainton, Massingberds of Bratoft, Disneys of Norton Disney, and Billesbys of Bilsby.[2] It is possible that their departure from the county at the end of the century is connected with the fact that Edward Forsett was in trouble with Lord Chief Justice Popham in April and May 1600 for denying that the Queen was the rightful heir to the throne, and under suspicion as a recusant.[3]

In any case, Maddison's pedigree ends with Edward's daughter Mary, and the line is picked up in the Wisbech parish registers with her cousin Leonard Fassett, who died in 1629. This is the first time a spelling with an 'a' is recorded, but the present pronunciation Fossett corresponds better to the old spelling. After some inconsistencies in the Wisbech records around the middle of the seventeenth century, the modern spelling - Fawssett - continues without interruption within the family, but the historian has to be aware of 'corrections', e.g., Fawcett, in records made by outsiders.

One of Leonard Fassett's great-grandsons, Richard Fawssett, surgeon and apothecary, is the man who started the medical line. However, the practice at Holbeach was already in being in the name of John Spikis Bennett, who from 1733 was variously described in the parish registers as apothecary, surgeon, or gentleman. As Richard married Bennett's daughter Mary in 1770 when he was over thirty, it is likely that he had been an apprentice or junior partner of Bennett for some years before that point.

In the eighteenth century surgeons received their training through apprenticeships, the calling then being nearer to a trade than a fully established profession, and only a small proportion became members of the Company of Surgeons. Likewise, registration as an apothecary was not compulsory and there were few educational requirements for entrance to the London Society of Apothecaries before 1815. In a list of 115 Lincolnshire medical men in 1783, no less than ninety-four described themselves as surgeon-apothecaries, with only three using the terms 'surgeon' or 'apothecary' on its own.[4]

This helps to explain the inconsistency of description in other documents such as parish registers, and in turn is explained by the need for medical men to be able to prescribe and dispense medicines; and to carry out the limited, but widening range of surgery that was possible before anaesthetics became available in the middle of the nineteenth century. Much of the surgery consisted of simple dressings, which we would now manage within the family. The dispensing of medicines was probably their main source of income. In sum, the surgeon-apothecary was the 'general practitioner' of the eighteenth century, although this term was only to come into general use in the third and later decades of the next century.

The cost of apprenticing a son to a surgeon and buying a practice or partnership would have been beyond the reach of most tradesmen, so it is not surprising to find that there are signs of modest wealth in Richard Fawssett's family. His father, also Richard (1700-1781), lived at Walpole and Castle Rising in Norfolk, and there was enough money and sufficient social standing for his second wife to be buried in the chancel of West Walton church a few miles away. His first son, Thomas (1732-1798) was also buried there after practising as an attorney in Wisbech, where he lived in an important residence called Mumpesson's House, now demolished. Richard's other brother, William, the third son (1740-1809), was a gentleman farmer at Castle Rising and one time mayor of the 'town'. Leonard (1742-1823), their half-brother by Richard's second marriage, was a merchant in Lincoln and Holbeach, and later had a post in the Customs Office in London.

Nothing is known about Richard Fawssett's practice at Holbeach, except that he was described as a 'respectable surgeon and apothecary' at his death on 8 April 1811.[5] However, his two sons who survived infancy went to Louth Grammar School, Thomas (1775-1853) becoming a draper in Horncastle, and marrying Rose Seekamp, daughter of Frederick Seekamp, surgeon of Ipswich. John (1774-1823) is described in numerous documents as an MD or physician. In his day nearly all physicians were men with a university degree, usually a doctorate in medicine (MD). This may not have been acquired by residential study and was more often the result of writing a dissertation presented to a university, frequently one of those in Scotland. Thus if he could afford the fee, it was possible for a man who had served his apprenticeship as a surgeon to qualify as a physician. This would enhance his status, as physicians were generally regarded as 'gentlemen', but in thinly populated areas such as Lincolnshire it may not have altered the balance of his professional life very much, and John Fawssett would probably have accepted the label 'physician in general practice'.

He practised in Horncastle and played a leading role in the setting up of the Lincolnshire Medical Benevolent Society in 1803-04, which in its formative years had a political, as well as a friendly society-type role. Fawssett enthusiastically supported another Horncastle physician, Dr Edward Harrison, who with help from Sir Joseph Banks, squire of nearby Revesby and President of the Royal Society, was prominent in the campaign for more stringent entry requirements to their profession. They were disappointed in their main objectives, but the Act which set up the licensing of apothecaries in 1815 was a first step towards the wider reforms of the mid-century.[6]

In 1789 Harrison had also set up the Horncastle Dispensary for the treatment of poor persons, one of the very earliest in England. John Fawssett gave his services here free, as a consulting physician. Harrison and Fawssett kept a small private lunatic asylum in a Horncastle house and seem to have been well abreast of developments in mental health. It is even possible that John Fawssett assisted the Rev. Dr Willis in the latter's treatment of George III's mental illnesses, as the present family has a compass said to have been given by the king to Dr Willis.[7]

It was from John's marriage to Charlotte Clitheroe, daughter of a Horncastle solicitor, that a dynasty of clerical Fawssetts sprang,[8] but three of her sisters married medical men. Elizabeth (1813-57) married Richard Horton, surgeon of Leeds, Sarah (1815-54) married Thomas Smith, MD of Patrington, Yorks, and Charlotte (1809-82) married Dr Barnard Boulton of Horncastle in 1833. Charlotte was almost certainly the 'C. Fawssett the younger' who conducted the research for the family tree, probably with help from her Clitheroe relatives, who included her solicitor grandfather, as well as Robert Clitheroe, attorney, husband of her sister Jane (Fig. 1).

In addition to the galaxy of medical husbands, these women had a medical brother, William (1812-*c.*1890-91), who practised at Binbrook from at least 1836. As a surgeon he may still have been apprenticed, but by now it had become usual for surgeons to take the examinations of the Royal College of Surgeons of London, preparation for which was frequently achieved at least in part by working in a large

Fig. 1: This painting of about 1846 represents a medical marriage alliance and another medical dynasty, showing Mrs Charlotte Boulton with some of her eight children. Charlotte was a daughter of Dr John Fawssett, who in 1833 had married Dr Barnard James Boulton, also of Horncastle. One of their sons - Albert Edward - continued the practice, and in turn his son Arthur carried it on down to 1932. (Mr and Mrs N. Boulton)

teaching hospital which organized lecture courses for surgeons in training. So in the 1851 census William described himself as MRCS, as well as a licentiate of the London Apothecaries' Company, that is a general practitioner in all but name. At the same date his household contained two female servants and a groom. The latter would be needed to keep William mobile around the thinly populated catchment in which his patients lived. He took on work as medical officer for the poor law authorities (Caistor and Louth Unions), which provided a steady if unspectacular source of income with the prospect of a pension and the chance to advertize his services more widely. He and his wife also helped with charitable activities such as clothing the poor. In the 1871 census William described himself as 'General Practitioner, MRCP, LAC' and his servants numbered as in 1851. In 1881 he described himself as 'Retired Surgeon and General Practitioner'; by this time he was widowed, and having no practice he had dispensed with his groom, having just two female domestic servants living-in.[9]

Dr John Fawssett's brother, Thomas, draper at Horncastle, had one daughter, Mary Ann who in 1831 married William Ward of Horncastle, MD and surgeon (notice the combination, which again implied 'general practitioner'). Thomas also had two sons, one of whom, Frederick (1807-), became a surgeon and practised in Wisbech, living in Mumpesson's House, the residence of his great-uncle Thomas, the attorney. He became known as Frederick the elder and was the instigator of Charlotte's researches which led to the 'tree'. He also kept up with his Lincolnshire roots by marrying Susanna Briggs, daughter of David Briggs, a 1,000-acre gentleman farmer at Oxcombe Hall, between Horncastle and Louth.

In 1851 Frederick actually described himself as a 'GP' on his census schedule, and it is interesting to see that he was qualified in similar terms to his cousin William, although the initials MRCSL and LSA do not correspond exactly. These were the commonest combination of qualifications for young men training as GPs in the 1830s, when the physicians were still a distinct breed of university-trained men, and the GP relied on his training as an apothecary for knowledge of 'physic' (i.e., medicine as opposed to surgery). At the same census Frederick's household contained a governess (he had several children, William remained childless), a groom and five female servants, as well as his aged parents who had moved from Horncastle.

Frederick I's son, also baptized Frederick (1835-1918), was born in Wisbech, but educated at King's School, St Albans; King's College, London; Edinburgh University and Paris (Fig. 2).[10] He was the first of the Fawssetts not to train as an apothecary - this branch of the profession was to become quite separate from 'doctoring', adopting the label of pharmacist. Instead the GP now took the 'modern' double qualifications at university in surgery and medicine at first degree level, but leading to the courtesy title of doctor (Dr), taken over from the physicians in general practice. In the case of Frederick II, his King's College course (1855-58) led to membership of the Royal College of Surgeons of England (1858). At Edinburgh in 1859 he took the degree of MD, which as a doctorate in medicine give him academic, as well as traditional claims to the title of Dr.[11]

Fig. 2: Dr Frederick Fawssett (1835-1918) of Louth, from W. T. Pike, 'Lincolnshire at the Opening of the Twentieth Century', 240 (Lincolnshire Libraries.) The inclusion of Frederick's portrait in this prestigious publication is a mark of his high social standing in the county.

From 1860, when he was twenty-five he practised in Wisbech. In 1867 Frederick married a Wisbech woman, Ellen Eliza, daughter of Charles Boucher, JP, who brought some property to the marriage. In 1868 or 1869 Frederick II moved to Louth and lived from then until 1918 in The Mansion, Westgate, a substantial early Georgian house in its own grounds of two acres, equipped with a range of stables and having two service cottages. His grandson, Edward, remembered that the house had a 'surgical annexe', reached through Frederick's study.

At the 1871 census Frederick described himself as 'Physician, MDEdin, MRCS England and Landowner' and the household contained a footman, cook, kitchenmaid and housemaid. The three latter posts held good in 1881 and there was also a nurse, probably for Frederick and Ellen's young children, rather than connected with the practice. As in 1871 a coachman lived nearby, possibly in Fawssett's employment (eventually a Model-T Ford came into use instead of horses). In this census Fawssett favoured the description 'Surgeon Major, Magistrate, Physician, MDEdin, MRCS', whilst in 1891 he was content with 'Registered Practitioner Physician'. Registration had become a significant term as early as 1858 under the Medical Act of that year, which allowed existing non-registered medical men to continue in practice, but abolished apprenticeships and allowed new practitioners to practice only on the basis of a formal medical qualification. In 1886 registration was made more demanding, as qualifications in all three of the disciplines of general practice became necessary: medicine, surgery and obstetrics. This change possibly explains Fawssett's choice of term in 1891. In the census of that year the household included four female servants, one designated as lady's maid. There was also a medical son at home, Leonard Alston Fawssett, aged twenty-two, 'Student of Medicine': however, asthma prevented him from completing his course at the Middlesex Hospital Medical School.

From 1873, as well as a GP, Frederick was also honorary consulting physician at the newly opened Louth Hospital in Crowtree Lane, which runs at the back of the The Mansion. By this date the hierarchical relationship between consultants as an upper echelon of the profession and the GPs as a lower echelon was rapidly developing. Frederick's MD was probably important in his appointment on the usual part-time basis to this higher level post. In this period many market towns acquired a voluntary hospital, sometimes as a logical extension to the work of a dispensary. The County Hospital at Lincoln was founded in 1769, the next Lincolnshire hospital following at Stamford only in 1828. After another long pause came a sudden spate, which included Market Rasen 1869, Boston 1871, Louth 1873 (dispensary 1803), Grantham 1874, and Spalding 1881. Originally, the voluntary hospitals treated mainly the sick poor, or at least not the well-off sections of the population, since the latter could afford to pay for treatment at home, including surgery. It was only with the development of anaesthetics that hospitals were generally frequented by the middle- and upper-classes.

In the meantime, from 1834 paupers were provided for in Poor Law Union infirmaries, and not merely paupers, since where the facilities could cope persons willing to agree to a legal fiction that they could not afford treatment elsewhere were admitted to a Union infirmary. In the large towns, owing to the weight of numbers, the workhouse infirmaries became well-equipped in different specialties, the best example in Lincolnshire being at Grimsby, where the Scartho Road Hospital was founded in 1866, after Grimsby was separated from the Caistor Poor Law Union. In Louth too the Union infirmary was well enough developed to become the County Hospital in 1930, when the local authorities replaced the Poor Law Guardians.[12] It would be to this hospital that William Fawssett's patients came from the Binbrook area, so we can imagine that William would have found it convenient to see his nephew Frederick when paying them visits. Under the National Health Service the County Hospital at Louth has continued to attract development and the voluntary hospital in Crowtree Lane, after a period of disuse, is now a boarding house for Louth Grammar School.

Frederick II was a man of wide and sometimes expensive interests, holding the rank of Surgeon-Lieutenant-Colonel in the Cambridgeshire Militia (Fourth Battalion, Suffolk Regiment) for many years. He joined his father in riding to hounds, and rode regularly with the Southwold from 1868-69 to at least 1909, when he could still manage two days a week. How he kept his practice going is not clear, but presumably he employed junior doctors to do a great deal of the work. As well as hunting, Frederick also went shooting and fishing, in Scotland and Norway. He was interested in local history and was a member of the Lincolnshire Archaeological and Architectural Society. He became a JP in 1873 and subsequently the senior JP for Louth. Frederick's obituary shows that he was deeply involved in the affairs of the Church of England and the Louth Conservative Association, the Louth Habitation of the Primrose League and the Louth Social Club. He was a commissioner for sewers and of the Louth Navigation, trustee of charities, and a school manager and governor, among other interests and positions. As a long-serving churchwarden, Frederick Fawssett is remembered on a memorial on a pier opposite the main door of the parish church; there is also a brass to him in Ely Cathedral.

After Frederick died on 6 August 1918, the main Fawssett sequence came to an end, the sale of his house occurring on 2 October. This home was well remembered by one of Frederick's grandsons, Edward Leonard, son of Leonard Alston Fawssett, who continued the medical tradition elsewhere, following a well-established training route. He went up to Gonville and Cauis College, Cambridge, in 1931, taking first and second MB exams (which included elements of both medicine and surgery) and part I of the Natural Sciences Tripos (the usual procedure for medical students at Cambridge) to complete his BA degree in 1934. He undertook hospital training at the Middlesex Hospital and in 1937 became an MRCS and LRCP (Licentiate of the Royal College of Physicians). Following a period in the RAMC and as a GP/consultant in Worcester, a Diploma in Public Health of Bristol University (1950) allowed specialism in that field as an assistant Medical Officer of Health for Somerset.[13]

Mention can also be made of a distant cousin of Edward and Frederick II, namely Francis William Fawssett, MB, MRCS, LRCP, who practised at Grimsby from *c.*1920 to *c.*1945, following service in the RAMC from 1915 to 1918. He was the great-grandson of Dr John Fawssett of Horncastle and belonged to the Leicestershire branch of the family begun by John's son Richard. Francis William was born at Laughton, where his father was the incumbent, but was educated at Felsted School and Guy's Hospital.[14]

The long span of nearly two centuries of medical life in one family, all starting from a common ancestor, Richard Fawssett (surgeon), illustrates changes in medical training and experience, and in medical institutions. It also illustrates the propensity of medicine to run in families. In addition to seven medical Fawssetts, eight female Fawssetts married medical men, one of whom was the son of a doctor, and three male Fawssetts (one a surgeon) married doctors' daughters. Finally, Dr E. L. Fawssett married Dorothy Hubbard, whom he met during war service with the RAMC, when she was a member of the Queen Alexandra's Nursing Service (QAIMNS-R).

Notes

1 I wish to record my warmest thanks to Mrs Peggotty Graham for drawing my attention to the Fawssett family tree, and to her parents, Mrs Dorothy Fawssett and the late Dr E. L. Fawssett, for access to this important document. In the absence of contrary indications genealogical information has been derived from the family tree and its annotations; and from parish registers, Kirkby Pedigrees (L.A.O. Dixon 15/1), county directories, land tax assessments, and the census enumerators' books. Comments on medical qualifications are based loosely on Irvine Loudon, *Medical Care and the General Practitioner 1750-1850* (Oxford, 1986) and Ivan Waddington, *The Medical Profession in the Industrial Revolution* (Dublin, 1984). Dr Loudon kindly checked the penultimate draft of this paper.

2 Confirmed by A. R. Maddison, *Lincolnshire Pedigrees*, Harleian Society, 4 vols (1902-06), II, 365-66.

3 *Calendar of State Papers Domestic*, 1598-1601, cclxxiv, 423-25, 430, 434.

4 Dennis R. Mills, 'A "directory" of Lincolnshire medical men in the late eighteenth century', *L.H.A.*, 23 (1988), 59-60, quoting Joan Lane, 'The medical practitioners of provincial England in 1783', *Medical History*, 28 (1984), 353-71.

5 Obituary notice for Richard Fawssett in *Gentleman's Magazine*, 81, n.s. 4, I (1811), 494. He owned property in Holbeach and Whaplode: L.A.O. M.C.D./164.

6 Loudon, *Medical Care*, 138-47; A. H. Briggs, 'The Lincolnshire Medical Benevolent Society', *Lincolnshire Poacher*, 2, 3 (Summer 1955), 29-35; *Rules of the Lincolnshire Medical Benevolent Society* (Stamford: J. E. C. Potter, 1903); circular from Dr E. Harrison, 23 September 1809, Local Studies Library, Lincoln, U.P. 1587.

7 J.N. Clarke, *Horncastle Dispensaries and Hospitals, 1789-1981, with Notes on the Lincolnshire Medical Benevolent Society* (League of Friends of Horncastle Hospital, 1981); bill of 1805 printed by Weir of Horncastle, in the possession of Mrs Mary Boulton; and letter from Dr E. L. Fawssett, 29 March 1985.

8 Dr John Fawssett's eldest son Richard, born 1807, became a clergyman first in Leicester, later at Smeeton Westerby (Leics). His eldest son John Barratt Fawssett held livings at Longworth (Oxon), Stafford and Laughton (Leics) and one of his sons, Father Leonard Fawssett (brother of Dr F. W. Fawssett mentioned later) worked at the Calcutta Mission. John Barratt had a brother, Richard Andrew, who was rector of Broadstairs in the 1880s. This clerical dynasty also included Dr John Fawssett's second son John, born 1810, rector of Waddingworth, vicar of Great Sturton with Baumber and incumbent of other parishes nearby, to the west of Horncastle, and his son Humphrey Sandwith Fawssett, born 1861, who was curate to his father at Baumber and subsequently held the livings of New Bolingbroke and Aswardby with Sausthorpe, south and east of Horncastle respectively. Finally, Dr John Fawssett's brother Thomas (the Horncastle draper) had a grandson, Robert Fawssett Ward (b. 1833), who dropped the name Ward in 1883, taking Fawssett as his surname, who was rector of Salmonby (1871-75), a parish north of Horncastle. This tally of seven clerical Fawssetts over three generations is a more intensive concentration than the medical Fawssetts with seven men spread over six generations.

9 Jean Stovin, ed., *Journals of a Methodist Farmer 1871-75* (1982), 83; and *Louth and North Lindsey Advertiser*, 16 November 1861. My thanks to Dr C. Rawding for the latter reference.

10 W.T. Pike, *Lincolnshire at the Opening of the Twentieth Century* (Brighton, 1907), 240; *British Hunts and Huntsmen* (London: Biographical Press, 1909), 53, *per* T. R. Leach; *Domesday of Owners* (1873) Cambridgeshire, gives Ellen's estate as 263 acres, with a gross estimated rental of £416. Her family owned a brewery in Wisbech, see the photo, c. 1854 in M. Millward and B. Coe, *Victorian Townscape: the Work of Samuel Smith* (1974), 46. D. N. Robinson, *The Book of Louth*, (Buckingham, 1979), 34-35. Frederick was also joint owner of ninety-seven acres of pasture land at North and South Somercotes from 1895 to 1910: L.A.O. A.H. 1/10/1/3/76. Some of the information in these paragraphs comes from Frederick Fawssett's obituary in the *Louth and North Lincolnshire Advertiser*, 10 August 1918, 3 - my thanks to Christopher Sturman for this article.

11 While this paper was in preparation a collection of two dozen documents relating to Frederick II's medical education came to light, and I should like to thank the Fawssett family for access to them. The largest group are attendance records and certificates issued by King's College, London, 1855-58. Subjects studied were anatomy, physiology, chemistry, medicine, surgery, midwifery, materia medica, botany, forensic medicine, and practical chemistry. Frederick also attended medical and surgical clinical lectures and his practice in King's College Hospital took the following form: dresser of surgical out-patients (November 1856-April 1857) and in-patients (November 1857-April 1858); physicians' clinical clerk (May-November 1857); and assistant house-surgeon (May-November 1858). Being a student of King's he also had to take a theological course (autumn 1856), and on 31 July 1857 he was awarded a second class college scholarship on the Warneford Foundation, which presumably lightened the burden of fees. In May 1858 Frederick graduated in medicine and surgery and became an Associate of King's College. On 21 May 1858 he was admitted Member of the Royal College of Surgeons.

The MD course at Edinburgh lasted only the session 1859-60 and was more like the modern taught Master's course in Arts or Social Sciences, than the three-year period of research for the PhD. Frederick attended lecture courses in natural history, general pathology and materia medica in a class of sixty candidates, and he wrote a dissertation 'On the nature and treatment of cholera'. On 13 April 1859 he was admitted to the Royal College of Physicians of Edinburgh. From that city he went to Paris, which is represented in the collection by an informal hand-written statement that he had followed a course of operative surgery, and had 'performed several times all the operations on the dead body'. The final document appointed Dr Fawssett to be a surgeon-major in the Militia Medical Department from 1March 1873.

12 Dennis Mills, 'Dispensaries and hospitals to 1937', in Stewart Bennett and Nicholas Bennett, eds, *An Historical Atlas of Lincolnshire* (Hull, 1993), 128-29.

13 Information partly from Sarah Wheeler, Gonville and Caius College, quoting the *Gonville and Caius College Biographical History*, V (1948), 386 and VI (1958), 96.

14 *Who's Who in Lincolnshire* (Worcester: Baylis, 1935), per T. R. Leach.

A Small Sketchbook

Jean Howard

Bennett Hubbard, son of Matthew Barton Pollard Hubbard, hairdresser, and Catherine his wife, was baptized at Louth on 20 October 1806.[1] He attended Louth Grammar School from Christmas 1816 till 1820, as did Alfred Tennyson. A sketch of him in the possession of Louth Museum, is signed by Arthur Tennyson, one of Alfred's brothers.

Bennett studied art under William Etty RA and John Varley and set up a studio in Chequergate, Louth, painting portraits of many local people. (It was said that when painting, Bennett wore a flowered dressing-gown).

There is no doubt he enjoyed considerable success: between 1839 and 1864 seven of his works were exhibited at the Royal Academy: three were of human subjects, including what was considered his masterpiece 'The Artist's Mother in her eighty-seventh year' (1855); the others were of ponies, a spaniel, and 'Feeding Time', presumably an agricultural scene. Some of his paintings were engraved, including that of the prize heifer 'Flower' bred by Thomas Moses of Stenigot (1846). The artist died on 10 April 1870 apparently lamenting that he had so much work to finish.

The contents of his studio were sold on 26 May and the notice of sale in the *Louth and North Lincolnshire Advertiser* (14 May 1870) lists a 'quantity of curious and interesting sketch books'.

Perhaps this is when a small green sketchbook, still bearing the ticket for lot number 206, was sold. This is in the collection at Louth Museum. It is signed 'B Hubbard 1844' inside the cover, and still contains twenty-one leaves, though some have clearly been removed. The sketches, many embellished with watercolour, are of a variety of subjects, in several locations, and dated from 1851 to 26 December 1854.

A view of a postmill, marked 'Bexwill Road near Downham, Norfolk' and three of the moors near Sheffield show that he carried this book on his travels, but the remainder are of local subjects. A particularly fine series was sketched in October 1852 at Cleethorpes and includes three seascapes; one with bathing machines (Fig. 1), two studies of saddled horses, a donkey (Fig. 2), a mother nursing a child, and a very appealing study of a boy with a model sailing boat (Fig. 3). Two studies, intriguingly described as 'near Louth', show a pollarded willow tree, and willows by a meandering water course (Fig. 4). A single sketch of a graveyard gives no clue as to location.

Fig. 1: Bennett Hubbard, 'At Cleethorpes Oct. 1852'

Fig. 2: Bennett Hubbard, 'Study at Cleethorpes Oct. 1852'

Fig. 3: Bennett Hubbard, 'At Cleethorpes Oct. 5 1852'

Three illustrations of cattle, and one of terriers, are precisely dated and located, showing that on Boxing Day 1851 and 1854 Bennett was at Tathwell Grange, the home of Philip Meredith whose spaniel, Bustle, was the subject of the second painting he exhibited at the Royal Academy (1842).

Fig. 4: Bennett Hubbard, 'Study near Louth 1854'

It was said of his professional career that Bennett Hubbard

> valued himself upon the excellence of his flesh-tints, and... that when visitors went to his studio, he would hold the back of his hand near a painting, begging them to compare the two in order to notice how true to nature was his work.

His oil portraits may be seen in Louth Town Hall and are found in a number of family homes in the area. This work would be produced to satisfy the customer's requirements, perhaps vanities, and the necessity of earning a living from painting. It is surely something of a comfort to find that in relaxation the artist chose to depict a similar range of subjects in his sketchbook, but with a freshness and spontaneity which perforce is not evident in his studio work.

Notes

1 All biographical details have been taken from Richard W. Goulding, 'Louth Grammar School Boys. Part V. 1815-1820', *Goulding's Louth Almanack 1930* (Louth, 1929), 108-09.

The 'Archaeologians' Visit Lincoln

Neville Birch

One of Terence Leach's great delights was to organize and lead an historical excursion. If he had been active in 1848 it is most likely that he would have been heavily involved in the visit of the Archaeological Institute of Great Britain, to Lincoln in July of that year: a meeting that was to last some eight days and encompass a multiplicity of lectures, visits and public dining. A considerable museum was also established for the duration.

The Institute was ultimately spawned from the moribund state of the Society of Antiquaries in the first decades of the century. A number of eminent men including some Fellows, decided to form a new society that was less aristocratic, more energetic, and migratory in the venue for their annual meeting. The British Archaeological Association was, for a time, quite successful but a further split took place and a third body, the Archaeological Institute, was formed in 1843. So, in 1848 one finds the Association holding its congress in Worcester whilst the Institute was at Lincoln.[1]

It was in 1846 at the Institute's gathering at York, that Lincoln was first suggested as a suitable venue:

> Sir Charles Anderson, Bart., presented a requisition from the county of Lincoln, signed by the Earl Brownlow, Lord Lieutenant, and principal gentry of the county, the municipal authorities and chief inhabitants of the city of Lincoln.[2]

Norwich had already been selected for 1847, so the meeting at Lincoln was agreed for 1848.

The local committee for the Lincoln meeting, who worked with the mayor, consisted of two bankers (Richard Carline and Leslie Melville), two architects (William A. Nicholson and Edward J. Willson), the Town Clerk, Richard Mason, the precentor of the cathedral, Richard Pretyman, and Captain Arthur Trollope of Casewick, near Stamford, who was also secretary of the Institute's Early & Medieval Antiquities Committee.[3]

The visit was keenly anticipated:

> Great preparations are making in Lincoln for the assembling of this learned body in this city, and many distinguished men are expected. The Lord Lieutenant, the Right Hon. Earl Brownlow, will, we understand, sojourn at the Bishop's Palace during his stay; and the following noblemen and gentlemen are expected to attend:- The Marquis of Northampton, Earl Yarborough, Lord Monson, Sir Richard Westmacot, the Dean of Westminster, Mr. Bancroft (the American Minister), Mr. Hallam, Sir J. Bolleau, the Dean of Hereford, M. Guizot, M. Van de Weyer (the Belgian Minister), Mr. Hawkins, Rev. Jas. Hunter, Mr. Buckler, Mr. H. Wyatt, Mr. Britton, Mr. C. Robinson, &c., &c.[4]

At a meeting of the local committee held in the Guildhall on Monday the 21st, it was reported that the Lincolnshire Topographical Society had donated £5 towards clearing out and exploring the Roman tunnel in the groined roof cellar of the old inn once called the Antelope, in days of yore, and that the Society was to be solicited to give £5 towards the same object. In addition, the same Society had donated £2 towards, 'cleaning the end of the old Norman house called the Jews House' and again the Institute were asked for a donation.[5]

The *Stamford Mercury* and the *Lincolnshire Chronicle* separately published the following comprehensive advertisement on 21 July 1848:

> *ARCHAEOLOGICAL INSTITUTE of GREAT BRITAN and IRELAND - for the Encouragement of Researchers into the Arts and Monuments of the Early and Middle Ages, especially in England - Fifth Annual Meeting, 1848, to be held at LINCOLN, commencing Tuesday July 25, and terminating Monday July 31.*
>
> The following is the general programme of the proceedings of the week, as published by the Committee:-
>
> TUESDAY - Reception room at the Railway Hotel. Introductory Meeting at 12 in County Assembly room, near the Cathedral. Visits to antiquities and objects of interest in Lincoln: remains of the Bishop's Palace - the Castle - Mint wall and Roman gate - vestiges of ancient Lindum - the Jews' House - John of Gaunt's House - the Mechanics' Institute, an ancient monastic building, &c., &c, Opening of the Archaeological Museum at the Assembly room. Excursion to Monk's House, and other objects adjacent to Lincoln. Public Dinner at the Corn Exchange (Earl Brownlow, President, in the chair), at six: tickets, including a pint of wine, 10s 6d each person.
>
> WEDNESDAY - Sectional Meetings at the County Assembly room and Stone Bow. Professor Willis's lecture on the Cathedral, at the County Assembly room, at 12. Visit to the Cathedral. Conversazione in the evening, at 8, at the County Assembly room.
>
> THURSDAY - Excursion to Stow and Gainsboro', returning by Torksey. Conversazione and Sectional Meeting in the

evening at County Assembly room at 8.
FRIDAY - Excursion by rail to Southwell Minster, Newark Church, and Castle Wollaton. Soiree given by the Mayor and Corporation at County Assembly room.
SATURDAY - Excursion by special train at 9 in the morning to Tattershall Castle, Kirkstead Abbey and Boston, Early and Medieval Section at the County Assembly room in evening.
MONDAY - Sectional Meeting at the Assembly room. Visit to Temple Bruer. Excavation at the Round Church of the Templars, starting from Lincoln at 9. General Meeting at the County Assembly room at 1.
CENTRAL OFFICE at the Guildhall in the Stone Bow, at the foot of the High Street; where every information may be obtained regarding the proceedings of the week.
The MUSEUM is at the County Assembly Rooms near the Cathedral, where the principal meetings will take place during the week.
The RECEPTION ROOM on Tuesday, will be at the RAILWAY HOTEL (near the Station), where tickets for the Meeting will be issued, price one pound; Ladies tickets (transferable) Ten Shillings. The Minster, the Castle, and principal Churches and objects of Interest in Lincoln, the Museum of the Institute at the Assembly room, &c., will be open, free of charge, to the bearer of such ticket. Tickets are also issued at the Apartments of the Institute, 12 Haymarket. After the commencement of the Meeting, the GENERAL RECEPTION ROOM and Central Office will, by permission of the Mayor and Corporation, be open at the GUILDHALL in the Stone-bow, the ancient City Gate at the foot of the High-street, and near the Saracen's Head Hotel. Tickets will be issued there, and every information given regarding the daily course of proceedings, excursions, &c., &c., during the week.
The Lodgings are numerous. Beds will be charged - in the Hotels, 2s 6d; in Private Lodgings 4s 6d. Daily Ordinaries, Breakfast and Dinner, will be provided at moderate charges. The temporary Museum of the Institute is at the County Assembly-room, near the Cathedral. All persons disposed to contribute antiquities or works of art for exhibition, are requested to communicate with Rd. Carline, Esq.; E. J. Wilson, Esq., Minster Yard; or any Member of the Local Committee in Lincoln, as early as possible. All precautions will be taken to ensure the safety of objects thus entrusted, and glazed cases provided for their exhibition. Every care will be taken of the articles forwarded, and a receipt given for their return carriage free.

The temporary museum soon expanded into a second room at the County Assembly Rooms. The exhibits were recorded in a Catalogue of Antiquities that was divided into nine categories.[6] The Lincolnshire exhibitors included T. M. Keyworth, the Right Hon. C. T. d'Eyncourt, the Rev. H. and Mrs Sibthorp, Major and Richard Ellison, E. A. Bromhead, S. Paddison, and the Lincoln Permanent Library. Others contributed more than one exhibit: A. Trollope with five entries; J. Dudding (three): E. J. Willson (twelve): Sir C. Anderson (four); Dr Charlesworth (two); R. Carline (two); Lord Monson (two); Sir E. Firench Bromhead (two); whilst clergy associated with the Cathedral submitted ten exhibits.[7]

Amongst the names contributing towards the local expenses of the meeting were the Bishop, and the Archdeacon of Lincoln, together with the Lord Lieutenant and High Sheriff of the county. A further list of thirty-two gentleman supporters reads like a Who's-Who for Lincolnshre.[8] Two local men were heavily involved in organizing the Lincoln meeting: Sir Charles Anderson of Lea Hall, near Gainsborough, and Edward James Willson, of Lincoln. The former was a prominent member of the Institute being president of the Architecture Section; the latter, a Roman Catholic, was secretary of that section.

It was in 1847, at the Norwich meeting, that railways and river-boats were utilized for the first time by the Institute. There were three full day excursions by special train from Norwich. The first on Saturday, 31 July, left at 8 a.m. bound for Binham Priory and Walsingham, visiting on the way East Dereham, Fakenham, and Little and Great Snoring. On the following Monday a train conveyed members to Berney Arms Station, where steamers took them on by water to Yarmouth. Here was held a public dinner followed by lectures before the party was brought back to Norwich by train. On Wednesday, 4 August, shortly after 9 a.m., a special train started for Ely, conveying the President and about one hundred and fifty archaeologists. On the way the train stopped at Wymondham to allow a visit to be made to the priory and the church.[9]

When the Institute accepted Lincoln's invitation for the following year it was hoped that the railways planned for the Lincoln area would be in place. Sir Charles Anderson expected that the newly opened Nottingham & Lincoln branch of the Midland Railway would adequately connect Lincoln to many parts of the British Isles, and it was anticipated that Lincoln would be linked to other county towns by the summer of 1848. However when the Lincoln meeting convened on Tuesday 25 July no more railways were open.

There were two railway excursions during the Lincoln meeting: the first on Friday the 28th, the other on the following day. On the Friday the Midland Railway, provided a special train to carry some 200 participants, first to Newark, and thence to Nottingham. At Newark, its church and castle, together with nearby Hawton church, and Southwell minster were visited. In Nottingham the excursionists made their way to Wollaton Hall, where Lord Willoughby, 'had made the most hospitable preparations for the entertainment of his numerous guests, and had arranged, with great kindness, every facility for their gratification'.[10] Initially it is puzzling as to why an excursion into Nottinghamshire was arranged, until one recalls that the county at that time was in the Lincoln diocese.

The Saturday excursion was to Kirkstead Abbey, Tattershall Castle, and Boston. The party travelled by train from Lincoln, presumably from an incomplete Great Northern station. Departing at 9 a.m. they passed down the Witham Bank to Bardney, along a line that was yet to be opened to the public. The special train, 'had been liberally supplied by the Directors of the Great Northern Railway, who conveyed the party to and from Tattershall, and also very hospitably entertained them at luncheon'.[11] At Bardney the party transferred to a steamer on which the luncheon was provided as they proceeded down the River Witham. The boat stopped at Tattershall bridge on its journey to Boston, in order to allow the party to go ashore and visit Kirkstead abbey, and Tattershall castle and church. The excursionists arrived at Boston at 4 p.m., and after visiting the 'Stump' boarded a ballast train an hour later, for a more rapid return to Lincoln. Although the Institute had not asked for, nor expected, a public reception in Boston, the *Stamford Mercury* explained that,

> Some of the 'very respectables' of the town were anxious that a public reception and entertainment should be given by the corporation to those lovers of the antique; but the worthy Mayor, although approving the objects of the Institute, did not consider the Corporation were called upon to take the steps hinted at.[12]

Boston's corporation, like Lincoln's, had little money to spare. Certainly the rail journey between Boston and Lincoln proved that the wooden bridge across Bardney deeps was in use.

There were two other day excursions, by carriage: on the Thursday, and on the second Tuesday. The first was to Stow, Lea, Gainsborough, and Torksey. At Stow the party found a badly neglected large cruciform church with much Saxon work in evidence. It had been recommended for restoration and the Lincolnshire Architectural Society had granted £10 towards a trial excavation to discover the extent of the damage. A consequence of this survey was the lecture given by the Rev. G. Atkinson to that Society.[13] During May 1847 Mr. Railton, an architect for the Ecclesiastical Commissioners, surveyed Stow chancel and suggested that 'the cost of putting the fabric into a due state of repair would be about five hundred pounds'. He proposed that the Ecclesiastical Commissioners contribute £300, the remainder coming from the Prebendary's Lessee,[14] It follows that the adverse comments made by Institute members during their visit encourage Atkinson and others urgently to seek for the financial means. The prolonged struggle to achieve its complete restoration is well told in Spurrell's account.[15]

The party were offered hospitality, including a cold collation, at Lea Hall by Sir Charles Anderson before continuing to the Old Hall at Gainsborough: it proved to be another badly neglected building. On their way back to Lincoln the party paused at Torksey to view the castle ruins and other sites, and at Kettlethorpe to view the gateway associated with Catherine de Swinford. The Gainsborough correspondent of the *Mercury* tartly commented that the visit by the Institute to Gainsborough, 'was not remarkable for any incident worthy of record. They visited the 'Old Hall' in a somewhat hurried manner, and took a cursory view of the exterior on the north.' In the banqueting hall, 'a learned discussion arose as to one word in the Old English character on the wall, several of the learned antiquaries being of the opinion that it is 'peace', others 'years'.' On viewing the exterior of the tower some of the party, 'entered an onion garden, and an old lady having more regard for her onions than for antiquities read them a severe lecture, till finding herself overcome by the numbers and the laughter of the antiquaries, made a hasty retreat'.[16]

The excursion planned for the Monday was postponed for a day, until after the official end of the Institute's meeting. So Tuesday, 1 August, saw a small party of members view and discuss the excavations taking place at the circular church at Temple Bruer. They were shown a skeleton recently discovered near its walls (no marks of violence were evident). The party then went on to dine with Earl

Brownlow.

On the first two days of the meeting several excursions took place within the city: to the cathedral, the old Bishop's Palace, the castle, the Mint Wall, the Roman Gate, the Jews' House, the Monks' House, and the former Greyfriars building then housing the Mechanics' Institute.

Many of the lectures given at the meeting were printed in the *Memoir* which appeared in 1850 (though this included several additional papers). It is perhaps appropriate that E. J. Willson headed the list of well-know Lincolnshire antiquarians with four contributions: on the Old Bishop's Palace, Lincoln castle, the old Deanery, and St Mary's Conduit; F. C. Massingberd, the Chancellor, had two papers published: on the Grecian Stairs and the Battle of Winceby. A good number of papers concentrated on the cathedral. Lord Monson produced an account of old Lincolnshire family feuds; the Rev. W. Moore dealt with the Spalding Gentlemen's Society. George Boole, soon to become Professor of Mathematics at the Queens College at Cork, furnished a description of a Bishop Grosseteste manuscript.[17]

The traditional dinner, presided over by Earl Brownlow, took place in the large rooms of the recently opened Corn Exchange. It commenced at 6 p.m.: 'the culinary arrangements, made by Mr. Heseltine of the Saracen's Head, were of the most sumptuous character... 265 noblemen and gentlemen were present, including several ladies.'[18] On the top table, to the Earl's right were the Bishop of Lincoln, Lady Mary Ann Alford, the Earl of Yarborough, Lady Amelia Cust, Lord Monson, Miss Mortlock, the Dean of Lincoln, and W. Marshall, Mayor of Lincoln. To the Earl's left were Lady Monson, the Duke of St Albans, Countess Brownlow, the Marquis of Northampton, Miss Kaye, the Bishop of Norwich, Lady Buxton, the Dean of Westminster, and the Precentor.[19]

Two of the many speeches are of interest: The Bishop of Lincoln suggested that:

> There was one branch of archaeology which must ever possess high interest for the Christian minister-that which related to ecclesiastical architecture. Let me be permitted to say that the religion of this land was necessarily connected with tradition and history-still it was a religion founded on facts which occured 18 centuries since.

He went on to defend the current interpretation of Christianity.[20] Later on in the evening Sir Charles Anderson rose to put the case for Lincolnshire: he hoped, 'that the learned body would in their excursions be something surprised to see what change agricultural enterprise had effected'; he went on to give examples of such improvements.[21]

The soiree given by the mayor and corporation on the Friday evening was held at the County Assembly Rooms. Its sponsorship of the event was achieved against council opposition at a meeting held on Monday 17 July. It appears that the advertising of the Institute's programme was the first intimation to councillors of such an expense. Mr Carline,

> presumed the publication of this soiree... arose from some private conversation he had with Mr. Weigh [Way], in London... the members of the Corporation having in committee expressed the impression that it would be desirable for the Corporation to entertain the Institute.[22]

At previous meetings, according to the Town Clerk, the relevant corporations had not entertained the Institute with council funds. One councillor, Mr Williams, stated it was illegal to finance such entertainment: he understood that at the York meeting held in 1846, 'the Institute was entertained by the Mayor personally, and by public subscription'. However, according to Mr Calder,

> the Mayor of York and other places had an allowance, and it made no difference which way the sum was given. In Lincoln, the Mayors had been noble enough to serve the office without making any charge at all, or calling upon the Corporation for an allowance; but it could not be presumed that the Mayor was to entertain the Institute at his own expense.

After being interrupted Mr Calder continued,

> that he should be the last person to desire to expend the Corporate funds profligately; but any expenditure of the Corporation for the entertainment of the Institute would be repaid to the town three or four fold.

After a long discussion the proposal, 'that £100 be placed in the hands of the Mayor and Committee' was carried.[23]

The soiree, having been put back a day, now had to follow closely the tiring excursion to Newark and Nottingham. It was 'given in the most liberal manner... The whole suite of the Assembly Rooms was brilliantly illuminated, the Temporary Museum was thrown open, and a band of music enlivened the scene.'[24] The company included:

> The Duke and Duchess of St. Albans, the Marquis of

Northampton, Earl and Countess Brownlow and Lady Cust. the Hon. the Champion, the Bishop of Lincoln, the Dean of Hereford, Lord Monson, G. T. W. Sibthorp, Esq., the Archdeacon of Lincoln, the Mayor and Mayoress, and most of the members of the Corporation: the company amounted to 400. Dancing was commenced by the Mayor and Lady Cust at 1/2 past eight, and a delightful ball was kept up for several hours. An abundance of refreshment of the richest kind had been provided, comprising the choicest fruits of the season, and altogether the alternation of pleasure with the rapid wheel of intellectual excitement was found a most agreeable and joyous relaxation.[25]

It was on the Saturday evening that members of the Mechanics Institute of Lincoln were invited to the Assembly rooms, to listen to the lectures, and to be shown round the conference museum. They were welcomed by the Marquis of Northampton, who in turn was later thanked by Sir Charles Anderson for the invitation and, 'of the kindness with which the curators had consented to explain all matters of archaeological interest which might excite their attention'.[26]

R. A. Cracroft of Hackthorn reported that he had never seen so many county people in Lincoln, and that the meeting had, 'excited a great deal of interest even amongst people not much given to antiquarian study. They seem earnest in pursuit of the ancient, and mixed much less humbug with their proceedings than I expected would be the case.'[27] However this has to be contrasted with Henry Crabb Robinson who confessed that he was only at the Lincoln meeting for mutually shared social pleasures, being, 'one of the least learned Archaeologians who attend'.[28]

As a consequence of Institute visits Gainsborough Old Hall and Stow church were given much publicity, the former as to its dating and sequence of building: it was reported that (to confound the Institute's theories?),

> a Memoir will very shortly be published by Mr. Bowden of Gainsboro', from the pen of Mr. Stark, in which it will be tolerably satisfactorily shewn that the Old Hall, as now existing, has been erected at least at four different periods, and these somewhat remote from each other.[29]

At Stow the visiting experts were astonished: it *was* an important Saxon church. There is no doubt that this visit stirred up a hornet's nest, to judge from the minutes of a vestry meeting held in October:

> it is evident... that a class of men calling themselves Archaeologists have resolved to fasten upon the Church of Stowe and the Parish funds, that they may use *both* for the display of their skill in the Science of Antiquities... to spend the money of hard working men in pursuit of the luxurious and refined pleasures of the wealthy would be a crime...[30]

The *Mercury* supported Earl Brownlow's proposal that a subscription fund should be established for the restoration of Stow's church, 'at once to leave a permanent record of the visit, and to show the important benefits that may be derived from the labours of such a society.'[31]

At this time work was proceeding on the cathedral, especially the central tower's western side, and the roof of the Morning Prayer Chapel. The cathedral was open daily; special arrangements were made for the inspection of the West Front - a contemporary time sheet records 'fixing a scaffold in the Church for Rev. Proff. Williss and Archaeologists by order of the Precentor.'[32] At the concluding general meeting of the Institute the Dean and Chapter were thanked, 'for the facilities afforded in the examination of the Minster, and their hospitality and friendly encouragement'.[33] In reply the Dean expressed their appreciation of the Institute's visit to Lincoln: 'they had received many valuable hints as to their cathedral, by which they hoped to profit'.[34] He may well have been alluding to the argument concerning the great east window, whose eighteenth-century glass was criticised in Charles Winston's lecture.[35] At their next meeting the Lincolnshire Architectural Society, after reference to their involvement in the Institute's visit, considered the replacing of, 'the very bad stained glass in the east window of the minster, with the very best that can be procured'.[36] The committee launched their appeal with a donation of £250 from the Dean and Chapter: it was 1855 before the glazing was complete, with a design setting forth 'the Scheme of Human Redemption'.[37]

So, with the departure of the Institute party two public subscriptions were underway. The meeting was a great success despite the inclement weather which saw much rain and little sunshine.[38] 'The learned men assembled all acknowledged that the Institute had never met with so hospitable a reception as in old Lincoln... all parties are loud in their praise of the liberality and good taste displayed by the ancient city.'[39] Earl Brownlow was so delighted that he invited the mayor to spend a few days with him at Belton; Terence would have been well satisfied.

Acknowledgement

I am grateful to Christopher Sturman for commenting on an earlier draft of this paper.

Notes

1 See *L.R.S.M.*, 4 August 1848. For the origins of the Institute see Philippa Levine, *The Amateur and the Professional: Antiquarians, Historians and Archaeologists in Victorian England 1838-1886* (Cambridge, 1986), *passim* and David Wehterall, 'From Canterbury to York: the foundation of the Institute', in *Building on the Past. Papers Celebrating 150 Years of the Royal Archaeological Institute*, edited by Balise Vyner, (1994), 8-21.

2 *Memoirs Illustrative of the History and Antiquities of the City of York, Communicated to the Annual Meeting of the Archaeological Institute of Great Britain, held at York, July, 1846* (1848), xv.

3 For a fuller account of the Trollope family, see T.R. Leach, 'Edward Trollope and the Lincoln Diocesan Architectural Society', in *Some Historians of Lincolnshire*, edited by Christopher Sturman, Occasional Papers in Lincolnshire History and Archaeology, 9 (1992), 13-26.

4 *L.C.*, 21 July 1848.

5 *L.R.S.M.*, 21 July 1848. The Lincoln Topographical Society presents something of a problem for local historians: the printed *Transactions* indicate that it flourished in the early 1840s.Could the donation from them in 1848 be that of a moribund printing society with a healthy bank balance? See Christopher Sturman, 'Lincolnshire', in *English County Histories. A Guide*, edited by C. R. J. Currie and C. P. Lewis (1994), 251.

6 These categories were Antiquities From Foreign Countries; Early British & Roman Antiquities Discovered in Great Britain; Anglo-Saxon & Early Irish; Ornaments of Gold; Medieval Antiquities, Arms & Armour; Sacred & Personal Ornaments; Seals & Signet Rings; Paintings, Sculpture, & Sepulchral Brasses Out of County; and finally, Sepulchral Brasses of Lincolnshire. See *Memoirs Illustrative of the History and Antiquities of the County and City of Lincoln Communicated to the Annual meeting of the Archaeological Institute of Great Britain, held at Lincoln, July 1848* (1850), xxvii-lx.

7 Philip N. Brockeden submitted rubbings of inscriptions in St Peter at Gowts' church, Lincoln: could this be of the Mr Brockeden who was then employed as an assistant engineer in the Lincoln area during the construction of the Great Northern Railway (*Illustrated London News*, 11 November 1848, 304)?

8 *Memoirs... Lincoln*, xxvi, ix.

9 *Memoirs Illustrative of the History and Antiquities of the City of Norwich. Communicated to the Annual Meeting of the Archaeological Institute of Great Britain, held in Norwich, July/August, 1847* (1848), ix.

10 *Memoirs... Lincoln*, xvii.

11 *ibid.*, xvii & xviii; according to *L.R.S.M.*, 4 August 1848, the special train was made up of carriages lent by the Midland Railway.

12 *L.R..S.M.*, 4 August 1848.

13 See *Lincolnshire Architectural Society. Third Report*, 1846, (1847) 11-26; also *Memoirs... Lincoln*, xxxiii.

14 L.A.O. Cor. B 5/4/63/1/19.

15 *Stow Church Restored 1846-1866*, edited by Mark Spurrell, L.R.S., 75 (1984), *passim*.

16 *L.R.S.M.*, 4 August 1848.

17 *Memoirs... Lincoln*, 140-44.

18 *L.R.S.M.*, 28 July 1848; *Memoirs... Lincoln*, xvi, states that over 300, including over 50 ladies attended.

19 See *L.R.S.M.*, 28 July 1848.

20 *ibid.*, for more detail.

21 *ibid.*

22 *L.R.S.M.*, 21 July 1848; *L.C.*, 21 July 1848.

23 *ibid.*

24 *Memoirs... Lincoln*, xvii.

25 *L.R.S.M.*, 4 August 1848.

26 *Memoirs... Lincoln*, xix.

27 Sir Francis Hill, *Victorian Lincoln* (Cambridge, 1974), 80, quoting ms Cracroft diary.

28 Hill, *Victorian Lincoln*, 80, quoting *Diary of Henry Crabb Roninson* (1872 edition) II, 294-95.

29 *L.R.S.M.*, 11 August 1848. I have not been able to trace Stark's pamphlet, though the following year (1849) his *Visitor's Guide to Gainsborough and Neighbourhood* was printed by Bowden.

30 Spurrell, *Stow Church Restored*, 28.

31 *L.R.S.M.*, 11 August 1848.

32 L.A.O. D&C Audit Papers C iv 58, Artisan Weekly Bills, 22 July 1848; this work is not costed nor is its removal recorded. See also D. M. Williamson, *Lincoln Muniments*, Lincoln Minster Pamphlets, 8 (1956), 11.

33 *Memoirs... Lincoln*, xxiii.

34 *ibid.*

35 *Memoirs... Lincoln*, 95.

36 *The Lincolnshire Architectural Society. Fifth Report*, 1848, (1849) 3, 4; see also Terence R. Leach [edited by Christopher Sturman], 'One hundred and fifty years: the origins of the Society for Lincolnshire History and Archaeology', *Lincolnshire Past & Present*, 18 (Winter 1994/95), 3-7.

37 Hill, *Victorian Lincoln*, 265.

38 *Illustrated London News*, 30 September 1848, 293.

39 *L.C.*, 4 August 1848.

'Much Ceremony and Aplomb': The Visit of the Lincoln Diocesan Architectural Society to Market Rasen and Neighbourhood, June 1862

Douglas Boyce

In September 1993 Terence gave a talk to the Market Rasen Society about this 1862 visit. He was in his element, referred to his own long membership of successor societies, and enjoyed reading from the original scroll presented to the parish during the visit. It was his intention to write up the excursion for *Lincolnshire Past & Present*, but he was unfortunately unable to do so.

The major source for this article is the 13 June 1862 issue of the *Lincoln, Rutland and Stamford Mercury*. The visit was also formally recorded in the *Reports and Papers* of the Associated Architectural Societies.[1] The newspaper account, taking up most of a page, gives a much fuller and more lively account.

> 'In Trollope's day, meetings of the Society were always conducted with much ceremony and aplomb, and attracted considerable publicity in the local, and sometimes the national press.'[2]

About 9 a.m. on Thursday 5 June 1862, a large gathering assembled in Market Rasen. No doubt some people had stayed the previous night at the White Hart, a coaching inn near the market place, and others had arrived by early morning trains from either Lincoln or Grimsby. The district had been chosen for the Lincoln Diocesan Architectural Society's June visit. (It also managed to make an excursion to Leicester and Bosworth Field in August.) In 1861 the Society had given five pounds towards the restoration of the parish church. (This gift however was omitted, with some other donations, from the framed printed list which was placed in the church.) Possibly knowledge that this work was then in progress, according to the plans of James Fowler, a professional member of the Society who had joined in 1860, the fairly recent restoration of Tupholme church at Middle Rasen, as well as the possibility of access by train, would have suggested the area as being ripe for a visitation. There had been a preliminary meeting at the Corn Exchange on Wednesday 19 March to make arrangements, but unfortunately the honorary secretary, the Rev. Edward Trollope, MA,FSA, honorary prebendary of Lincoln (Fig. 1), was not present so the clergy and gentry assembled had to adjourn their meeting until the following Saturday.[3] The setting up of the local committee would probably have been done at this meeting and perhaps early ideas on the accommodation, transport, ceremonies and the places to be visited. It seems that the Society at this time could not function without the presence of its honorary secretary, and many members would have been in awe of him. It would not have been wise to say, or think, anything contrary to his thoughts.

Fig. 1: Edward Trollope, 1817-1893. (Lincolnshire County Council, Libraries)

The visit started with the shell of the parish church and there the secretary read his notes. These always started with the Domesday entry. This was followed by a few facts then known of the manorial history of the town and the features of the church. At the time of the visit the wall of the north aisle had been demolished and a new one constructed. The wall on the south side remained propped up while new windows were being inserted. Subscribers to the restoration funds had complained of 'the impolicy of sewing a piece of new cloth to an old garment'. Others had thought the tower needed restoration more than the church.[4] Their guide pointed out that 'the external features of the late nave, and especially the north aisle, were not only of a poor, late character, but were also in a most dilapidated condition...' (Fig. 2). He wished that there were even more new work by lengthening the nave and rebuilding the chancel. A drawing in the Ross manuscripts[5] shows rather pleasant Perpendicular windows on this side, but the new work was 'made to correspond to the earlier and better proportions of the old fabric...', in this case Early English, which the Society promoted as being the most suitable style for small village churches. The visitors then looked at the 'St. Poll almshouses' not realising that much brickwork as well as the stone quoins remained from the original building. The 'humble row' in fact remained much as it was first built, despite its restoration after a fire in 1822 when the thatched roof was destroyed. They were also told that 'the new school a little way out of town, off the Willingham Road, under the direction of Mr James Fowler' was 'worthy of a visit on the part of such of our members as have time for the purpose'. Mr Fowler thus had two major commissions in the town at the same time. He was also busy nearby with the rectory at Linwood and the parsonage at Snelland. It seems that he was not present at the outing. Members cannot have had time that day to visit De Aston School because shortly after 10 a.m. the party took to the well filled carriages, of various descriptions, provided for the journey. (Presumably some mem-

Fig. 2: Market Rasen Parish Church 1853, showing the new porch; a pencil sketch by E. G. S. Scobell, probably the father of the vicar. (The vicar and churchwardens of Market Rasen)

bers used their own; it would be interesting to know how the others were recruited.) The details of the notes read show that Trollope must have spent time earlier in the year visiting on his own each of the sites on the tour; for Market Rasen he must have come once more, as the published paper describes the church after the completion of the restoration in October (Fig. 3).[6] In this he only added one complaint, about the pulpit, 'the effect of the whole is not altogether satisfactory'. It seems to have been moved to the south side when further alterations took place in 1877 but otherwise remains in the form that was criticised.

As the weather was fair there was some competition for outside seats. The procession received curious looks from the inhabitants, who seemed to them to be just waking up. Further carriages and some outriders joined the procession during the morning.

At Middle Rasen the bells were ringing to greet the visitors and also at Kirkby following the call at West Rasen. Some of the party were now wet from the driving rain and sharp shower. A small group was in the church to receive the visitors. The drive on to Kingerby was also spoilt by rain. The rest of the morning session was spent at Thornton-le-Moor and South Kelsey. The party then headed for Holton-le-Moor:

> HOLTON - A Sumptuous Luncheon. To this place the excursionists proceeded ... at the invitation of T. J. Dixon, Esq., the High Sheriff. After passing through the church which had been re-built by Mr. Dixon, that gentleman met them at the entrance of his grounds and conducted them to a spacious marquee decorated with festoons of evergreens, flags &c. Over the entrance were the words in ivy leaves "Welcome to the Architectural Society", and right glad and fortunate were the visitors to meet with so cordial a reception, for the rain had fallen faster and heavier for the previous hour, damping the spirits of even the most jolly, the Sheriff presided at the cross table, and Mrs. and the Misses Dixon were also present. The "creature comforts" of the visitors - about 130 in number, having been most liberally supplied, and the time for departure drawing near, the Sheriff drank to the health of his numerous and grateful guests. He expressed himself as exceedingly happy to see them all, and regretted very much that they must take their departure so quickly, as

Fig. 3: Market Rasen Parish Church, an architect's print published by R. Hackett of Market Rasen, showing Fowler's intended plans. (The vicar and churchwardens of Market Rasen)

> the arrangements of the day's programme, he suggested could not be altered. The society, whose members had done him the honour to partake of his hospitality, was of great utility and value, and he trusted it might continue to prosper. He also hoped that they might have the pleasure of meeting together on many similar occasions.

In the leader paragraph the *Stamford Mercury* had said:

> The High Sheriff... entertained them... in a princely style, the elegant and sumptuous banquet provided for them in a spacious marquee... causing them to forget the pitiless storm that was raging without. The marquee was full fifty feet in length, and about 130 ladies and gentlemen partook of the Sheriff's unbounded hospitality. The tables were covered with delicacies and vases of flowers, and wines were pressed upon the guests by attentive waiters ad libitum, while a band unseen "voluptuous music breathed". The appointments were all of the best quality and the admiration of everybody, the pleasure and comfort of the guests having been anticipated in every possible way.

Trollope in his reply said that Mr Dixon had the honour of occupying the highest post in the county and his kind and cordial recognition of the Society gave *éclat* to the gathering. The county was renowned for its hospitality, though some people considered it a mark of their barbarity. He was proud of it and hoped they would continue to be guilty of such barbarity. The Rev. C. J. Myers, of Flintham, Notts., proposed the health of the High Sheriff and Sir Charles Anderson, Bt., of Lea, that of Mrs Dixon; he felt sure that some delicate hands had superintended the arrangement of the delicacies and the decorations. The sumptuous repast had not been surpassed at any of their peregrinations. The Rev. J. Brown, of Great Limber, proposed the health of the Misses Dixon.

As the rain continued the guests then heard the paper on the Roman villa at Walesby read by the Rev. W. B. Philpot, rector of Walesby. The Rev. Felix Laurent, of Saleby, then proposed the health of Mr Philpot with thanks for his interesting paper and Mr J. Dixon, of Caistor, proposed prosperity to the Society making comments at some length on its great utility and the good it had already effected. The rain had by then ceased and the visitors, except for those in a few carriages which then left the group, drove to Nettleton in bright sunshine. After his visitors had departed Mr Dixon made the most of the marquee and entertained about seventy of his labourers and, on the Friday, their wives and children. It appears that the church at Holton was only briefly inspected: Mr Dixon had rebuilt this a few years earlier and they did not expect to find any ancient features there. Caistor was the next stop on the itinerary where two fragments of the old wall were examined. The party then went on to Walesby and, as the weather stayed fine, could visit both the Roman villa and the church.

At 6:30 p.m. the group returned to Market Rasen, after covering about thirty miles, being played in by the Rasen Volunteer Corps band. Following tea at the White Hart the visitors proceeded at 8 p.m. to the Market Hall where the Society's temporary museum had been set up. Sir Charles Anderson took the chair as the bishop had unfortunately had to go to Eton on business. He reminded those present of the objects of the Society, including the production of a complete history of the county. They should try to exact all the information they could about ancient remains and monuments. After a short discourse on the history of the English nation he referred to a book in the temporary exhibition, a history of drainage in 1660 and gave a list of food bought for a dinner the commissioners had in London. The vicar, S. G. Scobell (Fig. 4) then read an address from the inhabitants of the town to the Society hoping that the Society and the inhabitants would be gratified by the visit. Irvin Eller, rector of Faldingworth and one of the local secretaries for the Stow Archdeaconry, responded reading from the scroll with decorative bobbles which was presented to the town and still remains in the parish chest. The Society was pleased that one of its own professional members was superintending the restoration of the church. The next item was Trollope reading his paper 'Anne Askewe, the Martyr'. The Rev. H. R. Lloyd, of Owersby, in proposing a vote of thanks to the honorary secretary, thought that they could congratulate themselves on the better feeling at that time than when Anne lived under such persecuting laws; Canon Sing seconded the vote.[7] It is interesting that a Roman Catholic clergyman was present let alone speaking. Membership of the Society was not open but by election and this meeting does not seem to have been open to the public. Trollope returned thanks. Their meetings

> brought men of all classes together - men of old and esteemed families, such as their chairman represented, and men of the middle classes, and with these two classes, amongst whom he had found men of as gentlemanly and noble a nature as amongst those who were considered their superiors... so long as they were Christians they might sink their differences and make friends with one another, so long as conscience was not compromised.

Fig. 4: Sanford George Scobell (c.1822-1868), vicar of Market Rasen (1846-66). (The vicar and churchwardens of Market Rasen)

(The lower classes had to wait until the public meeting the following evening before they had a chance to join the gathering.) The Revs Irvin Eller and A. S. Wilde proposed a vote of thanks to the chairman and he also returned thanks agreeing with the sentiments expressed by the various speakers that evening. 'The meeting then broke up, and the excellent Volunteer band played some spirited music in front of the White Hart until the hour for retiring to rest had arrived.'

The proceedings resumed on the Friday. After a few miles the scenery improved. (The scenery in the immediate vicinity of Market Rasen was not really up to the standard approved of by the Society!) The weather 'which was fair during the morning, became hostile as the day wore on, the rain descended in torrents, and the wind blowing almost a hurricane'. The party started off at Linwood and proceeded to Snarford, Holton Beckering, West Torrington and at last found a haven at Hainton where they arrived cold, wet and hungry. They took tiffin at the Commercial Hotel but felt sure that if the Heneage family had been at home they would have received a hearty welcome there. (Had they also hoped to be invited for a meal?) Calls for bitter were incessant. In the afternoon they went on to Sixhills and Tealby where they visited Bayons Manor and approved of the architecture, its setting and the good taste and liberality of the late Mr d'Eyncourt. (Charles Tennyson d'Eyncourt had died the previous year.) They would have spent longer looking around the outer walls if it had not been raining. No doubt the party was again disappointed that George Tennyson d'Eyncourt, a member, was not at home. The greater attendance on Thursday was attributed to the hospitality of Mr Dixon.

As the party returned to Market Rasen it was met by the Volunteer Rifle Corps headed by its band. The carriages followed them to the market place, lined up, saluted the passing carriages and fired three rounds of blank cartridges. This all took place during a drenching downfall.

The excursionists were allowed a short interval to perform their ablutions and make their evening toilets before the remaining seventy sat down to dinner at the White Hart. Henry Boucherett, Esq. presided and Trollope officiated as vice chairman. 'Several ladies were present.' The public meeting started at 8 o'clock so speech making was limited (in their view). The band of the Rifle Corps played during the meal.

The chairman proposed the Queen, the Prince of Wales with the rest of the Royal Family. S. G. Scobell in proposing the toast of the Society, the Bishop (the absent president) and the Secretary, admitted he knew little of architecture and archaeology. He had much to learn from the Society. He thanked them for subscribing to the restoration fund 'and also for the instruction given to him and the restoration committee by the secretary'. Trollope rose to his feet and spoke on behalf of the Society; he had been asked to answer for the laity, high and low, 'for many working men were members' so he had to answer for every class of man. He was convinced that as long as the Society continued to be a working society and did not meddle with what did not concern it, 'the members would ever receive the good of their fellow men and women on occasions like the present'. This was greeted with loud cheering. The chairman proposed the Local Committee of Market Rasen coupled with the name of Mr Saffery. Mr George Saffery, a local solicitor, responded. The Rev. H. R. Lloyd proposed the Lincolnshire volunteer movement. Captain Goodson had provided their dinner, being the publican at the White Hart, and the excursionists had been inspirited by the band meeting them in the rain. Lieutenant Sharpley replied to the toast.

The Rev. George Atkinson, of Stow, proposed the chairman and he replied, admitting that he was extremely ignorant of all matters relating to architecture, but the Society was doing a good job. William Waldo Cooper, vicar of West Rasen and brother-in-law of S. G. Scobell, gave 'the ladies' and Ensign Goodson responded on their behalf and concluded by singing 'The Peasant Man'. (This was not the first occasion on which he had responded for the ladies.) The company arrived a few minutes late at the Market Hall which was filled to overflowing. A large portion of the audience belonged to the working classes. Members of the Society sat on the platform and Sir Charles Anderson again presided. In his introductory remarks, referring to the brass rubbings taken from monuments which were displayed on the walls, he mentioned humorously the scantiness of the ladies' dresses, compared with the amplitude of the 1860s. It was then Trollope's task to talk on the curiosities on show:

> These consisted of the rubbings aforesaid, of engravings and photographs of ecclesiastical buildings, books and sundry antiquities; a Cranmer bible of 1572, a translation of Doomsday for Lincolnshire, &c., a processional cross (found in the coffin of an Abbot of Lincoln cathedral), Roman urns and other pottery, bracelets, some curious keys, Nuremberg salvers and a peg tankard from Bayons Manor, an ancient British shield found in the Trent in 1842, two gad whips... &c., &c.. Mr. Trollope commenced with the most ancient Egyptian curiosities, and passed thence to the Roman, Saxon and Mediaeval specimens concluding with some remarks to the value of such studies. His remarks extended over a considerable time, and yet were necessarily brief accounts of each article. They were lucid, and consequently easily understood, and were listened to with marked attention. At the conclusion a vote of thanks was unanimously accorded to Mr. Trollope on the proposition of the Rev. W. B. Philpot and Rev. H. R. Lloyd and a vote of thanks with three cheers having been given for the chairman, on the motion of the Rev. W. Cooper and the Rev. S. G. Scobell, the meeting terminated.

By modern standards the Society had a great jumble of exhibits on show but few present would have been familiar with photographs of buildings on the continent or in Egypt. Nor would most have seen the artefacts dug up in their own locality as there was at that time (as at present) no museum for archaeology in the county. The Society's report gives further details of the exhibits: photographs and prints of Rome, plans and pavements of Roman country houses in the county, other illustrations 'exhibiting the mode in which such buildings were heated, roofed, furnished, and drained', statues, personal ornaments, glass, weapons and implements of Roman times, photographs of 'the most remarkable buildings' of Rome, Florence, Pisa, Caen, Bayeux, Rouen, Paris, etc., views of English cathedrals and Lincolnshire churches, Saxon spear heads, shield bosses, knives, girdle suspenders, clasps, pins, combs beads and scissors.

The meeting had ended but the press had some further comments. The visit had not been so well attended as some previous ones and the 'specimens composing the museum' were not so attractive as on some previous occasions, but the meeting was considered a success. Those in the party had arrived and made themselves sociable to one another. The comforts at the White Hart made up for any discomfort on the journey. Trollope was the 'life and soul' of the Society and the trouble he had taken over its organisation was a 'labour of love'.

Notes

1 *A.A.S.R.P.*, VI, 2, xciv-viii, 117-75

2 The quotation is taken from T. R. Leach, 'Edward Trollope and the Lincoln Diocesan Architectural Society', in *Some Historians of Lincolnshire*, edited by Christopher Sturman, Occasional Papers in Lincolnshire History and Archaeology, 9 (1992), 21.

3 *L.R.S.M.*, 28 March 1862.

4 *L.R.S.M.*, 30 May 1862. No mention is made anywhere of the disappearance of an old piscina and the remains of the Perpendicular roodscreen which were recorded in 1846: see N. S. Harding, ed., *Bonney's Church Notes* (Lincoln, 1937), 62

5 In the Local Studies Collection Lincoln Central Library, Vol. 4 Walshcroft, after p.152.

6 *A.A.S.R.P.*, VI, 2 (1862), 140

7 Thomas Sing was the first diocesan priest to serve the Church of the Holy Rood Market Rasen. He was there from 1859 to 1864. (Information from Fr. P. Bailey). For Sing, I follow the formal report in A.A.S.R.P., VI, 2 (1862), xcvi. The *Stamford Mercury* account mentions, presumably erroneously, 'The Rev. Canon. Long'. See Philip Bailey, *The Roman Catholic Mission and Church of the Holy Rood Market Rasen Lincolnshire* (Market Rasen, 1995).

Travels with an Aunt: Mary Bourne Revisited

Valerie Purton

The time is ripe for a paper on the role of aunts in literature: E. M. Forster, Joseph Conrad and Graham Greene would figure in it and certainly Tennyson would loom large. Alfred's first recorded letter was to his aunt, Mary Anne Fytche. John Waite, his headmaster at Louth, observed that the Tennyson boys' poetic genius was 'inherited and fostered by their parents, and excited by a good and kind aunt'.[1]

This paper is not, however, about Mary Anne, nor about the other obvious contender for aunt-as-muse, the celebrated Elizabeth Russell, but about the most obscure of Tennyson's aunts, the 'mad Calvinist', Mary Bourne. It is therefore also about the arbitrariness and unfairness of history, where cheap epithets are attached to and grow like barnacles around the names of the dead, obscuring their identities. Thus Peter Levi in the most recent Tennyson biography indulges in caricature rather than historical analysis: 'Mary was morose, a hypochondriac, a wanderer between health resorts and an addict of dramatic quarrels with landladies and intimates. She was a crazy Calvinist...' [2] I hope to free Mary Bourne from such crippling exaggerations and to suggest that there is need for a re-reading of many of the characters in the Tennyson story, to open the way for a more flexible approach to both life and works.

Mary was the oldest of the four children of George and Mary Tennyson and was born in 1776. Her sister Elizabeth was born in 1777 and her brothers George and Charles in 1778 and 1784. Much has been made of the fact that Mary and George, thought of as the least happy of the children, were the two who were boarded during their early years with their grandparents. Elizabeth and Charles, who stayed at home, were the most obviously well-balanced and successful. However there is much evidence, both historical and literary (one thinks of Fanny Price in *Mansfield Park*) that the 'boarding out' practice was widespread and that it was in the interests of bonding different generations of a family. The concept of the 'nuclear family' is after all very much a twentieth century one. There is no real evidence that George's unhappy temperament in particular would have been less unhappy had he remained as a child under his father's critical eye. There is evidence to the contrary, indeed: grandparents could be particularly doting and young George is known to have been tenderly treated by his widowed grandfather, old Michael Tennyson.

Mary grew up, no doubt, in the shadow of her beautiful younger sister Elizabeth, but history has tended to present the two as opposites rather than seeing a shared set of family characteristics in both. Elizabeth's letters can indeed dance on the page. One is reminded of Beatrice in *Much Ado About Nothing*: 'a star danced, and under that was I born'. It does not follow though that Mary was at the opposite extreme - a sort of sullen Martha to Elizabeth's Mary.[3] In Mary's letters too there is wit and a wry self-deprecation. After her marriage to the dissenter, John Bourne, she wrote frequently to her mother. When her mother died her main correspondents became her sister and brothers, whom she addresses warmly and affectionately: 'Dearest, kindest brother and sister' is a typical beginning. Her letters to her father, on the other hand share the querulous, self-justifying tone that seems to have come over all his children when they addressed him. It is almost as if they mimic his own characteristic voice. Mary describes herself in one letter as 'one already trampled upon by most of her kindred, my foes are truly those of my own house' and even joins the 'begging letter' queue dominated by her indigent brother George.[4] She is negotiating with Elizabeth (made financially secure by her marriage to Matthew Russell) to accept some coach horses and has the temerity to ask her father for money for their harness: 'a Hundred Pound to my private purse would much lighten my wordly cares'. Old George points out, reasonably enough, that '[I] have great advances to make to your brothers, who have both large families, you have none...'[5]

When writing to her siblings she is full of a gentle, self-deprecating humour which suggests her character more nearly than the letters to old George. Thus she tells Charles:

> I am groaning under mumps and dissappointment in being obliged to relinquish the hope of seeing yourself and my dear

> father at present. My face is half enveloped in flannel and though I might travel, I am not *viewly* for any but the eyes of love, and you might have other optics than your own at Tealby.[6]

Her love and admiration for Charles in particular are evident. She is proud of his worldly success: 'we did during your late campaign especially trudge after you most eagerly'; 'your affairs are so connected with the topsy turvy world!... you are at present in the foreground of a terrific picture.'[7] When Charles found himself embroiled (uncharacteristically) in a duel, she wrote a letter which is evidently tear-stained, about 'my dear brother and his persecuter... the Stamford affair... my eyes are nearly closed with weeping.'[8]

This interest in worldly affairs tempers her Calvinism at every point. Even her most fervent letters to her father begin with references to the weather: 'The weather promises to cheer up and renovate people and things, but I believe the Lord's Judgements are at present on the earth may his people learn thereby...'[9] She refers to herself as a 'solitary pilgrim', but the letters are far too concerned with earthly matters - servants, health, the plumbing - to suggest a spiritual nature. Even the famous anecdote which has guaranteed her place in history - 'Alfred, Alfred, when I look at you I think of the words of Holy Scripture - "Depart from me, ye cursed, into everlasting fire"' - when read in the context of the letters, acquires a tinge of humour - lugubrious, melancholic, but strangely innocent too - not at all the humourlessly vindictive comment it seems out of context.[10]

The Bournes seem to have lived a relatively settled married life emotionally, though there were no children, possibly because Mary did not marry until she was in her mid thirties. Mary travelled widely (as did her sister Elizabeth) for the sake of her health, but again, in the context of an age terrified of consumption, this was fairly common practice. Throughout her travels she wrote affectionately to her husband, who followed her progress and sent her gifts of game. Her letters to him are warm, affectionate and largely about her health (inevitably, as that is the reason they are apart). When he was ill with gout she nursed him assiduously, but again deprecated her own powers: 'I am become... a "Body Servant" but so insufficient that I fear he may shortly be obliged to have recourse to your prophetic council.'[11] When her husband died in 1851 she did seem to find comfort in her faith: 'I am borne up miraculously under my accumulating trials - the last of which cannot be worse.'[12]

It was in her last decades that Mary Bourne came into her own - no longer a daughter or a wife, but a dedicated and loving aunt. The recipient of the last two letters quoted was brother Charles's eldest son, George Hildeyard Tennyson d'Eyncourt. He was a quiet, dutiful, rather sad figure whose life was blighted by the death of Emily Lytton with whom he had been deeply in love. He never married and he and his aunt seem to have found in each other a quiet comfort, as of two gentle characters overshadowed by brighter stars. It is to her nieces and nephews that 'Aunt Bourne' writes most cheerfully and humorously. She seems to have been godmother to several of Charles's children - writing proudly of 'my four' - but young George inspired the best letters of all. I shall quote two at length to give their flavour. The first thanks George for sending John Bourne some tobacco from the Ionian Islands:

> My dearest George, I have heard of pleasure pipes and medicinal pipes; your whiffs of extended essence bear no such circumscribed limits, their exhilarating fumes now stimulate my heart to transmit you volumes of [happy] returns, but the immense distance between the deputy King of Greece and poor old Aunty of Dalby has paralysed my coarse and frivolous mind and rendered my ink stagnant.[13]

She involved young George in her activities and could be positively light-hearted when writing to him:

> My dearest George,
> I see good judgement in attending to your humble request of two lines when two hundred could not explain the whys and wherefores respecting our vacillating movements after people places and things... we have much pleasure at the thoughts of receiving you soon at the Sea and of giving you a good ducking. The shore here is too flat for the purpose but Worthing is a quiet, pretty, healthy little place and plenty of fish...

She encouraged him with her attention:

> You speak of invitations but no *accomplishment*! Now I am meditating a Christmas or New Year's invitation in which my poor dear husband joins me in requesting the pleasure of our dear Nephew Mr. George D'Eyncourt's company... and we are at Home to him at this time to next New Year's Day and hope for an early and favourable answer.'[14]

After John Bourne's death she retained her keen observation and sense of humour, describing (on black-edged mourning paper) her trials with her landlady - 'my smiling lady': 'if permitted I should fly through the roof of the house to escape. Miss Cole's countenance is eligible as far as smiles - wide mouth and wondrous strong teeth can make her but evidently a confirmed Toady!'[15] Even when she admits her desolation to Charles, she remains determined not to be a nuisance to him: 'I am occasionally at my wit's end - I am a stricken deer and all but heart broken. I know for my only substantial consolation that I have *you* for my *Friend* and *Brother*. You could not think for a moment that my insignificant self would assume to intrude upon your host of coming Annual visitants.'[16]

There is no doubt that Aunt Mary Bourne was a grumbler - but even her grumbles have a saving sense of the ludicrous and a Jaques-like relish to them, as when she describes one lodging: 'The water is corrupt and the sewers fraught with putrefaction - what is next awaiting me perhaps I am happily ignorant.'[17] What is often forgotten is that she was for years fondly in touch with neices and nephews from both the d'Eyncourt and the Somersby sides of the family, taking no account of the family quarrel; that she was obviously close enough to Alfred for him to risk arriving, with sister Cecilia and brother Charles, on her doorstep in Dalby at 10 p.m. one night in June 1837 (after the family had moved to High Beech) and that she lovingly fed them, despite the lateness of the hour; and that she alone of his original family attended Alfred's father's funeral in March 1831.

Mary Bourne will always remain a peripheral character. Even in her own lifetime she was overshadowed by more obviously attractive members of her family. She was not the 'mad Calvinist' of the historian/caricaturist however, but a melancholic, loveable, wistful person with a genuine love of her family and a strong sense of duty. She referred to Alfred and his family as 'the dearest and most interesting of my connections' and Alfred spoke fondly of her after her death in 1864.

My starting point for this paper was an address given by Roger Evans at the Tennyson Memorial Service at Bag Enderby on 7 August 1994. In this address the speaker declared his intention to 'come face to face with the Somersby family as it were afresh' and confessed that he was haunted by the words of Elizabeth Russell: 'Don't give credit to all you may be told respecting individuals of the Somersby family.'[18] This modest 'rereading' of Mary Bourne is a contribution to a revisiting of Tennysonism tradition. We are all too aware today that history is a series of interlocking narratives, constantly changing according to the concerns of each new generation. It is important to scrape the barnacles from tradition frequently and, even in the case of minor characters like Mary Bourne, to listen afresh to the voices of the past.

Notes

1 Peter Levi, *Tennyson* (1993), 14.
2 *ibid.*, 16.
3 Elizabeth Russell's memorial window at St Brandon's church, Brancepeth, Co. Durham, is of Martha and Mary: family tradition may itself have tended to polarize the two sisters.
4 L.A.O. T.d'E. H159/4.
5 L.A.O. T.d'E. H159/4.
6 L.A.O. T.d'E. H159/30.
7 L.A.O. T.d'E. H159/29.
8 L.A.O. T.d'E. H159/26.
9 L.A.O. T.d'E. H159/9.
10 Quoted, for example, in Christopher Sturman and Valerie Purton, *Poems by Two Brothers: The Lives, Work and Influence of George Clayton Tennyson and Charles Tennyson d'Eyncourt* (Stamford, 1993), 1. Cf. however Arthur Hallam's comment in a letter to Emily Tennyson of 16 February 1833: 'I was indignant to hear of Mrs. Bourne's petty spite against Miss Fytche, & poor Mary. I give Mrs. Bourne up. Where's the good of all her ostentatious Calvinism, if it cannot teach her to restrain her temper or direct her affections?' *The Letters of Arthur Henry Hallam*, edited by Jack Kolb (Columbus, 1981), 731. The notion itself is borrowed from Henry IV Part 1, 3:3, 29-30: 'I never see thy face but I think upon hell-fire.' Could Alfred possibly have used his literary knowledge to *invent* an anecdote to epitomize his aunt's character? We only have his word for its veracity.
11 L.A.O. T.d'E. H146/5
12 L.A.O. T.d'E. H146/9.
13 Quoted by Roger Evans, *Tennyson Research Bulletin*, 6, 3 (1994), 187.
14 L.A.O. T.d'E. H146/5.
15 L.A.O. T.d'E. H146/8.
16 L.A.O. T.d'E. H146/10.
17 L.A.O. T.d'E. H146/14.
18 *Tennyson Research Bulletin*, 6, 3 (1994), 183-90.

The Dogs' Meat Man: The Origins of a Victorian Nickname

Jim Murray

The Tealby family of Charles Tennyson d'Eyncourt (1784-1861), MP, FRS, FSA, uncle of Poet Laureate Alfred Tennyson (1809-1892),[1] had a private language of nicknames for their friends, social acquaintances, servants and relatives. By and large these nicknames were apt, witty, amusing and incisive. They were mostly good-humoured and not malicious unlike the nicknames given to them by their Somersby cousins.[2]

Charles Tennyson (1808-1879), Alfred's elder brother, was known in Tealby as 'the Dogs' Meat Man'. This name was given to him by his naval cousin Edwin Clayton Tennyson d'Eyncourt (1818-1903) who described him as 'going round in a rabbit skin looking like the dog's [*sic*] meat man'[3]. Edwin, in his turn, was known by his Somersby relatives as 'The Snob' - probably with good reason.

After Cambridge and ordination Charles became curate at Tealby having been appointed in 1833 to the living by his irascible grandfather old George Tennyson (1750-1835) who allowed him the use of Grove House in the park of Bayons Manor. Arthur Hallam exulted, 'Charley is a Revd! and lives, poor fellow, at Tealby with the old brute who is bruter than ever'.[4] His beautiful cousin Julia said, 'Charles is very nervous in church and does not make a very active country parson.'[5] Old George deplored his 'hubble bubble method' of conducting church services.[6]

Generally, the socially conscious Tealby family disapproved of his presence so close to them. It was not so much that he was disliked personally - in fact his gentle disposition endeared him to his cousins - but that they feared an invasion of 'Goths and Vandals' from Somersby.[7] Cousin Clara wrote 'It would be very disagreeable in many respects to have a tribe of Somersby people near us, as of course Mary would expect to go everywhere we did.' There was also the embarrassing problem of Charles's alleged growing addiction to opium. 'Charles is almost killing himself with laudanum', wrote Clara to her brother George Hildeyard in Corfu.[8] Her younger brother Eustace (1816-1842), destined to die an early death of yellow fever as a captain in the 46th Regiment in Barbados, gave his verdict:

> I cannot help pitying him, poor fellow, for he is the most good-natured fellow in the world and I think he will kill himself soon. I have great regard for him and always shall have.[9]

On 9 March 1835 Charles's great uncle Samuel Turner, the profligate vicar of Grasby, died, leaving him property at Caistor, Nettleton, Cabourne and Grasby. Alfred Tennyson wrote to his friend James Spedding, 'I know not whether you are aware that Charles has become an independent gentleman living in a big house among chalky wolds at Caistor'.[10] On taking up his inheritance Charles adopted the surname Turner, gave up his position at Tealby and settled down to become the much-loved vicar of Grasby, with Louisa Sellwood whom he married on 26 May 1836. (Louisa was the sister of Emily Sellwood who was to marry Alfred Tennyson on 13 June 1850.) The Dogs' Meat Man remained at Grasby writing sonnets and caring for his flock until his death in 1879.

There are two reasons why Charles Tennyson was dubbed 'the Dogs' Meat Man' - one obvious, the other less so. Firstly his elegant Tealby relatives would find their cousin unacceptably scruffy. Secondly they would connect him with a popular music hall ballad of the period. Whilst both these reasons would account for the nickname there may be a deeper and more significant explanation which I shall consider later in this paper.

Among the throng of nineteenth century London street traders with their familiar cries the 'Dogs Meat Man' was prominent.[11] At one time there were upwards of a thousand 'carriers' retailing cats' and dogs' meat which they obtained from the slaughter-houses (knackers) at fourteen shillings per hundred-weight in winter and sixteen shillings in summer. The supply of carcasses to provide this meat came from the 100,000 horses and mules working daily in London for brewers, coal merchants and cab and bus companies. Many of these poor animals died in harness especially in cold weather. Seven hundred and twenty horses were killed each week in the metropolis. Men removing dead horses were a common sight on the streets of Victorian London. (A runaway horse once impaled itself on the railing of the Gloucester Place home of Clara Tennyson d'Eyncourt.)

In the early nineteenth century the cat population of the United Kingdom was estimated at some seven million. There were at least 300,000 in London. There was no shortage of customers and one 'carrier' reckoned he amassed a thousand pounds at the business. After a while, though, there were so many at the trade that there was barely a living in it. Often only a penny or halfpenny per pound could be reckoned on, and complaints of losses from bad debts were common.

A typical dealer wore a shiny hat, black plush waistcoat and sleeves, a blue apron, corduroy trousers, and a blue and white spotted handkerchief round his neck (Fig. 1). The dogs' meat man would push his gaudily painted large wheeled hand cart around the City and West End. The meat was carved up into square wafers, using the lid of the cart as a block, and sold in penn'orths on skewers. No doubt in view of the widespread poverty in Victorian London it would not be just cats and dogs but humans who enjoyed these wares. Food hygiene legislation was in its infancy.[12]

The dogs' meat man, like many London street characters, was the subject of popular songs. Many of these were in a long tradition of the broadside ballad. Favourite themes were Royalty, Rape and Murder. The ballads were printed on one side of a sheet of paper which sold for a halfpenny. Music was not

Fig. 1: 'Cats' Meat' Man, King William Walk, 1885. (Spurgeon Collection, Greenwich Local History Library)

printed but the ballads were set to tunes which everybody knew. These Victorian street ballads reflecting the social life of the times, found their way into the repertoire of the Victorian music hall.

The d'Eyncourt family were familiar with the dogs' meat man and his music hall character. Throughout his long parliamentary career Charles Tennyson d'Eyncourt had kept a house at 4 Park Street Westminster. The family knew the stark contrasts of London life. They would have often seen the dogs' meat man from their carriage as they made their way to balls, dinners, soirées, drawing rooms and theatre. Their friendship with the Duke of Sussex (nicknamed 'His Royal Hainess') assured them entry to court society.[13] D'Eyncourt's three pretty daughters Julia, Clara and Ellen were presented at Court; Julia once danced in the same quadrille with the young Queen Victoria and Prince Albert.[14]

Not only did the d'Eyncourts attend Italian opera, classical concerts, and serious (sometimes French) theatre during the London season, they were also avid patrons of the more frivolous vaudeville and music hall entertainments and were themselves no mean Thespians. The male members of the family would have been patrons of 'Song and Supper rooms' during their sojourns in the capital. The whole family was musically and theatrically talented and delighted in all things dramatic. Indeed, Charles himself displayed from an early age oratorical gifts which were to stand him in good stead during his long Parliamentary career.[15] Whilst a pupil at Lincoln School he had been chosen by its Headmaster, the Rev. John Carter, to declaim a poem of introduction at the annual Speech Day (Potation Day) on 12 February 1795 attended by ecclesiastical and civic dignitaries and, no doubt, his doting father, old George Tennyson. He was ten years old and carried out this daunting task with the charming panache which characterised his later life.[16] Later, as a zealous Radical politician Charles was a captable orator. An observer wrote of him:

> His voice is not strong, but it is pleasant. He is always audible except when there is a noise in the house, a circumstance of by no means infrequent occurrence.[17]

Charles Tennyson d'Eyncourt's eldest son, George Hildeyard (1809-1871, 'The Sot') was a great mimic whose sisters missed his amusing miming during his 'exile' in Corfu on the staff of Lord Nugent, High Commissioner of the Ionian Islands (nicknamed 'Lord of the Isles').[18] His brother Edwin Clayton although he was nicknamed 'The Snob', was happy to play the buffoon in furtherance of his naval career. As Mate of HMS Jupiter (50 guns, under the command of Captain the Hon. F. W. Grey) he escorted Lord Auckland to India in 1836. He wrote to his father from Calcutta on 7 September:

> We have had a delightful trip. We acted farces and comedies on the way out and I always took the most ludicrous part in each play... Lord Auckland's sister [Miss Eden] asked me to act on the stage in Calcutta in an amateur play but I thought I had already made sufficient fool of myself and declined.[19]

Surviving playbills from Burton Constable Hall show that Captain d'Eyncourt RN played Tom Small (a page) in 'You Can't Marry Your Grandmother' on 12 April 1849. Two days later in the comedy 'The Sheriff of the County' he interpreted the role of 'Pansy'.[20]

The third d'Eyncourt brother, Louis Charles (1814-1896), inappropriately nicknamed 'The Stone' by his Somersby cousins, was a natural clown belying his gravitas as a barrister and Metropolitan Police Magistrate. He was obliged to wear a toupée as a result of nearly having died of smallpox in his youth. One day whilst he was entertaining the children at a party by standing on his head, his toupée fell off and remained conspicuously on the carpet. Nonchalantly he replaced it amidst screams of delighted approval.[21]

The d'Eyncourt daughters Julia Frances (1810-1879, 'The Saint'), Clara Maria (1817--1863, 'Puss'), and Ellen Elizabeth (1818-1900 'The Shrew'), were all gifted musicians. Their drawing room singing talents made them attractive to their disreputable Somersby cousins Frederick, Charles and Alfred. There were frequent amateur dramatic productions at Bayons Manor in which the talented family coerced their friends to play. Some of these theatricals were very ambitious and required a good deal of organisation which the family thoroughly enjoyed. Typical of these elaborate productions was 'One Hour or The Carnival Ball' presented at Bayons on Tuesday evening 5 November 1839.[22] The cast consisted of Clara, Ellen, Louis and Eustace d'Eyncourt with house guests the Hon. Mrs Emma Hamilton[23] (their cousin) and Monsieur le Compte de Courson. Later the same evening they presented the farce 'The Widow of Wicklow' in which their elder brother, George Hildeyard, and Mr Heneage of Hainton performed (Fig. 2). Notably absent was Julia (Edwin was away serving on HMS Calliope on the South American station).

The lyrics of the Dogs' Meat ballad with which the d'Eyncourts were familiar were written by Thomas Hudson, a comic song-writer and singer of the early nineteenth century. He published many volumes of his own songs, the first of which was printed in 1818. Many of them were sung extensively by well-known comedians of the day such as Robert Glindon, Henry Howell, John Caulfield and Charles Sloman. Hudson was born in Mount Street, Lambeth in April 1791. He was apprenticed to a grocer but found his way as a talented vocalist and became a celebrated song-writer. He made many music hall ballads popular among fasionable circles. 'Tom' Hudson was a man of considerable ability. He was active at the Coal Hole in the Strand and Cyder Cellars in Maiden Lane and published his songs which were made popular by other singers at Sadlers Wells (then a music hall) and Vauxhall Pleasure Gardens. Hudson died in straitened circumstances on 26 June 1844, aged fifty-one, apparently a 'model husband and parent'. The 'Spider and the Fly', 'Walter, the Tuppenny Postman' and 'The Dogs' Meat Man' were among his successes.[24]

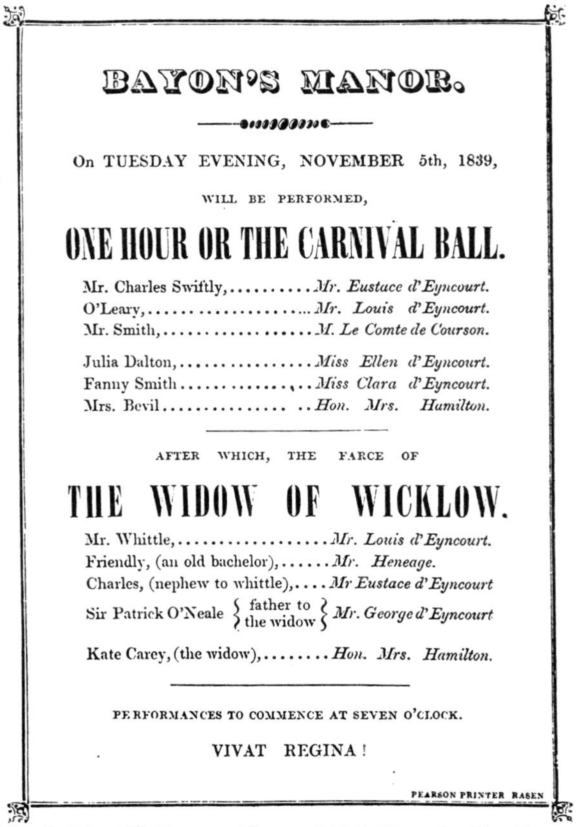

BAYON'S MANOR.

On TUESDAY EVENING, NOVEMBER 5th, 1839,

WILL BE PERFORMED,

ONE HOUR OR THE CARNIVAL BALL.

Mr. Charles Swiftly, ... *Mr. Eustace d'Eyncourt.*
O'Leary, ... *Mr. Louis d'Eyncourt.*
Mr. Smith, ... *M. Le Comte de Courson.*

Julia Dalton, ... *Miss Ellen d'Eyncourt.*
Fanny Smith .... *Miss Clara d'Eyncourt.*
Mrs. Bevil .... *Hon. Mrs. Hamilton.*

AFTER WHICH, THE FARCE OF

THE WIDOW OF WICKLOW.

Mr. Whittle, ... *Mr. Louis d'Eyncourt.*
Friendly, (an old bachelor), ... *Mr. Heneage.*
Charles, (nephew to whittle), ... *Mr Eustace d'Eyncourt*
Sir Patrick O'Neale { father to the widow } *Mr. George d'Eyncourt*

Kate Carey, (the widow), ... *Hon. Mrs. Hamilton.*

PERFORMANCES TO COMMENCE AT SEVEN O'CLOCK.

VIVAT REGINA!

PEARSON PRINTER RASEN

Fig. 2: Playbill, Bayons Manor, 1839. (Lincolnshire County Council Education and Cultural Services Directorate: Archives.)

'The Dogs' Meat Man' is a homely parable telling a familiar 'first he loved and then he left 'er' story, of the smooth-talking Cockney street seller. It was a great favourite reflecting Victorian popular morality:

In Gray's Inn Road, not very long ago
An old maid lived a life of woe;
She was fifty three, with a face like tan,
And she fell in love with the dogs' meat man.

He was a good-looking 'dandy':

That very evening he was seen
In a jacket and breeches of velveteen

The inevitable bogus proposal of marriage was followed by her lending him 'a five pound note':

He pocketed the money and went away
She waited for him all next day
But he never came; and then she began
To think she was diddled by the dogs' meat man.

Worse follows when she discovers that 'He'd got a wife and seven children':

So home she went with sighs and tears
As her hopes were all transformed to fears,
And her hungry cat to mew began
As much as to say 'where's the dogs' meat man?'
So you see just in one day's short span
She lost her heart, a five pound note and the
dogs' meat man.

What a cad! A familiar villain in Victorian culture at all levels. The word 'cad' meaning 'a low vulgar' man was current in Lincolnshire dialect in 1866. Cad was by dictionary definition carrion, stinking flesh or bad meat. The knacker or dogs' meat man was known as the 'cadman' and his ware was 'cadmeat'. Could there have been a connection with 'cadaver'? At all events all these Lincolnshire expressions would have been familiar to the d'Eyncourt family.[25] Cadmeat was fed to hunting dogs, and the d'Eyncourts were enthusiastic riders to hounds with County hunts. They kept a good number of dogs at Bayons.

The good-humoured dubbing of Charles Tennyson 'The Dogs' Meat Man' by his Tealby cousins can be traced to their knowledge of the reputed character, both in Lincolnshire and London, of this figure of the society they knew so well; also to their knowledge of and interest in contemporary music hall and drawing room ballads. Except perhaps for Edwin, who considered his Somersby cousins as 'really quite hogs' and referred to Alfred as 'that bloated ploughman',[26] there was no malice or spite, rather a good natured amused tolerance of the (to them) eccentric parson. Certainly the attitude of George, Louis, Eustace, Julia, Clara, and Ellen towards their cousin would have been no more than a feeling of snobbish superiority.

Not so their father, Charles Tennyson d'Eyncourt. He thoroughly disapproved of the Somersbyites particularly the three Tennyson brothers sniffing round his beautiful daughters. They were the least suitable suitors. In particular he felt the close proximity of his rather bohemian opium addicted nephew in Tealby to be dangerous. The feeling was mutual. Young Charles writing to a friend complained that in Tealby he was 'under my grandfather's [and uncle's] nose, which I call being too near'.

But 'Dogs' Meat Man' was of even more significance to d'Eyncourt. It went back several years when he had good reason to refer sarcastically to his uncle the Rev. Samuel Turner's dubious connection with the (legitimate) local meat trade.

As ordinary Mr Charles Tennyson, d'Eyncourt had been elected to Parliament in an expensively fought election at Grimsby in 1818. His father, old George, and brother in law, Matthew Russell had both been elected in the same general election for Bletchingly. The Parliament lasted from 4 August 1818 until the next general election in February 1820. Tennyson fought for re-election and retained his seat being elected member for Great Grimsby on 7 March 1820. Again it was a hard fought battle with the usual violence on the hustings. Accusations of bribery and corruption flew fast and furious.[27] Charles hard though he was politically, was particularly sensitive when he felt any disloyalty from his family.

A rumour came to his ears that his uncle Sam Turner had made a remark in Grimsby commercial circles to the effect that he 'would not give five pound [sic] to secure his (Mr Tennyson's) election'. Charles demanded an explanation. As was to happen so often in the future Charles' persistent and tenacious niggling precipitated a family row. The duel he fought in June 1831 with Lord Thomas Cecil over allegations of misbehaviour at the Stamford election, his single-minded defence of his son Eustace who was expelled from Sandhurst in 1834 for leading an affray at Bagshot, and his doggedly ferocious and passionate opposition to his beloved daughter Julia's entering a Roman Catholic convent in the late 1840s, vividly illustrate this trait of Charles' character which was a strength in public but a disasterous weakness in private life. He even later disowned Edwin after a row over some triviality (probably financial) which had escalated to such a pitch that he referred to his naval son as 'a venemous unnatural animal'.[28] Charles was very quick to take umbrage at the suggestion that his electoral chances in Grimsby were being put at risk.

The Rev. Sam Turner had been involved with a George Oliver of Caistor in victualling ships in Grimsby docks with beef. It was, he explained in a letter dated 2 April 1820 'an abominable lye' and a 'foul calumny' that he had compromised Charles' chances in the Grimsby election:

> Now, the fact is simply this. Being at Mr Oliver's the evening after our Ship-meeting, a conversation took place respecting the Beef supplied from Castor [sic]. I observed is that the Grimsby Butchers might have had the whole of the contract, it being first offered to them, that they had served the Ship with nearly two thirds of the quantity required at 61, that the Castor Butchers had contracted for the remainder at 56, equal if not superior Beef, and that it was a material saving to the Owners in general, and to me in particular as the principal; to which Mrs. O sagaciously remarked: "Aye, but by this you may throw away Mr. Tennyson's Election"; my answer was, "Indeed! If Mr. Tennyson's Interest stands on no better Foundation than a Bit of beef, *I would not give five pounds for it*". Now, my dear Charles, I should have treated this foul Calumny with the contempt it deserves, had you not mentioned the circumstances, - attaching to it an apparent degree of credit: Nay, I have it from the most respectable authorities that the ridiculous story of the Beef originated entirely with the Olivers, and otherwise it would scarcely have been noticed, but enough, for, -
>
> Sure such a Pair were never seen,
> He struts a King, she hops a Queen.[29]

But enough was not enough. This reasonable and charmingly disarming reply did not satisfy Charles. Like other real or imagined grievances in his life the beef affair would smoulder and rankle for years to come. He would be contemptuous of his uncle's 'cad meat' business and hence label him 'The Dogs Meat Man'. The nickname would have been transferred by association to young Charles when he came to Tealby in 1833. The d'Eyncourt children were very young in 1820 (the eldest, George Hildeyard being only eleven, and the youngest Ellen, only two) so they would not have known much about the row between their father and great uncle Turner. Perhaps they learned of this later as they grew up and understood the real significance of 'The Dogs' Meat Man'

Acknowledgements

The author wishes to thank the staffs of Lincoln, Grimsby and Nottingham Local History Libraries; Lincolnshire Archives Office, Sarah Ash of the Guildhall Library, London; the Museum of London; the British Music Library; Bob Harris, Essex Music Publishing Company; Charles Chilton; Dick Playle, British Music Hall Society. Particular thanks are due to Christopher Sturman, and Eric Fisher (butcher) of Tealby, Mark Tennyson d'Eyncourt and Juanita Lady Tennyson d'Eyncourt for help and encouragement.

Notes

1 For family background see Sir Charles Tennyson and Hope Dyson, *The Tennysons. Background to Genius* (1974), Robert Bernard Martin, *Tennyson: The Unquiet Heart* (Oxford, 1983), and Christopher Sturman and Valerie Purton, *Poems by Two Brothers: The Lives, Work and Influence of George Clayton Tennyson and Charles Tennyson d'Eyncourt* (Stamford, 1993). Charles Tennyson d'Eyncourt (1784-1861) served in ten successive Parliaments; he was MP for Great Grimsby, 1818-1826; Bletchingley, 1826-1831; Stamford 1831; and Lambeth, 1832-1852. He was nicknamed 'The Lambeth Spouter', and has been called the Father of Modern Reform. In the late 1830s he remodelled Bayons Manor, Tealby, into a 60-roomed Romantic Gothick mansion in preparation for the peerage he hoped to be given at Queen Victoria's Coronation in 1837. The peerage never came.

2 See J. Murray, 'The Tennyson d'Eyncourt nicknames', *L.H.A.*, 27 (1992), 34-39.

3 *Background to Genius*, 92.

4 *The Letters of Alfred, Lord Tennyson*, edited by Cecil Y. Lang and Edgar F. Shannon, Jr., 3 vols (Oxford, 1981-90), I, 80n.

5 L.A.O. T.d'E. H113/36.

6 *Background to Genius*, 82.

7 L.A.O. T.d'E. H117/64.

8 L.A.O. T.d'E. H116/22.

9 *Background to Genius*, 82.

10 *Lang & Shannon, Letters*, I, 130, 131.

11 Charles Hindley, *A History of the Cries of London Ancient and Modern* (1881; 2nd edn 1885); Charles Booth, *Life and Labour of the People of London*, 2 vols (1889-91).

12 Early food hygiene legislation included the Slaughter House Act (1847). The Adulteration of Food Act (1860) was the first major legislation although local laws were in operation before this. The Manchester Police Act (1844), for example, regulated the slaughter of animals, licensed slaughter houses, and gave powers to appoint inspectors.

13 Augustus Frederick, Duke of Sussex (1773-1843), sixth son of George III. He was a Freemason with Radical political tendencies. With Colonel Thomas Wildman (1787-1859) of Newstead Abbey, Nottingham, he founded the United Grand Lodge of England. Both men were friends of Charles Tennyson d'Eyncourt who was a Provincial Grand Master. In the 1830s he nominated Charles Tennyson d'Eyncourt to be the Vice-President of the Convent Garden Theatrical Trust.

14 Murray, 'Nicknames', 37.

15 Joseph O. Baylen and Norbert J. Gossman, eds, *Biographical Dictionary of British Radicals. Volume 1: 1770-1830* (New Jersey, 1979), 120-24.

16 Charles Garton, 'Lincoln School Speech Day, 1795: a Tennyson connection?', *Tennyson Research Bulletin*, 5, 5 (1991), 248-57.

17 'One of no party' [James Grant], *Random Recollections of the House of Commons...* (1836), 261-63.

18 George Nugent Grenville (1788-1850), Baron Nugent of Caranstown. In 1830 he was made one of the lords of the treasury. Resigned in August 1832 to become Lord High Commissioner of the Ionian Islands. He took with him George Hildeyard, the eldest d'Eyncourt son who was awarded the CSMG for his work there. See Murray 'Nicknames', 34 for an amusing caricature of the two.

19 L.A.O. T.d'E. H119/80. For Edwin's naval career see *Lean's Navy List* (1903).

20 L.A.O. T.d'E. H 9/8-9.

21 Sir Eustace H. W. Tennyson d'Eyncourt, *A Shipbuilder's Yarn* (1948).

22 L.A.O. T.d'E. H 9/7.

23 Emma Hamilton (died 29 April 1870) was the daughter of Charles Tennyson d'Eyncourt's sister, Elizabeth (1776-1865), wife of coal millionaire Matthew Russell MP of Brancepeth Castle, Co. Durham, one of the richest commoners in Britain. Emma married Gustavus Frederick Hamilton, 7th Viscount Boyne on 9 September 1828. He assumed the name Russell when Emma succeeded in 1850 to Brancepeth on the death of brother William.

24 For the life of Thomas Hudson (1791-1844) see Charles Douglas Stewart and A. J. Park, *The Variety Stage* (1893), and W. McQueen-Pope, *The Melodies Linger On* (1951). Hudson is referred to in Harold Scott, The Early Doors (London, 1928) as 'tainted with Regency Licentiousness'. Interestingly, one of his songs 'Jack Robinson', about a sailor returning to find his girl unfaithful and married to someone else, put a saying into the English language.

25 See J. Ellett Brogden, *Provincial Words and Expressions Current in Lincolnshire* (1866) and R. E. G. Cole, *Glossary of Words in Use in South-West Lincolnshire* (English Dialect Society, 1886).

26 Letters Alfred Tennyson, I, 134-35.

27 See Gordon Jackson, *Grimsby and the Haven Company* (Grimsby, 1971), 2-5.

28 L.A.O. T.d'E. H141/2.

29 L.A.O. 2 T.d'E. H61/25.

Edward Tennyson and Holbeck

Christopher Sturman

One consequence of the publication of the key biographical studies which form the nucleus of many a Lincolnshire book-collector's Tennyson shelf - Sir Charles Tennyson's *Alfred Tennyson* (1949) and *The Tennysons. Background to Genius* (1974), a work he wrote jointly with Hope Dyson, as well as Robert Bernard Martin's *Tennyson. The Unquiet Heart* (1980) - has been the revelation of the extent of the family's 'black bloodedness'. As Anne Colley has observed:

> [N]ow that the facts so long hidden from the public's eye are published, no biographical account can avoid the matter; few introductions to editions of Tennyson's work can close without alluding, at least to some degree, to the family's entanglement with epilepsy, melancholia, monomania, mania, hypochondria, hysteria, alcoholism, and drugs, and to its members' trials in public and private asylums.[1]

In this context, the sad life of Edward Tennyson (1813-1890), the fourth surviving son of the Rev. Dr George Clayton Tennyson and his wife Eliza, confined from 1832 until his death, in a private asylum at Acomb near York,[2] is of more than usual interest. It is the intention of this short essay briefly to review the facts known about Edward's troubled life, presenting some additional material to that hitherto available, as well as to examine Edward's literary work, and in particular his 'Sonnet upon Holbeck', a poem which provides a firm link with the late Terence Leach's interest in Lincolnshire houses.

In late February 1829, only days after a bitter dispute with his eldest son Frederick, Dr Tennyson wrote to his father about a proposed visit to Tealby:

> I shall bring Edward with me, as you have been so good as to interest yourself in his behalf. *At home* he will be *quite ruined*, & he is beginning to be what you call *chippy* & unmanageable. I shall however at all events bring him to you; he never will be well at home, & would fancy that he had a hundred complaints. He must be governed & know what it is to have a Master. He is already running restive & what am I to expect from a boy who has been at home nearly a year upon the *plea of ill health*, & encouraged as he is. He will stay at home all his life & be ignorant & impudent. Upon this subject, however, I shall converse with you, & you have shewn yourself so much the friend of my family that I will most willingly & confidentially trust to you, as to what is to be done with Edward, a very awkard [*sic*] & unlicked fellow who fancies himself to be a superior genius & who scarcely knows that two & two makes four. In short he is ruined here & must go from home.[3]

Although it could be argued, in the light of Dr Tennyson's temperament and the charged atmosphere at Somersby, that he might have been exaggerating the case, the key fact that Edward was at home and not at school cannot be challenged: the admission register of the grammar school at Louth shows Edward to have been entered only for the half year Christmas 1827 to Midsummer 1828 (indeed he may well have been withdrawn before the end of term).[4] In all probability he was never considered suitable for formal schooling: in November 1827, when Dr Tennyson was in Paris for the sake of his health, George Tennyson proposed placing Edward as a 'Clerk to a Solicitor'.[5] In the continuing absence of his father, Edward's entry to Louth school (with Septimus), seems to have been decided upon in some haste: his uncle John Fytche advised George Tennyson on 15 January 1828, 'I have seen Mr. Dale [the Usher] who will be happy to take the charge of the two boys, the school commences next Monday week.'[6]

The next letter that concerns us was written by Edward himself to his grandfather (his father was then in Italy), in March 1830:

> I should be exceedingly obliged to you if you would place me in some profession. I am quite certain a farmer would be the most suitable to my health as well as my choice, since a life of activity would enable me to shake off all lassitiude and despondency which I at present labour under from my want of employment. If some step is not immediately taken in my favour, I must inevitably resign all pretensions to any business, otherwise I must be an annuitant. My brothers all agree in saying that I ought to be put out to something. What do you think I should do? I have nobody to consult but you upon the subject my father being so many miles away from his native country: & it would gratify him to find that I was in some way of acquiring my livelihood. Since I have in a great measure recovered my health I think it would be a pity for me to remain at home inactive. I trusted by this time the Spring being so far advanced that something would have been done for me: I have waited for that crisis with anxiety & being indubitably assured from the benevolence of your disposition that you had my interest at heart & knowing that until my health was fully established, it would be useless troubling you, I will now consult you upon this occasion. As you say we cannot all be Collegians, I wish to know what you consider the best for me.[7]

In May 1831, some six weeks after the death of Dr Tennyson, his brother Charles wrote to their father, about Mrs Tennyson's finances and her children. The letter is well known; one passage in particular is relevant here:

> Edward is understood to be unfit for any *thrift* - and I fear must remain at home - but Alfred says he really fears that his mind will at length so prey upon itself, that he cannot answer for consequences. It is difficult to devise anything for him as an employment with a *real* object. Alfred says he should if possible, for the sake of his mind, go from home & be amused. He has often fancied he should like to be a farmer - but as farming requires as much wit as calling - I do not think we can look at that matter seriously. If Eliza should finally move to Buckden... then he might get into some variety of life which might relieve his mind - but I fear that if he were sent from home to mix with the world by himself - he would become unhappy from another source as he would find himself un[e]qual to his companions & perhaps be exposed to ridicule which his sensitive mind could not endure. Poor fellow! I feel for him - & will endeavour as far as I can to soften his existence for him - but that existence never, I fear, can be a happy one.[8]

In this instance Charles was almost prophetic.

By October 1832 Edward's mental state had deteriorated significantly. Thomas Probart, surgeon, of Tetford wrote, with Mrs Tennyson's permission, to George Tennyson concerning 'the extremely distressing state of mental aberration to which your Grandson Mr. Edward Tennyson is reduced', suggesting, 'since it appears to me the most judicious, humane and economical plan that can be adopted, his removal for a time to the Asylum at Lincoln where he would meet with every comfort and skill which an exclusive attention to diseases of the mind can afford'.[9] Such a recommendation did not find favour with Old George, who concurred in his son Charles's opinion 'that Lincoln would, on many accounts, be very objectionable & indeed injurious to the poor boy himself & to his Brothers and Sisters'[10] - of course Probart's scheme would have been equally 'injurious' to the Tealby branch of the family! It was decided instead to send him to York. Mrs Tennyson wrote to her brother-in-law Charles on 8 November 1832:

> The plan about to be adopted with respect to poor Edward, appears to me as far as I can judge to be a desirable one & I feel obliged to you for wishing to place him under the care of a humane person who will use him kindly, as I am convinced a contrary treatment would only aggravate his disorder. He weeps bitterly sometimes, & says his mind is so unnotched he is scarcely able to endure his existence & requires encouragement rather than severity. Perhaps you will be so good as to inform me by what Conveyance Mr Tennyson wishes Edward to be sent to York who is to accompany him & also to let me know the Gentleman's address under whose care he is to be placed.[11]

The Tennysons's choice - they had also relied on the advice of Dr Barton of Market Rasen and consulted the Rev. T. H. Rawnsley of Halton Holgate,[12] joint guardian with Mrs Tennyson and Charles of the Somersby children under Dr Tennyson's will - was a private asylum run by H. B. Hodgson, formerly Apothecary at the York Asylum, at Acomb. Although this fact is well known to Tennyson scholars, as far as I am aware no one has pointed out (despite the clues in the published correspondence) that Hodgson was the son of the Rev. Henry Hodgson, vicar of Tealby from 1779 to 1815. (Indeed there is something touching in the fact that Edward was surrendered to the care of the son of the man who in all probability in 1778, when curate of Market Rasen, had baptized Dr Tennyson.)

Edward was admitted to Acomb House on 1 December 1832 (the necessary 'Order' was perhaps significantly signed not by Charles, but by John Fytche[13]). It is clear that Edward had probably been persuaded that at last he was going to follow a profession, to judge from a letter Charles drafted to Hodgson on 13 November:

> Our plan is that the *young man should suppose* and also that others should suppose that he goes to you as a Pupil for the purpose of initiating him in the medical profession. He is perfectly capable of appreciating this difference between such a position, and the equivocal situation in which, without such an understanding, he would feel himself placed.[14]

In 1892 H. D. Rawnsley, gathering material eventually incorporated into *Memories of the Tennysons* (1900) was supplied a brief recollection of the Rectory family: 'Old Mrs Thompson aetat 82, who went to the Tennysons when 11 and stayed 7 years remembered them well - Mr. Arthur was a "Poor Creature", Mr Charles was very nice but Mr ___?___ he went to be a Doctor & died poor thing. He was nicest...'[15] If Mrs Thompson was remembering Edward (there could be some confusion with Septimus), it would suggest that people in the locality had been given a further gloss to Edward's departure: not only had he gone from home to study medicine, but that he had died. Such concealment of the true facts of Edward's position is, however, certainly evident in the final actions of Old George. Under his will, dated January 1834, by which time Edward's long term confinement would have been confirmed, the sum of £3,000 was placed in trust 'for the benefit of my Grandson

Edward Tennyson... and any woman he may marry, and any lawfull issue he may have'; the local solicitors who managed the fund could, of course, be relied on for their discretion in the matter. To the outside world, Edward ceased to exist.[16]

Edward was not completely forgotten by his family - his brother Charles recorded writing to him in 1866[17] - though one wonders whether such comments as

> Mr Edward Tennyson is at present much better than usual, more interested with passing events, much looking better in face - besides being in less depressed spirits than usual. (May 1856)

and

> Mr Edward is for him tolerably calm and well, still careless of his dress, and soon wearing out what he has, with the greatest care in watching him. He takes much exercise, walking out daily, and latterly he has amused himself more in reading, and other ways. (May 1857)

forwarded to the trustees with the half yearly statement of account[18] were passed on to his brothers and sisters. What is interesting is the fact that Alfred stayed for a night in York on his unconvincingly explained journey to Whitby in July 1852. Although there is no reference to his visiting Acomb in his surviving correspondence[19] he must have done so: H. B. Hodgson had died in May 1852, and it would seem probable that Alfred made this unaccompanied trip in part to ensure that Edward's future care was in order.

Any account of Edward's life must also mention Septimus (1815-1866), and in particular a letter Alfred sent to his uncle Charles in January 1834:

> I think it is my duty to inform you of Septimus's state of mind. My grandfather talks of letting him stop at home two or three months longer - if this be acted upon I have very little doubt that his mind will prove as deranged as Edward's, altho' I trust that his intellect may yet be preserved by getting him into some bustling[,] active line of life *remote from the scene of his early connexions*. I have studied the minds of my own family - I know how delicately they are organized - & how much might be done in this instance by removing Septimus from all those objects & subjects with which he has been familiar and upon which he has been accustomed to brood, into some situation where he might be enabled to form his own friendships with those of his own age & to feel that there is something to live & to care for - but this, if done[,] should be done immediately, because every hour which he wastes at home tends to increase his malady. At present his symptoms are not unlike those with which poor Edward's unhappy derangement began - he is subject to fits of the most gloomy despondency accompanied with tears - or rather, he spends whole days in this manner, complaining that he is neglected by all his relations, & blindly resigning himself to every morbid influence.[20]

On T. H. Rawnsley's recommendation, Septimus was sent to study with the family physician, Dr Bousfield of Horncastle, remaining for at least a year[21] - though at this stage it is uncertain if his medical studies were cut short on Dr Bousfield's death in 1836, or (as Tennyson biographers suggest) whether on receiving a legacy under his grandfather's will, he had earlier decided to discontinue his apprenticeship.

The 'black bloodedness' of the family certainly dogged Septimus. On several occasions in the late 1830s and early 1840s he was a voluntary patient under the care of Dr Matthew Allen at his asylum in High Beech.[22] A telling comment on his medical state only a few years before his death is recorded by Mrs Tennyson's sister-in-law, Anne Fytche (widow of John), following a visit to London in the early 1860s:

> Poor Sep is after his best fashion[,] he upset the regularity of Eliza's house so much, she was obliged to part with him, & he is in lodgings in London not far from Mother, he came 3 times during my visit & the last day dined with us - his face is much enlarged, & he struck me as looking much like poor Edward. I fear he has not nor can he altogether, give up [*sic*] his unfortunate habit.[23]

Even after the interval of nearly thirty years, Edward's physical appearance still lingered in the minds of his close family.

Like many of his brothers and sisters Edward wrote verse. In August 1831, Alfred sent one of Edward's sonnets, 'Why do I weep when gazing on that field' to his friend William Henry Brookfield for publication: it appeared, with Alfred's 'There are three things which fill my heart with sighs' in the *Yorkshire Literary Annual* for 1832, published in October 1831.[24] Fortunately a number Edward's verses are preserved: Alfred's Cambridge contemporary J. M. Heath in the period 1832-c.1834 transcribed three of Edward's sonnets into his 'Commonplace Book';[25] in 1879 Mary Tennyson (1810-1884) added seven of Edward's poems into a collection of her 'Sonnets and fugitive pieces' dedicated to Frederick.[26] (It is perhaps worth stressing that both these manuscripts also contain sonnets by Septimus). Several of Edward's poems hint, as indeed do Septimus's, at his mental state, but it is his 'Sonnet upon Holbeck', a work

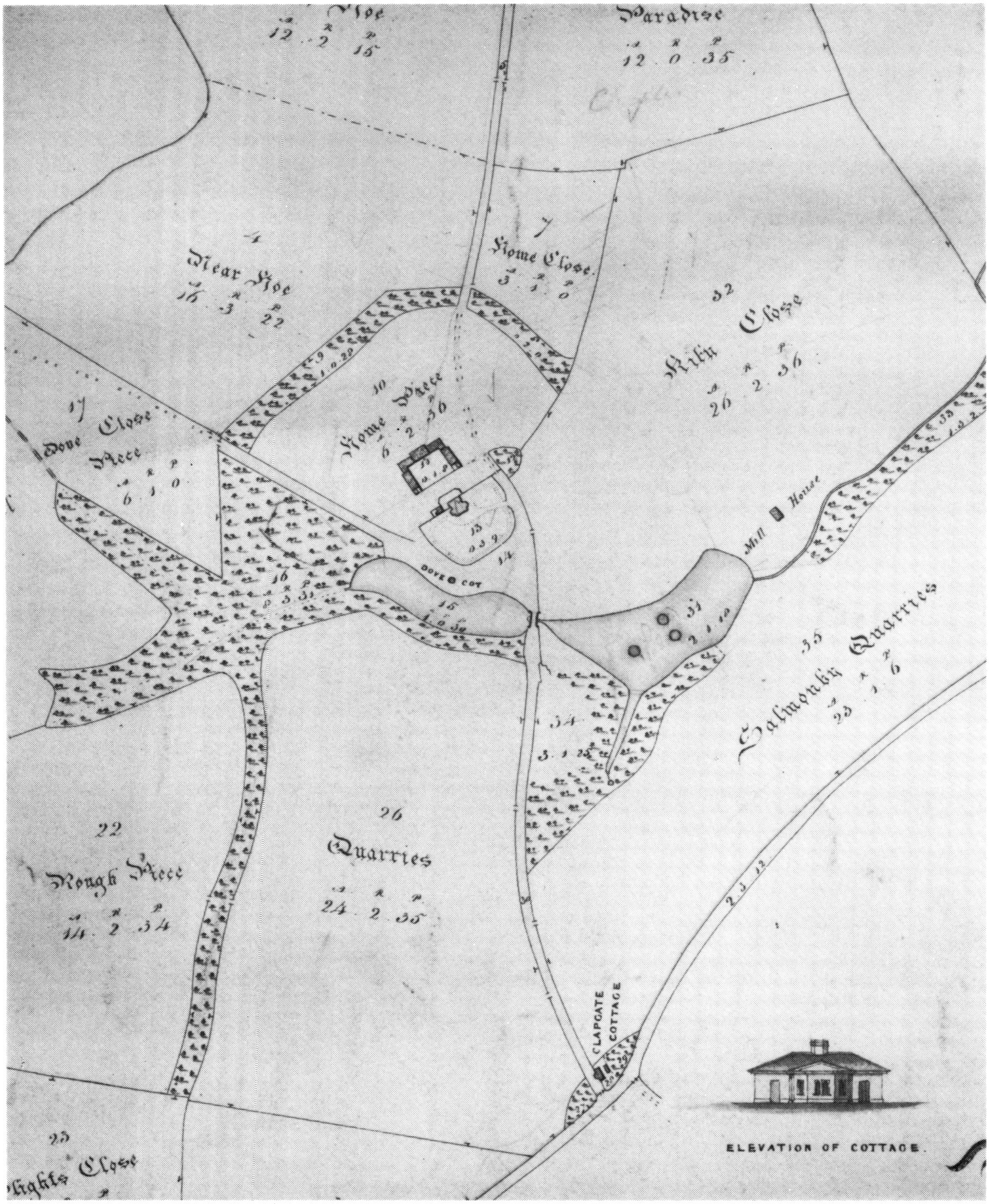

Fig. 1: John Fardell's landscaping at Holbeck, 1833, as surveyed by R.T. Blythe. (Lincolnshire County Council Education and Cultural Services Directorate: Archives)

(apparently on the surface) free from such melancholic introspection, which is of particular interest and merit.

Holbeck, in the parish of Ashby Puerorum, lay some two miles to the west of Somersby. In 1828, several large estates of 2,300 acres, 'comprising the Manor or Lordship of Greetham, with the Graveship and Bailwick [*sic*]of Greetham; the Manors, or Lordships, of Ashby Puerorum, Holbeck, and Scamblesby...' were offered for sale in London.[27] Much of this land was purchased by John Fardell (1784-1854), who from *c.*1829 began tranforming the Holbeck estate for his own residence (he became MP for Lincoln in 1830). The former farmhouse was demolished and rebuilt (the 1828 sale catalogue had noted of Ashby Puerorum and Holbeck, 'there are several delightful situations on which a Mansion House might be erected'), and the grounds, which contained two lakes (it is thought these were originally the quarries for the Roman fort at Horncastle) were landscaped.[28] In 1833 the estate was surveyed by R. T. Blythe (Fig. 1) and his map also contains a ground plan of Fardell's new villa, with front and east elevations (Figs. 2-3).[29] Henry Winn, who recorded a visit to view the 'pleasure gounds' and the exterior of the hall in his diary of 1844, commented, 'It is indeed a beautiful rural retreat'.[30] Later in the century Winn described Holbeck more fulsomely:

> It may be described as *Multum in parvo*, or a conglomeration of rural beauties, comprising a genteel residence, approached from a neat lodge through a beautiful avenue of elms, and embellished with extensive ponds, well stocked with fish, and ornamented with artificial islands and cascades, bounded by picturesque rocks and thriving plantations. There are also pleasant lawns, conservatories, and gardens, the whole surrounded by a productive farm. The capabilities of the estate were perceived and developed by the Fardel [*sic*] family...[31]

(The process of change has continued: the present Holbeck House was built in *c.*1873[32] - though it is uncertain whether Fardell's villa was demolished or just remodelled - and it has been further enlarged during this century; in the 1930s several follies were built in the grounds.)

The Tennyson children knew the environs of Somersby well. John Lewis Fytche recalled in a letter to Henry Winn of 1885 how

> As I boy I have often walked over the historic field [of Winceby] with Alfred Tennyson and my other cousins. It was our favourite walk from Somersby, and the tradition of Slash Lane running down with blood used to startle us.[33]

Clapgate Lodge, part of the Holbeck estate, also had Civil War associations;[34] whilst it cannot be proved that the cousins' 'favourite walk' detoured to Holbeck, the rectory children would have known the estate (one of the tributaries of the Somersby 'Brook' ran

Fig. 2 Front elevation of Holbeck Lodge, 1833, by R. T. Blythe. (Lincolnshire County Council Education and Cultural Services Directorate: Archives)

through the property). It was Fardell's landscape changes, and the building of his new residence, that caught Edward's imagination. His 'Sonnet upon Holbeck' cannot be dated precisely, though c.1831, that is after the house was completed, ties in neatly with his one published sonnet. Edward Tennyson responds rather like John Clare, acutely sensitive to the transformation of a familiar landscape. The imagery of destruction might be considered emblematic of Edward's deteriorating mental state, as might the unusual rhyme scheme, with the couplet 'recess/press' placed at the beginning rather than the end of the sestet, suggesting as it does a central collapse - though equally it might be an example of a free and easy experimentation with form. Whatever the case, Edward's sonnet is a work of great charm, even beauty, and certainly deserves to be more widely appreciated:

Sonnet upon Holbeck

The purple foxgloves long have ceased to bloom
Holbeck, upon thy windy range of hills
The hare no more lurks in its haunts of broom
Or curlèd fern beside thy sparkling rills
The plough hath levelled all with general doom
Only long sighing reeds remain to tell
How that the fairies left their shady home
When this sad change the rushy spot befell.
Now will they seek some other green recess
Which mortal footstep never dared to press
As if their free souls sickened at the view
Of toiling masonry and busy hands
That with such earnest cost of gold upthrew
This human pile upon their charmèd lands.[35]

Fig. 3: East elevation of Holbeck Lodge, 1833, by R. T. Blythe. (Lincolnshire County Council Education and Cultural Services Directorate: Archives)

Acknowledgements

Edward Tennyson's 'Sonnet upon Holbeck' is reproduced by permission of the Syndics of the Fitzwilliam Museum. I am grateful to Valerie Purton and Roger Evans for their comments on an earlier draft of this article.

Notes

1 *Tennyson and Madness* (Athens, Georgia, 1983), 34. See also Kay Redfield Jamison, *Touched by Fire: Manic Depressive Illness and the Artistic Temperament* (New York and Toronto, 1993), 196-201.

2 See in particular two articles by Christopher Daniell, 'Edward Tennyson in York: 1832-1833' and 'Edward Tennyson in York 1832-1890', in *Notes and Queries,* n.s. 34, 1 (March 1987), 32-35 and 35, 3 (September 1988), 315-17. In his second article Daniell suggests Edward had been moved to Lime Tree House by 1861. This is not the case. In November 1858 Edward's brother Charles advised Charles Tennyson d'Eyncourt, '[Edward] is now safely housed with the new man at the old house now called Lime Tree House instead of Acombe house', Tennyson Research Centre (hereafter T.R.C.), Lincoln, Edward Tennyson Trustees papers.

3 L.A.O. 2 T.d'E. H86/20, printed in *The Letters of Alfred, Lord Tennyson*, edited by Cecil Y. Lang and Edgar F. Shannon, Jr., 3 vols (Oxford, 1981-90), I, 29, though 'awkard [*sic*] & unlicked' is read as 'awkward and unlikable [?]'.

4 L.A.O. L.G.S. C/I/1.

5 L.A.O. T.d'E. H114/12, printed in Lang & Shannon, *Letters*, I, 17.

6 L.A.O. 2 T.d'E. H 85/5 (this section of the letter was not printed in the extract given in Lang & Shannon, *Letters*, I, 21). Edward and Septimus were then staying at Tealby. Before their departure in December, Mrs Tennyson advised her father-in-law, 'Poor Edward has complained lately of a giddiness in his head - should it get worse perhaps you will have the goodness to consult Mr Barton respecting it. I think he does not pay sufficient atention to his bowels which are in a confined state...' (L.A.O. T.d'E. H128/24, printed in Lang & Shannon, *Letters*, I, 21).

7 L.A.O. 2 T.d'E. H87/52.

8 L.A.O. 2 T.d'E. H91/63, printed in Lang & Shannon, *Letters*, I, 59-61.

9 L.A.O. T.d'E. H110/25, printed in Lang & Shannon, *Letters*, I, 81.

10 L.A.O. T.d'E. H110/27, printed in Lang & Shannon, *Letters*, I, 81 note 2.

11 L.A.O. T.d'E. H110/28, printed in Lang & Shannon, *Letters*, I, 81 note 2, in an incomplete version and with a number of significant errors of transcription.

12 L.A.O. T.d'E. H110/31.

13 York City Archives K 124, printed in Daniell, 'Edward Tennyson in York: 1832-1833', 33-34. Roger Evans observes, 'It is apparent that [Edward's] certification was an embarrassment to the Tealby family for any suggestion of lunacy in their number was to be suppressed; Charles Tennyson of Tealby would indeed assist the Somersby family, but he was by no means prepared to put his name or position in jeopardy.' ('Secret Rooms: The Life and Work of Charles Tennyson Turner', unpublished Ph.D. dissertation, University of Hull, 1993, 156). Although this may undoubtedly describe Charles's attitude, it must be borne in mind that the document is undated and that he left Lincolnshire for London on 23 November 1832 remaining out of the county - delayed by the fall of the government and its aftermath - for some three weeks (L.A.O. T.d'E. H111/84-88).

14 L.A.O. T.d'E. H110/24, printed in Lang & Shannon, *Letters*, I, 83-84.

15 Rawnsley family papers. I am grateful to Ann Thwaite for this reference which will be included in her *Emily Tennyson, the Poet's Wife* to be published in late 1996.

16 L.A.O. L.C.C. Wills 1835/326. T.R.C. Edward Tennyson Trustees papers, which contain accounts and correspondence from 1836.

17 T.R.C. Memorandum Book, 15 March 1866, cited in Evans, 'Secret Rooms', 156-57.

18 T.R.C. Edward Tennyson Trustees papers. Both letters are from J. W. Metcalfe to Thomas Rhodes of Market Rasen.

19 Lang & Shannon, *Letters*, II, 31-34.

20 L.A.O. T.d'E. H147/9, printed in Lang & Shannon, *Letters*, I, 106.

21 See L.A.O. T.d'E. H 116/9 and 118/26-29.

22 Robert Bernard Martin, *Tennyson. The Unquiet Heart* (1980), 237 and 253.

23 L.A.O. Dixon 14/1/3/1, undated letter (?c.1861) to John Lewis Fytche.

24 Lang & Shannon, *Letters*, I, 64-65.

25 Fitzwilliam Museum Cambridge. See Charles Tennyson, 'Tennyson papers. II. J. M. Heath's "Commonplace Book"', *Cornhill Magazine*, 153 (April 1936), 426-49.

26 T.R.C., which also holds a copy of Edward's 'Thoughts on Pre-existence'.

27 L.A.O. Padley III/93.

28 J. Conway Walter, *Records, Historical and Antiquarian, of Parishes Round Horncastle* (Horncastle, 1904), 11-12. See also *Some Correspondence of John Fardell, Deputy Regis trar, 1802-1895*, edited by Mary E. Finch, L.R.S. 66 (1973), 50-51. Nikolaus Pevsner and John Harris, rev. Nicholas Antram, *The Buildings of England: Lincolnshire* (1989), 106, erroneously date the house to 1823; they note further: 'The landscape of 1834 [*sic*] in the best Salvator Rosa taste, craggy, planted with firs and bracken, with a romantic lake...'

29 L.A.O. Misc. Dep. 102/1.

30 L.A.O. Winn 1/1, p.41.

31 'Old Lincolnshire Villages. II. Ashby Puerorum', undated newspaper cutting (?mid 1880s). L.A.O. 2 Binnall, Hill Hundred, Ashby Puerorum notebook.

32 Lincoln City Library, Green's Town & Village Life in Lincolnshire, 3, 40-41 [cuttings of early 1900s series from the *Lincolnshire Times*].

33 L.A.O. Winn 5/1, p.71, printed in Christopher Sturman, 'Tennyson studies: the local historian's role', *L.H.A.*, 22 (1987), 9-14.

34 Conway Walter, *Records... of Parishes Round Horncastle*, 10.

35 Fitzwilliam Musuem Cambridge, J. M. Heath Common place Book, p.26, (Edward is identified only by his initials, 'E.T.'). It was included, with additional punctuation, by Sir Charles Tennyson in 'J. M. Heath's "Commonplace Book"', 431. This version, with brief historical notes by Peggy Allso, was printed in *Lincolnshire Life County Annual 1965*, 127.

The Lincolnshire Booktrade

J. S. English

The history of local printing and the county's booktrade is a comparatively neglected area of Lincolnshire studies. Unlike Shropshire, Norfolk, Derbyshire, or Nottinghamshire, for example, no general survey of the county's booktrade has been published.[1] Booktrade histories of only two towns, Louth and Gainsborough, have been published,[2] and so far as individuals are concerned only the Grantham printer and bookseller Edward Pawlett, and the Mozley family of Gainsborough have been the focus of serious research.[3] Studies of Lincolnshire library history, in Lincoln, Stamford and Gainsborough, contain some incidental material on other aspects of the booktrade,[4] while light on another facet of the trade is shed by histories of the county's newspapers. However apart from Boston and Stamford, these are mainly to be found as centenary or other anniversary histories in the newspapers themselves.[5]

These isolated studies serve only to illustrate the lack of work that has been undertaken in this field, a neglect further illustrated by a 1981 bibliography of the provincial booktrade[6] where only twelve Lincolnshire entries are listed (seven of them relating to newspapers), compared with, for example, eighteen for Cheshire and twenty-one for Norfolk. To be fair, however, it must be said that there are merely seven entries for Nottinghamshire and only a single entry for Leicestershire. Even the Lincolnshire contributions to the ongoing British Book Trade Index[7] have been culled mainly from national published sources and from the British Library's Eighteenth Century Short Title Catalogue with, until recently, little local input from within the county.

The national map of provincial booktrade history is very patchy, depending as it does on the enthusiasm of individuals researching particular localities, and the same applies locally. The sources vary widely and are often 'difficult' to consult - parish registers, local newspaper advertisements, census returns, passing references (not always accurate) in town and other local histories, the surviving products of local printers, surviving wills and probate inventories, and so on - and such detailed information is readily available for only a few places in the county. What follows, therefore, is merely an attempt to synthesize an outline of the Lincolnshire booktrade while realising that it must be imbalanced, and acknowledging the many gaps that exist both in actuality and in the present state of my own knowledge.

Where and when, then, did the book trade originate in Lincolnshire? It would appear that Lincoln and Stamford were among the earliest centres in the county, with Boston, Gainsborough and Grantham also represented before 1700. In a lecture, 'The Romance of Bookselling' given at a summer school at Stoke Rocheford in 1928, W. P. Woolston said, 'The earliest known English booksellers were in Oxford in 1358 and one Johannes Liberarious in Lincoln in 1359' but he gave no reference for this assertion and so far it has not proved possible verify it. A more plausible starting date is 1571 when Charles Browne was said to have been a bookseller in Lincolnshire, and in the same year Edward Rockadon was listed as a Lincoln stationer who had paid the tax of scot and lot. Rockadon had been apprenticed to the London stationer Thomas Hackett, and had been admitted freeman of the Stationers' Company in September 1570. Nearly fifty years were then to pass before the next known booktrade reference for the county, when in 1615 the burial of the son of the bookbinder Henry Eshe (or Ashe) was recorded in the Gainsborough parish registers; that, however, was an isolated mention of Eshe so it is possible that he was a visitor rather than a resident of the town.

From that time the known references to booktrade personnel increase - two further isolated entries for stationers in the Gainsborough parish registers (1651 and 1686); John West, a mercer in Louth, supplying a prayer book to the Churchwardens in 1661 and another Louth mercer, Thomas Barker, supplying a Bible in the following year. Some years earlier, in 1638, Henry Browne (originally of Loughborough) was admitted to the freedom of Grantham as a bookseller and bookbinder; in 1639 William Mallory (or Malory) was admitted to the freedom of Boston, also as a bookseller and bookbinder; in 1671 Samuel

Wolly paid 20s. on gaining the freedom of Louth to trade as a bookseller (according to Goulding the first definite booktrade reference for that town); then the freedom of Grantham was granted to Edward Pawlett to trade as a bookbinder in 1660. Pawlett later added bookselling to his activities and in 1686 issued one of the earliest provincial book auction catalogues, a practice usually restricted at that time to the London trade. Three Lincolnshire booksellers issued trade tokens during the seventeenth century - Samuel Williams of Lincoln a farthing token in 1657, William Mallory of Boston one (and possibly two) farthing tokens in 1662, and Edward Pawlett of Grantham a half-penny token in 1666 - signs, perhaps, that they were traders of some consequence in their localities.[8]

By the eighteenth century the booktrade was becoming more widely established in the county and a more coherent pattern began to emerge, with signs of dynasties being founded, short-lived though they may have been, and of stationers and booksellers trading in other goods to make a living. Many were patent medicine sellers, some ran circulating libraries, some traded in secondhand as well as new books, the sale of music and musical instruments was added by some as a sideline, sometimes bookselling appeared to be little more than a sideline to trading as drapers or general merchants - combinations of trades which survived well into the nineteenth century when, from the evidence of the county directories, they became even more varied. The surviving trade-card of Oswell Carlton of Gainsborough (he died in 1730) can serve as an example of the range of books and stationery carried by a small-town bookseller.[9] In time some became printers.

In 1785 the first booktrade directory was compiled and issued by John Pendred;[10] this listed seven Lincolnshire towns - Boston, Castor [sic], Gainsborough, Grantham, Lincoln, Spalding, and Stamford. It was a pioneer attempt to collate and publish information on the provincial booktrade, but the listing of firms is by no means complete (it was intended to include only the main booktrade distributors) and of the nineteen names for Lincolnshire a couple (tanners and fellmongers) were only marginally connected with the booktrade; on the other hand nine were said to be printers. *The Universal British Directory*, published in the early 1790s, listed twelve county towns with booktrades - Barton-on-Humber, Boston, Castor [*sic*], Gainsborough, Glamford Briggs [*sic*] , Grantham, Horncastle, Lincoln, Louth, Sleaford, Spalding and Stamford. As booktrades became more widespread, and as the directories became more efficiently compiled, the number of booktrade entries multiplied, and an analysis of the Lincolnshire directories from White's of 1826 to Kelly's of 1861 produced a listing of nearly four hundred booktrade names for the county. These ranged from fifty two people in Lincoln to, for example, Jonathan Davison as a bookseller in Waltham in 1842, and William Drakard as a bookseller and stationer in Colsterworth between 1856 and 1861.[11]

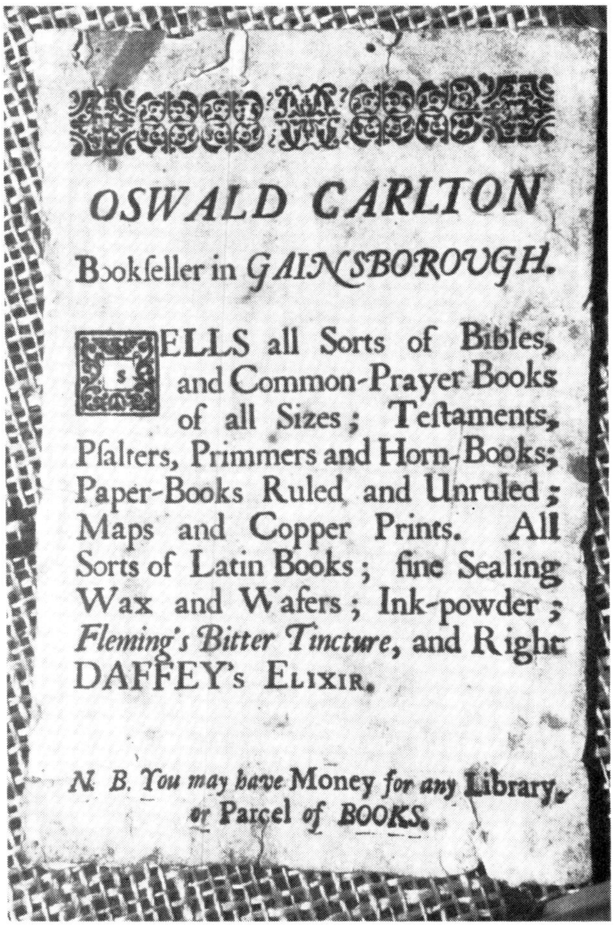

Fig. 1: Trade Card of Oswald Carlton, bookseller and stationer in Gainsborough from at least 1710 to his death in 1730. (Lincolnshire County Council)

It is interesting again to see some of the combinations of trades. In 1826, for example, the Alford bookseller John Joseph Brian was also a perfumer; John S. Sharman of Boston was a schoolmaster in 1849 but also ran a registry office for servants and apprentices, as well as being a bookseller, stationer and binder; in the same year Thomas Wigelsworth of Caistor was a bookseller and stationer, an ironmonger, and a clock and watch maker; in 1835 Richard Brown of Grantham was a binder and a bird-stuffer, while in 1826 William Hoff had a tea-warehouse in Spilsby as well as being a bookseller. When the Horncastle printer James Babington published the new catalogue of his circulating library in about 1832,[12] he described himself on the title page as:

> Printer, Bookseller, Binder and Stationer, Dealer in Perfumery, Patent Medicines, Paper Hangings, Jewellery, Fancy Ornaments, &c &c. Agent for the London and County Newspapers.

On a billhead dated 182213 Adam Stark of Gainsborough described himself as 'Printer, Bookseller, Stationer, & Binder', a seller of 'Genuine Patent Medicines', and went on to describe his services in the following terms:

> PRINTING of all sorts expeditiously and carefully executed_Writing and Shop PAPERS, wholesale and retail_STATIONERY_Ledgers, Day, Shop, and Counting-House Books &c ruled to any pattern_Music and Musical INSTRUMENTS__Prints and Medallions_Magazines and Periodical Publications_NEWSPAPERS procured, and ADVERTISEMENTS forwarded_CIRCULATING LIBRARY_SCHOOLS supplied on the most reasonable terms_Bookbinding, &c.&c.

John Feather has suggested that to be successful provincial printers needed to be involved in one or more related activities - they should produce a newspaper, they should specialize in jobbing printing (probably the backbone of the majority of provincial firms), or they should specialize in the printing of chapbooks and other popular (though ephemeral) small books; in addition a few firms went in for the printing and publishing of 'proper' books.[14] The Lincolnshire booktrade included examples of all of these.

So far as newspapers are concerned the *Stamford Mercury* must take pride of place as being the oldest surviving Lincolnshire newspaper, but Stamford was also the home of other early (though mainly short-lived) newspapers - the *Stamford Post* (1710-11?), for example, and William Harrod's *Stamford Herald* (1793-97), John Drakard's Stamford News (1809-34) and his *Stamford Champion* (1830-33). Other early newspapers included Adam Stark's *Lincoln and Hull Chronicle* (1807) and Henry Brook's *Boston Gazette*, (1810), but it was not until the abolition of newspaper stamp duty in 1855 that local newspapers began really to flourish. In that year, for example W. H. Caldicott founded the *Retford, Worksop and Gainsburgh News* after earlier experiments in the late 1840s with such titles as the *Gainsburgh & Epworth Press*; other newspapers founded in this period include *The Boston Guardian & Lincolnshire Advertiser* (1854), *The Grantham Journal* (1855), *The Louth & North Lincolnshire Advertiser* (1859), *The Market Rasen Weekly Mail & Lincolnshire Advertiser* (1856), and *The Spalding Free Press & Eastern Counties Advertiser* (1847).

Although files of some early newspapers are incomplete, and many are in a very poor state, enough have survived and have been documented to make the study of Lincolnshire newspaper history possible. This cannot be said about jobbing printers and their work, for most of their products were by their very nature not produced for survival, yet as trade in the county's towns expanded so the need for printed matter grew also. Some firms kept stock books and scrapbooks of their products and some of these have survived, notably the Skelton Collection in Grimsby Library; theatre and similar posters, billheads, handbills, broadsheets, and other examples of early jobbing printing can be found in museums and libraries (and in private hands), but in many cases their survival has been a matter of chance and it is questionable whether anything like a coherent history could be compiled from them. In some cases an odd poster, or a slim report of a local organisation, might be virtually the only remaining physical evidence of a printer/stationer/bookseller's activities. Such a one is John Knaggs of Gainsborough, active in the town from at least 1812 until his death in 1821, and described on his marriage in 1805 as being a bookseller in Market Rasen. His only known surviving work is a trade-card, a couple of posters and *Brighter Prospects for the Town of Gainsborough*[15] which he printed and sold for James Cox, headmaster of the local grammar school - yet in the decade or more that he traded he must have printed much more. Perhaps a further search of the files of the ESTC and a search of the Nineteenth Century Short Title Catalogue files might reveal more of his and other local printers' activities. Certainly interrogation of the former has already thrown up some early songsheets and other ephemera dating from the 1790s printed, for example, by J. Weir of Horncastle.

Histories of chapbooks, such as those by Victor Neuberg,[16] give the impression that none were printed in Lincolnshire; this was, however, not the case for - even if there were no others elsewhere in the county - the Mozleys of Gainsborough printed at least two dozen or more, many of them emanating from the delightfully named Mozley's Lilliputian Book-Manufactory. Such productions are supposed by some commentators to have had a fairly local distribution, and if so it would seem likely that these little books for popular consumption could have been printed in various parts of the county, but being so ephemeral comparatively few have survived. In fact, apart from those issued by the Mozleys, only two have so far been identified. One of these, *The History of Adam Bell, Clim the Clough, and William of Cloudeslie*, a copy of which survives in the University Library at Harvard, was printed in about 1760 by Henry Thompson, who was a printer in Gainsborough between at least 1754 and 1760; the other was *The Atheist Converted*, a twelve-page duodecimo printed by William Wood in 1748, and long thought to be 'the first effort of the press in the city of Lincoln' - in fact a book was printed in the city (also by William Wood) at least fifteen years earlier. Further research might show that Lincolnshire chapbook printing was more widespread than has hitherto been suspected, and that these ephemeral local products were an important factor in the county's social and educational development, as well as in local booktrade history and economics.

How was the booktrade regarded, and what of the dynasties? From the evidence of surviving records it would appear that boys from 'respectable' families were apprenticed to the booktrade. From a list of 120 boys apprenticed to country booksellers from 1710 to 1760, compiled from the records of the Stationers' Company,[17] their fathers included a 'gentleman', an 'esquire', three yeomen, and a clergyman, the rest being tradesmen of various kinds. None of these included Lincolnshire boys, but in 1773 Richard Newcomb, the son of Richard Newcomb, gentleman, of Billingborough, was apprenticed to the Cambridge printer and bookseller Thomas H. Fletcher for a premium of £40. He was freed in 1784, and had set himself up - whether with or without financial help from his father is not known - in Stamford by 1785 when he took on his first apprentice, a boy from Market Deeping; the son of a London bookseller followed and in 1798 his son, another Richard Newcomb, was bound apprentice to his father. This was the beginning of a comparatively short dynasty; others were longer lasting.

In 1687 Dickinson Boys was admitted to the freedom of Louth to trade as a bookseller and bookbinder, and when he died in 1719 he was succeeded by his nephew, also Dickinson Boys, who concentrated on the wholesale stationery trade which he developed into a major concern (supplying paper to, among others, John Clay of Daventry in Northamptonshire); after he died in 1763 his widow married Robert Sheardown, who added printing to the firm's activities, took his son into partnership by 1796, and retired in 1800 leaving his son to carry on until 1807 when he sold the business to Henry Hurton. A Gainsborough dynasty had a shorter time-span (at least in Lincolnshire), but the family details were more complicated and their productions more numerous. It began in about 1740 when Henry Mozley came to the town from Doncaster, where he had been employed in an office, and after various occupations set up as a bookseller; his son, John Mozley, added printing in about 1776, and his grandsons carried on the business under several guises (including J. & H. Mozley, J. M. Mozley, J. M. Mozley & Co., Mozley & Co., and H. & G. Mozley), until the grandson Henry Mozley took sole control. He removed the business to Derby in 1815 and it continued there under his, and later his sons' control until the late nineteenth century. Before the firm's removal, Henry Mozley's sister had married Adam Stark, a bookseller and printer in Gainsborough (and previously in Lincoln), and their son, John Mozley Stark carried on the business after his father's retirement in 1844, but he went bankrupt in 1846 through injudicious speculation in the railways. He later traded as a successful and respected printer and bookseller in Hull for many years. Several instances can also be found in various parts of the county of the marriages of journeymen (who were often former apprentices) to their former masters' surviving widows.

But in general, according to John Feather, book printing was not the economic base of most provincial printers, the country booktrade being based on distribution rather than production. Some Lincolnshire printers did print books, of course, but many of them were very local in character - sermons by local clergymen, such as *The Greatness of God in the Vegetable World...*, a sermon preached by Charles LaMotte in Stamford in 1740 and printed in the town as a twenty-four-page pamphlet by Francis Howgrave, or verse by local poets, such as *Tetford Club, A Poem by W.E.P.L.* issued in 1772 by the Boston printer Caleb Preston, or books and pamphlets by local antiquaries such as Adam Stark's *Visitor's Pocket Guide to Gainsburgh and Neighbourhood* printed by J. W. F. Bowden of Gainsborough in 1849, or pamphlets on matters of local dispute and concern, the handbooks essential to local businesses (such as catalogues of local circulating libraries) or to local societies (rules of friendly societies or savings banks, for example), and the numerous companions to the almanacks (packed with local information) which were printed in several Lincolnshire towns in the nineteenth century. The parochial nature of these publications is evident from their title-pages, for very often the person who printed and published them was also the main, if not the sole, distributor or retailer. Obviously a very limited business base, hence the selling of London-published books, stationery and other booktrade-related sales, jobbing printing of bills and posters, and the retailing of many and varied non-booktrade products. Patent medicines were particular popular lines, so much so that the companions to the almanacks often contained several pages of lists and advertisements for elixirs and other panaceas.

Yet some book publishing had a wider significance than the purely local already noted, illustrated again by the title-pages. *A Lincolnshire Freeholder, on the Thoughts of a Reverend Author, Respecting Sir Gilbert Heathcote's Address to the County Freeholders,* a twelve-page pamphlet, was printed in 1795 by and for B. B. Kelsey and sold by him in Spilsby and Boston and also by W. Wood of Lincoln and by Peat & Newcomb in Stamford, and *Theological Converse in a Dialogue Between Juventus and Puber, by Philanthropos*, a book of 286 pages printed in Gainsborough by J. Mozley and sold by him and by J. Weir of Horncastle in 1785. Sometimes the local men were involved with London publishers, with books printed in the capital for local booksellers such as *The Folly of Excusing Ourselves and Condeming Others*, a sermon preached in Lincoln Guildhall by John Garmston in 1715 and printed in London 'for John Knight, bookseller in Lincoln'; sometimes it was the other way round with books printed locally for London publishers such as John Smith's *A Discourse on Trade, Liberty and Taxes, Addressed to All Land-owners and Traders in Great-Britain...*, a forty-eight-page work printed in 1733 by W. Wood in Lincoln 'and sold by A. Bettesworth and C. Hitch, and S. Austen, London'. In some cases many booksellers were involved as with George Stinton's *A Sermon Preached in the Cathedral Church of Lincoln, Before the Governors of the County Hospital... November IX 1769* which was printed in Lincoln by W. Wood & Son and sold by three London booksellers and one each in Oxford, Cambridge and Exeter - an unusually wide distribution for what would appear to be a very local publication. Sometimes, however, title-pages are not all that they seem: between about 1782 and 1797 the Mozleys printed books for London publishers W. Osborne and T. Griffin - but although there were London booksellers with these surnames the initials do not tally with surviving records and they were, apparently, fictitious and used, presumably, to make the Mozleys' London connections appear better than they were; a few years later Henry Mozley used the names of J. Brambles, A. Meggitt and J. Waters as London booksellers on his title pages - fictitious again, as Brambles, Meggitt and Waters were all family names.

The Mozleys had no need, perhaps, for these fictitious London connections for they had plenty of proper connections both in the capital and in the provinces, and others were happy to trade on their reputation. In the *Yorkshire, Nottinghamshire and Lincolnshire Gazette and Universal Advertiser* for 28 March 1795, for example, the following notice appeared:

> W. Sheardown... determined to spare no pains or expense in extending the circulation and rendering it still more advantageous to his advertising friends and interesting to his readers has made the same a joint concern between himself and Messrs J. & H. Mozley, Gainborough, from whose extensive connections throughout the kingdom he trusts it will soon rank with any of its contemporaries. The partnership commences on Saturday the 4th of April...'

This partnership between these Doncaster and Gainsborough printers and booksellers was terminated on the 31 December 1796 after the death of John Mozley, his executor Henry Mozley and William Sheardown mutually agreeing to part company. The Mozleys had trade relationships in York, and also in north-east England, for Henry Mozley commissioned a number of blocks from the famous Newcastle engraver Thomas Bewick (he also saw a new printing press, a Stanhope, in North Shields, about which he waxed enthusiastic in a letter to his wife) and, according to title-page evidence, with booksellers in Oxford, Cambridge, Macclesfield, Nottingham, Leeds, Hull, Edinburgh, and elsewhere. They printed, published, or co-published, some three hundred or more books and pamphlets, and included catalogues of 'works newly published' in at least two of the books which they issued, and were without doubt the most prolific book printers and publishers in the county.

The Lincolnshire booktrade's long and varied history has been imperfectly studied and recorded, but it is hoped that this outline may stimulate further research both in recording titles produced, and also in discovering more about the people involved and the economics of printing and bookselling in a predominantly rural county.

Notes

1 Llewellyn C. Lloyd, 'The book trade in Shropshire. Some account of the stationers, booksellers and printers at work in the county to about 1800', *Trans. Shropshire Arch. Soc.*, 48 (1934-35), 65-142, 145-200. Trevor Fawcett, 'Eighteenth-century Norfolk booksellers: a survey and register', *Trans. Cambridge Bibl. Soc.*, 6 (1972) 1-8. Trevor Fawcett, 'Some aspects of the Norfolk book trade, 1800-24', *Trans. Cambridge Bibl. Soc.*, 4 (1968), 383-95. Norman Taylor, 'Derbyshire printing and printers before 1800', *Derbyshire Arch. J.*, 70 (1950), 38-69. John Walton, 'Survey of the printing trade and related occupations in Nottingham and Nottinghamshire to 1900' (unpublished thesis, Fellowship of the Library Association, 1968).

2 Richard W. Goulding, *Notes on Louth Printers and Booksellers of the Eighteenth Century* (Louth, 1917); his *Notes on Books and Pamphlets Printed at Louth, 1801-1850* (Louth, 1920) is a bibliography, not a history, but gives additional details of the Louth book trade. J. S. English, 'The Lincolnshire booktrade', in *Second Seminar on the Provincial Booktrade... University of Loughborough* (1983) 15-18.

3 John B. Manterfield, 'Edward Pawlett of Grantham: a provincial bookseller, 1660-1687'. *L.H.A.*, 29 (1994), 11-16. J. S. English, 'The Mozleys of Gainsborough', *Factotum Occasional Paper 3* (1983), 21-23. Christine Bowditch, 'Popular Literature and Literacy: a study of Gainsborough in the late 18th century', an unpublished B.A. dissertation, School of English, University of Leeds (1983), 14-30 explores the Mozleys' chapbook publications.

4 Elizabeth A. Melrose, 'Three 18th-century Lincoln libraries', *L.H.A.*, 19 (1984), 41-48. J. S. English, 'Books and libraries in Gainsborough: a short study with special reference to the nineteenth century', *Library Association Record*, 70, 3 (1968), 62-65. Michael J. Crump & R. J. Goulden, 'Four library catalogues of note', *Factotum*, 3 (October 1978), 9-13.

5 Lionel Robinson, *Boston Newspapers*, History of Boston, 11 (Boston, 1974). G. H. Burton, 'Notes on newspapers', *L.R.S.M.*, 20 March 1914. *Lincolnshire, Boston & Spalding Free Press Centenary Number*, 6 Oct 1947 is one such example.

6 John Feather, *The English Provincial Book Trade Before 1850: A Checklist of Secondary Sources* (Oxford, 1981).

7 Peter C. G. Isaacs, 'The British Book Trade Index', *Local Historian* (May 1994), 102-11. Professor Isaacs has written widely on many aspects of the provincial booktrade.

8 T. W. Townsend, *Seventeenth Century Tradesmen's Tokens of Lincolnshire: The Issuers* (Lincoln, 1983); for details of Mallory's supply of books to Alford Grammar School, see the article by Reginald C. Dudding on boys admitted to the school in *L.N.Q.*, XIII (1915), 181-83.

9 Copy in Gainsborough Library. Carlton's stock included Bibles, Books of Common Prayer and other devotional works, 'all sorts of Latin books', together with stationery, maps, prints and patent medicines. He also dealt in secondhand books - 'N.B. You may have Money for any Library, or Parcel of BOOKS.'

10 *The Earliest Directory of the Book Trade, by John Pendred (1785)*, ed. Graham Pollard, (1955).

11 J. S. English, 'The Lincolnshire Book Trade from the County Directories, 1826-1861', unpublished typescript (1967).

12 Copy in a private collection.

13 Copy in Gainsborough Library - Beaumont Street Independent Church archive.

14 John Feather, 'The country trade in books', in *Spreading the Word: Distribution Networks of Print, 1550-1850*, edited by Robin Myers and Michael Harris (Winchester, 1990). This thesis is further developed in his *The Provincial Book Trade in Eighteenth-Century England*, (Cambridge, 1985), the standard text on the subject.

15 Copy in a private collection.

16 Victor Neuberg, *The Penny Histories: a Study of Chapbooks for Young Readers over Two Centuries*, (1968). Victor Neuberg, Chapbooks: *A Bibliography of References to English and American Chapbook Literature of the Eighteenth and Nineteenth Centuries*, 2nd. edn. (1972).

17 John Feather, 'Country book trade apprentices 1710-1760', *Publishing History*, 6 (1980), 85-99.

The Fictional 'Apologia Pro Vita Sua' of a Lincolnshire Clergyman

H. B. Williams

Thomas Wimberley Mossman, of whom there is an entry in the *Dictionary of National Biography*, died in 1885, at the age of fifty-nine, when rector of two small villages on the edge of the Wolds in Lincolnshire, East and West Torrington. He was the author of doctrinal and theological works and a recipient of a Doctorate in Divinity from the University of the South in the United States. He is remembered as a leading ritualist of the Church of England and, as a high churchman, a member of the Order of Corporate Reunion within which, it is believed, he held the title of Bishop of Selby. He was received into the Roman Catholic Church by Cardinal Manning when on his death bed in the West Torrington Rectory.

In 1985, the centenary of his death, Mrs Barbara Mumford of West Torrington contributed an article on Mossman in the July issue of *Lincolnshire Life*, from which further biographical details are taken.[1] He was born in 1826, the eldest son of Robert Hume Mossman of Skipton in Yorkshire but was brought up by a maiden aunt, Miss Mary Ann Wimberley. After early scholastic promise he was a pupil of Peel Grammar School (presumably Isle of Man) from whence he proceeded to St Edmund Hall, Oxford, and became an adherent of the Oxford Movement.

Meanwhile his uncle, the Rev. Conrad Makyns Wimberley, rector of Donington-on-Bain, was growing increasingly unhappy with his ministry in that parish and seeking to escape on leave of absence. He awaited Mossman's graduation and arranged a Lincoln ordination as deacon with the title curate of Donington. Wimberley then left for London leaving the twenty-three year old Mossman in charge of a turbulent parish. It was in that respect that the writer of this paper first encountered Mossman who was curate there from 1849 to 1852. Subsequently he was curate of Panton, vicar of Ranby and finally, in 1859, rector of East and West Torrington.

Mrs Mumford recorded two aspects of Mossman of significance to this study; his sense of the failure of Christianity to accomplish its task and his identification with the interests of the Lincolnshire working man - the farm labourer. In the latter connection Mossman was an active Liberal, a supporter of the 1870 Education Bill, an opponent of means-testing and an advocate of the household franchise whereby the farm labourer finally won the right to vote.

There were other clergy sharing such views at that time. Mossman was marked out more by his ritualism, still somewhat unusual in the area, particularly so as extremely practised and openly advocated by him. *The Louth and North Lincolnshire Advertiser* in an October issue of 1867 carried a report of his West Torrington Harvest Festival. There was a processional cross with acolytes, incense was burned, the altar was 'illuminated' and Mossman wore 'a splendid cope made by the sisters of East Grinstead'. Strangely no hostile reaction followed this report. Earlier in the year there had been an antagonistic correspondence about his ritualism and an angry demonstration in Louth against his association with the Brotherhood of the Holy Redeemer - the 'Mossman Monks' - which he had established at West Torrington. Mossman was considered locally to be 'romanish in everything but name' and made no attempt to compromise with, or to appease, his opponents. Paradoxically Mossman was also of a decided ecumenical tendency. This may have been found even more peculiar in his day than ritualism. Mrs Mumford records that at the Diocesan Conference of 1877 he argued that nonconformists should be treated as Brethren of Christ. In 1881 he was advocating that an incumbent should be authorized, when he so wished, to allow other Christian denominations the use of his church for worship.

This paper is not intended to be a biographical study of Mossman. Its purpose is to examine the degree to which a novel *Mr. Gray and His Neighbours* throws light on the nature of this complex man and on his career in the Church of England. The foregoing sketch is no more than to provide the necessary information from which to proceed. What follows is drawn mainly from the novel and is limited to those aspects which can be considered to bear on Mossman's character and life. No attempt will be made to use the novel to illustrate Lincolnshire parochial and diocesan life in the third quarter of the nineteenth century, although it has a value in that connection.

The novel, purported to be by Peter Piper Esquire, was of two volumes published in 1876 by Hodges who were responsible for most of Mossman's theological works. The copy in the Golding Collection in Louth Library bears a note on the title page identifying the author as the Rev. T. W. Mossman of West Torrington. It is scarcely a novel in the conventional sense. It purports to be a life of a Reverend Theophilus Gray written by a lawyer who had, in earlier days, been a pupil of Gray during a period of convalescence between Rugby School and Oxford University. The style is anecdotal, interspersed by passages reflecting Mossman's known antiquarian interests and others of a homiletic nature.

The book did not go unnoticed, being praised in reviews of the day and going into a second [1877] edition. One reviewer even compared it with the work of Mr Anthony Trollope. It was not so well received in Lincoln clerical circles; *John Bull* had the following report:

> On Tuesday last, at a meeting of subscribers to the Lincoln County Library, it was proposed by the Rural Dean to expel it [*Mr. Gray*] from the library: a proposition which was carried by a majority of five to two.[2]

The Reverend Theophilus was rector of Irthling in Marshland with a hamlet Irthling Nook on the coast. The market town, Huddleborough, is identifiable with Louth, of which Hlud was an early spelling. The cathedral of St Guthlac corresponds topographically and architecturally with Lincoln Minster. The world was that of Mossman with the one difference that his parishes were of the Wold rather than of the Marsh. There is no plot until the second volume is reached when Gray's daughter Alice becomes betrothed to the son and heir of Lord Hogsthorpe only to discover that he had fathered a child on a maidservant with whom she had grown up in Irthling. Alice breaks off the engagement and devotes herself to good works. On an occasion when these take her to the fisherfolk of Irthling Nook a ship is wrecked off-shore. In an event reminiscent of Grace Darling, Alice assists in the rescue, from the exertions of which her death follows. Not, however, before a reconciliation with her lover who had, of course, been among those saved from the wreck.

Those elements of the novel that may be considered most pertinent in contributing to an understanding of its author are, apart from Gray himself, references to Marshland folk and the portraits of the two clerical neighbours who share the title with Gray. These will separately be considered in what follows. The somewhat critical passages relating to the Diocese of St Guthlac and its Bishop are less relevant although some reference will ultimately be made to them.

> Their hearts have a hard shell or crust upon them: and it is only after the crust has been broken that you find a heart, and sometimes a very warm one underneath. (I, 16)[3]

Marshland folk were not a demonstrative people although they could be swayed 'by the glowing appeals and prayers of a favourite revival preacher' (I, 15). The Church of England had lost its way to their hearts, however admirably it appealed to the educated and cultured. Nevertheless they retained a measure of respect and allegiance towards the Church and are frequently referred to as 'half Church - half Methodist'. Phrases are recorded which, one assumes, Mossman was familiar with : 'Not bigoted to no form of wasship'; 'Like to go to church and chapel'; 'So soon hear a sermon in church as in chapel provided it is a good 'un and the minister preaches the Gospel'. The essential element of an act of worship was the sermon and typical judgments were 'All jaw and no Gospel' with its antithesis 'All Gospel and no jaw'.

Marshland folk could respect their parson and his office even when doctrinally at odds with him. An illustration of this is told of the Rev. Nazianzen Applebee, of whom later as one of the 'neighbours'. Applebee was a scourge of Methodists against whom a field preacher set himself up in opposition. On one occasion Applebee stumbled upon one of the open-air field meetings in which the congregation were participating in a denunciation of Applebee's Papist tendencies. They parted to let him through and 'there was scarcely a man who did not raise his hat to him, or a woman who did not drop a curtsey' (I, 110).

Irthling was a Gray family living, still held although the great days of the family were past. It had long been Gray's ambition to be its rector; he was ordained as soon as possible after his graduation and assumed his Irthling charge the very next day at some time in the 1830s. This situation remained possible to the end of Mossman's time and even beyond. A patron of a living could reserve it for a member of the family, or indeed anyone whom he wished to oblige, by filling the vacancy, until the appropriate time, by a clergyman on an agreement to resign when required. Gray took over the parish as a deacon in very like manner as Mossman took charge of Donington although he was curate and not rector. Both began 'raw' with neither formal training nor supervisory counsel. Gray made his way slowly into the ministry 'after many sorrows and many sufferings, after many a long year of self-communing' (I, 19). He learned from his friends; and he learned even more from his foes.

He was the first resident rector of Irthling for over 200 years (which would have been almost true of at least three parishes with which Mossman was associated). As a result the parsonage had long since become a farm house and subsequently the home for three labouring families. These had to be rehoused and the parsonage restored before Gray could occupy it. During that time he lodged with a yeoman family of the village whose daughter he eventually married. It was that fortuitous situation that kept Gray from the 'Anglo-Catholic Revival Path' that he may otherwise have followed. No argument is given to substantiate this but the assertion is made that living in a Marshland yeoman's home led Gray away from concluding that the English Church, Protestant to the core, was devoid of Divinity and that the only place where true spiritual authority was to be found was that to which Newman and Manning had gone. Gray's future was not to be, as otherwise it may have been, theological study in a religious order.

Gray had been at Oxford during Newman's years. He was among those of his contemporaries who had come down believing that Anglicanism

> or the theoretical system of the Anglican Church as contained in the Book of Common Prayer was, if not absolute perfection, yet as near to it as it was possible for any system to be. (I, 39)

Those young pioneers of the Oxford Movement went out into their ministries with 'the resolve and the determination to make the system as perfect in practice and in real life as they believed it to be on paper'. (I,39) In that exalted mood Gray came to Irthling with the 'high resolve that he would make it a model parish'. (I, 39) It was not personal pride; it was a state of mind shared with hundreds like himself who were to be 'a spiritual arm, first regenerating English society by means of the English church - then the rest of Christendom - then the world'. (I, 39)

Gray anticipated that in his Irthling ministry he would

> convert all the Dissenters and Methodists from their schism, and make Marshland ploughmen devout, and Marshland maidens chaste, and Marshland bairns living exemplars of duty towards God and neighbour. (I, 40)

Gray began by re-introducing the daily offices in church which had not been exercised in living memory despite the rubrics of the Book of Common Prayer. This aroused criticism from neighbouring clergy, from the local gentry and even from the Bishop who, while admitting the precedent of the Book of Common Prayer, questioned whether it was prudent to re-introduce practices which had ceased to be part of established tradition. In Gray's earlier days there were parishioners who joined him in his worship; they gradually fell away over the years but were never among his critics for they accepted his church disciplines as 'a fad of our parson's' (I, 40).

The time came when Gray had to argue out his commitment to the Church of England with that friend and neighbour already referred to, the Rev. Nazianzen Applebee. He tried to convey the true nature of dissent to Applebee by taking him on a pastoral visit to one particular old lady of his God-fearing, half Church, half Methodist flock. He set out to draw from her the strands of her faith so that Applebee could learn 'the mind of the peasantry to whom he had been sent by the Anglican Church to minister in holy things' (I, 89). It was not the success for which he had hoped and Gray gradually came to realise that he and Applebee were not of like mind. When Applebee finally declared for Rome Gray was led to confess

> I can see there is nothing divine about the English church - I cannot see that any other church is more divine than the Anglican. (I, 186)

Perhaps this was the time of his decision and his Irthling ministry was to continue for a further forty years. During that time he came to understand that 'the common instinct of his race was wiser than the Church Principles as he used to call them' (II, 234). And he never failed to wonder that 'what he had arrived at after so many agonising mental throes, should have been attained by his humble friends as a heritage into which they had entered without either toil or pain' (II, 234).

During that long ministry Gray made no converts to Anglicanism, his people remaining Methodists in heart and feeling. But he was, for them, 'our Master Gray' or 'our parson' and when they heard the bell toll for his daily office they would say 'There is our Parson going into Church to say his prayers. Well, he'll think of us, bless him.' (II, 236) In the end he came to realise that Anglicanism was not a Gospel for the poor.

> The system, indeed, is most beautiful, as beautiful as moonbeams playing on the ice-bergs of a Polar Sea - and as cold. (II, 237)

There was no alternative church in which to minister; official Christianity strangles the religion of Christ by building itself up with the 'privileges of a sacerdotal clan'. (II, 239) Any church runs itself for its own benefit. So Gray, he who had been a Puseyite, an Anglo-Catholic, a High Churchman of High Churchmen, 'became what the world would say broad, but what he himself calls a liberal and primitive Christian' but yet one who 'clings close to Bethlehem and Calvary' (II, 237).

Some acquaintance has already been made with the Reverend Nazianzen Applebee, who came to the diocese shortly after Gray. He was a nephew of the Marquis of Carrowaysede which had earned him the privilege of being a guest of the bishop on the occasions of his deaconing and priesting; other candidates had to find themselves accommodation in the hotels and lodging houses of the town. Applebee held the valuable Carrowaysede livings of Spellow-doe and Willingdale-Bowels, worth £1,400 a year.

He was not a scholar but he came to his parishes knowing the Missal and the Breviary by heart. As far as Applebee was concerned Methodists were brands to be plucked from the burning or otherwise to be excommunicated by 'bell, book and candle'. This attitude was illustrated by a funeral sermon he preached following the burial of a devout old Methodist class leader. On the Sunday after the burial service the family, according to Marshland custom, attended church clad in decent mourning. As anticipated Applebee gave the funeral address - but not one to be expected. His theme was the misery and danger of dissent with its appalling after-death consequences. He never buried a dissenter without being aware of 'the enemy of man crouching and leering behind the nearest tombstone and saying "Ah! ah! my boy, I've got you at last!"' (I, 87).

While so he believed and so he taught, Applebee nevertheless tended his goats before their inevitable damnation. He never spent more than £200 in the year on himself; the remainder of his £1,400 went to the flock, much of it in tea and blankets. While this was well appreciated it did not draw them to share in his 'papist ways', among which were the administration of extreme unction and the practice of confession and absolution. He did not even succeed with elderly, deserving poor females normally the 'most promising materials for an earnest young cleric to work on' (I, 91). There was one occasion when he thought he had broken through. An elderly woman nervously asked for a private audience. Applebee welcomed her into his study, sat her down next to his prie-dieu, donned the stole he optimistically kept nearby in readiness, and waited on her words. Sadly they were a plea that she too should have a red flannel petticoat like her neighbour.

Applebee, weakened by such disappointments, had his scales tipped further to Rome by the promotion of the Rev. Anacharsis Backstairs Gunter. He was of an earlier generation of Marshland clergy than Gray and Applebee; rector of Potluc-le-Marsh, vicar of Borehole-in-the-Willows and licensed curate of Goosepool-le-Clay, these together bringing him £450 in the year. Since Mrs Gunter had presented him with an addition to the family for each of the past fifteen years that income was inadequate. In consequence he practised the 'hack-trade', reading prayers and preaching a sermon for a guinea and a dinner whenever he could relieve a neighbour absent on duty or pleasure.

Gunter had called on Gray in his early days to offer him such a service when required. He also took the opportunity of expressing his unease at the introduction of daily prayer, an 'unheard of innovation'. He was a high-churchman himself but a weak stomach inhibited him from fasting and his knees were too weak for frequent occasions of prayer. Gray found him uneasy at the use of the word 'priest' and even more so at 'Catholic'. It was from Gunter that he learned of the bishop's views on daily prayer; Gunter had heard these expressed when a fellow guest of the bishop's at a Passion Week dinner-party given by Lord Hogsthorpe. When Gray claimed to have met with some favourable response from his parishioners, Gunter's reaction was -

> What, the clodhoppers of Irthling, the chawbacons of Marshland, value and love daily prayers? I think, Mr. Gray, you must be amusing yourself at my expense this morning. (I, 55)

When Applebee arrived, and Gunter heard of the number of services he planned, he called in the full expectation that his assistance would be welcomed. He had no opportunity to introduce the topic for Applebee started a discussion on the relative merits of the Douai Bible and the Authorised Version making numerous references to alternative translations from the original Greek. For Gunter the only word to describe Applebee was 'mad'.

Gunter's promotion followed a bishop's visitation to Huddleborough when it fell to Gunter's lot to speak at the traditional clergy dinner which followed such an occasion. Gunter spoke so favourably of the bishop that he declared 'I knew he was a clever fellow from meeting him at dinner parties' (I, 155) and subsequently appointed Gunter rural dean and made him a canon. When Applebee resigned to enter the Roman Church (eventually a Franciscan) he offered his livings to Gray. To his astonishment Gray suggested Gunter. He needed the money but, more pertinently, he was an Anglican of 'the very spirit of the English Church - that great corporate entity expressing the religious convictions of the English people' (I, 194). He was popular with Marshland folk who 'reckon him quite particular in the pulpit' (I, 195). Relieved from his financial burdens Gunter blossomed. He became an authority on Education and an oracle on Dilapidations. He gave ruri-decanal dinner parties accompanied by a glass of decent port and ended his days 'a kind-hearted, genial cleric, a good parish priest, thoughtful for the poor, attentive to his schools' (I, 213).

In his earlier quoted article C. G. Barton noted that the 'incumbent of Biscathorpe wrote indignantly that he had been caricatured'.[4] This would have been the Rev. Dennis Prittie O'Connor whom Wimberley had housed in the rectory at Donington when he left for London. One object of this was that O'Connor should ease Mossman into his ministry. The two appear to have got on well in earlier days but Mossman publicly expressed criticism of O'Connor in later years for levying burial fees at Donington.

Those two clerical neighbours of Gray are the only parish clergy to feature in the work. They were, no doubt, exemplars whom Gray chose not to follow but they are not discredited. Other than the bishop, Mossman did not pillory the clergy of his day. More significantly, perhaps, he did not choose to portray that counterpart to himself - the serious, committed evangelical.

It is first to be considered whether Gray can to any extent be identified with Mossman. Was there any autobiographical element in the novel? C. G. Barton, in the article previously quoted, believed there was. He referred specifically to traditions in the Wimberley family, that of Mossman's mother. They related to estates held in the Marsh in Saxon times and to the story of an ancestress whose ship was wrecked at Donna Nook.[5] Mossman was careful, however, to avoid too close an identification. In particular Gray, on arrival at Irthling, lived in a village home, the daughter of which he married, and as a consequence of which he retained his allegiance to the English Church. Mossman moved into the Donington Rectory and was subsequently to marry an Irish girl. Nevertheless some significant parallels between Gray and Mossman can be drawn.

Firstly, while Gray was under Newman's influence at Oxford, Mossman was under that of Manning, then occupying the pulpit of the University Church of St Mary. Mrs Mumford described Manning as Mossman's friend from his university days. The enthusiasm of Gray entering on his Irthling ministry and his aspirations therein were surely an echo of those experienced by Mossman fresh from the headiness of Manning's preaching.

Secondly, both men, working in strongly Methodist communities, earned the respect and affection of their non-conforming parishioners. There is evidence of this in the case of Mossman. His uncle had been driven from Donington on Bain by the 'taunts of an ungracious people'.[6] Mossman so won them round that thirty years later his popularity in the village was a factor in the electoral triumph of a parliamentary Liberal candidate.[7] It was about the same time that he wrote, in a different context:

> The parish of Donington on Bain and all its inhabitants are very dear to me, for it was there I was first privileged to preach the word of God and to break the bread of eternal life.[8]

At his funeral at West Torrington 'All the inhabitants of the village walked in the procession'.[9]

Thirdly, Gray's doctrinal position as revealed in the book is close to that which Mossman was to disclose of himself. Gray has already been quoted describing himself as a liberal Christian. A longer quotation in the context of a doctrinal discussion with Applebee spells his position more clearly.

> I could not say truly that I have abandoned my old church principles, or that I think them false. When I go over in my mind the logical arguments by which I was led to embrace them they appear to me as sound and as forcible as ever they were. But I cannot make up my mind that these principles are either so true, or so important, that it is my duty to leave the English Church because she does not authorise me to teach and enforce them upon all her members, still less to join a Church which teaches some things to which, so far as I can see, I could never give a consenting assent. (I, 193)

This can be compared with words that Mossman wrote arising from an 1867 election of a Proctor in Convocation. The candidates were an evangelical and a high churchman and Mossman was automatically assumed in the Louth area to be a supporter of the latter. Not so:

> I am very thankful to say that I am not a High Churchman. I wish and try to be a Catholic as far as I know how. But I would much rather be an Evangelical or a Low Churchman of any school in preference to being a Lincolnshire High Churchman.

He continued that since there were not enough Catholic clergy in the diocese to elect a Proctor to their mind:

> I myself would feel very much inclined to vote for some pious Evangelical of the school of Simeon and Venn if such is to be found within our borders.[10]

Such comments, linked with earlier evidence of Mossman's ecumenical attitudes, are compatible with the ideas attributed to Gray. Moreover the longer passage quoted above from Gray may be a pointer to why Mossman did not leave the English Church. It is reasonable to assume from the continued association with Manning following his move to Roman Catholicism, that there must have been an ever present alternative.

There is, then, good reason to believe that Mossman wrote some of himself into the fictional person of Gray. Why then did he write the novel? He was fifty years old, well established in his West Torrington Rectory and with the expectation that he would end his days there. The known public hostility towards him over ritualism and 'the monks' would seem to have died down but he was still a man in the public eye despite the obscurity of his ecclesiastic office. He wrote articles; he corresponded widely; he was active on the political stage and in diocesan life. He was surely aware that he was something of an enigma both to his Catholic friends and to his Evangelical critics. He may have felt a need to explain himself and it is possible that his novel was suggested to him by one that Newman had published in 1848 when Mossman was in his last year at Oxford. *Loss and Gain* had as its hero an Oxford undergraduate, son of a clergyman, who found himself drawn to Rome despite all the efforts of friends and teachers. The characters were 'drawn with satiric wit',[11] which might be said also of Applebee and Gunter. Mossman, whether this were a precedent or not, cannot have anticipated it being of much consequence to his neighbours; more probably it was a form of therapy for one who must often have felt at odds with his world.

The next questions which may be asked of Mossman are why he waited until his death-bed to be accepted into the Roman Catholic Church and why a man of his calibre should have spent all his working life in small out of the way parishes, offering only modest stipends and inhabited in the main by Methodists hostile to his Church, if not to him? And it might be considered that these two questions are linked rather than independent. He had a way out.

The answer to the former can be assumed to be that which Gray gave at the end of his debate with Applebee. The mystery may rather be why Mossman did eventually consent to be accepted into the Roman Church. On the assumption that he was honest to himself his Catholic ideas were compatible with the Book of Common Prayer and the Thirty Nine Articles.

The answer to the latter lies partly in the state of the clerical profession of his day. It was still difficult for a man to advance in the church if he was neither of birth nor of wealth. Mossman, himself, while appreciated by the Donington patron, Lord Monson, was informed that he could not expect Donington if it fell vacant and on two further occasions failed in his application for other Monson livings.[12] Mossman may have been somewhat resentful of such circumstances, the novel suggests this in places, but they were among the facts of life for a Victorian clergyman.

More positively there are two comments in the novel that bear on the question. Both have already been quoted; Gray attempted to instruct Applebee in 'the mind of the peasantry to whom he had been sent by the Anglican Church to minister in holy things' (I, 89) Mossman's vocation had led him to the rural poor of the Lincolnshire Wolds. There is no clue in the novel how it came about but from the earliest days Mossman developed a concern for them and established a rapport with them. The fact that he could not convert them to his particular faith did not diminish the relationship. It may have been less priestly than he could have wished but it was a pastoral reality.

> There is our Parson going into Church to say his prayers. Well, he'll think of us, bless him. (II, 239)

The interests and activities of Mossman reached far beyond the boundaries of his parish but it is possible to judge that his office as the shepherd of his flock was the anchor which held him in the English Church as long as he could so act.

There may have been another factor conducing to an acceptance of his lot. In response to Applebee's unreadiness to tolerate a bishop who gave a Visitation Address such as that he had heard at Huddleborough or to the promotion of such as Gunter, Gray had to admit that such things did not disturb him. He would put himself into the place of the bishop or that of Gunter 'and see things as well as I can from their point of view' (I, 166). If such a level of tolerance were also that of Mossman, and it would be in accord with his ecumenical thinking, then it would be the easier and the more natural thing for him to hold fast to his rural ministry.

Nevertheless there would have been times of doubt and perhaps of conflict. His Christian name, Thomas, may not have been inapt, although it would not have been of his Master that he had doubts. More fitting, perhaps his Methodist parishioners sensed, may have been that which he gave to his hero, Theophilus - one who loves God.

Notes

1 Barbara Mumford, 'Thomas Wimberley Mossman', *Lincolnshire Life,* 25, 4 (July 1985), 30-31.
2 C. G. Barton, 'Dr. T. W. Mossman', *Lincoln Diocesan Magazine*, LXXIII, 9 (September 1957), 130.
3 References in parentheses in the text are to volume and page of *Mr. Gray and His Neighbours.*
4 Barton, 'Mossman'.
5 *ibid.*
6 L.A.O. Cor. B/5/4/14/3.
7 R. J. Olney , *Lincolnshire Politics 1832-1885* (Oxford, 1973) 212.
8 *Stamford Mercury*, 24 July 1884. Mossman was writing in connection with a scandal concerning burial fees in Donington-on-Bain. Such were not a custom of the parish when he was there, nor would he have demanded them.
9 Mumford , 'Mossman'.
10 *Louth and North Lincolnshire Advertiser*, 29 June 1867, quoting from a letter Mossman wrote to the *Stamford Mercury*.
11 Margaret Drabble, ed., *The Oxford Companion to English Literature* (1985), 695.
12 L.A.O. Mon. 25/13/10/5/70, 25/13/10/10/103, 25/13/10/11/13. In all three cases Monson was selling the next right of presentation of the living.

Lincolnshire Drawings

Joan Mostyn Lewis

Grimoldby Church.

Kingerby Church.

Cottage Garden.

Lincolnshire Lanterns.